HOCCLEVE'S *REGIMENT OF PRINCES*
COUNSEL AND CONSTRAINT

Thomas Hoccleve's politics and poetics have often been viewed as conventional, servile and naive. In the first book-length study of Hoccleve's major poem, Nicholas Perkins argues that *The Regiment of Princes* is in fact deeply engaged in the political and literary currents of the early fifteenth century, combining the elaborate deference of a petition, the resistance of a complaint and the monitory authority of a *speculum principis* in its address to the future Henry V. Dr Perkins sets the *Regiment*'s production within a late-medieval economy of advisory speech, reassesses the poem's relationship to the Latin treatises on which it draws, and examines its hermeneutics of royal counsel, which challenges the prince to interpret and act on the advice he receives. Using evidence from the *Regiment*'s many manuscripts, he then reveals how Hoccleve's poem was refashioned for new audiences beyond the Lancastrian court in the fifteenth and early sixteenth centuries.

NICHOLAS PERKINS is a Fellow and Director of Studies in English at Girton College, Cambridge.

HOCCLEVE'S *REGIMENT OF PRINCES*
COUNSEL AND CONSTRAINT

Nicholas Perkins

D. S. BREWER

© Nicholas Perkins 2001

All Rights Reserved. Except as permitted under current legislation
no part of this work may be photocopied, stored in a retrieval system,
published, performed in public, adapted, broadcast,
transmitted, recorded or reproduced in any form or by any means,
without the prior permission of the copyright owner

First published 2001
D. S. Brewer, Cambridge

ISBN 0 85991 631 6

D. S. Brewer is an imprint of Boydell & Brewer Ltd
PO Box 9, Woodbridge, Suffolk IP12 3DF, UK
and of Boydell & Brewer Inc.
PO Box 41026, Rochester, NY 14604–4126, USA
website: http://www.boydell.co.uk

A catalogue record of this publication is available
from the British Library

Library of Congress Cataloging-in-Publication data
applied for

This publication is printed on acid-free paper

Printed and bound in Great Britain
by Antony Rowe Ltd, Chippenham, Wiltshire

Contents

List of Plates	vii
Acknowledgements	ix
List of Abbreviations and Note on References	x
Introduction	1

1. **Hoccleve's Writings and the Regulation of Language in Late-Medieval England** — 5

   Official Regulation and the Language of Rebellion — 6
   Family and *Familia* — 12
   Institutions and Associations — 24
   Parliamentary Address and Petitionary Culture — 29
   Verbal and Financial Exchange in the *Regiment* — 39

2. **'Th'entente is al': Princely Reading and Political Interpretation** — 50

   Musing on Mutability — 50
   The Historiography of Counsel — 57
   Richard II: Reading King to Political Exemplum — 61
   Reading in the *Regiment* — 70

3. **Voices of Translation and the Sources of the *Regiment*** — 85

   Introduction — 85
   The Major Sources — 87
   The Sources and the Structure of the *Regiment* — 93
   Tyrants and Philosophers — 99
   Exemplary Translation and Redirecting Advice — 103
   The Imagery of Counsel — 114

   Table of Borrowings for Lines 2017–5463 of the *Regiment* — 122

4. *Regiment* and the Governing Body	126
Theories and Definitions	126
The Special Body of the King	132
The King and the Body Politic	137
Hoccleve's Body in the Dialogue	143

5. The Afterlife of the Poem: Hoccleve Manuscripts, Readers and Critics	151
The Corpus of *Regiment* Manuscripts	151
The Picture Tradition	155
The *Regiment* and its Manuscript Partners	160
Production and Ownership	168
The Problem of Genre in the *Regiment*'s 'Prologue'	178
Schemes of Reading	186

Conclusion	192
Bibliography	195
Index	227

List of Plates

Between pages 116 and 117:

Figure 1   BL MS Arundel 38, folio 37r

Figure 2   BL MS Harley 4866, folio 88r

Both are reproduced by kind permission of the British Library.

In memory of my father

Alan Perkins

17. 6. 38 – 9. 7. 00

and of my stepfather

Michael Brandon

26. 10. 32 – 25. 3. 01

Acknowledgements

Many people have helped me in the course of writing this book, which started life as a Cambridge Ph.D. thesis. The person who helped most is James Simpson, who has been unfailingly generous with his insight and scholarship first as a supervisor, and now as a colleague. I am also very grateful to my examiners, Richard Beadle and John Burrow, for their advice and encouragement, and to A.S.G. Edwards, who made helpful suggestions for the transition from thesis to book. Other friends, colleagues and family read and commented on parts of the text in various incarnations, or answered questions, or just got me thinking. They include Richard Axton, Jessica Brantley, William Byrne, Morgan Dickson, Sarah Eaton, Robert R. Edwards, Rebecca Hayward, Alfred Hiatt, Martin Kaufmann, Linne R. Mooney, Jennifer Nuttall, Scott-Morgan Straker, Sarah Tolmie, Colin Wilcockson, Neil Wright, and medieval seminars in Cambridge and Oxford. They saved me from numerous errors and misjudgements; the many that no doubt remain are my own responsibility.

I carried out the initial research for this book as a graduate student at Corpus Christi College, Cambridge, with generous funding from the British Academy. Since then, grants from the Oxford Faculty of English, St Hugh's College, Oxford and Girton College, Cambridge have aided the production of the book, in particular the colour illustrations. I have been fortunate to complete this project in two stimulating and supportive environments, first at St Hugh's and now at Girton: I am especially grateful to Peter McDonald, Isabel Rivers, Abigail Williams and Anne Fernihough. Caroline Palmer at Boydell and Brewer has been a model of patience when deadlines came and went, and Katy Cooper gave expert assistance with preparing camera-ready copy. Finally, and most importantly, thanks to Sarah, for her love, wise counsel and practical help.

The following libraries and institutions kindly gave me access to their collections or provided material on microfilm: the British Library; the Bodleian Library; the National Library of Scotland; Cambridge University Library; Corpus Christi College, Cambridge; Magdalene College, Cambridge; Queens' College, Cambridge; St John's College, Cambridge; Trinity College, Cambridge; the Fitzwilliam Museum, Cambridge; Coventry City Archives; Edinburgh University Library; the Society of Antiquaries; the Newberry Library, Chicago; the Beinecke Library, Yale University; the Rosenbach Museum and Library, Philadelphia; Princeton University Library; the Huntington Library, San Marino. Special thanks go to the staff of the University Library and the English Faculty Library, Cambridge.

Abbreviations

BL	British Library
BN	Bibliothèque Nationale
BLR	*Bodleian Library Record*
ChR	*Chaucer Review*
CUL	Cambridge University Library
CUP	Cambridge University Press
DML	*Dictionary of Medieval Latin from British Sources*, ed. R.E. Latham, D.R. Howlett et al. (London: British Academy/OUP, 1975–)
DNB	*Dictionary of National Biography*, ed. Sir Leslie Stephen and Sir Sidney Lee, 63 vols (London: Smith, Elder, 1885–1900)
EETS o.s.	Early English Text Society, original series
EETS e.s.	Early English Text Society, extra series
EHR	*English Historical Review*
ELH	*ELH: A Journal of English Literary History*
EMS	*English Manuscript Studies, 1100–1700*
FCS	*Fifteenth Century Studies*
JEGP	*Journal of English and Germanic Philology*
Loeb	Loeb Classical Library
MÆ	*Medium Ævum*
MED	*Middle English Dictionary*, ed. Hans Kurath et al. (Ann Arbor: University of Michigan Press, 1952–)
NLS	National Library of Scotland
NM	*Neuphilologische Mitteilungen*
OUP	Oxford University Press
PBA	*Proceedings of the British Academy*
PMLA	*Publications of the Modern Language Association*
RES	*Review of English Studies*
RP	*Rotuli Parliamentorum*, 7 vols (London: n. pub., 1783–1832)

RS	Rerum Britannicarum medii aevi Scriptores, or Chronicles and Memorials of Great Britain and Ireland during the Middle Ages (Rolls Series)
SAC	*Studies in the Age of Chaucer*

Note on references

Quotations from primary sources have been repunctuated where necessary, some spellings have been regularized and abbreviations have been silently expanded. Translations are my own unless otherwise stated. References to primary works are by author and short title or, for anonymous works, title and editor (for example: Ovid, *Ars amatoria*; or *Anonimalle Chronicle*, ed. Galbraith). References to secondary works are by author and date (for example: Walker 1995).

Introduction

> How so it be that som men hem delite
> With subtyl art hire tales for to endite,
> Yet for al that, in hire entencioun
> Hire tale is al for som conclusioun.
> *(Troilus and Criseyde*, II. 256–9)

In Book VII of John Gower's *Confessio amantis*, Genius, the priest of Venus, tells the story of a king who wants to know how he is regarded amongst his people (lines 3945–4026). His councillors, too afraid to tell the truth, claim either that the king is honoured, or that he simply requires better counsel. The king's fool – totally ignored until now – is the only one to speak out, correctly informing his master that if he himself were good, he would not have to worry about bad counsel. In the story, of course, the fool's words work a transformation in the king, who recognizes his faults and stops oppressing his people. The emblematic quality of this narrative, however, serves to emphasize its fictive nature; there are in fact few councillors who would copy the wise fool's actions, and even fewer rulers who would listen to his warning. This narrative of counsel and constraint thus takes its place in a tradition of advisory literature whose rhetorical manoeuvres reflect the ongoing dilemma of the courtier: if only a fool would tell the plain truth, how can anyone give meaningful counsel to a ruler? Thomas Hoccleve (c. 1367–1426) has been assigned the roles of loquacious fool and of timid counsellor – sometimes both – by readers of his longest poem, *The Regiment of Princes*.[1] This book examines how Hoccleve represents and responds to these pressures in addressing his future king, combining the voices of outsider, servant and advisor in a poem that itself encompasses a complaint, a petition for payment and a mirror for princes.

Hoccleve wrote the *Regiment* in 1410–11 and addressed it to Henry, Prince of Wales, who became King Henry V in March 1413 on the death of his father, Henry IV.[2] The *Regiment* is a work of 5463 lines composed in rhyme royal stanzas. The first 2016 lines contain a dialogue between

---

[1] W.J. Courthope, for example, describes Hoccleve's poetic persona as 'half-moralist, half-buffoon' (Courthope 1895–7, I, 334).
[2] See Burrow 1994, 18. The events to which Hoccleve refers seem to fix the imagined moment of the poem's creation in early 1411, but it was probably completed and presented to Prince Henry late in 1411 or in 1412.

the melancholy Hoccleve and an old man whom he happens to meet. The rest of the poem forms a book of advice for Prince Henry, drawing on influential works in the Latin advisory tradition. It was one of the most widely copied English poems of the medieval period, and still survives in over forty manuscripts.

To many modern readers, however, Hoccleve's apparent mixture of conventional morality and confessional autobiography merely confirm his admission of having 'lerned lyte or naght' from Chaucer's literary example.[3] In the words of one standard reference work: 'Even by the lowly standards of fifteenth-century verse, Hoccleve achieved no great distinction.'[4] Critical discussion of Hoccleve was until recently dominated by three linked preoccupations: his friendship with Chaucer, his value as a witness to historical events and mores, and his relationship with the royal court. In the last of these categories, the key word is 'princepleasers', coined by Richard Firth Green in his influential study of writing and the court in the fifteenth century. In this formulation, poetry written for or around the royal household could be viewed as a fashionable accessory passed around a small noble clique.[5] Meanwhile, the term 'political' has usually been applied to topical writing commemorating or commenting on particular events and people.[6]

Such a division into 'courtly' and 'political' (or 'topical') literature masks the underlying process of commentary and engagement in which so many medieval English texts are involved, a process that now figures more prominently in studies of 'Ricardian' writers such as Langland, Gower, Chaucer, Usk and Clanvowe.[7] Strategies for avoiding censure, the questioning of authoritative political and rhetorical positions and the manipulation of traditional generic boundaries have all been recognized as part of the ambivalent relationship that poets enter with the court and court-sponsored culture. But whereas 'Ricardian poetry' may be thought of as sharing certain thematic or stylistic practices, within which positions either of authority or dissent may be adopted, the term 'Lancastrian poetry' can still approximate to

---

[3] *Regiment*, line 2079. All quotations of the *Regiment* are from Blyth's edition, and subsequent references will appear in the text.
[4] Matthews 1972, 754.
[5] Green 1980; my description crudely simplifies the argument of his valuable book. Nevertheless, the term 'princepleasers' has become a kind of shorthand for the image of fawning ineptitude often applied to Hoccleve and his contemporaries.
[6] Surveyed in Scattergood 1971; see also *English Historical Literature*, ed. Kingsford, and *Political Poems*, ed. Wright.
[7] For example (and respectively) Baldwin 1981 and Simpson 1990a; Peck 1978 and Simpson 1995b; Wallace 1997; Strohm 1990; Patterson 1992. Middleton 1978 has given a strong impetus to studies of the public concerns of Ricardian writers.

Introduction

Lancastrian propaganda.[8] Hoccleve and the *Regiment* are at the centre of this historical and critical disjuncture.

Hoccleve's poetry as a whole has attracted growing interest in the last twenty years. Alongside questions of autobiography, historicity and tradition, other concerns have emerged – petitionary poetry, textuality, gender – and Hoccleve's works have been re-edited.[9] Recent studies of the *Regiment* are beginning to address its thematic and rhetorical complexity, for example through the relationship between the two parts of the poem (Hoccleve's Dialogue with the Old Man and the *Regiment* proper) or through the philosophical traditions that Hoccleve invokes.[10] The *Regiment*'s relationship to the Lancastrian regime has also come under scrutiny; here Hoccleve has most frequently been characterized as profoundly conservative, a willing agent of Lancastrian power. Larry Scanlon views the *Regiment* as revealing, but at the same time reinforcing, the ideologically constructed nature of monarchic authority. Derek Pearsall describes the *Regiment* as controlled by and contained within Prince Henry's self-representation as an ideal future king. In his recent work, Paul Strohm has traced with great intricacy the fears and pressures that run through texts on Lancastrian kingship. For him, though, Hoccleve remains innocent of any troubling potential in the *Regiment*; it is the unconscious anxieties of the text that betray him. Of one of the central narratives in Hoccleve's poem, Strohm concludes: 'However complicit his intentions [...] Hoccleve thus proves unable to give us a tale which suspends reference or stops meaning things.'[11] These and other treatments have opened up the *Regiment* to a

---

[8] This imbalance is partly due to the background of the terms themselves. 'Ricardian poetry' was coined by J.A. Burrow in order to emphasize some common characteristics in the works of Chaucer, Gower, Langland and the *Gawain* poet (Burrow 1971). 'Lancastrian' is also borrowed from history, but comes freighted with polemical associations; it is defined by its opposition to 'Yorkist'. The difference between 'Ricardian' and 'Lancastrian' poetry is thus something like the difference between 'Victorian' and 'Soviet' literature.

[9] On petitionary verse see Burrow 1981; on textuality in Hoccleve's writings, Burrow 1984, Greetham 1989 and Simpson 1991; on gender, Torti 1992, Winstead 1993, Batt 1996 and Nissé 1999. The traditional concerns of Hoccleve scholarship may be represented by Jerome Mitchell's book (Mitchell 1968), which established a framework for much subsequent discussion. New editions of Hoccleve's works have been made by Charles Blyth (the *Regiment*), J.A. Burrow (the *Complaint* and *Dialogue*) and Roger Ellis (a selection to be published by Exeter University Press).

[10] I refer to the first 2016 lines of the poem as the 'Dialogue with the Old Man', not the 'Prologue', for reasons discussed below, pp. 178–85. Valuable studies of the reflective interplay between the poem's two parts can be found in Torti 1991 (enlarging on Torti 1986) and Hasler 1990. Hoccleve's deployment of Boethian and Aristotelian traditions is analysed in Simpson 1995a.

[11] Scanlon 1990 (reprinted and revised in Scanlon 1994); Pearsall 1994; Strohm 1998, 1999 and 2000 (quoting from Strohm 1998, 269, note 57, where he discusses

fertile theoretical and critical debate about the relationship of the artist to governing ideologies. Yet by portraying Hoccleve as an agent of monarchic power, Lancastrian rule or Prince Henry's reputation, they ironically replicate the traditional image of Hoccleve as a poet at the mercy of his material, unable to control the literary or political forces that occupy his text.

I would not wish to close off unintentional or unconscious meanings in Hoccleve's writing, some of which may expose the inconsistency of his ideological positions. Nevertheless, I believe that Hoccleve's intentions go beyond the complicit, and that some of the *Regiment*'s most powerful and disturbing messages are generated by design.[12] The chapters that follow investigate these possibilities from different methodological perspectives. In Chapter 1, I describe historical and traditional constraints on public or advisory speech within an economy of advisory language, locate Hoccleve's own productions amongst those constraints, and investigate how he resists them in order to subsidize the poetic investment that the *Regiment* represents. Chapter 2 focuses on the genre of mirrors for princes and the process of royal reading, suggesting that the model of a reading king has significant implications for the practice of advisory literature. Chapter 3 analyses Hoccleve's translations of authoritative texts and images (the major Latin sources of the poem and two early manuscript illustrations), suggesting how they contribute to his advisory strategy. The representation of royal and political bodies in the poem occupies Chapter 4 and, finally, in Chapter 5 I discuss the *Regiment*'s many manuscripts, asking how and in what contexts Hoccleve's readers copied and interpreted the *Regiment* in the hundred or so years after its composition. These approaches will, I hope, be of individual value to a poem that remains comparatively little studied. Collectively, they focus on the relationship between language and governance, asking how Hoccleve responds to historical and textual pressures, how he formulates his approach to Prince Henry and how the *Regiment* and its meaning are, in turn, received and reshaped by its readers, medieval and modern.

Hoccleve's tale of John of Canace). Hasler 1990 has also been influential in portraying the tensions of the *Regiment* as a form of textual unconscious.

[12] In this sense, my reading shares more with the (relatively few) critics who find elements of resistance or threat in the *Regiment*, for example Simpson 1995a, Ferster 1996 and Tolmie 2000. A fine article by David Lawton (1987) has influenced this alternative view of fifteenth-century poetry.

Chapter 1

Hoccleve's Writings and the Regulation of Language in Late-Medieval England

Thomas Hoccleve's life spans a period of intense literary activity and intellectual inquiry, but also one of increasing censorship, religious conflict and political instability.[1] These conditions contribute to many of the anxieties over public speech and political advice that are revealed in Ricardian and early Lancastrian literature. The issue includes but goes beyond a narrowly defined 'problem of counsel' of the kind Gower dramatizes in *Confessio amantis* VII.[2] Giving advice to the king was an important arena of political activity, real and imagined, but the means of controlling language were a vital point of struggle or negotiation both between and within many political and social groups. After outlining some of the 'external' regulation imposed by law against unauthorized speech and writing in this period, I shall examine ways in which speech was regulated within relationships such as the family and household, institutions and associations (including the Church, guilds and fraternities), and the king and Parliament. These groups participated in what may be termed a 'verbal economy', in which the value of speech, and indeed silence, fluctuated according to the status of the speaker and the attitude of the listener.[3] The coinage of this economy was the vocabulary of loyal advice, of instruction and of complaint. Its currency was not, however, restricted to words, since words could

[1] Hoccleve was probably born in 1367, or perhaps 1366, and died in 1426. Burrow 1994 includes a succinct account of his career, along with life records. The period 1370–90 has been described as a 'phase of experimental ferment' in religion and writing, followed by increasing repression (Somerset 1998, 17).

[2] For this phrase, see Ferguson 1955 and 1965. Ferguson identifies some of the tensions inherent in medieval advice literature, but draws a misleading distinction between (undeveloped) medieval and (sophisticated) Renaissance habits of political thought. For a more recent discussion of early modern censorship and 'conditions of writing', which can illuminate several areas of debate in the medieval period, see Patterson 1984.

[3] The concept of a verbal economy has been developed by Pierre Bourdieu (1991, esp. 43–65). Bourdieu posits a symbolic capital based on social standing and the 'distinction' of a particular group's language. Bourdieu's work informs my discussion of medieval linguistic exchange, though his theories of linguistic *'habitus'* are too restrictive to be helpful here.

themselves be exchanged for money and influence, for example through the circulation of petitionary texts, discussed below.

This chapter will not be a historical survey of the conditions of political writing, but rather a study of how linguistic constraints are represented and challenged in Hoccleve's own works and those of his contemporaries.[4] Hoccleve himself was deeply involved in the social and verbal relationships that this chapter explores: he employs in his writing the proverbial rhetoric of speech and silence familiar from instructional texts; his work at the Privy Seal placed him in close contact with both the political and textual activities of government and Parliament; he belonged to a class of educated bureaucrats whose identity, political views and literary interests became increasingly visible during the late fourteenth and early fifteenth centuries. Hoccleve was thus ideally positioned to take part in the sensitive negotiations necessary for writing public poetry in the early fifteenth century; in the final section of the chapter I shall ask how constraints on speech are represented in the opening Dialogue of *The Regiment of Princes*, and how Hoccleve attempts to overcome or subvert them in order to advise, criticize, and petition for his overdue annuity.

I. OFFICIAL REGULATION AND THE LANGUAGE OF REBELLION

During the reigns of Richard II and Henry IV, political and religious instability, combined with growing vernacular articulacy about social and doctrinal problems, made public speech a contentious issue. The period has been described as 'a world where political debate was more heightened and criticism of royal government more widely disseminated than at any previous point in English history'.[5] At the same time, however, a series of legal constraints was being placed on that criticism. Here I shall outline both those constraints and the way in which control of language was vital to the struggle of dissenting groups.

Royal and ecclesiastical legislation against dissenting speech has been listed and discussed elsewhere,[6] but it will be helpful briefly to summarize the official measures in place against slanderers and heretics in the period. In 1378, a statute against 'controvours de faux novels et

---

[4] Such a survey is offered, for example, in Ferster 1996, 15–38. I adopt the word 'constraint' here as more flexible and less bound by implications of official policy than 'censorship', a word which carries the danger of an over-confident analogy with post-medieval surveillance and control. For an exploration of 'constraint' in the context of medieval satirical writing, see Simpson 1990b.
[5] Harriss 1985a, 1–2. For the rapid exchange of political information in this period, see Richmond 1988.
[6] See Aston 1960, Hudson 1988 and Simpson 1990b, 15–21.

countours des horribles et fauxes mensonges' was enacted.⁷ This strengthened a law of 1275, which had protected 'the great men of the realm'. The 1378 statute went further by specifying particular men and groups for protection, including the Clerk of the Privy Seal, where Hoccleve was later to work:

> [...] Prelatz Ducs Countes Barons et autres nobles et Grantz de Roialme, et auxint del Chaunceller Tresorer Clerc de Privie Seal Seneschal del Hostiel nostre Seigneur le Roi Justices del un Bank et del autre et dautres grantz Officers du Roialme.⁸

> [Prelates, Dukes, Earls, Barons, and other noble and great men of the realm, and also the Chancellor, Treasurer, Clerk of the Privy Seal, Seneschal of the Household of our lord the King, Judges of one bench or the other, and other great Officers of the Realm.]

The statute was again reinforced in 1388 (when Hoccleve would have been a new clerk in the Privy Seal)⁹ and, as in 1378, those arrested were to identify the person who first spread the lies ('celuy dont le parole sera moevez') before they could be released.¹⁰

This legislation registers disturbances in the relationship between, on the one hand, magnates and royal officers, and on the other the commons within and outside Parliament. Between the two enactments of 1378 and 1388, however, a much more shocking event – the so-called Peasants' Revolt of 1381 – showed how the control and dissemination of speech (and writing) could move to the centre of political dispute. An economic crisis precipitated the revolt, but the targets of the rebels' attacks also reveal a deep mistrust of official documents and their

---

⁷ 2 Ric. II, Stat. 1, ch. 5 (*Statutes of the Realm*, ed. Luders, II, 9): 'authors of false tales and tellers of terrible and false lies'.

⁸ Ibid.

⁹ In the *Regiment*, Hoccleve states that he has worked at the Privy Seal for twenty-four years 'come Estren, and that is neer' (805). He most likely refers to Easter 1411; see Burrow 1994, 18.

¹⁰ 12 Ric. II, Stat. 2, ch. 11 (*Statutes of the Realm*, ed. Luders, II, 59). On the parliamentary context of the statutes, see Roskell 1981-3, I, ch. IV, 46-7. It should be noted that in both 1378 and 1388 the government was in the hands of the King's Council, either because Richard II was a minor (1378) or because he had been deprived of power by the Lords Appellant (1388). That the legislation specifically mentions those classes of people serving on the King's Council might suggest an insecurity about their position rather than simply royal anxiety. See below, pp. 61-5, for additional orders against criticism said to be issued by Richard II himself, who also resorted to the Court of Chivalry as a means of suppressing criticism (for which, see Saul 1997, 441, note 21). The idea of the first instigator (*novus auctor*) of a story is developed both in the proverbial and satirical traditions; see below, pp. 22-3. Of course, the impact of these laws depended on the speaker's social standing and rhetorical position; see Grady 1995, 553-4.

promulgators, whom they saw as the agents of oppression. A bonfire of such records in Chelmsford set the pattern for numerous other burnings.[11] The documents produced by the rebels themselves press the question of written authority and public speech. A letter published under the name of 'Jakke Trewman', for example, quotes the motto 'Speke, spende and spede', making explicit the connection between corrupt payments and the ability to be heard in high places. His assertion that 'trewthe hat bene sette under a lokke' articulates the linguistic exclusion that the rebels felt (many documents kept under lock were, of course, destroyed in 1381).[12] The renegade priest and rebel leader John Ball uses terms culled from Wyclif and Langland to support his call for rebellion, while the insurgents' letters and actions both imitate and usurp the procedures and authority of royal administration.[13] On the other side of the lines, monastic historians and commentators consistently attempt to deprive the rebels of a clear voice, instead characterizing them as an unreasoning and inarticulate mob.[14]

Victims of the rebellion in 1381 included Simon Sudbury, Chancellor and Archbishop of Canterbury, and Robert Hales, the King's Treasurer, as well as the many rebels executed in the months that followed, once the charters of manumission granted to them had been revoked. Struggles for social and linguistic control were not, however, only the concern of large uprisings. At this time a labourer named John Shirley was hanged for speaking against the King in a tavern on Bridge Street, Cambridge. Ralph Hanna has drawn attention to the descriptions of Shirley's crime in the official records, which connect the danger he presents by his unruly speech with the social unease felt about him as an itinerant labourer.[15] The presentation of Shirley's crime as treasonous speech in a tavern helps to make it conform to an establishment paradigm about the lower orders. In a letter of 11 May 1402, for example, Henry IV complained specifically about malicious comments against him made 'in tabernis'.[16] This association of drinking and

---

11 See Crane 1992, Hudson 1994 and Justice 1994 (151–3 for the Chelmsford fire).
12 I quote from *Peasants' Revolt*, ed. Dobson, 382. The 'letters' are recorded in Henry Knighton's *Chronicle*.
13 See Hudson 1994 and Justice 1994, 67–70 and 83–110. For the connection between Lollard writings and political dissent see Aston 1960. Langland's views, though not specifically Wycliffite, came to be associated with Lollardy; see Hudson 1988, 401–8; Gradon 1980; Lawton 1981; Simpson 1990a, 179–80 and 227–8. The influence of Wyclif's ideas was by no means confined to those conventionally thought of as political and religious dissenters. In 1404, the House of Commons was alleged to have made an outright demand for the confiscation of Church property; see McNiven 1987, 73–7.
14 See Strohm 1992, 33–56 and Justice 1994, 17–19 and 204–14.
15 Hanna 1992.
16 Rymer, *Foedera*, IV, part 1, 27; see Simpson 1990b, 20, note 29.

unlicensed speech is neatly made by Hoccleve against himself in *La Male Regle de T. Hoccleue* of 1405–6:

> Of him that hauntith taverne of custume,
> At shorte wordes the profyt is this:
> In double wyse his bagge it shal consume,
> And make his tonge speke of folk amis.[17]

Hoccleve's saving grace, he claims, was that he was too much of a coward to get into drunken fights. In 1381, the speech of the rebels is devalued in establishment accounts by this very formulation, portraying the rebels as drunken idlers whose violence betrays a lack of reason. These linguistic constructions at the same time draw on and reinforce legal constraints on unauthorized speech. Whether by appropriating official formulae or invoking common beliefs about peasant speech, both rebels and establishment writers sought to gain control of the discursive field in order to secure their own political and linguistic position.

In the case of religious disputes, speech or writing is central – often constituting the act of rebellion in itself. This makes official action against heresy more explicitly directed to the control of language.[18] At the same time, however, the threat of heterodox opinion was conceived by the authorities as a political threat, a view which encouraged the association of heresy and rebellion.[19] In 1382 a statute condemned itinerant preachers who spread 'heresies and notorious errors'.[20] In 1388 a commission was set up to secure the suppression of heretical teaching and writings, under the control of the King's Council.[21] A presentation manuscript of Roger Dymok's *Liber contra XII errores et hereses Lollardorum* depicts Richard II crowned and enthroned, raising an admonitory finger at the reader.[22] Richard's credentials as an anti-Lollard crusader are, however, overshadowed by his successor, Henry IV, under whom the statute 'De haeretico comburendo' was enacted in 1401, allowing for those who preached illegally and those with heretical views to be handed over to the secular authorities to be burnt if they

---

[17] Hoccleve, *Minor Poems*, III (*Male Regle*), lines 161–4. Subsequent references to the *Minor Poems* will appear in the text.

[18] For legislation against Lollard heresy see Aston 1960, Hudson 1988 and Simpson 1990b, 17–19.

[19] See Aston 1960. Wyclif's own writings had large political implications, but the initial association of Lollardy and sedition was made by his detractors. Aston notes that renewed action against Lollards (for example in 1400–1) was due as much to government instability as religious conviction.

[20] 5 Ric. II, Stat. 2, ch. 5 (*Statutes of the Realm*, ed. Luders, II, 25–6).

[21] Richardson 1936, 25.

[22] Cambridge, Trinity Hall MS 17, made for Richard II in about 1395 (fol. 1r, reproduced in Gordon 1993, 32).

refused to recant. The first person to fall victim to this law was John Badby, whose execution is described in Hoccleve's *Regiment*, lines 281–329.[23] Meanwhile, ecclesiastical legislation in 1368 (against Pelagians), 1377 (a papal bull condemning Wyclif) and 1382 (the Blackfriars Council) inveighed against unorthodox opinions.

These circumstances made the production of Lollard texts a vital and contested field. As Anne Hudson has shown, Lollard writing adopts a characteristic vocabulary and style that distinguishes it from orthodox prose, and yet forms a unified body of work, whose individual authors are very difficult to identify.[24] In addition to the practical value of this identity/concealment, the formation of a semi-independent linguistic system marked the Lollard refusal to exchange their opinions on terms controlled by the established Church. In particular, the use of English in reading and discussing scriptural texts was perceived as a threat to the hegemony of an orthodox, Latinate, establishment. One response to this was perhaps the promotion of English as an official 'national' language of government (and poetry) by, for example, Henry V;[25] another, conversely, was the suppression of theological discussion in the vernacular.

Shortly before Hoccleve wrote the *Regiment*, Archbishop Thomas Arundel produced his Constitutions (drafted in 1407, enacted 1409), which attempted more comprehensively than before to limit vernacular discussion of theology, and to outlaw the ownership and production of suspect books.[26] The impact of Arundel's Constitutions has recently been analysed by Nicholas Watson, who argues that, while aimed initially at heretical writing, they inevitably affected the production of 'vernacular theology' as a whole.[27] Stringent limits were applied to written translations of scripture, whether or not they contained heretical views, a policy that could potentially have brought under suspicion such texts as *Piers Plowman, Pearl, Cleanness, Patience* and *The Scale of Perfection*.[28] The Arundel Constitutions both expressed and attempted to counter the perceived connection between vernacular

---

[23] For the political background to the burning, see McNiven 1987, 199–217. In 1401, William Sawtre had been tried and executed as a relapsed heretic just as Parliament was deliberating the statute. For Richard II's less draconian position and its political implications, see most recently Staley 2000, 86–7.

[24] See Hudson 1988, 20–9. Hudson's investigation of Lollard 'sect vocabulary' has implications for other texts with a coterie audience; see also Annabel Patterson's valuable formulation of 'functional ambiguity' in early modern texts (Patterson 1984, 8–23).

[25] See Richardson 1980, Fisher 1992 and Pearsall 1994.

[26] Printed in *Concilia*, ed. Wilkins, II, 314–19.

[27] Watson 1995.

[28] For ways in which *Piers Plowman* could be regarded as suspect under these rules, see Simpson 1990b, 18–20.

writing and Lollard belief. In trying to eradicate the latter, it affected the former too:

> If the evidence of Lollard trials is to be trusted, it remained dangerous throughout the [fifteenth] century for those beneath the ranks of the gentry and the urban elite to be known as a reader of texts as diverse as *The Canterbury Tales, The Prick of Conscience, Dives and Pauper* and *The Mirror of Sinners*.[29]

Both in *The Regiment of Princes* and in his *Remonstrance to Oldcastle* (1415), Hoccleve echoes the anxiety of the Constitutions about lay discussion of religious questions, in language ('strecche', 'enclyne', 'meeue') that suggests a fear of unstable, unauthorized religious investigation:

Sum man for lak of occupacioun
Musith ferthere than his wit may strecche,
And at the feendes instigacioun
Dampnable errour holdith. (*Regiment*, 281–4 (the Old Man speaking))

Lete holy chirche medle of the doctryne
Of Crystes lawes and of his byleeue,
And lete alle othir folke ther-to enclyne,
And of our feith noon argumentes meeue. (*Minor Poems*, II, 137–40)

Here Hoccleve participates in an attempt to close off religious discussion and its political implications (though in the *Regiment* this assurance of orthodoxy in fact clears the way for the revelation of social divisions). Watson's assessment of the production and circulation of vernacular texts after 1410 suggests that the Constitutions did indeed have their desired effect, in that both the quantity of material and its questioning spirit declined:

> Once its effects had taken hold, the commonest and most influential response to the legislation amongst writers and their scribes was silent compliance. For the most part, it seems the Constitutions worked (as was, no doubt, the hope), not by being wielded in public, but by

---

[29] Watson 1995, 831. See Pearsall 1994, 397–404 for a discussion of vernacular writing and Lollard belief in the context of the *Regiment*. Pearsall argues that Hoccleve's veneration of Chaucer is part of an attempt to establish an orthodox vernacular literary tradition. This argument appears to conflict with Watson's findings that *The Canterbury Tales* could be held suspect under anti-Lollard legislation. Perhaps we should see here competing fifteenth-century readings of Chaucer either as a figure of the establishment or as a subverter of orthodoxies. A wider struggle between orthodox and dissenting vernaculars in the fifteenth century is energetically analysed in W. Bennett 1992.

creating an atmosphere in which self-censorship was assumed to be both for the common good and (for one's own safety) prudent.[30]

Such caution in discussing controversial topics, as well as in stylistic experimentation, has been perceived as one characteristic of fifteenth-century habits of reading and writing. Paul Strohm, for example, has argued that the fifteenth-century interest in Chaucer's more 'conventional' Canterbury tales, such as *The Clerk's Tale*, *The Tale of Melibee* and *The Monk's Tale*, testifies to a narrowing of cultural horizons in this period.[31] While this phenomenon cannot be ascribed wholly to Arundel's legislation, the Constitutions seem at least to have played their part in a more wary approach to religious authority in fifteenth-century literature, driving the discussion of hazardous material further into the modes of dark prophecy and protective ambiguity.[32]

Control of the spoken and written word was, then, a contested issue in the late fourteenth and early fifteenth centuries. While expectations and pressures differed widely between rebellious peasants, vernacular authors and heterodox theologians, the writings and actions of each could affect the safety of the others, and constraints on speech influenced them all. Such public monuments as statutes and the Constitutions do not, however, occupy the whole landscape of late-medieval linguistic constraint. Regulation began at home, in the private exchanges of the schoolroom and household.

II. FAMILY AND *FAMILIA*

The previous section dealt with the effect of breakdowns in negotiation over linguistic constraints. This kind of public challenge and attempted suppression was, however, the exception; while the threat of legal sanction always hung over the production and dissemination of unauthorized speech and writing, constraint also operated much more subtly in the family and household, arenas that are often ignored by large-scale studies of political writing and censorship. The noble household was based on a family unit, and was also the centre of local

---

[30] Watson 1995, 831.
[31] Strohm 1982b; see also Spearing 1985, 89–92, Lerer 1993, 85–116 and Silvia 1974. Strohm accounts for this change by social and economic retrenchment and the break-up of the literary group connected with Chaucer, rather than external legislation. The Constitutions can none the less be seen as a public symptom of unease about social, political and religious debate in the early fifteenth century.
[32] These strategies reached an apogee in the Tudor period, but are already well established in texts such as *Piers Plowman*, *Mum and the Soothsegger* and the prophecies attributed to John of Bridlington (for whom, see Rigg 1992, 265–8). See Patterson 1984 for the role of 'functional ambiguity' in early modern writing.

politics, while the royal household was, in turn, the focus for national policy. Domestic structures and relationships were thus vital to the management of political life at many levels.[33] For example, one of the most widely read medieval mirrors for princes, *De regimine principum* by Aegidius Romanus, organizes its discussion into three books that deal in turn with the prince's own moral life, the management of his family and household, and the best forms of government. The regulation of the family and the household naturally precede, and are fundamental to, the government of the nation. Exactly this Aristotelian division is outlined in Gower's *Confessio amantis*, where 'Practique', the third science of Philosophy, is split into 'Etique' (personal governance) 'Iconomique' (household management) and 'Policie' (governing the realm).[34] In this section I shall begin by discussing the earliest educational texts to which children would be exposed, and go on to consider the regulation of speech and writing within the noble and royal household.

Parental Instruction and Proverbial Constraint

Learning some Latin and acquiring the skills and manners associated with the administration of a household were prominent parts of the education of a young boy (and it would be almost always boys) from medieval noble or gentry families.[35] Texts of instruction for children frequently reserve an important place for the control of speech. The ubiquitous textbook for elementary Latin, for example, was a late-Antique collection of proverbs and epigrams known as the *Disticha Catonis*. Knowledge of Cato was synonymous with an elementary education. The *Disticha Catonis* is related as a set of precepts passed from a father to his son, and includes the following:

> Uirtutem primam esse puto, conpescere linguam:
> Proximus ille deo est, qui scit ratione tacere.
>
> [I think that the first virtue is to guard your tongue: he is nearest to God who knows how to keep quiet by reason.]
>
> Rumores fuge neu studeas nouus auctor haberi;
> Nam nulli tacuisse nocet, nocet esse locutum.
>
> [Flee rumours, and do not wish to be regarded as their source; for to keep quiet harms nobody, but something spoken is harmful.]

---

[33] For the court as *familia regis*, see Green 1980, 3–37, Green 1983 and Starkey 1981.
[34] VII. 1641–710; all quotations of the *Confessio* are from Gower, *English Works*.
[35] For a general study of medieval noble education, see Orme 1984.

> Sermones blandos blaesosque cauere memento:
> Simplicitas ueri forma est, laus ficta loquentis.[36]
>
> [Remember to beware of soft and flattering speech: simplicity is the form of the true man, and the praise of the garrulous is untrue.]

The *Disticha* has two complementary functions here. It is 'regulating' the language of the pupil in that it teaches correct Latin grammar and the rules of syntax and metre, rules and forms that give access to the privileged arena of Latinate expression. But these examples also show how warning and advice about the control (the 'regulation') of language were instilled through educational literature. The reader is at once empowered by learning the language, and constrained by the knowledge which that language imparts. The imagined relationship between parent (the speaker) and child (the hearer or reader) provides a paradigm for the role of language and access to it in many other texts of instruction, while the *Disticha*'s imagery of guarding or binding the tongue finds its way into discussions of speech at all levels. Hoccleve himself employs such ideas when he warns Prince Henry that 'Unbrydlid wordes ofte man byweepith' (*Regiment*, 2433).[37]

Peter Idley's *Instructions to his Son* typifies the tradition in which the *Disticha* play a founding part. This parental advice text of the mid-fifteenth century includes a long passage on keeping quiet, full of proverbial sayings including 'Restreyne and kepe well thy tonge' and 'Be not autour also of tales newe.'[38] Idley draws on a wide range of instructional models to instil that awareness of language and its dangers that was required of the educated man. One of Idley's major sources is the thirteenth-century Lombard lawyer Albertanus of Brescia (active 1226–51).[39] Albertanus was widely read in England and his *Liber consolationis et consilii* lies behind Chaucer's *Tale of Melibee*.[40] Each of Albertanus's literary works is couched as instruction to one or other of his sons. The *De arte dicendi et tacendi* specifically addresses the problems of when and how to speak. Albertanus bases his argument around six conditions for speaking, which raise questions of self-knowledge, of

---

[36] *Disticha Catonis*, I. 3; I. 12; III. 4.

[37] Hoccleve's immediate sources for this passage are two other influential textbooks: the Bible and the *Secretum secretorum*.

[38] Idley, *Instructions*, I. 50–567, especially 50–98. The lines quoted are 69 and 76. See also *How the Wise Man Taught his Son*, in *Manners and Meals*, ed. Furnivall, 48–52, and *The Good Wyf Taught her Daughter*, ed. Mustanoja (who gives an account of medieval literature of parental instruction, 29–78).

[39] For Albertanus's background and writings, see Powell 1992 and Wallace 1997, 213–23.

[40] Chaucer's immediate source for *Melibee* was the French translation of Albertanus by Renaud de Louens. For Albertanus's influence in England, especially on Chaucer, see Wallace 1997, 212–46.

the value of one's speech, of the potential audience and its reaction: 'Quis, quid, cui dicas, cur, quomodo, quando, requiras.'[41] The sixth section of *De arte dicendi et tacendi* includes advice on different genres of address, including preaching, letters and legal language, and Albertanus finally tells Stephanus that everything he has taught about speaking can equally be applied to actions:

> Hanc igitur doctrinam super loquendo vel tacendo, breviter comprehensam, tibi et aliis tuis fratribus litteratis scribere curavi, quia vita litteratorum potius in loquendo vel in dicendo, quam in faciendo consistit [...] Si autem etiam super faciendo volueris habere doctrinam, detrahatur de hoc versiculo istud verbum, *dicas*, et in loco illius ponas hoc verbum *facias*.[42]

> [Therefore I have taken trouble to write this teaching about speaking or keeping quiet, briefly recounted, for you and your other educated brothers, because the life of the educated consists more in speaking and talking than in doing [...] If, however, you also want to have advice about doing, remove the word 'dicas' [you should say] from this pamphlet, and in its place put the word 'facias' [you should do]].

In this text the habits of thought necessary for verbal interaction (*dicas*) can be projected as a complete scheme of social relationships (*facias*). Speaking is an action that has a particular effect on individual listeners; thus in section III Albertanus warns Stephanus to discover whether someone is a friend or stranger, foolish or wise, before conversing with them, and to avoid talking to the mocking ('irrisore'), the long-winded ('linguoso vel loquali') or the spiteful ('malevolis').

Albertanus's attention to self-awareness and the effect of the audience on how and when words should be spoken gives a nuanced view of the dangers and possibilities of public speech. These ideas are echoed in many advisory texts, often using the 'conditions' he specifies as a shorthand for taking care when speaking:

> Yf that thow wolte speke A-ryght,
> Ssyx thynggys thow moste obserue then:
> What thow spekyst, and of what wyght,
> Whare, to wham, whye, and whenne.
>   (*Whate-ever thow sey, avyse thee Welle*, 57–60)[43]

This inelegant poem of the mid-fifteenth century was part of a widespread proverbial and instructional tradition, epitomized by the

---

[41] 'You should ask who [you are], what, and to whom you speak, why, how and when': Albertanus, *De arte dicendi et tacendi*, XCIII.
[42] Ibid., CXVIII–CXIX.
[43] *Manners and Meals*, ed. Furnivall, 356–8.

Disticha Catonis and Albertanus of Brescia.[44] Neither were proverbial phrases on speech and silence limited to private, social encounters. They formed units of authority, applicable both to personal ethics and political governance, and so could be applied in different texts and circumstances to reinforce a moral or political argument at any level. For example, *Whate-ever thow sey, avyse thee Welle* connects hasty speech to political problems:

> Yf euery man had thys woord yn thowght
> Meny thynggis had neuer be by-gunne
> That ofte yn Ingelond hath be y-wroght. (50–2)

Many other topoi of caution familiar from proverbs, courtesy books and political literature are also employed in the poem. For instance, lines 3–4 warn 'A man that schold speke, had nede to be ware, / ffor lytyl thyng he may be schente'. The related proverb 'who sayth soth he schal be schent' is deployed in many contemporary political texts, for example as the refrain to a poem in the Vernon manuscript.[45] Hoccleve, too, fears that he and his fellow clerks will be 'shent' for complaining about a corrupt official:

> What shul we do? We dar noon argument
> Make ageyn him, but faire and wel him trete,
> Lest he reporte amis and make us shent. (*Regiment*, 1513–15)

Hoccleve highlights the dangers of speaking out by juxtaposing two competing values and consequences of speech. The 'argument' of the powerless clerks, though true, carries no weight beside what the lord's retainer will 'reporte', while the word 'amis' implies both that the report will be false, and that it will nevertheless be damaging to the clerks. In the *Regiment*, 'shent' carries with it an unspecified threat, but in the contemporary alliterative poem *Mum and the Soothsegger* the word is accompanied by some all-too-physical punishments for anyone telling political truths:

> And yf a burne bolde hym to bable the sothe
> And mynne hum of mischief that misse-reule asketh,
> He may lose his life and laugh here no more,

---

[44] Another English example is the anonymous poem *Lerne say wele, say litel, or say nogt*, in *Twenty-Six Political Poems*, ed. Kail, 14–22.

[45] *Who Says the Sooth He Shall be Shent*, in *Religious Lyrics*, ed. Brown, 152–4. Wawn (1983, 273–7) perceptively discusses the meanings of 'schent', and several poems that employ the proverb or its antitype '*But* he sayth sooth, he schal be schent.' The proverb is listed in Whiting 1968, S 492.

> Or y-putte into prisone or y-pyned to deeth
> Or y-brent or y-shent or sum sorowe haue. (165–9)[46]

The poet of *Mum and the Soothsegger* here uncovers the political force of 'shent', which is normally masked by its proverbial status. Through educational, rhetorical and political texts, the proverbial tradition is used to regulate and restrict the circulation of speech. In *Mum and the Soothsegger*, this tradition is exposed and satirized, but the burden of proverbial wisdom was behind a policy of judicious silence; alternative traditions of truthtelling had to be carefully chosen and subtly deployed to overcome the weight of advice against speaking.

The Household

A practical impetus to proverbial teaching was provided in courtesy books. Since the noble household was based around a family, texts dealing with household etiquette naturally complemented books of parental instruction, often adopting the same model of advice from father to son.[47] In household manuals the practical and moral virtue of keeping quiet is firmly promoted. The mid-fifteenth-century *Book of Curtesye*, for example, advises those waiting at table: 'What ye here there, loke ye kepe hit secre [...] Passe forth youre way in silence and in pees.' The author then lays down the 'condicions' to observe before speaking.[48] Interrupting other people is specifically condemned:

> Undrestondeth therfore or than ye speke,
> Printyng in youre mynde clerely the sentence,
> He that useth a mannes tale to breke
> Lettyth uncurtesly the audience,
> And hurteth hymsylf for lacke of silence. (281–5)

---

[46] In line 169, the word 'y-brent' is added by the manuscript's corrector beside the scribe's 'y-blent'. Barr, following Lawton, accepts this correction, and suggests that the passage alludes to the 'De haeretico comburendo' statute of 1401; see *Mum and the Soothsegger*, ed. Barr, note to 165–7, and Lawton 1981, 788. The poem's author was familiar with legal and parliamentary procedure, and may have worked at Westminster or attended Parliament. See Barr 1989, 34–5 for the poem's date (she argues that it alludes to events as late as 1409). For the relationship between *Mum and the Soothsegger* and *Richard the Redeless*, see Embree 1975, Barr 1989, 1–20 and 186–221, and *Mum and the Soothsegger*, ed. Barr, 14–17.

[47] For works of education and etiquette, see Orme 1984 and Nicholls 1985. For the structure of the noble household, see Given-Wilson 1986 and Mertes 1988. On the development of the household in the fifteenth century, see Starkey 1987, Horrox 1995 (who rightly questions Starkey's distinction between a 'medieval' military household and a 'Tudor' political court) and Morgan 1987.

[48] *Book of Curtesye*, ed. Furnivall; Oriel text, 134, 140, 143.

Once again, the relationship between speech, meaning and its effect on the hearer is recognized; the control of speech takes its place amongst the intricate systems of honour, deference and exchange inherent in the noble household.[49] There is no doubt that the structure of the household demanded a rigorous attention to rank and etiquette, while words spoken out of turn could damage the honour of individuals and the 'worship' of the household as a whole.[50] In the Black Book, a manual for the household of Edward IV compiled in the early 1470s, provision is made for the 'marchals of the hall' to monitor the speech of those 'vnder the astate of a baroune', in order to prevent swearing.[51] The privacy of royal counsel was also protected. Those servants responsible for the laundry 'owe and be sworne to kepe chambre counsaile', and in the ordinance of 1478 the ushers of the chamber are ordered 'that yee suffer noe man to come to our chamber when wee bee at our councell'.[52] Control of speech and its arenas was an integral part of relations between the king, courtiers and servants, allowing for private advice and discussion – 'privy counsel'. The Black Book also, however, records the custom that members of the court would represent the household by talking to and entertaining visitors:

> Thes esquiers of houshold of old be acustumed, wynter and somer, in after nonys and in euenynges, to drawe to lordez chambrez within courte, there to kepe honest company aftyr theyre cunyng, in talkyng of cronycles of kinges and of other polycyez, or in pypyng, or harpyng, synging, other actez marciablez, to help ocupy the court and acompany straungers, tyll the tym require of departing.[53]

The courtier's dual role as advisor and entertainer forms a vital tension in the production of court poetry in the Middle Ages. The dilemma is represented in the alliterative poem *Richard the Redeless*, which claims to be written to Richard II by a loyal servant. Richard is encouraged to read the rest of the poem only if he enjoys it: 'And if ye sauere sum-dell

---

[49] On the importance of exchange in medieval households, see Heal 1996. Verbal exchanges are often imagined as part of an overall household economy, as in, for example, the elaborate linguistic negotiation that accompanies the exchange of winnings in *Sir Gawain and the Green Knight*.

[50] For the duties and strictures imposed by the royal household, see Green 1980, 18–20. Hoccleve, of course, not only worked for the court in Westminster, but for much of his life lived with other clerks in a hostel, a 'household' paid for by the Keeper of the Privy Seal; see Burrow 1994, 7–8.

[51] *Household of Edward IV*, ed. Myers, 165. Though the Black Book was compiled rather later than some of the other texts that I consider here, it probably formalizes long-standing customs.

[52] Ibid., 197 and 202.

[53] Ibid., 129.

se it forth ouere' (I. 55), and the poet adopts the fiction that his work is private and open to correction:

> And if ye fynde fables or foly ther amonge [...]
> Lete youre conceill corette it and clerkis to-gedyr [...]
> For yit it is secrette and so it shall lenger,
> Tyll wyser wittis han waytid it ouere,
> that it be lore laweffull and lusty to here. (I. 57, 59, 61–3)

The paradoxes of court advice are encapsulated in the last line here, where the alliterating 'lore', 'laweffull' and 'lusty to here' are held in tension; the 'lore' which the poet could give seems to be compromised by its need to be acceptable. The passage negotiates a narrow rhetorical space where the poem's recipient must apparently allow advice to be given, and the text itself lies open to alteration and censure.[54]

The potential conflict between the inventive display that characterized court life and the political role of the royal household allows two models of speech to be set against one another: plain unadorned words, associated with the simple truth, and elaborate eloquence, associated with flattery and dissimulation. This opposition is exploited throughout the Middle Ages in writing on the court, which often presents its anti-rhetorical case in extremely sophisticated forms.[55] In the *Male Regle* Hoccleve condemns flattery, which can 'glose in contenance and cheere' (266). As a result the plain truth is rejected:

> But whan the sobre, treewe and weel auysid,
> With sad visage his lord enfourmeth pleyn
> How that his gouernance is despysid
> Among the peple, and seith him as they seyn –
> As man treewe oghte vn-to his souereyn,
> Conseillynge him amende his gouernance –
> The lordes herte swellith for desdeyn
> And bit him voide blyue with meschance. (*Minor Poems*, III, 273–80)

---

[54] The complications of *Richard the Redeless*'s audience have recently been addressed in Kerby-Fulton and Justice 1997. They argue for an initial 'coterie' readership of London bureaucrats, a group to which, of course, Hoccleve belonged. For the redirection of this poem's advice from Richard II to Henry IV, see below, pp. 65–6.

[55] The idea is ubiquitous in writing about the court, from Walter Map and John of Salisbury in the twelfth century to *Winner and Waster*, Alain Chartier's *Curial* and Skelton's *The Bowge of Courte*, as well as *Richard the Redeless* and *Mum and the Soothsegger*. For the argument that Richard II promoted a distinctive 'court style', see Eberle 1985, but note also the cautionary comments in Horrox 1995. The tensions of courtly style are explored in Patterson 1992 and Barr and Ward-Perkins 1997.

This passage transposes into a minor key the ideal of loyal advice represented by Gower's story of the fool and the king, examined in the Introduction. Hoccleve exploits the fact that although the counsellor is knowledgeable ('weel auysid'), he is in practice extremely ill-advised to tell the truth directly to his lord. Plain information is not enough in the court environment, but has to be adapted according to its audience. Indeed, Hoccleve's own 'information' in this passage is placed at several removes from the direct speech of the unfortunate counsellor. The poem is addressed ostensibly to the personified figure of Health (though its target is, in fact, the Treasurer Lord Fourneval). Its apparent subject is Hoccleve's own misrule, from which the idea of political misrule is an apparent digression. Hoccleve's ultimate intention is to remind Fourneval that his annuity is overdue, but he does not mention this directly until the final four stanzas of the poem. The issue is itself deferred, while Hoccleve's autobiographical admissions deflect the political implications of the poem's misrule into the trivia of the poet's unregulated past.[56]

The prospect of judgement by a powerful audience that is raised in *Richard the Redeless* and deferred in the *Male Regle*, is, of course, a common medieval poetic device; literary reception by the audience of the court is frequently portrayed as a matter for poetic anxiety. In the Prologue to *The Legend of Good Women*, Chaucer portrays the God of Love as a censorious lord who finds Chaucer guilty of 'heresye ageyns my lawe' by translating *Le Roman de la Rose*; the poet is saved only by the intercession of his Queen, Alceste.[57] Alceste places Cupid's reaction to Chaucer's misdemeanour in a clearly political context. She counsels her husband not to be 'lyk tyraunts of Lumbardye, / That usen wilfulhed and tyrannye' (G. 354-5) in censoring the speech of their subjects. Alceste deploys the vocabulary of the mirrors for princes tradition to remind him of his duties:

> [H]im oweth, of verray duetee,
> Shewen his peple pleyn benygnete,
> And wel to heren here excusacyouns,
> And here compleyntes and petyciouns,
> In duewe tyme, whan they schal it profre.
> This is the sentence of the Philosophre,

---

[56] For autobiography as a petitionary strategy, see Burrow 1982b, Burrow 1981, Knapp 1994 and below, pp. 37-8.

[57] G-prologue, 256 (all Chaucer quotations are from *The Riverside Chaucer*). Burrow (1981, 71-4) discusses the petitionary tone of Alceste's intervention at this point, and see Strohm 1992, 95-119 on queens as intercessors. For the political undertones of the *Legend*'s Prologue see Wallace 1997, 349-56 and Simpson 1998b. Chaucer's portrayal of the dangers of poetry is discussed in Hanning 1984 and Simpson 1986a.

> A kynge to kepe his lyges in justice;
> Withouten doute, that is his office. (G. 360-7)

The affinity between discourses of love and of politics is highlighted here by the bureaucratic categories 'excusacyouns [...] compleyntes and petyciouns' (new in the G-prologue), while the 'Philosophre' referred to is Aristotle, presumed author of the best-known book of royal advice in the Middle Ages, the *Secretum secretorum*. Alceste's speech brings us uncomfortably close to the world of the *Male Regle* when she suggests that Cupid may not be getting a true account of Chaucer's crime:

> Al ne is nat gospel that is to yow pleyned,
> The god of Love hereth many a tale yfeyned.
> For in youre court is many a losengour. (G. 326-8)

The Legend of Good Women imagines the court as a site of fraught negotiation between a misunderstood poet and a judgemental courtly readership – a depiction that must have seemed more ominous as the 1390s wore on. Chaucer is cut short by Alceste when he tries to explain his motives for writing; he must simply be grateful for the penance that she imposes. In the *Regiment*, Hoccleve fears a similar response from a female audience for mentioning the topic of obedience, once again employing 'shent' as the unspecified but disturbing consequence: 'If that this come unto the audience / Of wommen, I am seur I shal be shent' (5104-5).[58] These menacing, misunderstanding audiences form a dark counterpart to the benevolent commissioning patron portrayed in so many poetic prologues, or the close reading communities to which, it has been argued, Langland and Chaucer released some of their works.[59]

In *The Legend of Good Women*, Chaucer's alter ego can atone for his crime with a literary penance. Chaucer's awareness of the dangers of household speech are portrayed more pessimistically in *The Manciple's Tale*. Conflicting considerations of service, loyalty, audience and proverbial constraint are explored here, and telling the truth to a ruler is shown to have devastating consequences.[60] The crow in the god Phebus's household has the role of a court poet who can 'countrefete the speche of every man [...] whan he sholde telle a tale' (IX. 134-5). By informing Phebus of his wife's adultery the crow destroys the fragile

---

[58] See also the *Series*, where Hoccleve's friend advises him to placate women who, he claims, objected to his *Letter of Cupid* (*Minor Poems*, XXI, 743-826).

[59] See Kerby-Fulton and Justice 1997 and Hanna 1996a, 10-11. Writers could, of course, be under genuine threat, too. Thomas Usk's *Testament of Love* is partly an *apologia pro vita sua*, but did not save him from execution in 1388; see Strohm 1990.

[60] On speech, silence and truth in the tale, see Scattergood 1974, Fradenburg 1985, Patton 1992 and Craun 1997, 187-230.

harmony of the court. Phebus kills his wife, abandons his music, and deprives the crow of his beautiful voice:

> 'O false theef!', seyde he,
> 'I wol thee quite anon thy false tale.
> Thou songe whilom lyk a nyghtyngale;
> Now shaltow, false theef, thy song forgon,
> And eek thy white fetheres everichon,
> Ne nevere in al thy lif ne shaltou speke.' (IX. 292–7)

Phebus's insistence that the crow has spoken a 'false tale' articulates the discrepancy between the duty of service that the crow owes to his master, and the accuracy of his allegations: he cannot be both a 'true' servant and tell a 'true' tale.[61] The collapse of Phebus's household suggests how dangerous it is for a courtier to shift genres from the love songs of the nightingale to the uncomfortable truth represented by the cry of 'Cokkow' (IX. 243). Indeed the crow's punishment for betraying the adultery ironically echoes the traditional fate of the nightingale, supporter of illicit love. The crow's attempt to tell the truth is in accordance with the Manciple's own insistence that 'The word moot nede accorde with the dede' (IX. 208), but the crow shows how this precept leads to disaster when blindly followed. David Wallace argues persuasively that it is the crow's lack of self-knowledge, and his failure to take into account the effect, or context, of his speech, which precipitates the destruction of Phebus's household. In effect, the crow ignores the advice of Albertanus's *De arte dicendi et tacendi* to take account of one's own position, choice of words and the audience when deciding to speak.[62] The conclusion of the tale, however, is equally unsatisfactory. A string of proverbial warnings put in the mouth of the Manciple's mother seems to mock the crow's conflicts of loyalty and representation by their one-dimensional repetition:

> The firste vertu, sone, if thou wolt leere,
> Is to restreyne and kepe wel thy tonge.
>
> My sone, be war, and be noon auctor newe
> Of tidynges, wheither they been false or trewe. (IX. 332–3, 359–60)

These two examples are, of course, culled from the *Disticha Catonis*, while the rhetoric of parental instruction is gratingly emphasized by the

---

[61] For a detailed exploration of the shifting meanings of 'true' and 'truth' in this period, see Green 1999. The use of 'false' in Phebus's speech corresponds to two competing meanings of 'truth' that Green analyses: factual accuracy and loyalty.
[62] Wallace 1997, 252–6.

repeated 'My sone', 'sone, if thou wolt leere'.⁶³ However, the garrulity of the Manciple's mother (her advice to keep quiet occupies over forty lines) undermines the message itself, and instead draws attention to its unthinking application.⁶⁴

The same unresponsiveness in the proverbial tradition is encountered by the narrator of *Mum and the Soothsegger* when he attempts to argue for the value of a 'soothsegger' at court in opposition to Mum, the personification of self-serving flattery and judicious silence:

> And euer he [Mum] concludid with colorable wordes
> That who-so mellid muche more than hit nedeth
> Shuld rather wynne weping watre thenne robes.
> And cleerly Caton construeth the same,
> And seyth soethly, I saw hit in youthe,
> [Nam nulli tacuisse nocet, nocet esse locutum]
> That of 'bable' cometh blame and of 'be stille' neuer,
> And a wise worldly worde, as me thenketh,
> Of the whiche I was hevy and highly abawyd. (286–93)⁶⁵

The narrator attempts to penetrate this wall of self-serving wisdom, but he finds only 'homely vsage of the olde date, / How that good gouuernance gracieusely endith' (312–13).⁶⁶ The allusions to childhood education and home truths ('I saw hit in youthe'; 'homely vsage of the olde date') reinforce the narrator's inability to participate as an adult in the debate, while his description of a 'soothsegger' as a 'barn vn-y-lerid' (50) suggests both his untutored style and his ability to escape proverbial strictures in order to tell the truth. Here, the educational tradition is briefly exposed as another stone in the edifice of linguistic constraint, whose traditional nature masks its ideological construction.

---

⁶³ The biblical book of Proverbs lies behind this form of address; see for example Proverbs 1: 7, 'My son, hear the instruction of thy father, and forsake not the law of thy mother', and the openings of chapters 2, 3, 5, 6 and 7 in the same book.

⁶⁴ For Chaucer and Cato see Hazelton 1960, and on Chaucer's use of proverbs, MacDonald 1966.

⁶⁵ Barr prints the Latin glosses in smaller type; here, I place the gloss from Cato in square brackets. In the unique manuscript, BL Add. 41666, the glosses are written in the margin, but markers beside the text give a reference point for the Latin lines.

⁶⁶ The poet is, however, quite willing to use the same tradition to support his case against the spread of lying rumours: 'Lesingz been so light of fote, thay lepen by the skyes [...] As falsely forgid as though a frere had made thaym [Rumores fuge ne incipias nouus auctor haberi]' (1402, 1404). The manuscript's corrector has added to the gloss 'but caton is all contra and his consail bothe'. Barr (note to line 1404) suggests that this comment is meant to tone down the implied criticism of the friars, but it also neatly expresses the irreconcilable complexity of the tradition as a whole.

The Manciple's Tale and *Mum and the Soothsegger* bring us full circle, from the *Disticha Catonis* itself to its redeployment in vernacular texts that explore the constraints of speech in a royal and political household. Between the imposition of silence that Mum and the Manciple's mother call for, and the idea of unadorned truth that the 'soothsegger' represents, the relationships of the household are ones of hierarchy and accommodation. Hoccleve's sensitivity to the effect of speech on particular audiences can be illuminated in the light of such unofficial negotiations.

III. INSTITUTIONS AND ASSOCIATIONS

While royal and noble households provide influential models for the ways in which the production and value of language were regulated, they were not the only institutions that attempted to influence the exchange of speech and writing. We have already seen how, as a result of vernacular (and specifically Lollard) religious activity, the Church sought to limit any discussion of religious questions outside its own discursive and doctrinal boundaries.[67] So too the hold of other institutions on a particularized language and its deployment could come under attack. In addition, established relationships between the Church, law and government were joined in the late-medieval period by groups such as professional guilds and religious fraternities, which developed their own hierarchies of association and of language.

The narrator of *Mum and the Soothsegger* initially recommends a truthteller for the king's household but is silenced by Mum. He then turns to other institutions to see if there is a place for a 'soothsegger' there. First he goes to the universities (321–91), whose self-serving, closed discourse the poem mocks:

> Rethoric-is reasons me luste not reherce,
> For he conceyued not the caas, I knewe by his wordes [...]
> But he wolde melle with Mvm ner more ner lasse,
> So chiding and chatering as choghe was he euer.   (340–1, 344–5)[68]

The search continues with bitter criticism of the friars for their deceitful and grasping activities (392–535), and the soft ways of monks and

---

[67] For the Church's attempts to control 'deviant speech' through penitential discourse and the idea of 'sins of the tongue', see Craun 1997.

[68] On criticism of academic and other privileged discourses in *Mum and the Soothsegger* and other poems of the *Piers Plowman* tradition, see Barr 1994, 42–50, and Barr 1995. The idea that *Piers Plowman* itself challenges institutional discourses is developed in Simpson 1990a.

priests (536–787). The narrator goes to church and hears a priest list the produce owing to the Church in tithes: 'Of hony in your hyves and of your hony-combes, / Of malte and of monaye and of all that multiplieth' (608–9). The excessive verbal expenditure of this speech, concentrated as it is on items of food and money, suggests the material wealth of the Church as an institution, but the narrator looks in vain for a return on these goods, material or spiritual:

> And euer I waitid whenne he wolde sum worde moeve
> How hooly churche goodes shuld be y-spendid,
> And declare the deedes what thay do shulde
> To haue suche a harueste and helpe not to erie. (613–16)

As elsewhere in the poem, the elaborate rhetoric and procedure of the Church is crucially undermined by its silence on matters of practical and spiritual importance. The mention here of ploughing ('helpe not to erie') is an appropriate way for the poet to mingle the literal and figurative, since the Church's income from agriculture is not repaid by the spiritual ploughing that should be expected of it.[69] Mum exerts an equal force over the court and the towns:

> I askid of a eldryn man as I beste couthe
> Yf any sothe-sigger sate in the halle,
> And he answerid sharply that 'the sothe-sigger
> Dyneth this day with Dreede in a chambre,
> And hath y-drunke dum-seede, and dar not be seye
> Sith Mum and the mayer were made such frendes'.
> Thenne waxe I woundre wrothe, as I wel might,
> And drowe me to the doreward and dwelled no lenger,
> But romed forth reedelees, remembring ofte
> That Mvm was suche a maister among men of good. (835–44)

The fate of the 'sothe-sigger' is highlighted in this passage by the inversion of proper customs and duties. Instead of the meeting-place of the hall, he dines shut up 'in a chambre'; rather than drinking wine, he has 'dum-seede'. Institutions of local government, like the universities and the Church, have been overturned by the stifling presence of Mum. The phrase 'dar not be seye' neatly captures the double meaning of the description, 'seye' carrying the echo of its meaning 'say', as well as the primary meaning here, 'seen'. The fate of the 'sothe-sigger' is mirrored in the effect which the old man's words have on the narrator. He too is left excluded by the pact between Mum and the mayor: 'I drowe me to the doreward and dwelled no lenger.' The inclusion here of the word

---

[69] For the image of ploughing and preaching, especially in *Piers Plowman* (to which this passage clearly alludes), see Barney 1973.

'reedelees' is especially apt, for it conveys both the narrator's own bewilderment and the more general lack of counsel that the poem seeks to redress. 'Reedelees' is also, of course, charged with political force, being the epithet already applied (probably by the same author) to Richard II in *Richard the Redeless*.

The poet of *Mum and the Soothsegger* gives an extended critique of institutions such as the universities, Church and court that control access to linguistic exchange and political influence. However, these institutions were joined in increasing numbers in the late fourteenth century by groups such as fraternities and guilds, based on religious community or professional interests. The establishment of such associations involved the construction of new types of social relationships, often portrayed (by themselves and by later historians) as 'horizontal' rather than 'vertical' or hierarchical. In practice many such organizations still paid careful attention to rank and precedence, but nevertheless the involvement of many unlanded men and women, particularly from the urban mercantile class, encouraged these associations to develop new models of social exchange and interaction.[70]

Hoccleve himself was a member of an association called the 'Court de bone conpaignie', for which he wrote a light-hearted balade to the Chancellor of the Exchequer, Sir Henry Sommer (*Minor Poems*, XVII). The poem adopts a mock-formal tone. Stanzas 2–6 summarize a letter sent to the group by Sommer, which apparently expressed concern about how much he would have to pay to subsidize their next dinner. Each of these stanzas employs quasi-legal syntax and starts with a bureaucratic connective phrase ('Rehercynge how'; 'Yee allegge eek'; 'Yee wolden'; 'Vn-to that ende'; 'In your letre contened is also') to reinforce its pseudo-official tone. In the opening lines of the poem, however, Hoccleve subtly suggests the shifting relationship between the members of the 'Court' and Sommer: 'Worsshipful sir, and our freend special, / And felawe, in this cas we calle yow' (1–2). This remarkable movement of address shows how the existence of a fraternity or association could, albeit temporarily, redraw the design of social interaction, allowing Hoccleve to speak to his superior as if to an equal. The final stanza of the poem seems to re-establish Sommer's superiority; 'Ensaumpleth vs [...] and vs miroure'; 'Reule that day' (64, 66). However, this authority relies on Sommer performing his duty as their fellow: 'But keepith wel your tourn how so befalle, / On thorsday next, on which we awayte alle' (69–70).

---

[70] For theories of 'horizontal' social organization and their influence, see Strohm 1979, 21, and Strohm 1989, 145–51. The importance of 'associational forms' in Chaucer has been investigated in Wallace 1997. On guilds, see Black 1984, and Rosser 1988 for the relationship between guild and parish organization.

Hoccleve's 'Court de bone conpaignie' seems to have been primarily a dining club, and indeed guilds and fraternities frequently organized social and religious gatherings. In addition, however, most promoted the interests of a trade or church and helped members in time of difficulty. The larger trade guilds were also deeply involved in urban politics and royal finance; indeed, suspicions about the activities of such associations led to a call at the Cambridge Parliament of 1388 for all guilds to submit an account of their constitution and purpose.[71] While the gentry classes represented in the Commons saw guilds as a threat to their position, guild ordinances themselves betray an anxiety to protect the private 'counsel' of the group. A relationship of trust existed between members, which was violated by unchecked speech about the secrets of the trade or the deliberations of the group. The ordinances of the Guild of St George the Martyr (a religious fraternity) in Bishop's Lynn include this stricture:

> Also that no brother no sister ne schalle discuse the counseil of this fraternite to no straungere, vp the payne of forfeture of the fraternite for euermore, bot if he haue grace.[72]

In the case of trade guilds, such rules undoubtedly had some practical use in guarding professional integrity. Just as important, they enabled the group to act together and maintain a bond of loyalty that mirrored relationships of family, the religious orders and household service.[73] Indeed the very wording of the ordinances, with their references to brothers and sisters and insistence on the secrecy of counsel, evokes both religious rules and political language.

The betrayal both of 'professional' secrets and the bond of service is acutely dramatized in *The Canon's Yeoman's Prologue* in *The Canterbury Tales*. The Yeoman is the servant of the Canon but is also an initiate in his practice of alchemy ('somwhat helpe I yet to his wirkyng' (VIII. 622)); they form both a hierarchical and fraternal/professional unit. When they encounter the group of pilgrims, the Yeoman begins his well-practised sales pitch about the Canon's powers:

> 'Nay, he is gretter than a clerk, ywis,'
> Seyde this Yeman, 'and in wordes fewe,
> Hoost, of his craft somewhat I wol yow shewe.'   (VIII. 617–19)

---

[71] See Wallace 1992, Simpson 1993, Wallace 1997, 83–103, and on guild politics more generally, Black 1984, 66–75.

[72] *English Gilds*, ed. Smith and Toulmin Smith, 76. Similar prohibitions occur in numerous ordinances.

[73] For the social regulation that some guilds attempted to impose, see McRee 1987.

However, the Host's shrewd assessment of the Canon's unkempt appearance brings the truth to light: 'Why is thy lord so sluttish, I the preye [...] If that his dede accorde with thy speche?' (VIII. 636, 638). The dislocation between the Yeoman's words and the Canon's deeds punctures the Yeoman's attempt to impress the Host; the Yeoman betrays their true status as impecunious charlatans, but his revelations are accompanied by references to the very codes of speech, loyalty and betrayal that he is breaking: 'But I wol nat avowe that I seye, / And therfore keepe it secree, I yow preye' (VIII. 642–3). When the Canon overhears what is being said, both his response and his actual words echo the *Disticha Catonis*:

> This Chanoun drough hym neer and herde al thyng
> Which this Yeman spak, for suspecioun
> Of mennes speche evere hadde this Chanoun.
> For Catoun seith that he that gilty is
> Demeth alle thyng be spoke of hym, ywis [...]
>
> 'Hoold thou thy pees and spek no wordes mo,
> For if thou do, thou shalt it deere abye.
> Thou sclaundrest me heere in this compaignye,
> And eek discoverest that thou sholdest hyde.' (VIII. 685–9, 693–6)

The Yeoman's unchecked speech has broken the bonds of master and servant and of professional loyalty; it has also, the Canon claims, disturbed the social order of the pilgrims' own 'compaignye'. However, it is the Host, the self-appointed leader of the company, who encourages the Yeoman to reveal what he 'sholdest hyde'. In doing so, the Host shows the Canon's own authority to be based on false promises and conspiratorial secrecy. The tale's *Prologue* ends with the Yeoman employing a standard rhetorical invention:

> Now wolde God my wit myghte suffise
> To tellen al that longeth to that art!
> But nathelees yow wol I tellen part. (VIII. 715–17)

This topos of inexpressibility is immediately given a telling social perspective, however, by the Yeoman's plainer gloss: 'Syn that my lord is goon, I wol nat spare; / Swich thyng as that I knowe, I wol declare' (VIII. 718–19).

It is, then, the Yeoman, not his master, who is licensed by the pilgrim company to speak about his 'craft'. The *Canon's Yeoman's Prologue* brings together the anxieties and possibilities inherent in new sets of associations and the linguistic relationships that they create. The construction of authority, of who has the power to speak, is momentarily disturbed, revealing deep fissures in the Canon's edifice of professional secrecy. The tale itself shows how the delusory power of words supports dubious claims and criminal practice.[74] A gullible priest is sworn to silence lest the secrets of the alchemical process be revealed; in fact, the attempt to 'multiply' precious metal is just a multiplication of words – the metal itself, in the form of the priest's money, disappears.

This sample of late-medieval institutions suggests that new, and potentially more open, forms of association were being developed for religious, social and professional reasons in the late fourteenth and early fifteenth centuries. Their establishment, however, also created new motives for keeping quiet and fears of betrayal. It is to another rapidly developing institution – Parliament – that I shall now turn, as it occupied an important place as a site of financial and verbal exchange in the later Middle Ages.

IV. PARLIAMENTARY ADDRESS AND PETITIONARY CULTURE

Parliament

Amongst the institutions and associations that we have encountered, Parliament, and specifically the House of Commons, has an unusual place. It is (in theory) an association of equals, representing the king's subjects and speaking on their behalf. It is also part of the hierarchical structure of the royal household, above it the Lords and the king himself. This dual axis of common representation and hierarchical engagement makes the language of parliamentary exchange particularly sensitive to interpretation and audience.

The principal exchange which Parliament negotiated was that of money and speech. Kings required assent from the Commons to introduce taxation; in return, the Commons presented complaints, petitions and advice to the king. In effect, they were paying for their speech, and the value of their words varied according to the king's financial needs on the one side, and the Commons' determination to see 'good and abundant government' on the other.[75] During the late fourteenth and early fifteenth centuries, the importance of Parliament to formal legislation and financial management was growing. The period also saw a series of conflicts between the Commons and the king, heightened by the costs of the French war and unease over the system of justice. Henry IV's reign suffered from continuing instabilities, as arguments

---

[74] On verbal dissimulation in the tale, see Edwards 1991a, 66, and Patterson 1993b.
[75] A phrase used in the 1406 Parliament; see Brown 1964, 28.

over taxation and the cost of the household, along with revolts and conspiracy, threatened the Lancastrian regime.[76]

Parliament is the final institution to be investigated in *Mum and the Soothsegger*. The gardener whom the poem's narrator meets in a dream takes Parliament as a pattern for truthtelling:

> And principally by parlement to proue hit I thenke,
> When knightz for the comune been come for that deede,
> And semblid forto shewe the sores of the royaulme
> And spare no speche though thay spille shuld.   (1118–21)

This is the theory, but again the practice falls short of it. Deploying the etymology of 'parliament', the gardener complains that 'souuerayns and the shire-men the sothe haue eschewed / Yn place that it proprid to parle for the royaulme' (1131–2). The 'fautes' of the kingdom are not addressed: 'Thay wollen not parle of thoo poyntz for peril that might falle' (1136).[77]

The fear of reprisals against those who speak can be substantiated from the records of parliamentary proceedings, and the vocabulary that the poem uses is rooted in the diction employed in Parliament itself. Anxiety about public speech is epitomized in an account (probably derived from an eyewitness description) of the 'Good Parliament' of 1376, preserved in the *Anonimalle Chronicle*. This Parliament sat at the end of Edward III's reign, when the King, in failing health, was said to be influenced by a coterie of advisors, notably his mistress, Alice Perrers. I quote at length here because the account provides an important model for parliamentary engagement in this period as a whole:

> Et fuist assigne a les chivalers et communes le chapiter del abbeye de Wymouster, en quel ils purrount lour conseil privement prendre saunz destourbaunce ou fatigacion des autres gentz. Et en le dit secunde iour toutz les chivalers et communes avauntditz assemblerent et entrerent en chapiter et ses assistrerent en viroune, chescune pres de autre; et comencerount de parlere de lour mater de les poyntes de le parlement, disoyunt qe bone serroit al comencement destre iurrez chescune a autre de tener conseil ceo qe fuist parle et ordine entre eux et loialment treter et ordiner pur profit de la roialme saunz conselement; et a cestez choses parfourner toutz unement assenterent et firent bone serement pur estre loialles chescune a autre. Et donques une de eux dist qe si ascune de nous sciet ascune chose dire pur profit del roy et roialme qe

---

[76] Brown 1989, 156–237, contains a careful account of the development, members and authority of Parliament in this period; see also Cam 1970.

[77] As Simpson notes (1990b, 20, note 29), *Mum and the Soothsegger* specifies Parliament as the legitimate site for speech and criticism, and condemns the spread of wild rumour and unlicensed speech by the lower orders.

bone serroit de moustrer soun sceue parentre nous, et apres, une apres autre ceo qe lour gist au coer.⁷⁸

[And the chapter house of Westminster Abbey was allotted to the knights and commons, where they could take counsel privately without being interrupted or wearied by other people. And on the said second day all the aforesaid knights and commons gathered and entered the chapter house and sat down together, each next to another; and they began to talk about their business and the issues of the parliament, saying that it would be good at the outset to be sworn each to another to keep counsel about what was said and decided amongst them, and to speak and determine loyally for the profit of the realm without concealment; and everyone unanimously agreed to these things being carried out, and made a solemn vow to be loyal to one another. And then one of them said that if anyone of us knows anything to say for the profit of the King and realm, that it would be good to reveal his knowledge amongst us, and afterwards, one after another, [to reveal] what lies in their heart.]

This passage emphasizes the competing obligations felt by the Commons: they can speak openly only when their proceedings are private. The fraternal nature of their enterprise is reinforced by the detail that the members sat 'en viroune, chescune pres de autre', while their oath to one another binds them as a unit, rather than as individuals whose loyalty is to the crown; one historian has described it as 'a significant act of community for such a large body from all over the country'.⁷⁹ Here the account echoes the social and fraternal bonds that characterize professional and religious associations.

Such collective spirit had two important functions. First, a unanimous view was far more authoritative than a majority one; 'comun conseil' thus means more than merely 'general opinion', but rather gives the Commons a unified voice. Secondly, unanimity would make the task of presenting their advice less perilous. The Speaker acts as mouthpiece for the whole Commons; their speech is directed through him.⁸⁰ The power of speaking for others echoes that of the King, who

---

⁷⁸ *Anonimalle Chronicle*, ed. Galbraith, 80–1. Galbraith notes (xxxiii–xxxiv) that the *Chronicle*'s use of English vocabulary suggests that this section was translated from English.

⁷⁹ Brown 1981, 124.

⁸⁰ There was always a danger that a king might be informed about the Commons' private discussions. In 1401 the Commons 'showed the King how it might happen, in regard to certain matters which were moved amongst them, that one of their members should tell about such matters to the King, to make himself agreeable to the King and obtain advancement [...] By this, the Lord King might be grievously disturbed in mind towards the Commons or some one of them' (*RP*, III, 456; translation from *Constitutional History*, ed. Wilkinson, 299–300). The poet

ultimately has to unify the voices of his counsellors and represent the whole realm.

The concern of the Commons for collective thought and speech is reflected in the language of the petitions that they present to the King. They establish a tension between the value of common good and the suspicion of individual profit:

> Pur singuler profit et avantage d'aucuns Privez entour le Roi, et d'autres de lour covyne, si est le Roy et le Roialme d'Engleterre grandement empovriz.[81]

> [For the individual profit and advantage of people close about the King, and others of their cabal, the King and Realm of England is so greatly impoverished.]

The symbiosis between money and words, part of the economy of parliamentary procedure in the late Middle Ages, is here transferred to the language of the Commons' complaint. It is by the bad advice of councillors that King Edward is materially impoverished, but it is also because of their financial profligacy that the realm is held in low esteem; the passage signifies both on literal and figurative levels. The language of the parliamentary proceedings is closely paralleled by the narrator of *Mum and the Soothsegger*:

> But I dreed me sore, so me God helpe,
> Leste couetise of cunseil that knoweth not hymself
> (Of some and of certayn, I seye not of alle)
> That of profitable pourpos putteth the king ofte,
> There his witte and his wil wolde wirche to the beste. (227–31)

At this moment Mum appears, stifling the criticism of Henry's court and advisors, but the division established here between 'couetise of cunseil' and 'profitable pourpos' hangs over the whole poem. The idea of 'common profit' was central to political exchange in this period, and brought into focus the claims made by the Commons, the Lords and the King to speak on behalf of the realm. Hoccleve employs the same key words in the *Regiment*, blaming civil war in Rome on those who 'drow to profyt singuler, / And of profyt commun nat weren cheer' (5249–50) in his call for peace between France and England.

Three further passages of the *Anonimalle Chronicle* illustrate models of late-medieval political discourse that are developed in many con-

---

of *Richard the Redeless* puts the problem more bluntly: 'somme were tituleris and to the kyng wente, / And formed him of foos that good frendis weren' (IV. 57–8).

[81] *RP*, II, 323 (also recording the 1376 Parliament). Ferster 1996, 78–9, notes the different senses of 'profit' employed in the *Anonimalle Chronicle* account.

temporary literary texts. The Speaker, Sir Peter de la Mare, aims his attack not at the King himself, but at 'certains conseilers et servauntz' who take personal advantage 'par sotilte endesceit de nostre seignur le roy' (85). The attack on evil councillors is, of course, a way of censoring the King indirectly, and it constantly recurs in public and poetic complaints.[82] The second (and closely related) idea is that the good are prevented from telling the truth:

> [N]e nulle ne ad entour le roy qe luy voet dire la veritee [...] avaunt qe ceux soient remowez, nulle ne serroit si hardy de verite dire, ne de remedy fair.[83]

> [Neither is there anyone around the King who will tell him the truth [...] until these [the bad councillors] are removed, no one would be brave enough to tell the truth, or to make remedy.]

This charge is echoed in *Mum and the Soothsegger*, where the truthteller is 'a-frountid for his feithful tale, / And y-ferked vndre foote while falsenes goeth aboute' (54–5). Finding one who can 'dire la veritee' is, of course, the driving principle of the poem.

A third discursive model in the *Anonimalle Chronicle* is the Commons' protestation of simplicity and poverty in their address to the Lords and King. The remedy for poor counsel is not rule by the Commons, but more advice, taken from the great men of the realm: 'Et nous sumez si simples de sceu et davoir qe nous ne purroms redresser tiels graundes poyntes saunz conseil de sagez gentz.'[84] This attitude of deference was not merely a pretence; A.L. Brown argues that the Commons genuinely believed that 'a council formally appointed and charged to do its duty was the best guarantee that good government would be achieved'.[85] However, the pose of dullness was also a useful way of deflecting criticism; as such it becomes a characteristic part of the political and advisory rhetoric of fifteenth-century poets including Hoccleve.[86]

To summarize briefly: the *Anonimalle Chronicle* provides a template for the structures of parliamentary exchange. The Commons are seen as an association of equals (like a fraternity) who negotiate with the Lords

---

[82] See Embree 1985.

[83] *Anonimalle Chronicle*, 90, 91. The phrase 'si hardy' echoes the statute of 1275, which warns that none be 'si hardi de dire ne de contier nule fause novele' (3 Edw. I, Stat. 1, ch. 34 (*Statutes of the Realm*, ed. Luders, I, 35)).

[84] *Anonimalle Chronicle*, 84: 'And we are so simple in knowledge and possessions that we cannot redress such great issues without the counsel of wise men.'

[85] Brown 1964, 10–11. A similar concern with balancing a strong monarchy with accountability has been noted by Sally Mapstone in her valuable treatment of the Scottish advice tradition (Mapstone 1987, 5).

[86] See Lawton 1987.

and the King above them (as in a household). The terms of that negotiation essentially involve words (advice, support) and money (taxes, 'profitable' action). In addition, the Commons employ several paradigms for advisory and monitory speech from subjects to the monarch: an emphasis on common profit, speaking via an intermediary, employing rhetorical sleights of hand such as the King's ignorance and the pose of dullness. These paradigms are repeated, elaborated and questioned in politically informed poetry of the Ricardian and Lancastrian period, and are an essential part of the grammar of Hoccleve's advisory speech in the *Regiment*.

Petitions

The 'Good Parliament' of 1376 was exceptional in its strong opposition to Edward III's policies. However, the basic structure of parliamentary proceedings – the Commons debating and negotiating the King's request for money, and presenting their own petitions on matters of concern – was common to most Parliaments of the period, as was the tension between the need for redress and the fear of reprisals.[87]

The medium for the Commons' grievances was the petition, and its form institutionalized the language of deference for the expression of complaint and advice.[88] The ubiquitous nature of petitionary exchange in late-medieval political society has long been recognized, and has been re-emphasized recently by Gerald Harriss, who draws attention to the involvement of a growing number of people – royal bureaucrats, justices of the peace, the urban patriciate – in local and national

---

[87] Sir Peter de la Mare was imprisoned after the Parliament of 1376, but released following Edward III's death in 1377; see Ferster 1996, 27–9, who also discusses the case of Thomas Haxey, imprisoned by Richard II in 1397 for presenting a bill critical of the King's household (29–31). Haxey was exonerated at Henry IV's first Parliament. Given-Wilson suggests that the Commons were at greater liberty to criticize Henry IV – both because of his more amenable character, and because he had to secure their approval for taxes. Sir Arnold Savage voiced strong criticism of Henry's household in 1404. Savage was not punished, and likewise the Speaker in the reformist 'Long Parliament' of 1406, Sir John Tiptoft, who was appointed Keeper of the Wardrobe. Henry IV's poor health was a major factor in the power-sharing compromise worked out at this Parliament; see Pollard 1995. Thomas Chaucer, Speaker in 1407, 1410 and 1411, also voiced forthright criticism of the household, despite holding the post of Chief Butler from 1402 to 1413. See Given-Wilson 1986, 110–38 and 188–99, Brown 1964 and Brown 1981. On the other hand, the Commons asked in 1404 for protection against assault on their way to the chamber (*RP*, III, 542), and see above, note 80, for the fear that their deliberations might be betrayed to the King. Parliament was also the scene for bitter disputes over Church temporalities and Lollard sympathies; see McNiven 1987, 190–9.

[88] For the central role of petitions in parliamentary business, see Brown 1981, 125–8.

government.[89] This 'growth of government', fuelled by petitions, can be gauged by the development of the royal writing offices, including the Privy Seal. A department which, as its name suggests, had appeared initially as a private writing office for the king, was by 1400 a 'clearing house' for royal administration employing ten or twelve clerks, Hoccleve amongst them.[90] Though not as prestigious as the longer-established Chancery, it sent out many thousands of letters each year on all kinds of subjects, including making payments to officials, ordering the release of prisoners, seeking loans and inquiring into complaints, often as the result of petitions. Legal procedures were also changing, partly due to pressure from suitors: 'It was the receipt of *querelae*, or plaints, which extended the crown's criminal jurisdiction beyond felony to embrace many trespasses.'[91] In this system the administrative role of the King's Council became more clearly defined, and its responsibilities more regular: 'The council was [...] the nodal point for three elements of late medieval government: the royal will, the administrative machine and the concern of subjects for good governance.'[92] The petition can be taken as a symbol of that concern.

Hoccleve's poem *The Letter of Cupid* (1402) deploys the forms of this petitionary culture. Cupid responds to a complaint that he has received from one section of his subjects, namely women:

In general we wole that yee knowe
That ladyes of honur and reuerence,
And othir gentil wommen, han isowe
Swich seed of conpleynte in our audience,
Of men that doon hem outrage and offense,
That it oure eres greeueth for to heere.   (*Minor Poems*, part 2; VIII, 8–13)

This address assumes the authority of the monarch's spoken voice, but encloses it within a written form; such written appropriation of the spoken word is common to many of Hoccleve's poems. In *The Letter of Cupid* the process has another level, since the poem parodies a common bureaucratic (written) style, including a standard dating formula at the end: 'Writen [...] In our Paleys [...] The yeer of grace ioieful & iocounde, / M. CCCC. and secounde' (471, 472, 475–6). Hoccleve adopts the style

---

[89] Harriss 1993; see also Brown 1981 for parliamentary petitions. Burrow (1982b, 408–11) discusses Hoccleve's poetry in the light of medieval petitionary culture.

[90] See Tout 1920–37 (V, 54–112 on the Privy Seal), Griffiths 1980, Brown 1981, 44–52 ('clearing house' comes from 44) and Catto 1985, 79–83.

[91] Harriss 1993, 36, and see Powell 1989, 13. Cf. the narrator's promise in *Mum and the Soothsegger* to 'vnknytte [...] a bagge / Where many a pryue poyse is preyntid withynne' (1343–4), including complaints and petitions about the whole range of ecclesiastical and governmental abuses.

[92] Harriss 1993, 38; in the early fifteenth century Henry IV's poor health and a series of crises made the role of the Council more crucial.

from Christine de Pizan's *Epistre de Cupide*; in this he is doing what his job as clerk in the Privy Seal frequently involved: copying letters that impersonate the royal voice from French and Latin models.

Our knowledge of these bureaucratic models is due in no small part to a lengthy manuscript written mostly by Hoccleve himself in the early 1420s, known as the Formulary.[93] This provides well over a thousand examples of documents used in the Privy Seal, recording exchanges between central government and local magnates, between suitors and the court, between the King and his creditors. The Formulary has thirty-three sections, mostly relating to types of recipients, including 'Au Chanceller', 'Au Tresorers de les Guerres', 'Pur Venir au Conseil', 'Pur Monoie Apprester' and 'Irland'. Documents are included either as examples of forms or styles for common situations, or, it seems, as records of particularly significant events. In its mediation between the normative and the occasional, the Formulary echoes some of Hoccleve's poetic concerns – interspersing familiar or derivative forms or situations with the particular and remarkable.

The Formulary is not only a valuable record of the activities of the Privy Seal, but also displays those concerns over the production and direction of advice that are evident elsewhere in late-medieval society. Its function is, indeed, to distinguish the styles of address appropriate for different situations and recipients; while apparently a collection of standard letters, the Formulary actually allows for a sensitivity to small changes in tone and meaning. It includes, for example, a substantial section headed 'Exordies et extraits'. These are short rhetorical or proverbial phrases that can be used to embellish a letter, introduce a topic or adapt a document for a particular addressee. This part of the manuscript is in effect Hoccleve's own rhetorical florilegium, built up over the nearly forty years that he spent as a Privy Seal clerk. The extracts include quotations from *auctores*, proverbial phrases, and religious and moral epigrams. It was the job of the clerk to match the form of the letter to its recipient and to these rhetorical embellishments. Undoubtedly this was often a repetitive and tedious task, but the Formulary nevertheless contains those elements of the inventive and personal alongside the formulaic that mark the rest of Hoccleve's writing; while Hoccleve appropriates bureaucratic forms in his poetry, he also deploys rhetorical forms in his work at the Privy Seal.[94]

---

[93] London, BL Add. 24062, transcribed in Bentley 1965. For discussion, see ibid., i–xxxiv, Tout 1920–37, V, 54–112, Brown 1971 and Burrow 1994, 4–6.

[94] Knapp (1994, 67–71) discusses a point in the manuscript where Hoccleve includes his own initials in a sequence of three 'exaggeratedly impersonal' documents. 'Subjectivity in the *Formulary*', Knapp comments, 'can be represented only through an act of signification which is simultaneously an act of assertion and one of reticence' (69); see also Knapp 1999a. Another document in the Formulary that includes Hoccleve's initials has an even greater personal resonance. On fols 189v–

The nuances of the petitionary form of address were exploited, as John Burrow has shown, in many poetic guises.[95] The petition is Hoccleve's characteristic mode in poems such as the balades to the King (*Minor Poems*, XV), to John Carpenter (XVI) and to the Virgin (VII), and the *Male Regle* (III). Burrow links the act of naming oneself in a poem to the petitionary need: autobiographical revelation serves the aims of the petition because it identifies the person whom the reader is supposed to pay or pray for. The petition is thus a personal form which claims to reveal genuine facts about its author. Along with the self-identification that the petition involves, I would also draw attention to the way in which petitions explore the boundaries between writing and speaking. Just as a petition must bear the identity of the petitioner to ensure its success, it also requires a sense of urgency, of current need, if it is to have any force.

Oral forms of address most nearly approach this sense of need, 'present' both physically and temporally. For example, in a balade to Henry V (*Minor Poems*, XV), the King is addressed in repeated invocatory phrases: 'Victorious kyng' (1), 'o kyng pitous!' (3), 'Benigne lige lord!' (9), 'O lige lord' (17), 'O worthy Prince!' (24). In the *Male Regle* the opening invocation is even more elaborate, this time initially directed at the personified figure of Health. The demotic, confessional style that the poem fosters reinforces this impression of oral exchange rather than planned document:

> Ey, what is me that to my self thus longe
> Clappid haue I? I trowe that I raue.
> A, nay, my pore purs and peynes stronge
> Han artid me speke as I spoken haue. (*Minor Poems*, III, 393–6)

Any idea, though, that Hoccleve's petitionary poems are naively oral in design encounters problems. Many of the petitionary pieces are written in an established literary form, such as the balade or roundel.[96] As well as this formal textual basis, they also owe much to the traditions of poetic petition and impoverished poet exemplified in works by Deschamps, Machaut, and in Goliardic Latin poetry. The *Male Regle* signals this tension between oral and written when Hoccleve continues:

190r Hoccleve writes the introduction to a will, and includes his own initials as its testator: 'Eapropter ego, T.H. [...] testamentum condo in forma que sequitur et dispono. In primis etc.' (Bentley 1965, no. 982). This moving act of self-revelation gathers force from being concealed in a formulaic excerpt within a whole volume of such formulae.

[95] Burrow 1981; Burrow 1982a, 26–43; Burrow 1982b.
[96] For example, *Minor Poems*, XIII, XIV, XVII, all of which are called 'Balade' or 'Chanceon' by Hoccleve himself in San Marino, Huntington MS HM 111.

> Who-so him shapith, mercy for to craue,
> His lesson moot recorde in sundry wyse;
> And whil my breeth may in my body waue,
> To recorde it vnnethe I may souffyse. (397–400)

The play here between oral/physical ('breeth [...] in my body', and previously 'speke as I spoken haue') and written ('recorde') highlights how the poem is sliding between the two forms. Other poems display the marks of this friction. In the balade addressed to John Carpenter (*Minor Poems*, XVI), Hoccleve maintains the fiction of direct oral exchange, but the poem only makes sense as a written document: Hoccleve refers to his creditors 'whos names I aboue expresse', and indeed he has written 'A. d B & C. d D. &c' to stand for them in the margin of the manuscript.[97] In addition, the name 'Carpenter' in the first line has been written over an erasure; the original version must have contained a name of two syllables to accord with the decasyllabic line. The poem as a whole stands in a collection of similar pieces made by Hoccleve much later in life. All these factors complicate the vocal and present qualities of Hoccleve's petitions. While they seem to be striving for orality in effect, the poems are in fact deeply based in literary and documentary traditions. The written petition exists when the chance for an oral or physical plea is not possible; it thus constantly tries to recapture the physicality and proximity of the spoken request, but enclose them within a recorded, written form. Physicality is here provided by the document itself, which may at least come into the hands of the recipient.[98] The written text can in this way bridge the distance between writer and reader, while its vocal quality imagines the presence of the writer as speaking supplicant.

In both parliamentary exchange and in one of the characteristic literary forms of late-medieval government, the petition, the form and direction of address and the fiction of the spoken voice play a central role. Hoccleve's writing develops these concerns in his activities as a scribe and in his poetic response to bureaucratic forms. Hoccleve the clerk would have drafted an official reply to the kind of request that Hoccleve the petitioner habitually addressed to the King or Chancellor.[99] He stands between the two worlds, mimicking both the authoritative voice of government and the complaint of the petition.

---

[97] San Marino, Huntington MS HM 111, fol. 40r.
[98] Thus in the envoy to the *Regiment*, Hoccleve addresses the 'litil book' that must pronounce its words 'in the presence / Of kynges ympe and princes worthynesse' (5440, 5441–2).
[99] The Keeper of the Privy Seal had special responsibility for dealing with petitions from the poor; see Bentley 1965, xv.

V. VERBAL AND FINANCIAL EXCHANGE IN THE *REGIMENT*

This final part of the chapter asks how the conditions of constraint and the verbal economy are represented in *The Regiment of Princes*. Hoccleve in fact audaciously combines the voices of official advice, social criticism and petition that we have already encountered in various combinations in his other works. In the *Regiment*, Hoccleve must negotiate an exchange between his words and the hoped-for reward from Prince Henry. But as well as the implied threat that a personal petition may pose (that a lack needs to be rectified, in this case Hoccleve's overdue annuity), the *Regiment* contains more far-reaching complaints against social and political wrongs. These complaints are directed through the depression, poverty and exclusion from sites of verbal and institutional authority that Hoccleve's poetic alter ego experiences, and which are described during the Dialogue with the Old Man whom Hoccleve encounters outside the city, before the idea of writing a book of advice to Prince Henry has occurred to the impecunious Privy Seal clerk.[100]

From the outset of the *Regiment*, Hoccleve's poverty is entangled with his feelings of melancholy and isolation, and thus his inability to speak.[101] He paradoxically describes his anxiety (whose proximate cause is lack of money) as a surfeit:

> [Thought] that wikkid hyne
> Hadde beforn vexed my poore goost
> So grevously that of angwissh and pyne
> No rycher man was nowhere in no coost. (8–11)

Hoccleve's play here on 'coost' (meaning 'tribulation', 'circumstances', but also suggesting 'cost', 'expenditure')[102] is characteristic of the figurative richness — even excess – of his financial imagery.[103] In describing other symptoms of his melancholy, the vocabulary of riches and poverty continues to appear. Thought, for example, is described as exacting a payment from Hoccleve: '[Thought,] that fretynge adversarie / Myn herte made to him tributarie' (88–9), and three stanzas later,

---

[100] I call the author's persona 'Hoccleve', but he is not, of course, an uncomplicated autobiographical figure.

[101] Views differ as to the severity of Hoccleve's actual financial situation; even within the poem, the Old Man tells Hoccleve that he should be able to manage on his income (1212–18). I am grateful to Jennifer Nuttall for allowing me to read a striking discussion of fiscal regulation, tyranny and the *Regiment*, which will appear in her forthcoming Oxford D.Phil. thesis.

[102] *MED*, s.v. 'cost' (1), meaning 3; 'cost' (2), meaning 1a.

[103] For Hoccleve's verbal excess as part of his melancholy persona, especially in the *Series*, see Dunlop 1998, 105–39.

thought has 'despoillid' (111) his 'mazid heed [...] of konnynge / And wit' (110–11).

This network of images reminds the reader that Hoccleve's financial and literary 'worth' are at stake in the *Regiment*; in addition, financial constraint is closely linked to verbal and textual constraint. In lines 110–11 quoted above, Hoccleve has already claimed that anxiety has robbed him of 'konnynge' and 'wit'. Later in the Dialogue, Hoccleve implies that his poverty directly affects his ability to think and write:

> [W]hyl it with me stood
> So that I hadde silver resonable,
> My lytil wit was sumwhat covenable.
>
> But now, for that I haue a large lyte,
> And likly am heeraftir to han lesse,
> My dul wit can to me nothyng profyte;
> I am so drad of moneyes scantnesse,
> That myn hert is al nakid of lightnesse. (1237–44)

Here, lack of money is both cause and effect of Hoccleve's 'dul wit': he cannot turn his thoughts to 'profyte' because of anxiety over his empty purse. The phrase 'silver resonable' also mingles the semantic fields of wealth and mental capacity, since the effect of not having a reasonable income threatens to deprive Hoccleve of his reason. He tellingly returns to the theme just before the final section of the poem, on Peace, reminding the Prince that the material conditions that generated the poem have yet to be met:

> More othir thyng wolde I fayn speke and touche
> Heere in this book, but swich is my dulnesse,
> For that al voide and empty is my pouche,
> That al my lust is queynt with hevynesse,
> And hevy spirit commandith stilnesse. (5013–17)

Financial, literary and sexual impotence combine to impose silence on the poet. As in the previous quotation, Hoccleve's 'dullness' has here a much more concrete reason than the burden of literary inheritance which has been posited for these and similar confessions.[104] In these passages, Hoccleve is not so much suffering from an anxiety of

---

[104] See, for example, Spearing 1985, 88–110, on the looming figure of 'father Chaucer', or Lerer 1993, who characterizes the post-Chaucerian literary tradition as 'a phenomenon of subjugation' (5). Lawton's analysis of dullness as a shield for politically dangerous views is more apt here. Of Hoccleve, he says: 'The extravagant guise of dullness can hardly be overdone by a poet with a government position whose primary concern is public comment' (Lawton 1987, 764).

influence, as one of affluence. His uncertain prospects are themselves closing off the 'profyte' that may come from speaking and writing.

One of the most intricate of Hoccleve's monetary metaphors again involves the process of writing the *Regiment*. Here Hoccleve is introducing one of his major Latin sources, the *De ludo scaccorum*:

> There is a book [...]
> That the Ches Moralysed cleped is [...]
>
> And al be it that in that place sqwaar
> Of the listes – I meene th'eschequeer –
> A man may lerne to be wys and waar,
> I that have aventured many a yeer
> My wit therin, but lyte I am the neer,
> Sauf that I sumwhat know a kynges draght;
> Of othir draghtes lerned have I naght. (2109, 2111, 2115-21)

Here, of course, 'that place sqwaar / Of the listes' refers both to the jousting of the chesspieces and the name of the Exchequer, so called because money was traditionally tallied on a chequered cloth.[105] It was also the office from which payment for the Privy Seal clerks should come, and whose delays caused Hoccleve such anxiety. The Old Man has already acknowledged the problem: 'thow maist nat be payed in th'eschequer' (1877). For Hoccleve, then, the Exchequer 'listes' hold a more pressing personal significance; as well as an area for jousting, 'listes' could mean 'tricks' or 'cunning', and also a strip of cloth or vellum, perhaps like the rolls that should record payments to the Privy Seal clerks.[106] Hoccleve's observation that despite his labours 'but lyte I am the neer' can be taken as a pointed reference to his overdue annuity. The last two lines also carry a multiple charge. Hoccleve claims to know the moves appropriate to a king in chess – 'a kynges draght' – as a metaphor for the actions expected of a king in a mirror for princes. But 'draght', amongst many possible meanings, signifies a piece of writing; Hoccleve claims to know how to write on behalf of the King, how to adopt the style appropriate to his subject.[107] Of course, Hoccleve's job as a Privy Seal clerk involved precisely that, though the enterprise of

---

[105] *MED*, s.v. 'list(e)' (2), meaning 5a.

[106] Ibid., s.v. 'list(e)' (1), meaning b; 'list(e)' (2), meanings 2 and 3. The suggestion that Hoccleve could imply a written 'list' in the modern sense must remain tentative, since the earliest example of this usage recorded in the *MED* comes from 1439.

[107] Ibid., s.v. 'draught', meanings 3a ('A motion or movement, course'); 3b ('a move in chess'); 9a ('That which is drawn or written'); 9d ('a treatise'). Sarah Tolmie discusses the imagery of this passage in a fine essay (Tolmie 2000, 298-9). She also (300-6) explores Hoccleve's monetary language in a way complementary to the discussion here.

writing a full-scale mirror for princes is much more public and hazardous than Hoccleve's routine tasks.

The relationship between money and writing is, then, at the centre of Hoccleve's figurative language as well as his alter ego's anxieties; financial constraint is projected as the textual and verbal constraint of Hoccleve's dullness. The idea that 'money talks' is explored throughout the Dialogue with the Old Man, since institutional and political wrongs are described in relation to a verbal economy controlled by those in power. Hoccleve and the Old Man see loyal service cheated, falsity rewarded, and a bureaucratic system that 'comaundith stilnesse' (5017).

Hoccleve describes his world as full of false exchange and unprofitable dealings. The problems of the Privy Seal clerks are, for example, exacerbated by a corruption of the textual-financial exchange that should support their work. The clerks are cheated out of their payments by 'sum lordes man' (1500), who asks them to write a letter for his lord, and then fails to give them 'that that is us due / For our labour' (1501–2). What the clerks lose is described as a combination of words and money: 'Thus bothe oure thanke and lucre goon aweye' (1544). As we have already seen, the clerks dare not speak out, 'Lest our conpleynte ourselven overthrowe' (1526). This passage draws on the proverbial expression of constraint and the experience of working in the highly regulated environment of the Privy Seal. While the clerks cannot speak for fear of being 'shent' (1515), there is no one prepared to speak on their behalf either:

> [F]ynde can they noon [...]
> That ones list for hem to ryde or goon,
> Ne for hem speke a word, but doumb as stoon
> They standen where hir speeche hem mighte availle. (1493, 1495–7)

The silence of these potential patrons ironically echoes the 'travaillous stilnesse' (1013) which, Hoccleve explains, writers must endure:

> We stowpe and stare upon the sheepes skyn,
> And keepe moote our song and wordes yn. (1014–15)

Paradoxically, the condition of writing is depicted here as a form of verbal constraint; the enclosed atmosphere of the office denies Hoccleve the chance to 'holde a tale' (1002) – one that, most likely, would expose his unfair treatment. Meanwhile, those who do have the power to effect change, whose 'speeche hem mighte availle', remain silent for different reasons.

The distorted relationship between words and money is broadened by the description of flatterers at court. Flattery is characteristic of the warped verbal economy revealed in the Dialogue. The Old Man begins by condemning those who wear elaborate clothes; their surplus and ostentatious cloth is implicitly connected to the surplus, and deceitful, textuality by which flatterers gain access to those in authority:

> But he that flatere can or be a baude,
> And by tho tweyne fressh array him gete,
> It holden is to him honour and laude. (547–9)

The importance of flattery as a form of textual misrepresentation is discussed in the next chapter. What I should like to emphasize here is the way in which flattery destabilizes the system of linguistic and financial exchange on which the master–servant relationship relies: linguistic, since the flatterer's words do not truly refer to the things they describe; financial, since the purpose of the flatterer is to receive undue reward.[108] The Old Man depicts flattery as disturbing the whole economy of the state. He paints a comically inverted picture in which the demand for excess cloth bankrupts the wearers:

> For thogh he gette foorth among the prees [...]
> His cofre and eek his purs ben penylees [...]
> For land, rente, or catel he may go light;
> The weighte of hem shal nat so moche peise
> As dooth his gowne. (428, 430, 432–4)

Tailors are forced to lay out their material in the fields because their workbenches are too small, and retainers are useless in a fight because they can hardly hold up their huge sleeves, let alone wield a sword. This passage entertainingly extends a traditional theme, part curial satire and part complaint over social mobility.[109] However, it also draws attention to the distorted relationship between verbal and financial expenditure, which disturbs the landscape of the Dialogue. Later in the *Regiment*, Hoccleve returns to this idea by describing the flatterer as a 'blynd marchant', who exchanges his master's and his own soul for worldly goods (3074–80).

The indignities that the Privy Seal clerks suffer and the warped economy of flattery are reinforced by the wider evidence of financial and verbal (mis)dealings described in the Dialogue. For example, courtiers are accused of taking benefices and doing nothing for their parishioners. Outlay on church repairs, or on sermons, is out of the question: 'The oynement of holy sermonynge / Him looth is upon hem for to despende' (1429–30). Meanwhile, veterans of the French war are neglected, receiving no reward for their long service: 'Now been tho

---

[108] In the *Male Regle*, Hoccleve describes how he paid boatmen handsomely and received flattering words in exchange; see Mills 1996, 102–3.

[109] For attitudes to clothing and medieval sumptuary legislation, see Sponsler 1991–2.

worthy men bet with the yerde / Of neede' (880–1). Another exchange *manqué* occurs in the passage describing the execution of the Lollard John Badby. In return for renouncing his heresy, Prince Henry (as the Old Man says) promised Badby 'souffissant lyflode [...] Unto the day he clad were in his grave' (307–8). This barter – the Prince's money for Badby's recantation – helps to underline the urgency of Hoccleve's own need for a profitable way of addressing the Prince. The Old Man implicitly compares Hoccleve with Badby, since they are both victims of 'perillous' (267) thought, which can lead to error.[110] The Old Man's aim is not, however, to apply undifferentiated lessons such as those of the proverbial tradition, but instead to build a positive model of speech: 'If that thee lyke to been esid wel, / As suffre me with thee to talke a whyle' (148–9).

Hoccleve believes that an injection of hard cash is the only answer to his problems. When the Old Man first offers to relieve his distress, he is scathing:

> Cure thyself that tremblest as thou goost,
> For al thyn aart wole enden in thy speeche.
>
> It muste been a gretter man of might
> Than that thow art that sholde me releeve. (163–4, 176–7)

Hoccleve exposes the apparent disjuncture between the fine words of the Old Man and the material benefit that he requires. These lines also evoke a wider anxiety that the 'art' of the petitioner, advisor or poet will end merely in words rather than effecting practical change. The value of words seems to operate in a closed system that has no referent in a political sphere dominated by men 'of might'. Despite Hoccleve's pessimism, however, the Dialogue does generate arguments and narratives that suggest an alternative to the 'travaillous stilnesse' to which Hoccleve would otherwise be condemned, and establish a fair rate of exchange between loyal speech and financial reward.

The Old Man begins by encouraging Hoccleve to speak openly about his anxiety. He compares Hoccleve to a beggar:

> Thow seest al day the begger is releeved
> That sit and beggith blynd, crookid, and lame;
> And why? For he ne lettith for no shame
> His harmes and his povert to bywreye
> To folk, as they goon by him in the weye. (248–52)

The story is ostensibly designed to encourage Hoccleve to talk openly to the Old Man, and thus have the catharsis of a consolatory dialogue.

---

[110] See Hasler 1990, 171–2.

However, the fictional beggar's position is not merely analogous to Hoccleve's need to speak to the Old Man, it is also directly applicable to Hoccleve's situation in the *Regiment* as a whole. The beggar has to speak in order that his poverty shall be relieved; he exchanges his verbal resources for cash. The Old Man's exemplum powerfully expresses the need to speak out, a need echoed in Hoccleve's *Male Regle*:

> The prouerbe is 'the doumb man no lond getith';
> Who-so nat spekith and with neede is bete,
> And, thurgh arghnesse his owne self forgetith,
> No wondir thogh an othir him forgete. (*Minor Poems*, III, 433–6)

The actions of the fictional beggar, exposing his ailments and proclaiming his poverty, are a powerful model of Hoccleve's strategy of revelation in the *Regiment*'s Dialogue, one that uncovers 'harmes' that the country suffers as well as the poet/beggar's individual poverty. The very casualness of the Dialogue (Hoccleve is indeed talking to someone who has '[gone] by him in the weye') enables Hoccleve's voicing of dangerous criticism against corrupt officials, unheeding lords and mismanaged royal finances.[111] As James Simpson has argued, it is important that this conversation occurs outside the city, in 'the feeld' (117), away from the pressures of the Privy Seal.[112] Here these two marginal figures can place a vernacular gloss on the highly regulated textual and political tradition that the mirror for princes genre represents. By speaking, Hoccleve can indeed, as the Old Man puts it, 'walke at large out of thy prisoun' (277).

The Old Man argues that Hoccleve should speak to him (and thus indirectly to the Prince) from practical need, but the Dialogue also contains suggestions that the act of speaking or writing is in itself generative: it makes something out of nothing. Hoccleve, as we have seen, describes himself as having 'a large lyte' – plenty of nothing. The Old Man poses a similar contradiction when he invites Hoccleve to inspect his own purse:

> Gold, silver, jewel, clooth, beddyng, array –
> Ne have I noon othir than thow maist see;
> Pardee, this bare old russet is nat gay,
> And in my purs so grete sommes be
> That ther nis contour in al Cristientee
> Which that hem can at any noumbre sette.
> That shalt thow see, my purs I wole unshette.

---

[111] The phrase also tellingly echoes the biblical 'o vos omnes qui transitis per viam / adtendite et videte si est dolor sicut dolor meus' (Lamentations 1: 12) [All ye who pass by the way, behold and see if there be any sorrow like unto my sorrow].

[112] Simpson 1995a, 159. I am indebted here to this insightful article as a whole.

> Come hidir to me, sone, and looke whethir
> In this purs ther be any crois or crouche
> Sauf nedel and threde and themel of lethir;
> Heer seestow naght that man may handele or touche. (673–83)

As noted above, the image of the empty purse can powerfully convey the idea of linguistic as well as financial constraint. But the Old Man does have something in his purse after all: a needle, thread and thimble, with which to mend the 'bare olde russet' (675) he is wearing. I think it is significant that Hoccleve places these productive tools in the Old Man's purse. As elsewhere in the tradition of political poetry, cloth and clothing have close links with words and speech-making. The wearing of a plain cloak identifies the speaker as a loyal, straightforward truthteller, in contrast to the finely dressed and linguistically devious courtiers who people the Dialogue of the *Regiment* as well as contemporary works of complaint such as *Mum and the Soothsegger* and *Richard the Redeless*.[113] In the *Regiment*'s envoy, Hoccleve similarly imagines his poem as 'nakid [...] of eloquence' and 'unclothid' except for a 'kirtil bare' (5443, 5445). Just as this covering, stitched from simple rhetoric, can implicitly protect the poem from hostile readings and produce moral and financial 'welth' for the Prince, so the Old Man's possession of needle and thread rather than silver suggests the generative power of verbal coinage. In this context, the Old Man's call to 'Assaye, assaye, thow symple hertid goost!' (1889) when telling Hoccleve to petition the Prince carries the stamp of financial as well as literary minting.

Later in the *Regiment*, Hoccleve relates a story in which making money out of nothing plays a crucial role. This is the exemplum of John of Canace, an old man whose daughters and sons-in-law ignore him once he has spent all his wealth on them (4180–354).[114] John remedies the situation by borrowing a chest of coins from a merchant friend, and ostentatiously counting them when he knows that his grasping relatives

---

[113] The same image is later invoked in Skelton's *Collyn Clout*, 53–8 (*Complete English Poems*, XIX):
> For though my ryme be ragged,
> Tattered and jagged,
> Rudely rayne-beaten,
> Rusty and mothe-eaten,
> Yf ye take well therwith
> It hath in it some pyth.

[114] This much-discussed exemplum is most recently analysed in Strohm 1998, 196–214. Strohm uses the 'emptiness' of John of Canace's money chest as a way of exploring what he sees as the effacement of political difficulties in Hoccleve's poem. My reading assigns a much more central role to the creative power of John of Canace's performance and, in turn, to the political agency that Hoccleve exercises in the *Regiment*.

will be watching. They are taken in by the scene and shower their father with gifts and affection until his death. The figure of a poor old man who generates a lucrative narrative in order to secure his retirement surely has resonances for Hoccleve's project in writing the *Regiment*. Indeed, Hoccleve specifically compares himself to John of Canace, and comments that 'The indigent men setten nothyng by' (4359): to be poor is to be ignored. Hoccleve's own effort to avoid this fate must, then, involve the ostentatious display of his verbal resources:

Thogh that my lyflode and possessioun
Be scant, I ryche am of benevolence;
To yow therof can I be no nygoun. (2031–3)

While speaking out about poverty and constraint can, then, be justified on the grounds of need, Hoccleve also develops the idea that speaking and writing generate value in themselves; the apparently empty purse still contains materials for stitching together a protective or productive text. Loyal advice can be assigned value in the same way; just after the stanza quoted above, Hoccleve introduces Aristotle's supposed letters of advice to Alexander, the *Secretum secretorum*, 'Whos sentence is wel bet than gold in cofre' (2040).

This vision of the social and political worth of true speech is reinforced by the Old Man in his eventual advice to Hoccleve to write to Prince Henry. While the Dialogue has so far revealed that Hoccleve's labours, like those of other loyal citizens (veterans, the other clerks), are undeservedly ignored and suppressed, a practical solution seems no nearer. At line 1814 comes a kind of recapitulation. The Old Man sees that his efforts to reconcile Hoccleve to his poverty have not been completely effective, and tells Hoccleve once again to 'awake!' (1818). It is at this point that several strands of the Dialogue are brought together: Hoccleve's labours as a writer, his need for money, and the involvement of Prince Henry.[115] The Old Man suggests the Prince as the most suitable target for a petition, which could secure Hoccleve's income with an investment of words: 'To hym pursue and thy releef purchace' (1848). Despite Hoccleve's weary doubts about the Old Man's proposal for a straightforward petition ('Swich an eschange gete I noon to yeere' (1893)), the plan for a literary work is not far behind. The Old Man admonishes Hoccleve once more: 'Wryte to him a goodly tale or two [...] And his free grace shal upon thee lyght' (1902, 1904). The advice to write a 'goodly tale' overturns Hoccleve's earlier complaint

---

[115] Simpson (1995a, 166–70) argues that Hoccleve rejects Boethian complaint as a philosophical model at the end of the Dialogue, turning instead to an Aristotelian tradition of political intervention. I accept this shift, but would also emphasize the value of the Boethian tradition in allowing Hoccleve's current complaints to be voiced.

that he could not 'holde a tale' (1002), while the idea of 'free grace' neatly sublimates the issue of the Prince's obligation to pay Hoccleve. The exchange of Hoccleve's words for Henry's money is again touched on several stanzas later, in lines that emphasize Hoccleve's status as a household servant, performing a duty rather than imposing a burden:

> Syn my lord the Prince is, God holde his lyf,
> To thee good lord, good servant thow thee qwyte
> To him, and treewe, and it shal thee profyte. (1944–6)

Here the bond of duty between servant and master can paradoxically free Hoccleve from both his verbal and financial constraints. The Old Man's comments here seem to answer his earlier question 'what profyt is for to be pensyf?' (231); by establishing writing as a valuable service, its profitability can be measured against the inward-regarding anxiety from which Hoccleve suffered at the start of the Dialogue. One further issue is recalled and turned to Hoccleve's advantage. The Old Man warns Hoccleve against flattering the Prince, and claims on the contrary that honest truthtelling is the only way to unmask the effects of flattery at court and to redress the corrupt value-system currently operating amongst the nobility:

> The mooste lak that han the lordes grete,
> Is of him that hir soothes sholde hem telle. (1926–7)

> They been so blent with Faveles gay speeche [...]
> That in hemself they deemen greet vertu,
> Whereas there is but smal or nat a gru. (1935, 1938–9)

It is entirely appropriate here that an argument for speaking uncomfortable truths is depicted as a physical or financial 'lak' in the lords themselves, a misrecognition of their true value because of the debased currency of flattering speech. At the end of the Dialogue, the two commodities at issue – speech and money – have been brought together, just as the figures of Hoccleve and the Old Man himself become integrated (the Old Man reminds Hoccleve that 'swich as that I am, sone, I am thyn' (1992)).[116] Hoccleve's need for money and his dangerous, melancholy silence can both be remedied by addressing 'a goodly tale or two' to the Prince. Meanwhile, however, the Dialogue has already broken Hoccleve out of his prison house of language at the Privy Seal, and revealed the nation's inequitable economy of flattering expenditure and moral bankruptcy.

---

[116] See Tolmie 2000, 296.

This chapter has shown how linguistic and textual regulation were not a matter of common consent during Hoccleve's lifetime, but a site of often fraught debate, where the production of language could itself become a point of political and social struggle. Such arguments were played out amongst people whom Hoccleve knew and worked for, in texts that he wrote and read. The context of linguistic regulation in which Hoccleve was writing energizes the *Regiment*'s concern with the value of words in both the private and the political arenas. Political and social constraint are explored in the *Regiment* through the idea of financial lack, while honest truthtelling is established as a 'profitable' alternative to the false economy of the flatterer. But of what does this truthtelling consist? Hoccleve's chosen vehicle for 'a goodly tale or two', the genre of mirrors for princes, has usually been dismissed as a transmitter of bland moral platitudes. In the next chapter I challenge that view, and ask how Hoccleve's own counsel is to be approached by his intended reader, Prince Henry.

Chapter 2

'Th'entente is al': Princely Reading and Political Interpretation

I. MUSING ON MUTABILITY

Chapter 1 suggested how intimately connected were the arenas of literary and political discussion in the late fourteenth and early fifteenth centuries, while traditional and institutional constraints were employed to limit the expression of advice and complaint. The king is frequently portrayed as the judge of such issues, whether issuing laws against slanderers (as Richard II's government did in 1388) or imagined as the angry God of Love, condemning Chaucer's crimes against his laws in *The Legend of Good Women*.[1] This judicial role requires a critical faculty, in order to distinguish the importance, intention and effect of a text. In addition, the king himself must become a writer, issuing documents in response to the information that he receives; Hoccleve was involved in this process of royal reading and writing through his work at the Privy Seal. In a further short step, spoken advice and actions can be figured as a kind of text that the king must interpret in the same way, paying attention to subject, author, effect and audience.[2] In this chapter, I examine more closely the relationship between advice and the kings who must read and act on it.

If a king is both a reader and writer in the political sphere, then what criteria should he apply to his reading, and by what rules should his writing be governed? One answer could be that, since the king controls the production of writing, he also controls the generation of meaning: royal hermeneutics would then be entirely at the whim of royal desire.[3] This is close to the position adopted by, for example,

---

[1] Royal judgement is also, of course, a common motif in French poetry of this period, as in Machaut's *Jugement dou Roy de Navarre*; see Kelly 1987. For the influence of French models on Ricardian court literature, see Butterfield 1997, and on Hoccleve's relationship to French poetry, Burrow 1997.

[2] These relate closely to the categories of interpretation developed by Albertanus of Brescia in his treatise *De arte loquendi et tacendi*, examined above, pp. 14–16.

[3] Simpson argues that this is indeed the situation described in the Prologue to *The Legend of Good Women*. Royal desire is embodied in the God of Love, who seeks to

Princely Reading and Political Interpretation

Derek Pearsall, who sees the *Regiment* as a cog in Prince Henry's formidable propaganda machine.[4] I propose a different model for royal reading and writing. Books written for kings are frequently concerned not merely to reinforce the arbitrary will of their royal readers, but to teach them how to act in the political sphere: that is, teach them how to read, interpret and write.

This instruction is supported by a threat, one that exemplary texts carry within their form, and which is inscribed in the very narratives of past kings that fill the pages of mirrors for princes. Such rulers, historical and legendary, are presented to the current reader either as ideal models to emulate, or as disastrous failures to avoid. The actions of past rulers are thus read by the present incumbent; they have become texts that approximate to the historical and literary formulae laid down for good or bad kings.[5] The threat is clear: the actions of current kings will also be written and interpreted in the way that their predecessors have been textualized. They too will become exempla, fashioned by the strictures of exemplary writing. Faced with the threat of being read in the future, kings must themselves learn to read now, in order to interpret the texts not only of historical exempla but also of current political action. The process of assimilation to a textual model is suggested in, for example, the Prologue to Lydgate's *Troy Book*, written for Henry V between 1412 and 1420. Lydgate, in a move to dignify the status of authors, enlarges on the value of their books in recording the truth about the deeds of heroes:

> For unto us her bokes represent
> Withoute feynynge the weie that thei [the heroes] went
> In her daies, whan thei wer alyve.
> Ageyn the trouthe who so evere stryve,
> Or counterplete or make any debate,
> The sothe is rad of highe or lowe estate,
> Withoute favour, who so list take hede. (*Troy Book*, Prologue, 177–83)

The historical nature of the deeds is balanced here by their re-creation in historical writing. They are 'represented': shown to an audience, but also made present once again, spatially and temporally. Lydgate boldly

---

impose his (naturally cupidinous) will on the production of the text (Simpson 1998b).

4 Pearsall 1994.
5 For the assimilation of royal figures to a literary genre (in his case the fall of princes) see Wallace 1997, 299–336. Chaucer portrays an equally inexorable assimilation in the figures of Criseyde and Dido, both of whom predict how their actions and intentions will be represented by future misogynist accounts (*Troilus and Criseyde*, V. 1051–64; *The House of Fame*, II. 345–63).

reverses Chaucer's vision of the Troy legend as a hopelessly corrupt, unreliable contest between partial accounts, including the charge that

> Omer made lyes,
> Feynynge in hys poetries,
> And was to Grekes favorable. (*The House of Fame*, III. 1477–9)

Instead, Lydgate posits a recoverable truth, echoing (or rather, contesting) this passage of *The House of Fame* when he says that his account will be 'Withoute feynynge' and 'Withoute favour'.[6] The truthful, 'historical' account is, however, one controlled by writers:

> For after deth clerkis lityl drede
> After desert for to bere witnesse,
> Nor of a tyraunt the trouthe to expresse.
> As men disserve, withoute excepcioun
> With lak or prys thei graunt hem her guerdoun.
> Wherfore me semeth every maner man
> Schulde be his live in al that ever he can
> For vertu only eschewe to don amys;
> For after dethe, pleynly as it is,
> Clerkis wil write – and excepte noon –
> The pleyne trouthe whan a man is goon. (*Troy Book*, Prologue, 184–94)

Far from being an uncomplicated apologist for royal power, here Lydgate quite explicitly claims for authors like himself hegemony over reputation and historical judgement.[7] It is significant that just after the passages quoted above, Lydgate goes on to discuss the value and honour properly accorded to writers: 'For they enacted and gilte with her sawes / Her [heroes'] hyghe renoun, her manhood and prowes' (198–9). The word 'enacted' hints that the writers not only put the glorious deeds of heroes in books of deeds (*gesta* or *acta*), but that they themselves brought to life and participated in those very actions. The 're-enactment' of such deeds deserves reward: whereas writers have the power to grant the subjects of their works 'her guerdoun' according to their deserts, so in return writers deserve to be 'cherisched' and 'honoured gretly' (196, 197) by their masters.

---

[6] Of course, Lydgate also attacks Homer, who 'feyned falsly' (272) that the gods were on the Greek side. However, Lydgate does claim that a true history of Troy is possible. For an analogy between Lydgate's imagined lineage of Trojan historians and the precarious dynastic claims of the Lancastrian kings, see Ambrisco and Strohm 1995. The anti-imperialist tradition of Trojan history in which Lydgate operates has been charted in Simpson 1998a.

[7] A recent assessment that does acknowledge the complexity of Lydgate's relationship with the Lancastrian kings is Patterson 1993a; see also Straker 1998.

The *Troy Book*'s Prologue thus establishes a potential exchange between 'clerkis' and rulers, underpinned by the threat of a historical verdict on royal (mis)deeds.[8] This model of literary judgement reverses the image of royal judgement on literature, which is invoked earlier in Lydgate's Prologue (Prince Henry is lauded as the originator of Lydgate's translation) and taken to a tyrannous extreme in the Prologue to *The Legend of Good Women*. The *Troy Book* Prologue shows that while some literary presentations show the court interpreting literature as a political act, political actions can also be figured according to the 'rules' of literature.[9] Lydgate himself enacts this idea in two poems in the *de casibus* tradition, one more than 36,000 lines long (*The Fall of Princes*), another of fewer than 50 lines (*Of the Sodein Fal of Princes in Oure Dayes*).[10] While the former is mostly concerned with biblical, Classical and other characters before Lydgate's own time, the latter brings the subject right up to the fifteenth century, with stanzas on Edward II, Richard II, and John, Duke of Burgundy. As David Wallace has argued of Chaucer's *The Monk's Tale*, such 'modern instances' of the fall of princes can recharge the political force of the genre, bringing current precarious rulers face to face with the fall of legendary figures.[11]

---

[8] The theme of political reading is developed throughout the *Troy Book*. Verbal interpretation and the power of rhetorical skill are prominent themes, but Lydgate's protagonists often disastrously misread the texts with which they are presented. See, for example, the passage where the Trojans deliberate about attacking the Greeks (II. 1745–3318). Paris's libido-driven reading of his dream of judgement (II. 2369–809), in which he rejects Minerva (prudence) to choose Venus (sexual desire), symbolizes the Trojan failure to understand political signs. In II. 3295–306, Lydgate points out that if only they had listened to reason (i.e. to Hector and Cassandra), the Trojans would have saved their city. After the decision to fight has been made, Lydgate notes ominously that Priam's folly 'schal be rad in story and in fable, / And remembrid, with dites delytable' (II. 1887–8). Meanwhile, the Greeks consult Apollo's oracle. They only take notice of the news that they will defeat Troy, ignoring the fact that it will take them ten years to do so (II. 5941–6076).

[9] This begs the question of a category of 'the literary' in the medieval period. I am arguing here that by writing poetry, Lydgate, and also Hoccleve, Langland and Gower, for example, consciously engage in a discourse that holds distinctive assumptions and possibilities. For discussion of how patterns of thought and writing interact in medieval poetry, see Burrow 1993 and Simpson 1986b.

[10] *Sodein Fal* is printed in Lydgate, *Minor Poems*, II, 660–1.

[11] Wallace 1997, 299–336, esp. 326–36. Wallace compares Chaucer's tale (elusive, politically uncomfortable) with Lydgate's *The Fall of Princes*, 'dead on arrival as a critique of princely excesses' (334). However, he does not mention *Sodein Fal*, and underestimates the troubling potential of the longer work. For a thorough appraisal of *The Fall of Princes*, see Mortimer 1995a. If, as Derek Pearsall suggests, *Sodein Fal* was written to accompany a monitory tapestry or procession, it would quite literally be bringing current rulers face to face with their discredited predecessors; see Pearsall 1970, 180–1.

Hoccleve's Regiment of Princes: Counsel and Constraint

Lydgate's *The Fall of Princes* was written for Humphrey, Duke of Gloucester, whose own political ambitions coexisted with generous patronage of humanist literary endeavours.[12] Humphrey was himself, however, to fall victim to a 'sodein fal'. His failed attempt to be declared regent during Henry VI's minority, along with his disastrous marriage to Jacqueline of Hainault, made him numerous enemies, including the influential Cardinal Beaufort. In early 1447, Duke Humphrey was arrested on a charge of treason, and died in custody. Humphrey's fall is commemorated along with those of his former wife, Eleanor Cobham (imprisoned from 1443 until her death in 1454)[13] and John, Duke of Somerset (died 1444) in an anonymous poem of the mid-fifteenth century, which brings home to its readers the frightening proximity of Fortune's wheel:

> Wee nede not nowe to seke the croniclez olde
> off the Romans, nor Bockas tragedye,
> to rede the ruyen and fallys manyffolde
> off prynces grett putt to dethe and miserye
> in sondrye landes.[14]

In this poem, Duke Humphrey is inscribed into a literary form that he himself made widely available in English by his patronage of Lydgate. The textual control of the commissioning patron has here been overturned by a rapacious literary and political tradition.[15]

While the political implications of the *de casibus* tradition have long been recognized, poems such as Chaucer's *The Legend of Good Women* and Lydgate's *Troy Book* have only fitfully been associated with the more overtly advisory mirrors for princes. Their paradigms of royal reading as part of a political sphere of action can, however, be helpfully applied to a tradition that has usually been regarded as narrowly conservative in its political outlook and virtually moribund as literature. If mirrors for princes are concerned with teaching the prince to read politics, then their lack of specific advice on policy, and also their traditional nature, become easier to explain: they are involved in a wider framework of interpretation and action, and do not require specific injunctions in order to bear a political charge. Though indi-

---

12 On Humphrey's career and humanist activities, see Vickers 1907, Weiss 1941, de la Mare 1988–91 and Harriss 1994–6.
13 She was accused of plotting Henry VI's death by sorcery; see Carey 1992, 138–45.
14 'Musyng uppon the mutabilitie', lines 9–13, printed in *The Welles Anthology*, ed. Jansen and Jordan, 110–14. The poem is in the tradition of *The Monk's Tale* and *The Fall of Princes*, but also seems to draw on Hoccleve's *Regiment*; see Perkins 1999b.
15 For Lydgate and Duke Humphrey, see Hammond 1914 and more generally Wilson 1975. Mortimer 1995a, 60, notes Duke Humphrey's appearance as a *de casibus exemplum* in several texts, including Chastellain's *Temple de Boccace* and the *Mirror for Magistrates*, but does not mention 'Musyng vppon the mutabilite'.

vidual texts inescapably register urgent contemporary pressures, they often resist attempts to historicize their prescriptions in a specific way.

Modern scholarly discussion of medieval advice texts has until recently tended to avoid such attempts. Initially, works in 'the advice tradition' were identified and placed in categories according to their political or philosophical affiliations. This is essentially the scheme of diachronic surveys such as Lester Born's 1928 article, and the substantial studies by Wilhelm Kleinecke and Wilhelm Berges.[16] Second, historians of political theory have followed a similar path in tracing schools of political thought, Aristotelian influences or scholastic debates behind political texts. This approach has much to teach us about the theoretical, historical and rhetorical elements of mirrors for princes, though texts in English have rarely been studied with the same attention as those in Latin or Italian.[17] Third, scholars such as Robert Steele and M.A. Manzalaoui have tracked the dissemination of a particular text – in their case the hugely popular *Secretum secretorum* in its many translations and adaptations.[18] These methods are primarily concerned with the tradition as a whole, rather than the context of individual works. Many English poems from this period have been termed 'political', and discussed individually, but in analysing advisory texts, as opposed to complaint or satire, problems emerge.[19] To some critics, the lack of specific advice on 'political' subjects has been frustrating, indicative of an undeveloped medieval consciousness that excludes advisory poetry from serious critical consideration.[20]

More recent work on advice texts has been informed by different theoretical alignments, including explorations of power relationships that owe a debt to psychoanalysis, Marxist criticism and to Foucault,[21] and new historicist accounts that posit a permeable boundary between written texts and their political and intellectual environments.[22] These

---

[16] Born 1928; Kleinecke 1937; Berges 1938. See also Bornstein 1976.
[17] See, for example, Wilks 1963 and Skinner 1978 for influential accounts.
[18] See *Secretum Secretorum*, ed. Steele, Manzalaoui 1961 and *Secretum Secretorum*, ed. Manzalaoui.
[19] Scattergood 1971 covers essential ground with propagandist and 'historical' texts, but rarely addresses their wider ideological implications. He has, however, subsequently discussed political currents in Chaucerian and other texts; see Scattergood 1974 and 1987. For the debate over what constituted 'political' literature in the Middle Ages, see Elliot 1973, Coleman 1981, Kane 1986 and Trigg 1986.
[20] See, for example, Ferguson 1965, who characterises the *Regiment* as a set of 'uncontested generalities' with occasional 'lapses into originality'. Ferguson grudgingly admits that these lapses 'indicate that Hoccleve, hack-writer and time-server that he was, could observe realistically and interpret the function of unsolicited written counsel to some extent in a practical light' (89).
[21] For example, Fradenburg 1984, Hasler 1990, Scanlon 1990 and Wallace 1997.
[22] For example, Justice 1994, Patterson 1991, 1992 and 1993a. A historicism both more eclectic and more 'historical' than Patterson's can be found in Strohm 1992.

readings have illuminated the dynamics between writer, text and extra-textual forces, but their application to the advisory tradition still presents problems. In the most recent book on the advice tradition in England, Judith Ferster recognizes that advice texts appear elusive because of their apparent lack of specific reference.[23] In response, she employs several theoretical models while also attempting to historicize the production of individual texts. This leads her, for example, to read Chaucer's *The Tale of Melibee* as a text 'about' the contradictions of advice texts, but at the same time to tie *Melibee* to a specific debate – that over Richard II's policy on war with France.[24] Ferster's book also includes a chapter on the *Regiment*, in which she (rightly, I believe) counters the view that Hoccleve's work merely contributes to a totalizing discourse of monarchical power. Hoccleve's project of advice, however, does not emerge as a convincing alternative to royal self-representation, but rather as a patchwork of conflicting signals. Ferster's comment on Prince Henry's reading of the *Regiment* is indicative: 'But there were other parts of Hoccleve's message, and the prince could take his pick' (145). Later in this chapter I hope to suggest a more consistent impetus for the production of Hoccleve's poem.

Perhaps my contention that advice texts are concerned with the process of reading appears dangerously close to the idea that they are simply 'about' giving advice; after all, both propositions may appear to be preciously self-referential.[25] I would counter this by saying that a theory of reading, far from locking the text into a treadmill of self-reference, may provide a way out of the constraints imposed by a tradition which otherwise seems merely to talk to itself. If a mirror for princes teaches a skill – a process of reading – then the king may have a chance of applying that skill more widely than in a narrow historical moment. In this way, the mirror-image changes according to the figure placed before it. This helps to explain why medieval advice texts are not, on the surface, books about current affairs,[26] and may also account for the enduring popularity both of the genre and of individual texts: the technique of political reading and interpretation was always in demand. In this sense, the advice tradition is concerned much more

---

[23] Ferster 1996, 2–3.
[24] Ibid., 104–5 on *Melibee*. Much more rewarding is her exploration of the political and monitory currents in James Yonge's 1422 translation of the *Secretum secretorum* for James Butler, Earl of Ormonde and Henry V's lieutenant in Ireland (55–66). *Melibee*'s intricate balance of textual interpretation and physical threat within a household has been more successfully explored in Wallace 1997, 234–46.
[25] But not out of the question: one poem that can certainly be described as 'about' giving advice is *Mum and the Soothsegger*.
[26] Another reason for this lack of specifics is, of course, suggested by the dangers and constraints encountered in Chapter 1.

with the broader notion of personal and national 'governance' than with individual policy decisions.

In summary, a mirror for princes provides a point of reflective exchange, where the king as reader of a literary text and as interpreter of the text of politics are brought face to face. In the act of being read, these works of political literature teach kings how to read; they also confront their readers with the textualized actions of royal predecessors, as positive or negative reflections of a process of political and literary interpretation. Reflection in the mirror can be oblique (forwards to an ideal vision, backwards to an exemplary past) or straight ahead, revealing current lack or promise.[27] If this interpretative model for mirrors for princes seems to be concerned more with our own desire as critics to place hermeneutics at the centre of textual and political activity, then we should remember that authors of advice texts (such as Trevisa, Gower, Hoccleve and, later, Ashby) were also intimately engaged in writing and interpretation. They had a motive for promoting their own kind of hermeneutics as a vital part of political debate.

II. THE HISTORIOGRAPHY OF COUNSEL

The role of counsel was agreed by medieval commentators to be vital to the health of the body politic, and the problems and benefits of counsel are discussed at length in medieval mirrors for princes. However, the actual content of this counsel is very rarely set out; advice books usually discuss not what the king should do, but how to evaluate advice from others.[28] The king's role thus emerges as one of verbal and literary interpretation. Another substantial element of advice texts, concentrating on the physical and moral development of the king, is usually dismissed by historians as a set of commonplaces, and ignored by most literary scholars.[29] Here I outline the historical debate over medieval royal counsel: was it based on a system of parliamentary representation, or small cliques of noble advisors, or a professional bureaucratic elite? How do mirrors for princes fit into the discursive system of royal representation and counsel? Historians have held widely differing views about the context and relevance of these medieval representations of counsel. After summarizing the debate I suggest how two

---

[27] On mirror imagery in medieval texts, see Grabes 1982 and Torti 1991, 1–35.
[28] As Strohm points out (1998, 173), kings would be constantly bombarded with advice and petitions, making the evaluation of that advice especially important.
[29] The circulation and popularity of advice texts have been discussed by Green (1980, esp. chapter 5), Orme 1984 and, for Richard III's reign, by Sutton and Visser-Fuchs (1997, 105–33).

recent interpretations may help in understanding texts of advice, and in particular Hoccleve's *Regiment*.

During the nineteenth and first half of the twentieth century, the dominant model of late-medieval history was a constitutional one. It depicted the steady accumulation by Parliament of legal authority and the rise of administrative institutions to prominence, and emphasized the curbs imposed on kings by custom and practical exigency. In this model, the King's Council had an important role in giving formal advice and in making decisions about policy. Constitutional interpretations of Lancastrian kingship were especially influential: Henry IV and Henry V were seen as instituting a programme of proto-democratic reform in the English political system, which prefigured a flowering of the constitutional monarchy in the Victorian era.[30]

The constitutional approach to medieval politics was challenged after the Second World War by K.B. McFarlane and his followers.[31] They located practical political power in the individual retinues and local polities of magnate families. Magnates used their power to further their own ends, and the king, though the most powerful magnate, was also involved in this essentially factional enterprise. Although McFarlane's own analyses of late-medieval politics are both subtle and wide-ranging, the growth of 'McFarlanism' encouraged the production of detailed local studies that emphasized a fractured system of loyalty and rule. This work has been very valuable, but has diverted attention from broader issues of governance and political *mentalités*; its influence can be seen in the focus on patronage and individual lordship in many studies of fifteenth-century history.[32] In this world, the value of advice is strictly limited to the interest of different noble factions, and advice texts are regarded as, at best, decorative.

In the last decade or so there have been attempts to shift the focus back from private polities and patronage towards a broader view of English political society.[33] Instead of applying nineteenth-century conceptions of the constitution to the fifteenth century, however, this model attempts to use medieval theories of government and their practice to construct a 'new constitutionalism'. This approach raises its own problems, but its value for literary study is that it pays attention to medieval public texts, both historical and literary, such as parlia-

[30] The seminal work is Stubbs 1874–8. The arguments are, of course, more complex than there is space to present here. For the historiography of fifteenth-century politics, see for example Richmond 1983, Powell 1989, 1–20, Powell 1994, Carpenter 1995 and Watts 1996, 1–12.
[31] For example, McFarlane 1973 and 1981. For his influence see Richmond 1983 and Carpenter 1995.
[32] Powell 1989, 3–5, especially note 23.
[33] See Powell 1994. Powell acknowledges here the influence of the work of Quentin Skinner (see, for example, Skinner 1988, 79–96 and 119–32).

mentary records, chronicles, and mirrors for princes, in order to understand the ideas and language that inform, and potentially shape, political action.

One historical study that takes careful account of such 'public' literature, and specifically advice literature, is John Watts's book *Henry VI and the Politics of Kingship*.[34] Watts argues that the state machinery was still small enough to rely on the personal leadership of the king. Counsel came to him mainly through the informal networks of the court, and the official Council was there to provide practical advice and administration. Royal will was the force by which policy was seen to be driven, and because the king was thought to embody the kingdom, his will had to express the interests of the whole people. The central role of the royal will in the structure of government meant that the character of the king and the correct use of counsel were of crucial importance. This accounts for the value accorded to personal virtue in royal advice literature: only by encouraging the practice of justice, pity, temperance and so on, could the realm be safeguarded, since the royal will could not formally be constrained. Thus political literature and advice books insistently return to the qualities that make the king most independent and yet representative. The vital role accorded to personal virtue in political thought helps to explain the enormous popularity of moral and didactic literature that relates political action to individual virtue. Ideas that made royal authority contingent on popular support were deployed as warnings, to prevent the king overstepping his jurisdiction. They acknowledge that alongside regal authority comes the responsibility for representing the views of his subjects.[35] This is why a rupture between the king and his people is so potentially devastating, and why he should be as open as possible to counsel.

Watts's book suggests that the main endeavour of political society was to direct the will of the king, not to reduce his importance or to divide the power of the executive by giving formal authority to a council.[36] Of course, this model of political exchange and representation was frequently subject to fracture by the promotion of individual or factional interests; such dangers are highlighted in texts such as *Mum and the Soothsegger* and *Richard the Redeless*. Despite (or rather because of) this potential for political fragmentation, mirrors for princes could perform a 'constitutional' function in guiding the king's will through the deployment of advice. There is, however, a further step to be made,

---

[34] Watts 1996. This paragraph crudely summarizes 1–101 of his book.
[35] On medieval representative traditions see Ullmann 1966, 150–92, Quillet 1988 and Dunbabin 1988.
[36] Later in the century, Sir John Fortescue proposed a shift towards conciliar government after the difficulties of Henry VI's reign had brought about a crisis in the system; see Watts 1996, 46–7 and Fortescue, *On the Laws and Governance of England*, xxxvi–xxxviii, 112–17 and 137–8.

which Watts's historical study does not explore: the correlation between directing the political will of the king through advice, and the medieval understanding of educational or philosophical reading, in which the will is 'informed' by the rational and imaginative faculties of the soul. This kind of reading has been examined in literary contexts by Alastair Minnis and James Simpson; particularly relevant here is the latter's study of Gower's *Confessio amantis*, a poem that Hoccleve certainly knew.[37] Simpson argues that Amans and Genius are parts of the same psyche, whose reading is initially guided by desire, and which eventually marries the impulse for imaginative recollection ('reading') with a rational faculty. Gower's love allegory cannot mask his primary interest in politics, which is prepared for in the Prologue to the *Confessio*, and displayed openly in Book VII. In addition, Amans is identified with the figure of Richard II, though having reintegrated his capricious will, the lover is revealed to be 'John Gower' himself.[38] This interpretation of the *Confessio* accords with Watts's view of counsel as educating the will of the king, and it is in Book VII of the *Confessio* (where the advisory tradition is incorporated into the poem's penitential scheme) that the relationship between royal reading and political action is most apparent.

In Book VII of the *Confessio*, the five 'points of policy' that come under the science of 'Practique' are introduced by a discussion of rhetoric: the power of the word precedes any lessons about the authority of the king. The passage on rhetoric (VII. 1507–640) is closely concerned with the dangerous, ambiguous force that words possess: 'Herba, lapis, sermo, tria sunt virtute repleta, / Vis tamen ex verbi pondere plura facit.'[39] Rhetoric and its interpretation are immediately linked to political action, or even supplant it:

> The wordes maken frend of fo,
> And fo of frend, and pes of werre,
> And werre of pes. (VII. 1574–6)

These questions of verbal potential spill over into the direct discussion of 'policy', for example in the comparison of the power of a king, woman, wine and truth (VII. 1783–984), the condemnations of flattery (VII. 2177–694) and the narratives of the courtiers and fool, and of

---

[37] Simpson 1995b, esp. chapters 5–7. See also Minnis 1984, Minnis and Scott 1988, Simpson 1986b and Simpson 1996. An insightful discussion of Gower's positioning *vis-à-vis* royal power and representation can also be found in Dimmick 1998, 183–210.

[38] Simpson 1995b, especially 263–71 and 279–84. In BL MS Add. 42131, fol. 115r, a miniature depicts Gower as a 'personal king'; see Wright 1992, 195–7.

[39] Before VII. 1507: 'Herb, stone, speech, these three are full of power, but the force of word's weight achieves more.'

Rehoboam (VII. 3945–4026; 4027–146). Gower turns repeatedly to the question of verbal power and interpretation when the subject of politics is directly addressed, and throughout the *Confessio* he places imaginative engagement with texts at the centre of any progress towards rational judgement or the control of wilful desire.

The work of Watts and Simpson independently suggests the importance of educating or directing the will to late-medieval conceptions both of political authority and psychological discourse. This is a potentially rich field for our own understanding of political and advisory literature from a period which saw a burgeoning debate in English on royal authority, representation and governance, including works by Trevisa and Lydgate as well as Langland, Chaucer, Gower and Hoccleve. Before examining the *Regiment* itself, I shall show how the actions of a particular king were presented as instances of wilful reading, and subsequently moulded to form exemplary texts and interpretative models. When Hoccleve was writing the *Regiment*, the last king to have died was Richard II, whose reign provides a striking example of this process of textual and historical assimilation.

III. RICHARD II: READING KING TO POLITICAL EXEMPLUM

The previous section suggested how advice literature may attempt to direct the will of the king. In the end, however, the power of interpreting and representing that advice is left with the king himself. Questions of understanding, of reading and responding to counsel, thus become crucially important, and moments of verbal exchange between subject and monarch are also points of tension. This section turns to representations of Richard II in narrative history and poetry, examining how these points of tension are shown, and how the King's actions are described in the language of counsel. Richard attracted partisan descriptions on both sides, but such deeply partial accounts themselves demonstrate what a central role textual interpretation played in the political ideology of late-medieval England.[40]

During the Parliament of 1383 the Speaker of the Commons, James Pickering, attempted to give some unwelcome advice to Richard II. While professing that the matter was really one for the Lords to consider, he recommended a less expensive campaign in France. Pickering

---

[40] For Richard's regime and deposition, see Saul 1997, Tuck 1971, Barron 1968, Gransden 1982 (chapter 6) and Barron 1990. Both Gransden and Barron give accounts of the narrative sources for the deposition and their biases. Relevant texts are translated in Barron 1990 and *Chronicles of the Revolution*, ed. Given-Wilson. The narration of Richard II's deposition through the frame of the *de casibus* is described in Wallace 1997, 335–6.

attempted to make a fine distinction between his own simple words and the threat that more formal counsel might pose to the King:

> Mais ils nel dient mye, ce dit le dit Monsieur James, par voie de conseil ent doner a Vous, einz soulement Vous ent monstrent lour plein advis sur lour dite Charge.[41]
>
> [But they are not saying it in the least, said the aforementioned Sir James, by way of giving counsel to you, but only by way of showing their full opinion about the said issue.]

The King, however, refuses to participate in the hermeneutic play that Pickering introduces:

> A quoy feust dit de par le Roi illoeques tantost, Q'ome ne purroit legierment mettre grant difference en celle partie; c'est assavoir, entre les ditz paroles, conseil, et advis.
>
> [To which was then said on behalf of the King straightaway, that someone could not easily make out much difference in this case, that is to say, between the said words, 'counsel' and 'opinion'.]

Richard, through his spokesman, is portrayed here as unmasking the verbal contingency of Pickering's distinctions, forcing a confrontation over the issue of Parliament's right to counsel the King. Fifteen years later, Richard is alleged to have disguised his own intentions to Parliament; Walsingham's *Historia Anglicana* relates that the King appointed a committee in 1398 to usurp some of Parliament's duties. The felony is compounded by Richard's attempt to hide his arrogation of power, by altering the official record of the proceedings:

> Et hoc de voluntate Regis, in derogationem status Parliamenti, et incommodum totius regni et perniciosum exemplum. Rex autem super hoc facto, ut videretur habere colorem et auctoritatem, fecit rotulos Parliamenti mutari et deleri, contra effectum concessionis praedictae.[42]
>
> [And this was by will of the King, to the derogation of the status of Parliament, and the distress of the realm and as a pernicious example. Even more than this, the King, so that he would seem to have the excuse and authority, ordered the Rolls of Parliament to be changed and obliterated, against the intention of the aforesaid grant.]

---

[41] *RP*, III, 145, reading 'nel dient' for 'ne l'diont'; the next quotation is ibid., 145–6. I am grateful to Sylvia Huot for advice on these passages; any remaining mistakes are mine.

[42] Walsingham, *Historia Anglicana*, II, 227. For the committee's actual operation, see J. Edwards 1970.

Princely Reading and Political Interpretation

Walsingham's use of 'colorem' – a word commonly employed in literary or rhetorical discussion – emphasizes the linguistic trickery of Richard's attempt to alter the official account. Richard is fabricating an excuse for his behaviour by changing the verbal record of his wilful actions (and in the process giving a 'perniciosum exemplum'). The accusation contrasts sharply with Richard's impatience over Pickering's subtle verbal distinctions in 1383. Walsingham's account is itself, however, not what it seems. It is copied nearly verbatim from the Articles of Deposition against Richard, a partisan Lancastrian document placed on the Rolls of Parliament well after the momentous events of 1399 that it describes.[43]

The Articles as a whole stand in apposition to Richard's coronation oath, which was entered on the Rolls of Parliament above them.[44] Besides portraying Richard's abuse of his own publicly stated words, the Articles also focus closely on his rejection of advice and criticism from others:

> Item: in many great councils of the kingdom [...] lords, justices and others, when offering their advice according to their discretion, were often so sharply and violently rebuked and reproved by the King that they dared not speak the truth in giving their advice on such matters.[45]

This accusation shifts the responsibility for poor government from the advisors (the apparent object of criticism during Richard's reign) to the King himself, ironically according the deposed King greater power than rhetorical tradition allowed him during his reign. Article 20 makes the widest charge of verbal coercion against Richard:

> Item: the King, wishing to be free to act according to his arbitrary will [*arbitrium voluntatis*] in all things, unlawfully commanded all his sheriffs to swear an oath which went further than their ancient and accustomed one [*ultra antiquum & solitum Juramentum*], namely that they would obey all and whatsoever mandates he sent to them under the great seal, the privy seal, or by signet letter. And if the sheriffs happened to hear of any person in their bailiwicks, of whatever status, who either publicly or privately was speaking ill of the King or saying things which redounded to his discredit or scandal, they were to have him arrested and kept securely in prison until they received further orders from the King. This can be found on record, and might lead to the destruction of many liegemen of the realm.[46]

---

[43] For the status of the Articles see Lapsley 1934 and Strohm 1992, 80–1.
[44] *RP*, III, 417.
[45] *Chronicles of the Revolution*, ed. Given-Wilson, 179; *RP*, III, 420.
[46] *Chronicles of the Revolution*, ed. Given-Wilson, 178–9; *RP*, III, 420.

The article creates a powerful contrast between Richard's wish to be free to act according to his desire, and the liegemen of the realm whom it imagines as 'kept securely in prison'. There is also a tension between Richard's 'arbitrary' will and the 'ancient and accustomed' oath that the sheriffs are commanded to replace with unquestioning obedience. Of course, the 'ancient and accustomed' oath that looms over the whole document is Richard's coronation oath; by making the sheriffs swear a new oath, Richard commits another act of perjury along with them. He forces them to speak, while they must force others to be silent. In article 16, Richard is portrayed as locating the country's laws in his own body:

> Item: the King, not wishing to uphold or dispense the rightful laws and customs of the realm, but preferring to act according to his own arbitrary will and to do whatever he wished, at times when his justices or others of his council expounded to him upon the laws of the realm and asked him to do justice according to those laws, frequently replied and declared expressly, with an austere and determined expression, that his laws were in his mouth, or at other times, that they were in his breast: and that he alone could change or make the laws of his kingdom.[47]

This article has been discussed in some detail by Larry Scanlon, who finds in it the component of power which, he argues, underlies the superficially constitutional formulations of medieval juridical and theoretical texts. Richard is guilty, Scanlon claims,

> not because he violated some explicitly established constitutional principle. It is because he declined to live up to the ideal of the corporate fiction. He refused to embody counsel and legal precedent in a single unifying voice: he literalized the body politic and thus revealed monarchical theory to be a metaphor – that is, a fiction.[48]

Scanlon's account sharply illuminates the relationship between a 'historical' document, which claims representational veracity (such as the Articles of Deposition), and a narrative fiction, which also usurps the voices of others to mask its own motives. However, this does not provide the whole explanation for the depiction of Richard here. There *is* a constitutional issue at stake, not in the sense of breaking a written code, but because the role of counsel and representation was essential to the practice of kingship. The fact that the Articles describe Richard's behaviour in these terms demonstrates the importance of counsel in contemporary political theory. The King refuses to put into action the texts 'expounded' to him, and so, crucially, rejects the role of reader that is demanded of him. As the Articles report it, Richard failed in his

---

[47] *Chronicles of the Revolution*, ed. Given-Wilson, 177–8; *RP*, III, 419.
[48] Scanlon 1990, 221.

responsibility to represent the kingdom, rather than merely embody it. The fiction of a king embodying the realm thus operates in both directions. It allows the king great power in unifying the interests of the realm, but it also relies on the king acting as the embodiment of the kingdom. To formalize this relationship as an 'explicitly established constitutional principle' would have been to sacrifice its flexibility and limit its scope. However, the prevalence of ideas and narratives about counsel, responsibility and representation encouraged an informal constitution that, in theory, allowed advice and complaint to travel from citizens to local magnates, to the courts and to the king. The importance of the royal will and royal reading in medieval political ideology explains why the Articles return again and again to the disjuncture between Richard's oath and his actions, his arbitrary will and the interests of the kingdom.

The image of Richard II as a wilful ruler quickly became established in the literary and political tradition. In Lydgate's *Of the Sodein Fal of Princes in Oure Dayes*, Richard II's demise is treated in one terse stanza, and attributed to the fact that 'yvel counseyle rewled him so, elas!'[49] Much earlier, the author of *Richard the Redeless* already employs the same topos to characterize Richard's misrule:

Now, Richard the redeles reweth on you-self,
That lawelesse leddyn youre lyf and youre peple bothe;
[...] from youre willffull werkis youre will was chaungid,
And rafte was youre riott and rest, for youre daiez
Weren wikkid thoru youre cursid conceill. (I. 88–9, 92–4)

This passage presses home the discrepancy between Richard's uncurbed will and the ideal of the king acting on loyal counsel. The poet tells Richard to read his own advice carefully: 'waite well the wordis and so werche ther-aftcr' (I. 45).

Such advice seems to offer Richard hope of regaining his authority. As Helen Barr has demonstrated, however, *Richard the Redeless* was written several months after Henry IV had come to the throne. The reference to Henry as 'Hieste of kynde / To kepe the croune as cronecle tellith' (III. 92–3) suggests that the poet had no realistic expectation that Richard could benefit from his advice in this life. Instead, the advice is to be 'overheard' and interpreted by Henry, so that he can avoid the same mistakes. The poet hints at this redirection early on, for he notes that his advice applies to 'euery Cristen kyng that ony croune bereth' (I. 43). Richard is thus addressed as a substitute for his successor; his real and imagined crimes are, as in the Articles of Deposition, redrawn

---

[49] Line 12. The poem is printed in Lydgate, *Minor Poems*, II, 660–1.

to refer more closely to the ideals that the informal constitution of counsel demanded of a king.[50]

Besides employing the idea of counsel in attacks on Richard II's misrule, the importance of counsel to royal government was recognized in Henry IV's own promises to the Parliament of 1399. An address by Archbishop Arundel stated:

> It is the will of the King to be counselled and governed by the honourable, wise and discreet persons of his realm and to do the best for the government of himself and of his realm by their common counsel and assent. He does not wish to be governed by his own will, nor by his wilful purpose or singular opinion, but by common advice, counsel and assent.[51]

This process of elaboration and conformity to the ideal of counsel was not, however, to remain completely under the control of the Lancastrian dynasty. The authorized version of Richard's reign and downfall could also serve as a stick with which to beat the new regime. In 1406 the rebel nobles Henry Percy, Earl of Northumberland, Edmund Mortimer and Lord Bardolf accused Henry IV of breaking oaths and ignoring loyal advice. The rebels demanded that

> wise men of the realm [...] be assigned to the King to give the counsel necessary to him, excluding from the King alien and greedy councillors who desire to tell and do those things which please the King, so that they may become rich [... and that] the barons, nobles and people may have free opportunity in their councils in parliaments to say what they will.[52]

---

[50] For the date of the poem, see *The Piers Plowman Tradition*, ed. Barr, 16. Another poet who redirects towards Henry IV material designed for Richard II is, of course, John Gower. Apart from the rededication of *Confessio amantis*, Gower also adapts material from the *Confessio* in his poem 'In Praise of Peace' (Gower, *English Works*, II, 481–92), written for Henry early in his reign; see Grady 1995. Finally, at the end of the *Chronica triperta* (written in about 1400) Gower addresses the poem 'Rex celi deus' to Henry IV. A previous version of this poem rounded off an *epistola* to Richard II, a small mirror for princes within Gower's *Vox clamantis*; see Gower, *Latin Works*, 264–6 and 343–4.

[51] *Constitutional History*, ed. Wilkinson, 43; *RP*, III, 415. The importance of counsel was again publicly acknowledged by Henry V at his first Parliament in 1413. The Chancellor, Henry Beaufort, took as a text for his opening address Ecclesiasticus 37: 20, 'ante omnem actum consilium stabile' [let there be wise counsel before every action].

[52] *Constitutional History*, ed. Wilkinson, 47. The failure of Henry IV to live up to his promises was eloquently put by the Commons in Henry V's first Parliament. Calling for a restoration of 'bone governance', they recalled the many promises made by Henry IV, 'mes coment y feust tenuz et perfourne en apres, mesme

Princely Reading and Political Interpretation

Neither was this sort of criticism confined to renegade nobles. In May 1401, Philip Repingdon, later Bishop of Lincoln, wrote to Henry IV warning of misrule and ascribing the kingdom's troubles to 'tyrannous will': 'et nunc pro lege sufficit tyrannica voluntas'. He also makes specific reference to Henry's predecessor:

> [S]icut, infra biennium, in rege Ricardo, tanquam in speculo stupendo, vidimus exemplatum, universo orbi et omnibus superviventibus indelebiliter et indefectibiliter memorandum.[53]

> [Just as, after two years, we have seen a model [of misrule] in King Richard, as if in an amazing mirror, to be recalled indelibly and completely by the whole world and everyone living.]

In this 'mirror for princes' Henry sees not the ideal reflection of a future dynasty but the image of Richard II's failures, an image that Henry himself helped to shape in the aftermath of his usurpation. At Henry IV's own death, Thomas Elmham addressed a poem to Henry V on his duties, particularly the dangers of misrule.[54] In the main part of the poem Elmham appropriates the voice of Henry IV himself, who is imagined as giving advice to his four sons on his deathbed. Before this Elmham warns the new King:

> Regis Ricardi crebro memorare secundi,
> Cujus fortunae sit cito versa rota.
> Henrici regis patris ipse tui memor esto,
> Nam sua fortuna carne supina ruit.
> Illius in speculo res extitit haec speculata,
> Haec mage quo fieret conspicienda tibi.[55]

Seigneur le Roy ad bone conisance' [but how they were later kept and performed, our lord the King well knows]: *RP*, IV, 4; see Powell 1989, 135.

[53] Repingdon, *Letter*, 154. Grady argues that this letter, since it invests Henry with the power to address the nation's wrongs, actually 'contributes to Henry's royal self-representation' (Grady 1995, 554). Strohm (1998, 174–9) has also questioned the critical power of the document, seeing it as deflecting the responsibility for current unrest away from the new King. Repingdon's attacks are certainly written as one member of an elite to another, but I am not convinced that Henry's image would have been enhanced by the letter, whose complaints about injustice and poor government were all too accurate. Whatever the monitory force of the letter, Richard II's reputation is here being employed in the public scrutiny of Henry IV's regime, and the phrase 'tyrannica voluntas' in particular repeats a specific, personal, criticism of Richard II.

[54] *Political Poems*, ed. Wright, 118–23. For Elmham's work in general, see Rigg 1992, 299–301. I am grateful to Neil Wright for advice on Elmham's idiosyncratic Latin; any remaining mistakes are my own.

[55] Lines 27–32, reading 'haec' for Wright's 'hoc' in line 31.

[Remember frequently King Richard II, the wheel of whose fortune was quickly turned. Be mindful of King Henry your own father, for his fortune fell down along with his flesh. In his mirror this thing is clear, because of which it should be keenly watched by you.]

Both Richard II and Henry IV have here been written into the roll-call of fallen or discredited rulers for the benefit of Henry V. The implications of Richard II's fall, assimilated by Elmham to the tradition of Fortune's wheel, threatened to destabilize the Lancastrian dynasty throughout the first decade or so of the fifteenth century. Despite Richard's death early in 1400 and the public display of his corpse, rumours that he was still alive began to circulate, and were connected to numerous rebellious disturbances.[56] In 1402 Henry IV made a proclamation about the rumours, and the Council sent messengers into each county seeking to punish those who spread them.[57] Having attempted to suppress rumour and dissent during his own reign, Richard thus became a focus for both, and a symbol of desire for better rule. When Henry V came to the throne in 1413, a counterfeit Richard (Thomas Ward of Trumpington) still resided at the Scottish court, and one of Henry's first acts as King was to move against Scottish and Ricardian conspirators.[58] The reburial of Richard's body in Westminster Abbey was also a priority for Henry V, an action designed to lay the ghost of Richard's deposition and assert Henry's own legitimacy as heir both to Henry IV and Richard.[59] Hoccleve's poem written on the occasion of the reburial in fact confines mention of Richard to just one of its six stanzas. He is kept firmly in the past: 'Our kyng Richard that was' (*Minor Poems*, VIII, 35). Hoccleve reminds us that Richard has not 'fled' from Henry's 'remembrance' (36), but rather has been 'in Toumbe leid adoun' (40). The pointed finality of Richard's poetic interment (it calls to mind the Clerk's reference to Petrarch as 'deed and nayled in his cheste', *Canterbury Tales*, IV. 29) is an attempt to lay his political threat to rest, but cannot help but register the potential of the ousted King to disturb the Lancastrian regime. The rest of the poem is occupied by the Lollard heresy, another threat to Henry's rule which had quickly become linked to Ricardian conspiracy.[60]

[56] See McNiven 1994, Morgan 1995 and Strohm 1996 on Richard II's troubling posthumous presence in Lancastrian politics.
[57] Strohm 1996, 93–4; see also Simpson 1990b, note 29. For the frequent accusations that friars were involved in fostering the rumours, see Barr 1989, 66, and Rezneck 1927–8, 547–9.
[58] Powell 1989, 134–9. Bills claiming that Richard was alive in Scotland were circulating at the time of Henry IV's death.
[59] See Strohm 1996, 101–5.
[60] See ibid., 105–10, for perceived connections between Ricardian rebels and Lollard suspects such as Sir John Oldcastle. Oldcastle's career and the anti-Lancastrian conspiracy are reassessed in Strohm 1997a.

Princely Reading and Political Interpretation

Another work that, like Elmham's, refers to the fall of Richard II in the context of advising Henry V is *The Regiment of Princes*:

> Me fil to mynde how that nat longe agoo
> Fortunes strook doun thraste estat rial
> Into mescheef. (22–4)

Derek Pearsall argues that this allusion would have been welcomed by Prince Henry, who as a boy had been close to the deposed King. The reference to Richard is like a reminder of a favourite uncle: 'This was very much to the prince's taste.'[61] I believe on the contrary that both here and in the other examples Richard's fate is an exemplum of the fall of princes too close to home to provide any comfort for Henry V or his father. In 1410–11, when the *Regiment* was probably written, the threat from Ricardian loyalists was still potent. From a poet who shows himself so alert to shades of meaning and address, to a Prince so renowned for political acuity and 'self-representation', it would seem implausibly naive if Hoccleve's reference to Richard did not carry some political charge. I read it as one of the signs of dangerous 'Thoght' that threaten to overwhelm Hoccleve, and which instead are channelled, directed into advice to Prince Henry.

Richard II's portrayal as a wilful reader of advice is, then, reformulated in surprising and potentially uncomfortable ways in the period following his deposition and probable murder.[62] At the time Hoccleve was writing the *Regiment*, Prince Henry may have appeared to be taking on the mantle of his discredited cousin, Richard. The Prince wrested control of the Council from his father in 1409–10, and the position of Henry IV himself came under scrutiny before the King regained his hold over the Council in late 1411.[63] Prince Henry's subsequent reputation as a successful military and political leader has tended to mask these signs of political wilfulness, but in 1410–11 they must have provoked alarm as well as hopeful expectations.[64] How

---

[61] Pearsall 1994, 391. The notion that Henry V was fond of Richard is also open to question; he spent time at Richard's court in the late 1390s, and accompanied the King to Ireland in 1399, but his position may have been closer to that of a hostage than a favourite.

[62] The process of turning a king's reign into an exemplary narrative was not, of course, confined to Richard II. A prose life of Henry V was written by Tito Livio Frulovisi for the instruction of Henry VI; see Rigg 1992, 310. Morgan 1997 shows how the reputation of Edward III (Hoccleve's 'worthy Kyng beningne, Edward the laste' (*Regiment*, 2556)) was also rewritten to conform to a historical ideal.

[63] See McNiven 1980, 1–3.

[64] Such signs were to continue after Hoccleve wrote the *Regiment*. The Prince's challenge to Henry IV over French policy in 1412 amounted nearly to outright rebellion, and his supporters were said to have suggested that the King abdicate in his favour; see McNiven 1980, McNiven 1987, 136–57 and 185–91, and Allmand

should Hoccleve attempt to steer Prince Henry away from the tyrannically wilful habits of reading that Richard II represents in the political and literary tradition? One answer lies in the examples of 'reading' kings that appear in Hoccleve's *Regiment*.

IV. READING IN THE *REGIMENT*

Kings as Readers

The relationship between a reading prince – in this case, Prince Henry – and written advice is present at some level throughout *The Regiment of Princes*: Hoccleve's awareness of the *Regiment* proper as written advice in the Latin tradition, and his frequent references to Henry as his reader, bring to the fore the act of royal interpretation that the work as a whole demands.[65] The allusion to Richard II and the 'estat rial' examined above alerts us to a further significance that the examples of past kings will carry in Hoccleve's book. While Richard himself is not mentioned again, the practice of exemplary kingship and royal reading is tellingly explored through the rulers and commanders who inhabit the narratives of the main part of the poem.

Chapter 1 showed how Hoccleve's play on the phrase 'a kynges draght' (2120) carries financial, written and political implications. Hoccleve continues to explore the value of royal language at the start of the *Regiment* proper, reminding Prince Henry of the need for integrity: 'Litil enchesoun hath he for to speke, / To whos wordes is geven no credence' (2220-1). The phrase is echoed when Hoccleve discusses the distribution of Church appointments: 'To kynges letters geven is credence; / Beeth waar how that yee wryte in swich mateere' (2927-8). Furthermore, the King's written words will be used as evidence on which to judge his character:

> [W]rytynge wol endure.
> What a man is, it prest is for to preeve;
> Outhir honure it shal him or repreeve. (2371-3)

The necessity for rulers themselves to engage in the hermeneutics of speech and writing is explored in an exemplum shortly before this

---

1992, 41–53. These accounts temper the overwhelmingly positive interpretation of Prince Henry's actions in Harriss 1985a. Pearsall 1994, 387–91 discusses this crucial period as the context of Hoccleve's writing the *Regiment*. For a revealing discussion of Prince Henry's reputation and the writing of Lydgate's *Troy Book*, see Straker 1998, 227–49.

[65] See Simpson 1995a, 177.

passage. Lines 2300–31 relate the story of Alexander the Great and a philosopher from the city of Lampsacus. The King, 'Meeved of ire and of malencolie' (2302), initially intends to destroy Lampsacus. Seeing a philosopher – his former teacher – approach from the city, Alexander realizes that the philosopher will try to avert the destruction: 'And as swythe as the kyng hadde of him sighte, / He knew him and his meenynge' (2314–15). So far, Alexander has read the situation correctly, and accurately interpreted the philosopher's intentions. But the King's pre-emptive effort to impose his will on events is outmanoeuvred by the philosopher. Alexander states categorically 'At thy prayere do wole I nothyng' (2318), and so the philosopher tells him to destroy the city. There comes a moment of insight that transforms Alexander's mood:

And whan the kyng his [the philosopher's] preyere undirstood,
Al his angire and his irous talent
Refreyned he. (2325–7)

Here the King engages in two acts of 'reading' – firstly of the philosopher's intentions, then of the meaning of his request. Alexander is correct in judging the philosopher's overall aim (to save the city) but he also has to interpret the words of his former master's 'preyere' in order to understand their true purpose. In this case, the philosopher's intention is served even when (or rather, especially when) his words have a radically different meaning. The King's anger is restrained, in deference to his oath to deny whatever the philosopher will request.[66]

This complex set of intentions, forms of words and moments of understanding is reinforced by the relationship between the philosopher and Alexander. They are not simply representatives of enemy factions, but re-establish their previous roles of master and pupil. The philosopher not only saves his town, but also teaches Alexander about words, intentions and their interpretation. The *Regiment* itself is partly based on the lessons supposedly given to Alexander by another philosopher, Aristotle.[67] In such a context, this tale of close reading and textual faithfulness has a resonance for the whole project of advisory literature. The clever philosopher restrains the King's anger, saves his

---

[66] Similar moments have been identified in Jean Froissart's portrayal of Edward III: 'Certain episodes [in Froissart's *Chroniques*] appear to highlight those critical moments at which the king *learns* how to reign – over his subjects, but also over his own passions and self-will' (Ainsworth 1990, 292; his emphasis).

[67] The *Secretum secretorum* tradition itself emphasizes Alexander's need to interpret Aristotle's letters. Take, for example, John Shirley's *The Governance of Kynges and of Prynces*, in which Aristotle writes to Alexander: 'And graunte the such grace, such vnderstondyng, and such engynous subtilté and science [...] that by thy self thou may conceyve and vnderstond all that thou desirest and askest forto witte and knowe' (*Secretum secretorum*, ed. Manzalaoui, 273).

city from destruction, and teaches the King how to move in a closely textual and densely interpretative world.

Another siege narrative in the *Regiment* mirrors the exemplum of Alexander and the philosopher. Lines 2584–646 relate the story of Camillus and the city of Falisk, where a 'maistir in the citee dwellynge' (2589) attempts to negotiate with the attacking leader. This time, however, the master intends to betray the city by leading out his pupils as hostages to Camillus and the Romans. Once again, the narrative turns on a moment of understanding, of 'reading' the master's intentions. Camillus rejects the traitor's offer: 'Nat were it knyghtly me to thee consente / That taken hast so traiterous entente' (2610–11). Instead, the master himself is bound and led back to the city by his former pupils. This story is a neat inversion of the exemplum of Lampsacus, showing how those who abuse the role of teacher should be punished, but it does not end with Camillus's noble action: a further act of interpretation follows. The inhabitants of the city judge Camillus to be a worthy lord because of his honourable actions, and surrender the city to him anyway:

> The duke commandith, shortly for to seyn,
> His handes him behynde to be bownde,
> And bad the children lede him hoom ageyn
> To hir fadres; which, whan that they han fownde
> So greet justice in this duke habownde,
> The senat clepte and this unto hem tolde;
> The hertes gan to chaunge of yonge and olde. (2626–32)

From within the exemplum itself, Camillus's deeds have become the subject of discussion and evaluation. Hoccleve reinforces this process when he imagines Camillus's future conduct:

> [W]hat was folewynge,
> Nat have red, wherfore I can nat seye.
> But this just duke, as by my supposynge,
> Was to hem swich in wil and in wirkynge,
> That he hem qwitte so as mighte hem qweeme.
> What sholde I elles of swiche a lord deeme? (2641–6)

Hoccleve bases his judgement on the written evidence of the story, implicitly encouraging Prince Henry to interpret the narrative according to the same historical-literary principles. But Hoccleve then goes further, by recalling the Prince's own ancestor, Duke Henry of Lancaster, 'Whos justice is written and auctorysid' (2648), and explicitly placing the Duke alongside his Classical examples: 'Why sholde I nat thee rekne amonges tho / That in hir tyme han justice excercysid?' (2649–50). This assimilation of the recent past to exemplary history directly engages Prince Henry in a moral and political hermeneutics whose progession will inevitably encompass the Prince himself.

After another story of a traitorous servant (this time a doctor) whose actions merely prove the virtue of the exemplary figure, Hoccleve includes an exemplum about a false judge, on whom the king in turn passes judgement:

> And whan the knowleche of this fals jewyse
> Was come unto the kynges audience,
> This doom he gaf as blyve and this sentence.
>
> He bad men fleen him qwik out of his skyn,
> And therwith kevere the judicial see,
> And made his sone to be set theryn,
> That juge aftir his fadir sholde be,
> To this ende and entencioun, that he
> Sholde be waar how he his doomes gaf,
> And lene alway to rightwisnesse staf. (2679–88)

In this exemplum, affinities between judicial, royal and literary interpretation emerge. The word 'sentence' (2681) has a rich usage in many Middle English texts: as a proverbial or authoritative utterance (directly equivalent to the Latin *sententia*); a form of counsel; a passage of writing; a legal judgement; or the meaning or significance of a word or action.[68] In the passage quoted above, the King 'gives a sentence' in several ways. He pronounces judgement on the judge and he expresses a general principle: that those giving judgement should be righteous. In the context of the *Regiment*, he also voices a piece of counsel to be studied by the poem's readers – especially Prince Henry, whose judicial role will be one of his most important functions as king.

Hoccleve's suggestive use of 'sentence' may be compared with a passage in Gower's *Confessio amantis*, Book VII, in which Julius Caesar uses his formidable powers of rhetoric to overturn a judgement against the traitor Catiline. Julius's opponents 'spieken plein after the lawe' (1623) but 'he the wordes of his sawe / Coloureth in an other weie' (1624–5). Julius's verbal skill persuades the judges to 'torne the sentence' (1620), a phrase whose judicial meaning mingles with the rhetorical sleight of hand by which leniency is achieved: to change the judges' sentence is also to corrupt the relationship between words and their referents. Gower's narrative betrays the destabilizing effect of rhetoric in the political sphere. For him, misreadings and the abuse of words are all too apparent in the imperfect linguistic system that mediates political relationships.

---

[68] *MED*, s.v. 'sentence'.

The King's 'sentence' in Hoccleve's story of the corrupt judge is less susceptible to the distortions of rhetoric than is Gower's exemplum but, as in the *Confessio*, carries both judicial and textual implications, and is closely linked to another word whose judicial and rhetorical applications Hoccleve explores: 'entencioun'. Intention is an important feature of political and legal discourse, but is also central to medieval discussions of literary production.[69] 'Entente' is a constantly recurring term in the *Regiment*, used to qualify or judge the integrity of literary and political language and action.[70] In the exemplum of Camillus and the corrupt master, the Roman leader rejects the master's plan on the grounds of its 'traiterous entente' (2611), and Hoccleve later echoes the story of the corrupt judge when he warns Henry to 'do lawe in no vengeable entente' (2811).

Intention plays a vital part in the exemplum of the brazen bull, made for a tyrant by a 'sotil werkman in craft of metal' (3009) as a cruel and unusual form of punishment. The next chapter discusses the implications of the bull as an instrument for distorting the voices of the dissidents to be placed inside it.[71] For the moment, consider the reaction of the ruler to the bull and its creator:

> For whan the kyng this cruel werk had seyn,
> The craft of it commendid he ful wel,
> But the entente he fully heeld ageyn,
> And seide: 'Thow that art more cruel
> Than I, the maydenhede of this jewel
> Shalt preeve anoon; this is my jugement.'
> And so as blyve he was therin ybrent. (3032–8)

The importance of this 'cruel werk' lies in its intention: however well-crafted it is, evil 'entente' undermines the work's reception and, ultimately, its value. An important and unremarked feature of this exemplum is the element of textual interpretation in which the ruler engages. The bull is described in literary terms; it is to all intents and purposes a 'rhetorical' invention that reformulates the voices of those who speak out according to its maker's own agenda. The lesson of the exemplum may be extended to include all those at court, especially

---

[69] For Sir John Fortescue, the *intentio populi* is the ultimate arbiter of political action: 'And just as in the body natural [...] the heart is the first living thing [...] so in the body politic the intention of the people is the first living thing' (*On the Laws and Governance of England*, 20–1). The concept of *intentio* was central to medieval biblical exegesis and literary theory, too; see Copeland 1991, 76–86.

[70] I count twenty-two appearances of 'entente' and words based on it in the *Regiment*; see lines 1346, 1355, 1419, 1469, 1581, 1596, 1620, 2041, 2355, 2611, 2686, 2811, 3034, 3393, 3591, 3666, 3725, 3766, 4039, 4679, 4791, 4950. Note also line 24 of Hoccleve's envoy to the Duke of Bedford (*Minor Poems*, XI).

[71] Below, pp. 104–5.

Princely Reading and Political Interpretation

writers, who approach the king with cruelty in mind. Significantly, Hoccleve follows this narrative with a long discussion of flattery – another type of rhetorical invention with which a false servant may seek to please a ruler. The passage has little to do with pity, the subject of this section of the poem, but everything to do with the production and reception of true and false advice at court.

These exempla from the *Regiment*'s section on pity explore the theme of royal reading and interpretation in close proximity. Suggestions of reading, listening and of the verbal engagement inherent in ruling, are, however, found throughout the *Regiment* proper. For example, understanding and accepting harsh words feature in numerous exempla, including those of Alexander (3496–512), Scipio (3529–35) and Antigone (3536–42), some of which are examined below in more detail in Chapter 3. Hoccleve mentions approvingly a story that Edward III disguised himself and went 'Into contree [...] To heere what men seide of [his] persone' (2561–2). Later Hoccleve defines the virtue of Prudence in terms that connect it to the practice of reading and interpretation: Prudence is 'vertu of entendement'; she gives 'light / Of conseil' to the other virtues, 'That they may wirke [...] Aftir hir reed' (4761, 4756–7, 4758–9). Her advisory role is strengthened by her knowledge of 'thynges past and been and that shul be' (4766). In the next section, on taking counsel (4859–5019), the interpretative skills of the ruler are more explicitly discussed. Hoccleve advises Prince Henry to treat counsel on its own merits and, unsurprisingly, not to disregard 'the poores sentence' (4893). Having received good counsel, Hoccleve tells the Prince to 'impresse it in the cheste / Of your memorie' (4898–9), tellingly combining an image familiar from discussions of textual interpretation and memorialization[72] with the implication that advice is more valuable than 'gold in cofre' (2040).

The *Regiment*'s section on counsel thus reinforces the examples of kings who prudently interpret the words of their advisors, though its generalized statements are less successful than the suggestive exemplary narratives at which Hoccleve excels. The longest of these, that of John of Canace (4180–354), hinges on the (mis)interpretation of words and actions. John deceives his greedy daughters by presenting a plausible fiction which they interpret according to their own expectations. He stages a scene in which he counts out his (borrowed) money on a cloth, while his relatives view the action through gaps in a partition. The story's denouement sees them opening a chest which they believe contains their (now dead) father's money. However, having obtained the key and unlocked the chest, they find only a riddling inscription attached to a mace. Such interplay between texts and treasure is characteristic of the systems of exchange encountered

---

[72] See Carruthers 1990, 34–45.

above, in Chapter 1. The key and chest are also, of course, common images for the process of unlocking textual meaning. As John of Canace says of his treasure-chest: 'By every keye writen been the weyes / Of my wil' (4329–30). Despite these hints, John's children still hope for real treasure. When instead they find a didactic text, the reversal of metaphorical expectations alerts the reader to the ambiguous coinage of political language with which so many of the *Regiment*'s exempla are involved. Interpreting according to the 'wil' of the writer, not the unchecked desire of the reader, is the key to this particular text, as in the exemplum of Alexander and the philosopher with which we began.

Verbal interpretation, whether of written or spoken texts, thus runs through the fabric of the *Regiment* proper. Moreover, the moment of royal interpretation in these stories is also the moment at which the fictional kings make a transition from reading texts to acting on them. In doing this, they too become 'texts': their own judgements and actions are recorded as part of an ongoing exemplary process, as with the narrative of Camillus, whose judgement against the false master of Falisk results in the citizens reading his intentions as honourable, and in Hoccleve predicting his future conduct. By reading and interpreting in the political sphere, kings themselves are liable to be read. Such a constantly shifting boundary of action, interpretation and inscription makes the exemplary narratives of Hoccleve's poem a fertile but unstable source of moral and political wisdom: their readers become part of the tradition even as they make judgements on the figures in the exempla, or on the current 'sotil werkman' presenting an example of his 'craft' to the ruler.

Hoccleve's Good Intentions

The individual narratives of interpretation and advice in the *Regiment*'s exempla constitute small mirrors for princes in themselves. They are also, however, fragments of a whole mirror, likewise being interpreted by the prince according to principles of political hermeneutics. Hoccleve emphasizes the importance of reading in the poem as a whole by the way in which he frames his advice. He draws attention to Prince Henry's position as reader by assuming that he already knows the three Latin texts on which Hoccleve's advice is to be based:

> I am seur that tho bookes alle three
> Red hath and seen your innat sapience;
> And as I hope, hir vertu folwen yee. (2129–31)

Hoccleve emphasizes here the process of reading, understanding and acting that characterizes royal hermeneutics in the *Regiment*'s exempla. He then turns to Henry's reading of the *Regiment*'s own stories:

Princely Reading and Political Interpretation

> At hardest, whan yee been in chambre at eeve,
> They been goode for to dryve foorth the nyght;
> They shal nat harme if they be herd aright. (2140–2)

These lines recall Chaucer's request in *The Book of the Duchess* for a romance 'To rede and drive the night away' (49) after insomnia brings 'melancolye / And drede [...] for to dye' (23–4). Chaucer's alter ego reads a book including

>   fables
> That clerkes had in olde tyme,
> And other poetes, put in rime
> To rede and for to be in mind [...]
> Of quenes lives, and of kinges. (52–5, 58)

Hoccleve's work also contains 'fables' of kings, which are designed to cure the poet's financial, and the realm's political, melancholy.[73] In Chaucer's poem (written for Prince Henry's grandfather, John of Gaunt) it is the writer himself whose reading of the story of Ceyx and Alcione leads him to dream of the Black Knight. Hoccleve's overtly political stories are presented to the Prince apparently without this extra filter of a remembered dream, but they nevertheless require interpretation: 'They shal nat harme if they be herd aright.' Hearing 'aright' is the key to the texts that Hoccleve presents to Henry, not just because some of the advice in them may be regarded as dangerous, but because the ability of a ruler to hear and interpret is what the poem as a whole tries to teach. Hoccleve underlines the self-consciously readerly cast of the *Regiment* proper with a repeated insistence on his good intentions as author:

> For thogh I to the steppes clergial
> Of thise clerkes thre nat may atteyne,
> Yit for to putte in prees my conceit smal,
> Good wil me artith take on me the peyne. (2150–3)[74]

He picks up the idea five stanzas later – 'thogh I be nat wys, / Wel willid am I' (2185–6) – and it is reinforced by the vocabulary of

---

[73] For the political implications of poetic melancholy in this period, see Dunlop 1998. She analyses, amongst other texts, Hoccleve's *Series* and *Regiment*, and Chaucer's *The Book of the Duchess*, arguing persuasively that their melancholy narrators pose serious questions about the realm's political health (though she does not discuss these passages together). Several other parallels between *The Book of the Duchess* and *The Regiment of Princes* are noted in Blyth's edition.

[74] In another self-conscious literary move, this passage alludes to *Troilus and Criseyde*, V. 1791–2, where Chaucer imagines himself to 'kis the steppes' of his own *auctores*.

'wholeness' with which Hoccleve characterizes his project: 'Me recommande unto your worthynesse, / With herte enteer' (2022–3). Goodwill returns in the *Regiment*'s final envoy. Addressing his book in a conceit popularized by the envoy to *Troilus and Criseyde*, Hoccleve hopes that Henry's 'humble pacience' (5446; a virtue taught by the poem itself) will embolden the book to go before the Prince. Hoccleve again draws attention to the meaning and intention of his project:

> I am so pryvee unto thy sentence,
> Thow haast and art and wilt been everemo
> To his hynesse of swich benevolence,
> Thogh thow nat do him due reverence
> In wordes, thy cheertee nat is the lesse. (5449–53)

Hoccleve's Latinate 'benevolence' does not mask the operation of goodwill, which he once again claims, while 'sentence' punningly conveys the sense of 'what the book says', 'the advice in the book' and 'the book's inner meaning'.[75] Similar concerns for the right reading of the poem are included in another envoy to the *Regiment*, this time written for John, Duke of Bedford.[76] Referring to 'maistir Massy', an official in the Duke's household, Hoccleve tells his book:

> I charge thee to shewe thow thy face
> Beforn my seid Maistir, and to him preye
> On my behalue that he peise and weye
> What myn entente is, that I speke in thee;
> For rethorik hath hid fro me the keye
> Of his tresor – nat deyneth hir nobleye
> Dele with noon so ignorant as me![77]

The intimations of goodwill and requests to 'peise and weye' Hoccleve's 'entente' in these introductions and envoys are, it might be argued, just traditional expressions common to texts that address those in authority. Here, however, they amount to more than the merely formulaic because of Hoccleve's repeated focus on questions of meaning, intention and reading throughout the poem, including the Dialogue with the Old Man, to which I now turn.

---

[75] There also seems to be a playful reference to the Privy Seal in 5449.
[76] This envoy survives in two *Regiment* manuscripts: BL MS Royal 17 D. xviii and Bodleian MS Dugdale 45. It also appears in Hoccleve's hand in Huntington MS HM 111.
[77] *Minor Poems*, XI, 21–7. The 'Massy' mentioned here became caught up in the debate over the identity of the *Pearl* poet; see Nolan and Farley-Hills 1971, Turville-Petre and Wilson 1975 and Peterson 1977. The evidence is too slight to make many literary claims about Hoccleve's 'Massy'; he was probably a household officer whom Hoccleve knew to be interested in poetry.

Reading Lessons in the Dialogue

So far, we have examined the experience of royal reading in the *Regiment*'s exempla and in the poem's framing addresses. I began with the exempla because those narratives seem to relate more nearly to the proposition about mirrors for princes that I outlined at the start of the chapter, and to the historical and textual legacy of Richard II. However, verbal and textual interpretation is also a cardinal concern of the Dialogue, opening the way to the political hermeneutics practised in the *Regiment* proper.

The start of the poem sees Hoccleve assailed by 'Thoght', which has placed him in a state of constant agitation:

> Bysyly in my mynde I gan revolve
> The welthe unseur of every creature,
> How lightly that Fortune it can dissolve
> Whan that hir list that it no lenger dure. (15–18)

Specifically, Hoccleve says that the 'thoghtful wight' (99) does not take in anything that is told to him: 'He heerith it as thogh he thennes were' (100). He lacks the faculty of reason and understanding: 'He undirstandith nothyng what men seye' (104). Hoccleve's meeting with the Old Man confirms the former's lack of reason, since he does not even notice his interlocutor at first:

> A poore old hoor man cam walkynge by me,
> And seide, 'Good day, sire, and God yow blesse!'
> But I no word, for my seekly distresse
> Forbad myn eres usen hir office. (122–5)

These images of incapacity and absence mark Hoccleve's unreasoning state. The Old Man quickly perceives that something is wrong, and asks Hoccleve if he can read: 'Art thow aght lettred?' (150). He then explains:

> Lettred folk han gretter discrecion,
> And bet conceyve konne a mannes sawe,
> And rather wole applie to reson
> And from folie sonner hem withdrawe. (155–8)

The ability to understand and interpret texts, to 'conceyve [...] a mannes sawe', is seen as vital to the re-establishment of Hoccleve's reason. Hoccleve, however, is still resistant to the idea that words can help:

> Cure thyself that tremblest as thow goost,
> For al thyn aart wole enden in thy speeche.
> It lyth nat in thy power, poore goost,
> To hele me. (163–6)

As I discussed in Chapter 1, Hoccleve's challenge to the Old Man is tested and modified during the Dialogue, which ends by claiming a direct relationship between Hoccleve's writing and his overdue annuity. But words cannot be weighed quite as easily as coinage; they must be assessed according to an interpretative system. During the Dialogue, the Old Man (whose role as Hoccleve's guide has been widely discussed)[78] touches on this question of how to 'conceyve a mannes sawe', with implications not only for Hoccleve's progress during the Dialogue, but also for Prince Henry's reading of the whole poem.

After the Old Man has drawn from Hoccleve an assurance of religious orthodoxy, he nevertheless suspects that the younger man scorns him:

> I woot wel, sone, of me thus wilt thow thynke:
> This olde dotid grisel halt him wys;
> He weeneth maken in myn heed to synke
> His lewed clap, of which sette I no prys. (400–3)

The Old Man imagines that Hoccleve judges the value of his speech (its 'prys') only by his age and poverty, but the Old Man quickly counters this superficial reading, presenting the traditional objection that one must not judge by appearances:

> But thogh I old and hoor be, sone myn,
> And poore be my clothynge and array,
> And nat so wyde a gowne have as is thyn –
> So smal ypynchid ne so fressh and gay –
> My reed in hap yit thee profyte may,
> And likly that thow deemest for folie
> Is gretter wysdam than thow canst espie. (407–13)

The Old Man brings together several strands of argument here. He sets out the straightforward warning that one should read not according to outward appearance, but the value of the words. The last two lines of the stanza deepen this commonplace by echoing the biblical sentiment that worldly wisdom is folly according to God, while the use of clothing as a sign for 'textual' style or value extends a theme found in numerous contemporary political and satirical texts.[79] The pun on 'profyte' also alerts us to the eventual goal of the Dialogue (some manuscripts understandably read 'perfet' here). After 150 lines spent condemning excess in clothing and speech, the Old Man returns to his argument, namely that young men should listen to the old and poor:

---

[78] See Torti 1991, 87–106 and Simpson 1995a.
[79] See I Corinthians 3: 18–19. For clothes and textuality, see above, pp. 42–3 and 46.

> For many a yong man, woot I wel certeyn,
> Of corage is so prowd and so hauteyn
> That to the poore and old mannes doctryne
> Ful seelde him deyneth bowen or enclyne. (557–60)

This passage as a whole operates on several levels. It outlines the simple point that virtue may exist in a poor guise. It connects this lesson to advisory speech ('reed' (411); 'doctryne' (559)) – implying, of course, that a rich prince should also listen to a poor advisor. It develops the fertile image of texts as clothing, showing how the misuse of either can threaten social cohesion. It suggests both metaphorical and direct connections between those who dress beyond their means (literally and rhetorically) and the generation of deceptive, flattering speech, which is tailored to elicit praise but in fact bankrupts its wearer/speaker and undermines the material and textual economy.

The warning here to investigate beyond the superficial appearance of words and actions is echoed by both speakers later in the Dialogue. Hoccleve admits to the Old Man that 'Yee been nat he whom that I wende han fownde' (772), while the Old Man recalls being taken in by Fortune's 'deceyvable cheere' (1360): 'I wend shee had been swich as shee seemed' (1368). The impulse to interpret, to 'conceyve', even brings the Old Man to read Hoccleve's marriage in intentionalist terms. He asks 'What was thy cause why thow took a wyf? [...] what was thy motyf?' (1556, 1559), before setting out the 'Three causes' (1573) that make intercourse allowable. Hoccleve is to lay aside 'othre ententes alle' (1581). Hoccleve is confused, and asks how children can be conceived without 'lust' (1587). The Old Man again bases his argument on the act's meaning. There is a crucial difference between 'leefful lust' (1590) and 'lust for lust oonly' (1592). This difference resides not in the action itself, but in its intention: 'Th'entente is al; be waar ay of folie' (1596).

For the Old Man, then, understanding intention is the key to unlocking the meaning of an action or text. This concern is then carried into the frame of the *Regiment* proper, where Hoccleve describes his own 'herte enteer' (2023) and Aristotle's 'treewe entente' (2041) in advising Alexander. By focusing on issues of intention and interpretation here, the Dialogue provides a guide to reading the rest of the poem. In this sense, the Dialogue recalls the Prologue to *The Legend of Good Women*, which, as Rita Copeland has suggested, deploys the vocabulary of academic *accessus* in order to establish a pattern for reading the stories that follow.[80] Hoccleve consciously uses this register too, describing the *Regiment* proper both as a compilation and translation, drawing attention to his *auctores* and quoting from them in the margin. In the Dialogue, Hoccleve takes the chance to construct his own

---

[80] Copeland 1991, 186–97; for *accessus* texts, see *Accessus ad Auctores*, ed. Huygens.

intentio auctoris, which also provides the biographical information of a *vita auctoris*.[81] It is no surprise that when the Old Man first introduces the plan of translating a 'tretice' for Prince Henry, he at once clarifies its intention: the work should be 'Growndid on his estates holsumnesse' (1950).[82] The last mention of the Old Man is as Hoccleve's *auctor* and surrogate patron, whose 'entente' is crucial to the undertaking:

> Recordyng in my mynde the lessoun
> That he me yaf, I hoom to mete wente [...]
> And to parfourme his wil and his entente
> I took corage, and whyles it was hoot,
> Unto my lord the Prince thus I wroot.   (2010–11, 2014–16)[83]

The Dialogue, then, serves as a reading lesson for Hoccleve, who begins unaware even of the presence of the Old Man, and ends by diligently recording the lessons that he has absorbed. Of course, Hoccleve is not the only person to whom the Old Man's advice is applicable. The topics of discussion in the Dialogue mirror the concerns of the *Regiment* proper;[84] indeed, contemporary abuses of authority are condemned more explicitly here than in the translated information of the formal treatise. In addition, the Dialogue is a lesson for Prince Henry in how to read the poem that follows. The Prince must live up to the Old Man's assumption that he has all the requisite interpretative skills to take advantage of Hoccleve's mirror: 'His hy prudence hath insighte verray / To juge if it be wel ymaad or nay' (1908–9).

These lessons in interpretation add up to a pattern for reading the *Regiment*: following one's reason, interpreting the intention of the speaker, avoiding flattery, listening to those on the margins of the text. They prepare the way for the tests of interpretation in which the rulers in the exempla must engage. The representation of taking counsel in the *Regiment* is crucial, because it is here that the two forms of reading are brought together: reading a book of advice, and reading the advice of one's subjects. It is the moment at which the political text of advice is turned into political action. Narratives that include the moment of giving and receiving advice thus mirror the process of reading the book itself. They create the effect of a *mise en abyme,* in which the production

---

[81] For the application of these terms, see Copeland 1991, 192–7, and Minnis 1984, 55–6 and 211–17.

[82] Compare Robert Copland's *The Secrete of Secretes of Arystotle*, whose verse preface merges the 'entent' of author and reader/ruler: 'Make your entent, as the auctoures was, / Which grounded it on right hie grauitie' (*Secretum secretorum*, ed. Manzalaoui, 229).

[83] For the Old Man as Hoccleve's surrogate patron, see Hasler 1990, 169.

[84] Torti 1986; Torti 1991, Hasler 1990.

of the text is also inscribed within the text.[85] The implications of such mirroring for Hoccleve's poem, and for the advisory tradition as a whole, are large. For in this perspective, the narratives contained in the *Regiment* are not merely repetitious calls for abstract virtues, but potentially unstable encounters between a reading king and a didactic tradition that reclaims the interpretative insights and errors of the ruler as grist to its historiographical mill. The kings that read advice texts now, will themselves be read by their subjects and successors. Of the textual instability that occurs when the boundaries between reader and actor are breached, Jorge Luis Borges has written:

> Why does it disturb us that Don Quixote be a reader of the *Quixote* and Hamlet a spectator of *Hamlet*? I believe I have found the reason: these inversions suggest that if the characters of a fictional work can be readers or spectators, we, its readers or spectators, can be fictitious. In 1833, Carlyle observed that the history of the universe is an infinite sacred book that all men write and read and try to understand, and in which they are also written.[86]

Hoccleve's fictional readers have an equally disturbing potential for his addressee: they suggest that Prince Henry cannot hope to escape from historical formulations of exemplary behaviour, only to inhabit and participate in them. An illustration in one of the earliest manuscripts of the *Regiment* shows a kneeling man, probably Hoccleve, presenting a book to a prince.[87] Perhaps it represents the actual occasion on which *The Regiment of Princes* was presented to Prince Henry. If the book shown in the illustration is *The Regiment of Princes*, then will it too include a presentation picture? And will the book in that portrait itself contain a portrait? At the vanishing point of this hall of mirrors the Prince has entered the book, the reader has become the exemplum. In

---

[85] The term was coined by André Gide; see Dällenbach 1989, 7–10 and 169–74. Dällenbach notes the close affinity between the *mise en abyme* and the idea of mirroring, and identifies three categories of the technique: simple duplication, paradoxical duplication and infinite duplication. An example of the first is *Hamlet*'s play within the play; of the second, the story in *The Thousand and One Nights* (the 602nd night) that relates the story of *The Thousand and One Nights* itself; of the third, the proposition formulated by the philosopher Josiah Royce, where a perfect map of England is created, on which every detail is accurate, and which must contain a map of the map, and so on. Hoccleve's text answers to all of these types. Firstly, exempla that portray the giving of advice to rulers mirror Hoccleve's advisory project as a whole. Secondly, the *Regiment* proper is framed by the Dialogue, which describes the origin and production of the text. Thirdly, an infinite regression of *Regiments* is implied in the presentation scene of the Arundel manuscript.

[86] Borges 1970, 231.

[87] BL MS Arundel 38, fol. 37r; see plate 1.

the next chapter, I shall continue to ask how Hoccleve engages Prince Henry in his text by examining the exempla that he translates from the Latin advisory tradition, assessing how far the Latin texts shape Hoccleve's work, and how he deploys their narratives to promote his own advisory concerns.

Chapter 3

Voices of Translation and the Sources of the *Regiment*

I. INTRODUCTION

The sources of *The Regiment of Princes* have not been the subject of much recent study. Hoccleve himself forestalls investigation by listing in his address to Prince Henry the three books on which he will base his own manual of advice:

> Aristotle, moost famous philosofre,
> His epistles to Alisaundre sente [...]
> Of which, and of Gyles of Regiment
> Of Princes, plotmeel thynke I to translate.   (2038–9, 2052–3)

> There is a book Jacob de Cessolis
> Of the ordre of prechours maad, a worthy man,
> That the Ches Moralysed clepid is,
> In which purpos I eek laboure ywis;
> And heere and there, as that my litil wit
> Afforthe may, I thynke translate it.   (2109–14)

The books in question are the pseudo-Aristotelian *Secretum secretorum*, *De regimine principum* by Aegidius Romanus and *De ludo scaccorum* by Jacobus de Cessolis.

Hoccleve also signals the kind of translation he will attempt: 'plotmeel' (2053); 'heere and there' (2113). In a characteristic use of a humility topos, he makes no higher claim than to collect what is 'scatered fer in brede' (2135). His work is 'avys / That I compyle out of thise auctours olde' (2187–8). Hoccleve's apparent role as compiler wards off the accusation that he is assuming unwarranted authority by taking the part of Aristotle in this mirror for princes, while he presents his compilation as if it were another piece of scribal, manual work like the tasks undertaken by the Privy Seal clerks.[1]

---

[1] For the role of the *compilator* and its literary uses, see Minnis 1979 and 1984 (for example Minnis 1984, 94–103).

Hoccleve's description of his role in this compilation may be compared to that of Genius in Gower's *Confessio amantis*, Book VII. Before starting the book, Genius disclaims expert knowledge of Aristotle's teaching, which is a 'hih aprise, / Which is noght unto Venus knowe' (VI. 2424–5). *Confessio* VII as a whole is, however, presented as Genius's own interpretation of Aristotle's teaching. The book's proximate sources, such as the *Livres dou Tresor* by Brunetto Latini, are not mentioned in the text. Hoccleve's specific citing of biblical and patristic texts in the *Regiment*'s marginal glosses, and his regular acknowledgement of sources for individual stories, makes him a more overt compiler than Gower.[2] Of course, the *Confessio*'s poetic persona, Amans, is the one receiving rather than giving instruction; this places the construction of authority in Gower's poem on a different basis. Hoccleve's presence in the *Regiment* is nearer the surface of the narrative, and so the protection granted by his role as a mere compiler is all the more valuable.

Hoccleve's guise of humility and dullness is designed to avert scrutiny from his own agenda in the *Regiment*, but one should not be misled into thinking that Hoccleve's translations from the Latin sources are simply verbatim reproductions. Medieval translation is also an act of interpretation, which involves both the reception of another text and the active appropriation of its meaning.[3] The transition from Latin to the vernacular itself comes freighted with significance, and features of the 'original' work, such as its rhetorical structure and manuscript context, affect its appearance in translation. With these aspects of medieval translation practice in mind, I introduce Hoccleve's three main sources for the second part of the *Regiment*, discuss their possible influence on the structure of the English poem and suggest how Hoccleve's adaptation of exemplary stories (from *De ludo scaccorum* in particular) contributes to a major feature of the *Regiment*, namely the representation of dialogue between subjects and rulers. Finally, I suggest how two pictures in early manuscripts of the *Regiment* may illuminate Hoccleve's relationship to textual authority and contribute to his advisory strategy.

---

2 Hoccleve makes references like 'as Valerie hath told' (3249), 'as seith Bernard' (3368), 'Senek seith' (3375) throughout the *Regiment* proper. The case for Hoccleve's responsibility for the *Regiment*'s marginal glosses is argued in Marzec 1987b. On the Latin apparatus of the *Confessio*, see Yeager 1987b.

3 See Copeland 1987, 41–3 and Copeland 1991.

II. THE MAJOR SOURCES

Secretum secretorum

All three major sources of the *Regiment* proper were widely known works, surviving in many manuscripts and in numerous vernacular adaptations. They were all at the height of their popularity in England in the early fifteenth century, and Hoccleve would not have had much trouble obtaining copies from which to work. The *Secretum secretorum* was one of the most influential didactic treatises of the later Middle Ages, surviving in two main Latin versions in at least 600 manuscripts.[4] The first of these versions (the 'short form') was translated from Arabic by Johannes Hispaniensis in the mid-twelfth century. A translation of the 'long form' was made, probably in the first half of the thirteenth century, by Philippus Tripolitanus. This is the version annotated by Roger Bacon, sometime before 1257.[5] The *Secretum secretorum* was believed to be a genuine work of Aristotle, representing letters written by the philosopher for the guidance of Alexander the Great. It had a great influence on other texts in the mirror for princes genre, including *De instructione principis* by Gerald of Wales, *De regimine principum* by Vincent of Beauvais and *De regimine principum* by Aegidius Romanus. The *Secretum* was itself frequently referred to as *De regimine principum*.[6] Gower made use of the *Secretum* in *Confessio amantis*, Book VII,[7] and the numerous English versions of the text testify to its continued popularity in the late fourteenth and throughout the fifteenth century.[8] The contents and order of material change in different versions, but overall the *Secretum secretorum* is characterized by its juxtaposition of material on diet, health and medicine, astrology and magic, as well as advice on kingship and governance.

Manzalaoui's study of the *Secretum* tradition gives a valuable introduction to the manuscript contexts in which the *Secretum* is found.[9] It was frequently copied alongside other 'regiminal' texts – that is, works teaching the reader about correct behaviour and moral standards, especially through the prism of royal governance. It occurs with texts

---

[4] See Schmitt and Knox 1985, 54–75.
[5] *Secretum Secretorum*, ed. Steele. The most authoritative discussions are ibid., vii–lxiv, and *Secretum Secretorum*, ed. Manzalaoui, ix–l.
[6] Gilbert 1928, 86 and 94.
[7] Ibid., 84–93, and Manzalaoui 1981.
[8] For late-medieval English translations, see *Three Prose Versions of the Secreta Secretorum*, ed. Steele; *Secretum Secretorum*, ed. Manzalaoui; and Lydgate and Burgh, *Secrees of Old Philisoffres*.
[9] *Secretum Secretorum*, ed. Manzalaoui, xix–xl.

on royal coronations[10] and education – one version was written for the education of Edward III when Prince of Wales[11] – and also appears in some manuscripts with versions of Hoccleve's other main sources.[12] The *Secretum* was, then, a text of royal instruction that could be associated in particular with the duties to be taken on by a new king. It was a natural partner both for the *De ludo scaccorum* and for Aegidius's *De regimine principum* in a compilation such as the one Hoccleve claims to undertake in the *Regiment*.

De regimine principum

The *De regimine principum* of Aegidius Romanus was in circulation by 1285, though it was written earlier, perhaps as a manual of instruction for the future Philip IV of France ('Philip the Fair', who came to the throne in 1286). The work became extremely popular.[13] Aegidius himself was a distinguished theologian and teacher; born in about 1243 in Italy, he joined the Augustinian house in Paris in 1260. While there, he may well have studied theology under Thomas Aquinas. Aegidius taught theology in Paris in the mid-1270s, but was forced to leave in 1277 when some of his teachings were condemned. His whereabouts from then until 1281 are unknown, but this was the period in which he wrote *De regimine principum*. He was in Italy in 1281, and stayed there until his return to the University of Paris in 1285. He was later elected Vicar General of the Augustinian Hermits and in 1295 was appointed Archbishop of Bourges by his friend, Pope Boniface VIII. He took the Pope's side in the disputes between Philip IV and the papacy, prompting Aegidius to write a defence of papal authority, *De ecclesiastica potestate*, in 1302/3. His numerous other theological and philosophical writings include commentaries on many works of Aristotle, most notably the *Rhetoric*. When Pope Boniface was captured and soon

---

[10] For example, BL MS Royal 12 D. xv (with a *Liber de administratione principum*); BL MS Add. 32097 (with *Processus factus ad coronacionem regis Ricardi Secundi*); Royal 12 D. iii (with *Modus coronandi regem*); Oxford, Bodleian MS Douce 95 (with *De coronatione regis*).

[11] Paris, BN MS fonds français 5. 71; see Manzalaoui 1981, 180, note 62.

[12] CUL MS Ff. i. 33 (written in Bourges in 1420) includes a French translation of the *Secretum* along with the *Livre de eschez*, Jean de Vignay's translation of *De ludo scaccorum*. In Oxford, University College MS 85 (s. xv²), an English version of the *Secretum* appears with a compilation of material from Aegidius, Vegetius and others entitled *Consideracions right necessarye to the good governance of a prince*.

[13] For Aegidius's career and the dissemination of the *De regimine principum*, see the valuable study by Briggs (1999). Previous discussions of manuscripts and translations include Bruni 1932, 346–68, Zumkeller 1961, 55–60 and del Punta and Luna 1993. There is no modern edition of *De regimine principum*, and little likelihood of one for some time. I have consulted a Venetian edition of 1502.

afterwards died Aegidius fell from favour, but at the time of his own death in 1316 his reputation as a scholar had been securely established.

The *De regimine principum* is divided into three books.[14] The first discusses personal conduct, virtues and vices. The second deals with the governance of the king's family and household. The third addresses the wider concerns of the state, including discussion of the political theories of Plato and Aristotle, the best form of government and the duties of the king in peace and in war (this last part is based on the *De re militari* by Vegetius). The Aristotelian structure of the work, moving from personal 'regiment' to affairs of state, draws attention to the bond between private and public governance. Aegidius also negotiates the dilemma of royal power and the need for restraint, arguing for a strong ruler who is kept in check by a 'commitment to moral law'.[15]

De regimine principum had already been translated into French in the 1280s, by Henri de Gauchi.[16] Other translations into French and Italian followed, and the Latin version quickly became a standard university textbook in Paris. By the late fourteenth century, it was also part of the English university curriculum. Manuscripts of *De regimine principum* were owned and read by clerics, aristocrats and educated laypeople, and Charles Briggs notes that the period between 1380 and 1430 shows the 'most accelerated proliferation' of copies in England.[17] Indeed, an English translation survives from about the mid-point of those fifty years. It was made by John Trevisa and appears uniquely in Bodleian MS Digby 233, along with a translation of Vegetius.[18] This impressive manuscript is dated c. 1410 (nearly contemporary with the *Regiment*), and the fact that no other copies survive has generated some debate, since Trevisa's other major translation projects seem to have been disseminated with the help of his patron, Sir Thomas Berkeley.[19] Most recently, Briggs has noted that the manuscript shows signs of correction and alteration, and has suggested that Trevisa left the translation incomplete at his death (by 1402), making the Digby manuscript a

---

[14] See Fowler 1995, 200–6.

[15] Ibid., 190. In Molenaer's judgement, Aegidius stresses the need for 'due recognition, on the ruler's part, of the *people's rights*' (Henri de Gauchi, *Livres du gouvernement*, xxi; Molenaer's emphasis). Molenaer's idea of 'rights' is somewhat anachronistic, but he raises an important question of the duty of kings to restrain their potentially absolute authority. Scanlon, by contrast, argues that Aegidius ultimately endorses royal power, despite acknowledging its artificial construction (Scanlon 1994, 105–18).

[16] Henri de Gauchi, *Livres du gouvernement*.

[17] Briggs 1999, 21.

[18] Trevisa, *The Governance of Kings and Princes*. For discussions of Digby 233 and its texts, see Childs 1932, Hanna 1989, 897–902, Scott 1996, II, 123–5 and Briggs 1998. The Vegetius translation is edited by Geoffrey Lester in Vegetius, *De Re Militari*.

[19] On Berkeley's patronage, see Hanna 1989.

problematic exemplar from which to disseminate the work.[20] Trevisa's *Governance of Kings and Princes* also provides some suggestive evidence about the interpretation of Aegidius in England in this period. In some places, Trevisa has added notes which pointedly address problems of tyranny and faction,[21] and which highlight the fact that Aegidius was not necessarily a comfortable read for those interested in the duties and power of kings in late-medieval England. Hanna has also speculated that Thomas Berkeley's very interest in Aegidius may have stemmed from his isolation from Richard II's circle of influence in the years from 1385 to 1398, giving him a personal stake in the work's distinctions between proper royal authority and oppression. These circumstances give Trevisa's translation a powerful contemporary resonance, and should encourage more careful thought about Hoccleve's use of Aegidius, too. The *De regimine principum* could be read not only as a textbook on Aristotelian ethics, or as a defence of strong monarchy, but also as a warning against royal tyranny.

De ludo scaccorum

The *Libellus de moribus hominum et de officiis nobilium super ludo scaccorum* is a collection of exempla, which, as its full title reveals, uses the premise of describing chesspieces to discuss the orders of society in a moral framework.[22] Its author, Jacobus de Cessolis, is identified as a Dominican by references in the incipits and Prologue to his work. Earlier scholars thought that Jacobus was based in northern France,[23] but Tommaso Kaepelli has made a convincing case for identifying the author as the member of the monastery of San Domenico in Genoa, who is mentioned in some documents in the cartulary of Ugolino Cerrino monastery dating from 1317 to 1322.[24] One refers to him as 'Jacobum de Cessora de Ast.', which would fix his place of origin as the town of Cessola near Asti, north-west of Genoa. Another mentions Jacobus de Cessolis as vicar of the inquisitor of Lombardy and the March of Genoa, Jacobus de Levanto. This is likely to have been towards the end of Jacobus's career. Kaepelli suggests a date of approximately 1300 for *De ludo scaccorum*.[25]

The monastery of San Domenico at Genoa was home to two other well-known author-compilers of the thirteenth century: Jacobus de Voragine (d. 1298), who wrote the *Legenda aurea* between about 1260

---

[20] Briggs 1998; Briggs 1999, 82–8.
[21] See Fowler 1995, 195–9, Somerset 1998, 76–8 and Briggs 1999, 80–1.
[22] For editions, see Jacobus de Cessolis, *De ludo scaccorum*, ed. Vetter, and Burt 1957; see also van der Linde 1874, I, supplement 2, 19–153.
[23] Mitchell (1968, 26) still calls him 'a Dominican friar at Rheims'.
[24] Kaepelli 1960.
[25] Ibid., 155.

and 1267, and Giovanni Balbi, who produced an extremely popular encyclopaedia, the *Catholicon*, in 1280. San Domenico's resources and literary traditions would, then, have been conducive to the production of a large-scale compilation of didactic exempla such as the *De ludo scaccorum*. The work's main sources are the *Speculum maius* of Vincent of Beauvais, John of Salisbury's *Policraticus*, Valerius Maximus, and the Bible; these account for two-thirds of the exempla.[26] Other sources include Jerome, Seneca, Augustine, Orosius, Paul the Deacon, Peter Alphonsus, Cicero and Justinian.

De ludo scaccorum quickly became very popular and was translated into several vernaculars. These include three versions in French, all made in the mid-fourteenth century, by Jean Ferron (started in 1347), Jean de Vignay (probably made in the 1340s), and an anonymous translation surviving in MS 275 of the Bibliothèque de la Bourgeoisie de Berne.[27] A conflation of the translations by Jean Ferron and Jean de Vignay also exists. This composite version was used by Caxton for his translation *The Game of Chess*, while a Middle Scots poetic translation of the Latin survives in the Asloan Manuscript (Edinburgh, National Library of Scotland, MS 16500).[28] There were several translations into German, too, including Heinrich von Berigen's *Schachgedichte* (dated to the early fourteenth century) and Conrad von Ammenhausen's *Schachzabelbuch* (1337).[29]

As with the *Secretum secretorum* and Aegidius, the manuscripts in which *De ludo scaccorum* appears can helpfully illuminate the genres and reading contexts in which the work was placed. *De ludo scaccorum* occurs alongside texts on politics and governance, such as the pseudo-Bernardus Silvestris *Epistola de cura et modo rei familiaris gubernandi*, Vegetius's *De re militari* and an anonymous treatise on counsel, the *Tractatus consiliandi*.[30] In Bodleian MS Bodley 58 the compilation includes a moral treatise (*De quatuor virtutibus cardinalibus secundum dicta principum et philosophorum*), a collection of exempla (*De ludo scaccorum*) and a work on practical medicine (*Tractatus de regimine sanitatis secundum Bartholomeum in suo breuiario*). The effect of this combination is to create a new version of a regiminal text, but one that as a whole still

---

[26] Mehl 1978, 233–7.
[27] See Rychner 1955 and Knowles 1954.
[28] Unusually, Caxton produced two editions of *The Game of Chess*, probably because he later gained access to an illustrated manuscript of the work. The first edition was printed in 1474 in Bruges; the second, illustrated, edition was produced in 1483 in London. For the Scots version, see *The Buke of the Chess*, ed. van Buuren.
[29] Vernacular translations and manuscripts of *De ludo scaccorum* are discussed in van der Linde 1874, I, supplement 2, 114–53, Murray 1913, 549–54 and Burt 1957, xxix–xxxviii.
[30] Vegetius is found in BL MS Royal 12 E. xxi, the *Tractatus consiliandi* in Bodleian MS Hatton 105 and the *Epistola* in both manuscripts.

corresponds to the mixture of science, moral guidance and narrative exempla found together in, for example, the *Secretum secretorum*. In BL MS Royal 12 E. xxi, the first nine items (written in the fourteenth century) provide a varied introduction to aspects of aristocratic education. The manuscript includes works on war, science, rhetoric, morality, natural history and exegesis.[31] The moral tales, *De ludo scaccorum* and the *Gesta Romanorum* provide narrative commentary on these pieces, presenting exempla of those who followed or broke moral codes, biblical figures, and victors and vanquished in war. A new section was added to the manuscript in the fifteenth century (items 12–15). This reinforces its religious character, but also introduces another regiminal text, the pseudo-Bernardus Silvestris *Epistola* also found in Bodleian MS Hatton 105. In the sixteenth century two works relating to chess were inserted after *De ludo scaccorum*, one a moral treatise, the other a practical guide.[32] These accretions make the manuscript an intriguing gauge of the practical and moral curriculum to which a late-medieval reader would be introduced.

A manuscript in Cambridge (Sidney Sussex College MS 56. 3. 11) represents one part of that curriculum: rhetoric. It begins with one of the most popular rhetorical treatises, the *Poetria nova* by Geoffrey of Vinsauf. This is followed by a poem from a similar rhetorical environment – the pseudo-Ovidian *De vetula* – along with a commentary on Ovid and a piece on writing a sermon. In such company, *De ludo scaccorum* could easily be read as a compilation of rhetorical exempla. The text is, indeed, introduced to the reader as a collection of narratives intended to have a particular effect on a particular king, though it is also more widely applicable. *De ludo scaccorum* includes dozens of self-contained vignettes portraying vices and virtues, employing numerous descriptive and narrative techniques. This is the kind of writing employed in rhetorical treatises, while the exempla themselves provide ample material for inclusion in a sermon or didactic piece. Manuscripts such as these can display in a fresh light *De ludo scaccorum*'s associations with works of governance, morality, rhetoric, science and storytelling.

---

[31] The manuscript contains:
1. Excerpts from Vegetius, *De re militari*
2. Excerpts from Macrobius
3. Parts of Alcuin, *Dialogus de rhetorica*
4. Ethical/rhetorical texts; quotations from Aristotle
5. Moral tales
6. John le Walleys, *Breviloquium de virtutibus cardinalibus*
7. Extracts from *Gesta Romanorum*; natural history etc.
8. Exposition on the book of Numbers
9. *De ludo scaccorum*
10. Hexameter verses on chess (copied s. xvi)
11. The 'Innocent Morality', a moral treatise based around chess (copied s. xvi)
12. *De oculo morali*
13. Theological commonplaces in Latin
14. pseudo-Bernardus, *Epistola de cura et modo rei familiaris gubernandi*
15. Theological sayings, prose and verse

[32] Burt 1957, x, notes that many manuscripts of *De ludo scaccorum* contain marginal annotations about the game and sets of chess problems.

To summarize, Hoccleve's major sources were extremely popular in Latin, and had all been translated into French during the late thirteenth and fourteenth centuries. All three were linked with advice to princes and young kings. The *Secretum secretorum* was associated with coronation texts and a copy was made for the young Edward III. *De regimine principum* was written for a French prince soon to become king. *De ludo scaccorum*'s initiating fiction is of a philosopher advising a young king; one of its French translations was made in the 1340s for Prince John, who became King John II of France in 1350.[33] In Hoccleve's *Regiment*, Prince Henry can take his place in a long procession of mythologized and historical princes who commissioned and are remembered in these texts. While the *Regiment* draws on this authoritative tradition, however, Hoccleve also incorporates it into the much more personal and unstable literary environment that the Dialogue with the Old Man has created. The next two sections of the chapter will focus on Hoccleve's response to his three Latin sources and their continuing structural and thematic presence in the English poem.

III. THE SOURCES AND THE STRUCTURE OF THE *REGIMENT*

Many have been content to take Hoccleve at his word and describe the *Regiment* proper as a straightforward translation. Each of the three main sources has at one time or another been claimed as the major influence behind the *Regiment*, usually without any substantiation. A traditional view was simply to regard Hoccleve's work as a translation of Aegidius. Thus H.S. Bennett writes: 'In 1411 or 1412 he translates the *De Regimine Principum* of Aegidius Romanus for Henry, Prince of Wales.'[34] A recent echo of this belief is voiced by M.C. Seymour: 'Hoccleve's book [is] ultimately based on Aegidius Romanus's work of the same title, supplemented by Jacobus de Cessolis's *De ludo scaccorum* and the *Secretum secretorum*, all of which he may have read in French or English translation.'[35] The status of Aegidius's work was effectively challenged by Jerome Mitchell over thirty years ago,[36] but the view that Aegidius was Hoccleve's main source is nevertheless still widely held. The case for the *Secretum secretorum* as Hoccleve's underlying model is put by Anthony Hasler: 'As Mahmoud Manzalaoui pointed out long ago, the

---

[33] This is Jean de Vignay's translation; see Burt 1957, xxxii.
[34] Bennett 1947, 148–9.
[35] Hoccleve, *Selections*, ed. Seymour, 255. Seymour's suggestion that Hoccleve may have used vernacular translations is possible but unnecessary. There is no reason to think that Hoccleve would not have been able to read the source texts in Latin.
[36] Mitchell 1968, 24.

overall pattern of the *Regiment* is founded on the pseudo-Aristotelian *Secretum Secretorum*.'[37] In fact, Manzalaoui gives equal weight to the three sources in the article that Hasler cites.[38] Sixteen years later, however, Manzalaoui does refer to the *Regiment* as 'Hoccleve's version of the *Secretum*'.[39]

If the only criterion for influence on the *Regiment* were the volume of borrowings from each source, any argument could quickly be settled in favour of *De ludo scaccorum*. Over a century ago, Friedrich Aster demonstrated how much Hoccleve took from each main source, printing passages of the Latin texts alongside the corresponding lines of the *Regiment*.[40] Aster's study is still the fullest treatment of the *Regiment*'s major sources, and shows that Hoccleve used *De ludo scaccorum* much more than Aegidius or the *Secretum*.[41] Much of the advice in the *Regiment* is in the form of exemplary stories, and Jacobus de Cessolis's treatise is a rich mine for these exempla, most of them originally drawn from biblical and Classical history. Aegidius Romanus adopts a scholastic style, much more dense and theoretical than *De ludo scaccorum*, and with virtually no illustrative exempla. Hoccleve uses *De regimine principum* for theoretical *sententiae* and particularly for the sections of the *Regiment* on Avarice and Prudence.[42] All but one of the parallel passages that Aster finds are taken by Hoccleve from *De regimine principum*, Book I, parts i and ii.[43] The *Secretum secretorum* is used least of all, providing some illustrative stories and a few *sententiae*.[44]

The Table of Borrowings sets out the distribution in the *Regiment* of quotations listed by Aster, Allan Gilbert and Marcia Smith Marzec from

---

[37] Hasler 1990, 166.
[38] Manzalaoui 1961, 95.
[39] *Secretum Secretorum*, ed. Manzalaoui, xxxviii, note 1.
[40] Aster 1888.
[41] He lists fifty-two correspondences between *De ludo scaccorum* and the *Regiment*, ibid., 28–50 (four of these occur in the Dialogue with the Old Man).
[42] Twenty-one correspondences, ibid., 22–8. This list can be supplemented, with caution, by reference to Marzec 1982. Marzec argues that Hoccleve used French translations of his sources alongside the Latin texts. Most of the extra borrowings that she proposes are due to parallels between the *Regiment* and French and English texts of *De regimine principum* and the *Secretum* respectively. These parallels may, as she herself concedes, be due to readings in the Latin texts from which Hoccleve worked.
[43] Briggs notes that the first three parts of Book I are the most heavily annotated in many manuscripts of Aegidius (Briggs 1999, 113).
[44] Eleven correspondences, Aster 1888, 17–22. Again, this can be supplemented by the references in Gilbert 1928, 93–8, and the parallels with English versions of the *Secretum* suggested in Marzec 1982, 18–19. Little other work has been done on the relative importance of the three works. Brief comments on Hoccleve's translation technique are given in Mitchell 1968, 85–6, Hoccleve, *Selections*, ed. Seymour, xxvii–xxviii, and now Blyth's edition of the *Regiment*, 8–12.

Hoccleve's three main sources.[45] It shows that Hoccleve rarely combines passages from all three sources in one of his sections. Usually, he relies on one major source for each of his sections, with occasional references to the others.[46] The pattern of use shows, as one would expect, that Hoccleve employs his 'narrative' sources mainly in the central, illustrative passages of the sections, using definitions and *sententiae* from the Bible and religious authors to define his topic or to sum up.

So far, I have considered the quantity and distribution of borrowings that Hoccleve makes from his sources. However, the relative number of borrowings does not necessarily show which of the sources influenced the structure of the *Regiment*. The borrowings from *De ludo scaccorum*, for example, are nearly all illustrative exempla rather than structural units. Another complication is that the *Secretum* was certainly an influence on Aegidius's work, and quite possibly on the *De ludo scaccorum* too.[47] However, a more detailed comparison reveals additional information about the structural influence of the three sources.

The assumption (already current in the fifteenth century) that Hoccleve's *Regiment* is a straightforward translation of Aegidius stems partly from Aegidius's reputation as a royal instructor and the popularity of his work. The fact that Hoccleve's poem shares Aegidius's title has also fostered the impression, though, as already seen, *De regimine principum* was a generic title for a text of royal instruction. Looking closer, Book I of *De regimine principum* does partly correspond to the *Regiment* in the subjects discussed and in their arrangement. For example, Aegidius warns against placing happiness in the flesh, in honours, in glory and reputation (Book I. i, 6–11). The second section discusses the virtues necessary in a ruler, including *prudentia* (I. ii, 6–9), *iusticia* (for instance, I. ii, 12: 'Quod maxime decet reges esse iustos et in suo regno iustitiam obseruare'),[48] *fortitudo* (I. ii, 13–15) and *liberalitas* (for instance, I. ii, 18: 'Quod reges et principes inpossibile est esse prodigos & quod maxime detestabile est eos esse auaros et quod potissime decet eos liberales esse').[49] Other attributes discussed by

---

[45] Below, pp. 122–5.

[46] For example, in the 'Paciencia' section he uses Jacobus, in the 'Avaritia' section, Aegidius.

[47] Aegidius's *De regimine principum* stands in the tradition of regiminal texts of which the *Secretum* is a seminal work. As noted above, Aegidius was familiar with the works of Aristotle (to whom the *Secretum* was attributed) and wrote a commentary on Aristotle's *Rhetoric*. Blake asserts that *De ludo scaccorum* 'was itself based on *De regimine principum* by Aegidius Romanus' (Caxton, *The Game of Chess*, first page of introduction), but provides no evidence for the claim.

[48] 'That it greatly behoves kings to be just and to uphold justice in their kingdom.'

[49] 'That it is impossible for kings and princes to be spendthrift and that it is especially despicable for them to be avaricious and that it is particularly appropriate for them to be generous.' (Aster 1888 notes nine borrowings by Hoccleve from this chapter.)

Aegidius here include *magnanimitas, humilitas* and *iocunditas*. The rest of Book I (sections iii and iv) deals with *passiones animae* (such as love, fear and hope, bravery and despair) and habits of the young and old.

There is also a verbal correspondence that suggests a link between Aegidius and one section of the *Regiment*. This is the heading commonly given to lines 4005–123 of the *Regiment*: 'Quod rex non debet felicitatem suam ponere in divitiis.'[50] The word 'felicitatem' is used in this way in numerous chapters of Aegidius's treatise; it becomes almost a catchword for the first part of his work, and may have influenced the heading in the English text. It has been suggested that the passage on peace which concludes the *Regiment* is a conscious response to the *De regimine principum*, which ends by describing the duties of the king in war.[51] Aegidius's work, then, has some suggestive parallels with the *Regiment* at the thematic and structural levels as well as verbal borrowings. However, the *Regiment* can in no way be described as a 'translation' of *De regimine principum*. Hoccleve's borrowings are, in fact, mostly from Book I, part ii of the Latin work; out of *De regimine principum*'s three books, Aster finds only one borrowing later than Book I, part ii, 23.[52]

The *Secretum* equally has chapters devoted to subjects that concerned Hoccleve. These include avarice and largesse, not speaking too much, chastity, mercy and taking counsel.[53] Hoccleve borrows numerous passages from these, but they do not amount to a sustained use of the *Secretum* as an immediate structural model. Its influence stems as much from its status as an originary work for the advice-giving tradition as from its textual presence in Hoccleve's poem.

---

[50] 'That the king should not place his delight in riches.'

[51] Blyth 1993, 351. Blyth does not mention that Aegidius also includes a section on peace, before his borrowings from Vegetius. Another potential influence on Hoccleve here is Gower's 'In Praise of Peace'.

[52] Of the twenty-one borrowings noted by Aster, fifteen are from I. ii; see Aster 1888, 22–8. Aster's tally of borrowings is possibly to be supplemented by two or three parallel passages that occur later in the French version of Aegidius (Marzec 1982, 17–18), but the general point remains valid.

[53] Respectively: 'Capitulum sextum adhuc de hiis que pertinent largitati et declinacioni prodigalitatis et avaricie' [Chapter six so far about these matters concerning largesse and avoiding prodigality and avarice]; Chapter 11: 'de ornamento regis et prerogativa et abstinencia a multiloquio et consorcio subditorum' [on royal distinction and prerogative and refraining from chatter and the company of subjects]; part of Chapter 13: 'De Castitate Regis'; Chapter 18: 'de regis misericordia, quod rex non sit facilis ad effusionem sanguinis' [about royal mercy, that a king should not be quick to spill blood]; and from Book III, Chapter 13: 'de specialibus condicionibus, sive de bonis moribus et virtutibus optimi bajuli' [about special agreements or about the good habits and virtues of the best councillor]. See *Secretum Secretorum*, ed. Steele, 44, 48, 51, 55, 141.

At first sight, *De ludo scaccorum* looks extremely unpromising as an influence on the structure of the *Regiment*, as opposed to the individual exempla within it. Rather than using abstract qualities as an organizing principle, *De ludo scaccorum* groups its stories around the pieces of the chessboard, with each chapter employing the illusion of describing one piece. The passages translated by Hoccleve are concentrated for the most part in Tractate II of Jacobus de Cessolis's work, which describes the pieces on the 'back row' of the chessboard, using their differing status as a means of discussing the behaviour of their human counterparts. Thus there are chapters on the king (II. 1), queen (II. 2), 'alphyns' (what came to be known in England as bishops, but described by Jacobus as judges, II. 3), knights (II. 4) and rooks (II. 5). The next book of *De ludo scaccorum* deals with the pawns, dividing them into eight types of workers, including labourers, merchants and smiths.[54] This pattern does not seem to match the *Regiment*'s division into the virtues that the ideal ruler should possess, and gives rise to the impression that Hoccleve built the structure of the *Regiment* around Aegidius or the *Secretum*, here and there dipping into *De ludo scaccorum* for stories to illustrate his theoretical points.

Within the chapters of his work, however, Jacobus de Cessolis pursues the same themes of justice, mercy and chastity that Hoccleve's other sources present. This makes it possible for Hoccleve to include in the *Regiment* several exempla one after another, straight from Jacobus.[55] A closer look at *De ludo scaccorum* also suggests that Hoccleve also owes it a debt of structure and organization. For example, *De ludo scaccorum* II. 2, 'De forma regine', has a prominent theme of chastity. From the chapter, Hoccleve borrows two exempla (numbers 12 and 13 in Aster) for his own section 'De castitate'. Equally, Jacobus's chapter on the king (II. 1) has a section illustrating mercy. Hoccleve uses three stories from this passage (numbers 3, 4 and 6 in Aster) in his own section 'De misericordia'. By far the most heavily used chapter of *De ludo scaccorum* is II. 5, 'De rochis', from which Aster notes twenty-one borrowings (his numbers 21–41). Rooks exercise authority on behalf of the king and thus require many of the same attributes. Their inclusion also widens the scope of Jacobus's treatise: rooks are not only figures for the king himself, but also ministers and bureaucrats in their own right. Jacobus lists their essential qualities: 'In hiis debet esse justicia, pietas, humilitas,

---

[54] Burt 1957, xvi–xvii, points to the unusual prominence of the pawns in *De ludo scaccorum*'s scheme, and their ability to improve by their own endeavours: if a pawn reaches the other side of the board, it can acquire the movements of any other piece.

[55] Thus *Regiment*, 3476–542, from *De ludo scaccorum*, II. 5. See Aster 1888, 34–7. This correspondence was noted by Kleinecke (1937, 115) but has not subsequently been explored.

patientia, voluntaria paupertas et liberalitas'.[56] These qualities are illustrated in turn. They are notably close to the first sections of the *Regiment*: keeping oaths and observing the laws, 'De pietate', 'De misericordia', 'De patientia'. This parallel is strengthened when we consider the passages that Hoccleve borrows from 'De rochis'.[57] Borrowings 21–4 in Aster come from Jacobus's passage on *justicia*. All four appear in the *Regiment*'s sections on laws and justice. Aster 25–30 are in Jacobus's passage on *pietas*; 25 and 27–30 are in the *Regiment*'s section 'De pietate' (Aster 26 is used in the next section of the *Regiment*, 'De misericordia'). Jacobus's passage on *humilitas* does not have a direct echo in the *Regiment*, though Aster 31 is used in the *Regiment*'s 'De paciencia' section, as are all *De ludo scaccorum*'s narratives about patience (Aster 34–7). In these sections of the *Regiment*, then, Hoccleve not only borrows quotations *en bloc* from *De ludo scaccorum*; he also uses Jacobus de Cessolis's arrangement of themes and exempla as a guide to organize his own work. The influence of this part of *De ludo scaccorum* is clearer than the presumed influence from *De regimine principum* and the *Secretum*, and can be substantiated by the volume and placing of passages that Hoccleve incorporates into the *Regiment*. This part of *De ludo scaccorum* seems, then, to provide the immediate model for the equivalent sections of the *Regiment*.

Tractate III of *De ludo scaccorum* (which deals with the pawns) also uses the chesspieces to illustrate particular virtues and vices. For example, Chapter 3, 'De lanificiis et notariis', is concerned with chastity. Hoccleve uses four passages from this chapter (Aster 43–6) in his section 'De castitate'. Chapter 6, 'De tabulariis et hospitibus', discusses gluttony and drunkenness. From this chapter, Aster 49–51 are used in the *Regiment*'s 'De castitate', which condemns excesses of the body. Chapter 4, 'De mercatoribus', concerns avarice. Two passages from this chapter (Aster 47 and 48) are included in Hoccleve's 'De vicio avaricie'. Chapter 8, 'De prodigis, ribaldis, lusoribus et cursoribus', warns against profligacy, and includes the story of John of Canace (Aster 52), which occurs in the *Regiment*'s section 'De virtute largitatis, et de vicio prodigalitatis'. These thematic and structural parallels counter the superficial impression that Hoccleve simply gathers stories from *De ludo scaccorum* to fit a design inherited from *De regimine principum* or the *Secretum secretorum*. Those two works do provide important models for Hoccleve, setting the parameters of virtue and vice; dealing with royal duties in peace and war; underlining the importance of counsel; linking bodily health to good governance and so to the health of the body

---

[56] Jacobus, *De ludo scaccorum*, II. 5 (ed. Vetter, below cols 303–4). I quote Hoccleve's sources from Aster 1888 (by borrowing number) where possible; when quoting passages not printed in Aster (as in this case) I shall note the edition used.

[57] See Table of Borrowings, below, pp. 122–5.

politic. It is *De ludo scaccorum*, however, that contributes most directly to the structure of the *Regiment* proper, especially in the discussion of justice through to chastity.

IV. TYRANTS AND PHILOSOPHERS

One aspect of *De ludo scaccorum* makes it a potentially significant, yet dangerous, source for Hoccleve's poem. Jacobus de Cessolis's work is supposedly a book on the chesspieces and their roles in the game, but this is, of course, an excuse for a political treatise on the roles of different social groups, in particular kings and others in authority. It would be very hard to use the book as a practical manual on chess. Indeed, the first chapters make the political purpose of the work clear. The first tractate explains the origin of the game and the book in a kind of inverted etiology. Instead of describing the text to come as a book of governance based on the game of chess (what *De ludo scaccorum* in fact is), chess is described as a game based on principles of governance,[58] and invented as a desperate attempt to correct the errors of an evil and tyrannous king.[59] The opening passage illustrates the background to the book's imagined origin:

> Inter omnia mala signa in homine unum est precipuum, quando aliquis non timet Deum offendere per culpam et homines per inordinatam vitam, quia non solum correptiones [*or* correctiones] negligit, sed correptores affligit. Quemadmodum de Nerone legimus inperatore, quod ipse Senecam magistrum suum occidit eo quod correptiones eius ferre non posset.[60]

> [Amongst all the evil signs in a man, one is pre-eminent, when someone is not afraid of offending God by sin and men by an unruly life, since he not only ignores rebukes [corrections], but attacks those

---

[58] Chess did have a strong connection with military strategy: the pieces originally represented parts of a traditional Indian army. They came to be identified with sections of western society when chess was adopted in Europe (it was well known there by the twelfth century); see Eales 1986.

[59] Tyrants were a familiar feature of Italian politics at the time when *De ludo scaccorum* was written. Genoa itself (where Jacobus de Cessolis probably lived) had a turbulent political history during the later thirteenth century. In 1257, a revolution put William Boccanegra in power, but his regime had no lasting support, and numerous revolts and conflicts ensued. Elsewhere in northern Italy, government by tyrants was common; see Armstrong 1932, Waley 1988 and Epstein 1996, 140–87 and 325. Epstein (160–77) also discusses Genoese culture in this period, but does not mention Jacobus de Cessolis.

[60] *De ludo scaccorum*, I. 1 (ed. Vetter, below cols 33–4).

chiding him. As, for example, we read about the emperor Nero, that he
himself killed his master Seneca because he could not bear his rebukes.]

This is hardly the relationship of benign master-philosopher and willing pupil-king in an ideal *Fürstenspiegel*. *De ludo saccorum* goes on to describe the wicked King Evylmerodach, who dismembered his father's body and fed it to vultures – it is for his instruction that chess was invented. A story about the councillor Theodorus Cyrenaicus is placed in this section; he is killed for attempting to reprove his king's vices while other advisors say nothing.[61] This and two other stories of the mutilation or death of philosophers give the invention of chess a background of tyranny and fear of giving advice. The philosopher Philometer ('quod idem est apud Latinos quam mensure vel iusticie amator')[62] invents chess as a way of taming King Evylmerodach's wickedness. By teaching the King about the pieces and their roles, he teaches the King about his own responsibilities. Philometer eventually tells the King why he invented the game:

> O domine mi rex! tuam vitam gloriosam desidero, quam videre non possum, nisi iusticia et bonis moribus insignitus a populo diligaris. Opto te ergo alium fore regimine, ut tibi prius domineris, qui non iure aliis sed violentia dominaris. Iniustum quippe est, ut aliis inperare velis, cum tibi ipsi inperare non possis, et memento: violenta inperia durare non possunt. Hec ergo tue correptionis causa existat. Patienter enim reges sapientum suorum correptiones ferre debent et ipsos correptores libenter audire.[63]

> [O lord my King! I wish your life to be glorious, something that I cannot see unless, outstanding in justice and good habits, you are loved by the people. I pray you therefore to take a different rule [of living], so that first of all you may govern yourself, who does not govern others by law but by violence. For it is unjust that you should wish to rule others, when you cannot even rule yourself, and remember: violent regimes cannot last long. This, then, is the cause of your reproof. For kings ought patiently to bear the rebukes of their councillors and freely to listen to their reprovers.]

The philosopher presents his argument for good governance as being ultimately also of political value to the King: he will be a more successful ruler if he is more moral. Analysing this exchange, Larry Scanlon comments that 'The *Ludus Scaccorum* leaves th[e] ambiguity between ideology and virtue unresolved, operating in the tension between the

[61] Translated in the *Regiment*, 2570–83.
[62] 'Which is in Latin, the same as a lover of moderation or justice'; *De ludo scaccorum*, I. 2 (ed. Vetter, below cols 45–6).
[63] *De ludo scaccorum*, I. 3 (ed. Vetter, below cols 59–62).

two.' But Scanlon then disregards such ambiguities when he argues that this passage of *De ludo scaccorum* ultimately endorses royal power: '[Philometer's] correction is framed entirely by his desire for the king's glory and he presents the change he recommends more as a self-generated ideological program than as a response to external constraint.'[64] Scanlon here underestimates the strength of the warning that Philometer gives, and the benefits that the philosopher himself hopes to receive from his advice. His colleagues have all been executed for trying to counsel Evylmerodach. Philometer therefore constructs a theory that kings are more successful when they are just, merciful and so on. His primary aim is not, however, merely to extend the King's power, but to bind it into a system of governance – an ideology – that is generated and regulated by people such as philosophers and councillors.

Jacobus's story of a tyrant and a philosopher is paralleled in another text of the late thirteenth century: the *Liber sancti passagii christicolarum contra Saracenos pro recuperatione Terrae Sanctae* by Galwan de Levanto. This was written between 1291 and 1296 for Philip IV of France, the dedicatee of Aegidius's *De regimine principum*. The text aims to persuade him to undertake a crusade. Its first tractate, however, is entitled 'De regimine principum atropologice educto de ludo scachorum'. The invention of chess is ascribed to a philosopher named Justus who wishes to reform a tyrant named Juvenalis.[65] Here, in a work contemporary with Jacobus's *De ludo scaccorum*, we have another scenario in which chess is a vehicle to curb tyranny – in particular, the tyranny of a young ruler. It is notable that Galwan came from Genoa, where Jacobus was also probably based. One can perhaps discern in these two works a north Italian anti-tyrannical narrative that was exported to the palaces of France, and, via translations of Jacobus, into numerous European vernaculars.

Jacobus's origin story makes the game of chess integral to the business of advising kings, rather than a mere pastime that happens to mirror human society. In *De ludo scaccorum*, inventing chess is equivalent to writing a book of advice. By such a pursuit, a king may be led to understand moral duties profitable to his reign and his soul. In Jacobus's fiction, to play the game of chess is also to read the book of advice, and to act out its principles. The philosopher involves the king in the rules and limitations of the game before the latter realizes that, as a king, he is also part of the game. This interweaving of play and advice should remind us of the alternatives of pastime and profit that Hoccleve

---

[64] Scanlon 1994, both from 315.
[65] See Murray 1913, 549–50. The unique manuscript is Paris, BN MS nouv. acquis. lat. 669. See Kohler 1900–6 for discussion and a partial edition of the text (not including the first tractate).

cautiously suggests Henry may gain from the *Regiment*: 'if yow list of stories taken heede, / Sumwhat it may profyte, by your leeve' (2138–9).

Both *De ludo scaccorum* and *The Regiment of Princes* are offered by nervous advisors as diversions for their rulers, in the case of Philometer to turn Evylmerodach from a path of wickedness. The atmosphere of tyranny and danger engendered at the start of *De ludo scaccorum* creates a disturbing background to Hoccleve's use of the treatise alongside *De regimine principum* and the *Secretum secretorum*.[66] No wonder, then, that immediately after introducing *De ludo scaccorum*, Hoccleve claims that Henry does not really need its advice: 'it be no maneere of neede / Yow to consaille what to doon or leeve' (2136–7). These phrases may simply be topoi of humility, but if Henry had indeed read 'the bookes alle three' (2129),[67] the implied parallel between himself and the tyrant parricide Evylmerodach could have been distinctly unsettling for a prince already rivalling the power of his ailing father. At the level of *De ludo scaccorum*'s initiating fiction, and within its exempla, Jacobus de Cessolis starkly depicts the dilemma of the subject wishing to advise or correct his king, and the possible dangers that such advice may incur. The next section examines the *Regiment*'s portrayal of royal advice in benevolent and dangerous situations, asking how Hoccleve represents the relationship between advisors and kings in the narratives that he adapts from *De ludo scaccorum*.

---

[66] I have already commented on possible anti-tyrannical readings of Aegidius in England (above, p. 90), and the *Secretum secretorum* tradition does not present an entirely untroubled image of the advisory relationship either. The text emerges as a series of letters that Aristotle sends instead of going to advise Alexander in person. In this sense, the *Secretum* is born out of disobedience to Alexander; see Ferster 1996, 44. The Aristotle–Alexander relationship as a whole also raises many questions about the effectiveness of philosophical advice. Take, for example, the ambiguous portrayal of Alexander in Gower's *Confessio amantis*, and the final comments on him in the *Regiment*, 5349–62 (for Gower's treatment of Alexander, see Dimmick 1998, esp. 183–8). It will be clear that I disagree with Scanlon's view that the *Secretum* simply preaches a more efficient way to control the people; see Scanlon 1990, 231.

[67] Not an unreasonable assumption, given their popularity. Prince Henry was said to have consulted Aegidius for the latter's comments (culled from Vegetius) on military tactics (see Pearsall 1994, 393–4), though this description may owe as much to literary as military traditions.

V. Exemplary Translation and Redirecting Advice

Relatively little work has been done on the affiliations of the Latin texts that Hoccleve used, his translation practice or the implications of his translations for the *Regiment's* advisory project. Here I shall consider one aspect of these questions: the alterations that Hoccleve makes to the exempla of *De ludo scaccorum*, and the theme of debate between subjects and kings that emerges as a result. Many of the changes made by Hoccleve to his sources are minor. For example, he often removes the names of characters and kingdoms from the stories, making them slip more smoothly into the current of the narrative, and presenting them as archetypal figures. Conversely, Hoccleve will sometimes add a detail or image, apparently to colour the narrative, connect it with other exempla in the section or make a specific didactic or topical point.

One passage that illustrates this technique comes in the *Regiment's* section on observing laws. The exemplum concerns a consul's son who is discovered to be an adulterer (lines 2731–68). *De ludo scaccorum's* narrative occupies one sentence; the consul is named Zaleucus; the action is all reported by the narrator (Aster 17). Hoccleve's story is more dramatic. It occupies thirty-eight lines, fifteen of which are taken up by the (here unnamed) consul's speeches. Hoccleve exploits the organizing potential of his rhyme royal stanzas, making each one introduce a new part of the narrative, or a significant change of direction. In the first, the law against adultery is made; the punishment is blinding, and we learn that a consul's son is found guilty. In the second, the people and other consuls ask that the punishment be excused because of their respect for the guilty man's father. In the third, the father speaks and refuses to bend the rules: 'to that may I nat enclyne' (2751). In the fourth, the combined pressure of the people and consuls forces him to give ground. The next stanza sees the father make his concession, again in direct speech. He will lose one eye, and his son another. The final lines summarize the situation. The consul and his son 'wole have but o mannes sighte' (2766), while the people are not entirely satisfied, but have to accept the compromise, just as the father is earlier 'overcome' (2756) by the will of the people. Hoccleve then poses the question:

> Now if tomorwe fil ther swich a chance,
> Sholde men fynde so just governance?
> Nay, nay, this lond is al to scars and lyte
> To fynde oon that so justly wolde him qwyte. (2769–72)

This exemplum is characteristic of Hoccleve's translation practice. The removal of names, addition of other details (especially the role of the common people) and the use of direct speech all dramatize and enliven the narrative, while Hoccleve invites his readers themselves to address the moral dilemma at the heart of the story.

In the exemplum of the brazen bull (an instrument of torture designed by a 'sotil werkman in craft of metal' (3009) for a tyrant) Hoccleve likewise removes the names of the tyrant and the workman (Phalaris and Perillus), partly perhaps because they are less well known than characters such as Alexander, Caesar, Scipio and Pompey who frequent the *Regiment*'s narratives. *De ludo scaccorum* describes why the bull was made: 'Perillus [...] credens complacere Phalaridi tyranno crudeli [...] fecit taurum aeneum.'[68] Hoccleve translates the middle phrase as 'His lord the kyng he thoughte plese and glade' (3011), reflecting the strength of the verb 'complacere' by two English words. But Hoccleve also makes more substantial changes to the exemplum. Later in his version, he returns to expand the idea of currying favour which the Latin 'complacere' suggests. The workman becomes a 'losengeour' (3027) and it is not merely the tyrant's whim to test the invention on its maker; instead, 'our lord God, of pitee the auctour' (3025) takes control of the workman's fate, punishing him for his flattery as much as his cruelty. The moral that Hoccleve draws from the tale moves away from pity altogether and introduces a passage about flattery: 'Men may seen heere how Favel him enclyneth / Ay to his lordes lust' (3039–40).

Chapter 2 showed how this narrative depicts a reading and interpreting king (albeit a tyrant), who rejects the cruel intention of the workman's invention. Hoccleve strengthens these associations in his translation from *De ludo scaccorum*. The dysfunctional relationship between flattering speech and royal power is suggested by the bestial noise that the bull's victim is heard to make: 'whan to crye hem conpellid hir wo, / Hir vois was lyk a boles everemo' (3021–2). Ironically, the workman intends this incoherent fate for those who displease the King – presumably by speaking the plain truth, rather than false flattery.[69] In fact, it is the workman himself whose flattery is turned into bellowing when he becomes the first victim of his own invention. His impending metamorphosis is further underlined by the sexualized language of the tyrant's judgement:

> Thow that art more cruel
> Than I, the maydenhede of this jewel
> Shalt preeve anoon; this is my jugement. (3035–7)

---

[68] Aster 9: 'Perillus [...] thinking he would please the cruel tyrant Phalaris [...] made a brass bull.'

[69] The Latin text makes its own play on the idea with a pun on *vociferarent*, 'they would cry out', and *vox feralis*, 'bestial voice': 'Cumque introclusi vociferarent prae poena, non videretur vox humana sed feralis' [And when those inside would cry out because of the torture, the voice would not seem human but bestial].

Here, in a reversal of an Ovidian rape, the flattering workman changes into a bull after he enters his creation. Hoccleve uses the same group of images elsewhere in the *Regiment*. Lechery is described as a 'hogges lyf' (3657); it is behaviour 'That beestes resonlees usen and holde' (3659). Lust is portrayed as burning – 'What prince that with unclennesse is brent [...] No parfyt dede or werk him folwe may' (3630, 3632) – and indulgence in the flesh makes one incoherent:

> And aftir moot he rowne with a pilwe
> His lyflees resons there to despende.
> We beestes resonable, allas, why wole we
> Ageyn resoun werreye and hir offende? (3893–6)

In an earlier exemplum, a knight tells Alexander that 'thy lust bestial and miserable / Hath qweynt thy reson and entendement' (3503–4). These links between flattery, sexual indulgence and bestial unreason, forged throughout the *Regiment*, colour the workman's fate.[70] As I have already suggested, the insistent identification of the workman's device with flattering speech suggests that the brazen bull is a 'rhetorical' work too;[71] it is made by 'sotil aart' (3020; compare the Chaucer quotation at the head of the Introduction, above, p. 1) and appropriates the voices of its subjects for new ends. The story of the brazen bull is, indeed, used by Ovid to illustrate linguistic trickery. Let women, he says, be cheated by promises just as they cheat men:

> Et Phalaris tauro violenti membra Perilli
> Torruit: infelix inbuit auctor opus.
> Iustus uterque fuit: neque enim lex aequior ulla est,
> Quam necis artifices arte perire sua. (*Ars amatoria*, I. 653–6)

[Phalaris also roasted in his fierce bull the limbs of Perillus. The unhappy author christened his work. Both [i.e. Phalaris and Busiris in Ovid's previous story] were just; for there is no fairer law than that contrivers of destruction should perish by their own skill.]

In the *Tristia*, Ovid (whose exile adds to the acuity of his views on verbal invention and political power) draws an even clearer parallel between making the bull and writing. He compares the attacks of an enemy to Perillus's invention:

> 'Pro quibus inventis, ut munus munere penses,
> da precor, ingenio praemia digna meo'

---

[70] Flattery and sexual indulgence were, of course, commonly associated; take for example the flattering Lady Mede, depicted as the Whore of Babylon at the start of *Piers Plowman*, B-text, passus II.
[71] Above, pp. 74–5.

dixerat. At Phalaris 'poenae mirande repertor,
ipse tuum praesens imbue' dixit 'opus'. (*Tristia*, III. xi, 49–52)

[He had said 'For this invention, so as to pay gift with gift, give me, I pray, a prize worthy of my skill.' But Phalaris said 'Wonderful inventor of punishment, dedicate in person your own work.']

In *De ludo scaccorum*, lines from the *Ars amatoria* are used as an epigram to the story of the brazen bull: 'Nulla enim lex equior, quam necis artifices arte perire sua, ut dicit Ovidius.'[72] Hoccleve's development of the story may well have have been directly influenced by the Ovidian reference in the Latin text, but even if it was not, both Ovid's 'auctor' and Hoccleve's 'sotil werkman' explore the dangers of brazen flattery at court, whether by means of sculpture or spoken words.

While the exemplum of the brass bull stands as a metaphor for dangerous speech, Hoccleve consistently adds direct speech to his sources, breaking open the constraining silence alloted to would-be counsellors in the *Regiment*'s Dialogue and in the *Male Regle*. *De ludo scaccorum* itself includes a good deal of dialogue. Many of its stories depend on the interpretation of a word or phrase, or a confusion of understanding.[73] Hoccleve takes up this theme and extends it in his translated exempla. His interest in the exchange of spoken counsel may be illustrated by three stories from *De ludo scaccorum* adapted in the *Regiment*'s section 'De paciencia'. In the first (3496–512), Alexander is reproved by an old knight. The Latin exemplum has no direct speech, reporting both the accusation of the knight Antigonus and Alexander's 'patient' reply:

De patientia Alexandri dicitur, quod cum Antigonus ei dixisset quod ei non competebat regnare [...] patienter duram reprehensionem tulit, nihilque praeterquam se corrigere et bonos mores et honestos assumere dixit. (Aster 34)

[It is said about the patience of Alexander that when Antigonus had said to him that he was not competent to rule [...] he accepted patiently the harsh reproof, and said nothing except that he would correct himself and take up good and respectable habits.]

This sentence involves three layers of reported speech – 'dicitur', 'dixisset' and 'dixit'. Hoccleve avoids the complex subordination of the Latin by putting the exchange into direct speech. He shows his alertness

---

[72] *De ludo scaccorum*, II. 1 (ed. Vetter, below cols 101–2). One of Vetter's manuscripts also quotes lines from the *Tristia* at this point.

[73] See Mehl 1978, 241. Antin notes this feature in Caxton's *Game of Chess*, with 'a strong tendency to restrict the meaningfulness of the solutions to a kind of purely verbal reality' (Antin 1968, 277). The use of dialogue in Hoccleve's translations has been noted in Mitchell 1968, 85–6 and Scanlon 1994, 315.

to different modes of address by his characterization of the knight and of Alexander through their speech. The former's moral outburst has strong overtones of a sermon against 'lust bestial and miserable' and 'leccherie' (3503, 3506), with the threat of damnation at the end: 'Repreef, I drede, qwyte shal thyn hyre' (3507). Alexander's response also uses religious language, that of a penitent:

> The kyng answerde, 'I knowe myn errour;'
> And paciently seide, 'I have offendid;
> I woot it wel, and it shal been amendid.' (3510–12)

Here, Hoccleve's use of direct speech enables him to imbue the short exemplum with a Christian–moral significance not present in *De ludo scaccorum*.

The *Regiment*'s next lines also introduce dialogue added from *De ludo scaccorum*. In a balanced sentence, the Latin text shows how Caesar patiently bears the revelation of his low origins: 'Cumque quidam maternam eius [sc. Caesaris] originem despexisset [...] ridendo pertulit.'[74] *De ludo scaccorum* quotes Caesar's reply directly, but Hoccleve puts the accusation in direct speech too, adding colloquial vocabulary: ' "Julius", quod he, "make it nat so tow, / For of thy birthe art thow nat worth a leek" ' (3516–17). This change likewise makes the exemplum more confrontational. The next stanza (3529–35; Aster 36) has exactly the same pattern of charge and response (this time involving Scipio Africanus) and again the accusation is made more direct. Alterations of voice such as these have a cumulative effect, placing dialogue between ruler and subject at the centre of the poem.

The involvement of 'the people' in political dialogue is once again achieved in the exemplum of Lycurgus (2950–89, Aster 20; Hoccleve says he is 'a knyght, I not what men him calle' (2950)). The story is told without direct speech in *De ludo scaccorum*. Hoccleve's version, however, creates a debate between ruler and subjects, who are this time represented by the mass of the people – 'the prees' (2967), 'the peple' (2986) – rather than one accuser. They are given a collective, colloquial voice: ' "Yee, yee, man, yee! We graunte it al and some" ' (2979). Charles Blyth notes the difference between Hoccleve's story and the version in *Confessio amantis*, Book VII, in which an ideal ruler goes into voluntary exile for the sake of just laws.[75] Hoccleve gives voice (though not necessarily endorsement) to popular complaint in his story, and the tale ends with no eulogy on the knight's actions, though he has earlier been called 'A just man and a treewe in al his deede' (2951). Hoccleve's

---

[74] Aster 35: 'And when someone mocked his [Caesar's] family origins [...] he put up with it with laughter.'
[75] Blyth 1993, 355–8.

Hoccleve's Regiment of Princes: Counsel and Constraint

exemplum, Blyth argues, is 'closer to the world of daily social and political abuse and deception' than Gower's.[76] This effect is partly achieved by Hoccleve's dramatization of the exchange between people and ruler. Here, as elsewhere, Hoccleve removes barriers between the common voice of complaint and the ruler, imagining a people far more articulate and powerful than Hoccleve and his fellow clerks are shown to be in the *Regiment*'s Dialogue.

By creating such public dialogues, Hoccleve sets subjects on a plane of discourse with the ruler, whether or not their advice is followed. The exemplum of Theodorus Cyrenaicus, for example, demonstrates how a voice of protest can be heard even amidst the imposition of silence by a tyrannous regime. Theodorus is executed for criticizing a king while other councillors keep quiet. He is crucified, lending an atmosphere of Christian martyrdom to his actions. What was reported speech in Latin has been turned into direct speech:

> Nat rekke I thogh I rote on hy or lowe,
> As he that of the deeth hath no gastnesse;
> I dye an innocent, I do thee knowe;
> I dye to deffende rightwisnesse. (2577–80)[77]

Rather than silencing him, the cross provides in effect a platform for Theodorus to denounce the cowardice of the flattering councillors. The narrative ends not with Theodorus's death, but with his defiant, unmediated words. Immediately afterwards comes the story of the treacherous *magister*, who offers Camillus his pupils as hostages (2584–642; Aster 23). Hoccleve puts the words of the traitor into direct speech; they can thus be set against those of the true councillor Theodorus, and of the honourable Duke Camillus. The story takes its place amongst the numerous dialogues within the larger dialogue of instructor and prince, poet and audience that the structure of the poem supports.

The implications of subject–ruler dialogue are widened by exempla that imagine a public audience for the exercise of kingly virtue and duty. In lines 3513–28, for example, 'a man' derides Caesar for being a baker's son. I showed above how the addition of direct address in these lines fits a pattern of kingly dialogue in the *Regiment*. The passage also changes the emphasis of the Latin story by assuming a wider constituency for the dispute. Whereas in *De ludo scaccorum* the man scorns Caesar for his lowly birth *per se* (Aster 35), in the *Regiment* the important factor is that 'men knowen wel ynow' (3518) about Caesar's family, and

---

[76] Ibid., 358.
[77] The Latin text (Aster 1) reads: 'Voluit dicere, quam parum curabat de ipsa morte et mortis modo, dum tamen innocenter et pro iustitia morerentur' [He wished to say how little he cared about death itself and the manner of death, since he was to die innocently and for justice].

that the man 'can tellen how / Thy fadir was a bakere' (3519–20). Hoccleve's narrative poses the threat of public knowledge for Caesar's origins rather than the private dishonour of the leader's low birth.[78]

Hoccleve adds more speech to the story in which Caesar is confronted by an old knight (3270–304; Aster 41). In *De ludo scaccorum*, only the knight speaks directly, but Hoccleve creates another dialogue between ruler and subject by having Caesar reply. As in the story of Lycurgus, Hoccleve also has an eye to the public effect of Caesar's actions, introducing 'the peple' as effectively another protagonist in the tale. *De ludo scaccorum* describes why Caesar eventually agreed to speak for his former soldier in court: 'Verebatur enim non tantum superbus sed et ingratus videri.'[79] The sentence implies that Caesar would seem proud and ungrateful to the veteran. Hoccleve expands and recasts the passage to include the public. In the *Regiment*, the knight has confronted Caesar 'On heighte wel, that al the peple it herde' (3278). For his part, Caesar

> dredde him, if he nadde thus ywroght,
> The peple him wolde han for a prowd man deemed,
> And ungentil, and that he cowde noght,
> As that it sholde eek have unto hem seemed,
> Thanke hem that worthy were to be qweemed. (3298–302)

The ideas of public pressure and duty to the people as a whole are new in Hoccleve's version and place a significant slant on the story, just as the active role of the people as speakers in the story of Lycurgus changes the focus of that narrative. The lines quoted above refer to 'hem that worthy were' in the plural, not just to the knight; Hoccleve, of course, wishes to establish himself as one of those worthy of reward.

The importance of dialogue and address is reflected in some of Hoccleve's own interventions in the poem. Shortly before the speech of Alexander's loyal knight, beginning 'O Alisaundre, it is uncovenable' (3501), the mention of the biblical King David draws from Hoccleve this apostrophe: 'O pacient, o humble kyng benigne, / O Kyng David' (3473–4). Hoccleve here assumes the same mode of address towards characters in his exemplum as they do towards one another. In lines 3200–27 Hoccleve includes an apostrophe to the city of Syracuse and to Marcus Marcellus: 'O worthy knyght, who shal thy steppes sue? / Thy successour halt him to longe in mue' (3219–20). Once again, Hoccleve intervenes in the exemplum, taking on the role of the subjects in the stories considered above by making a direct address to the historical Marcellus. In this case, the apostrophe is more than a conventional

---

[78] James Simpson (1995a, 174) plausibly suggests an allusion in Hoccleve's story to the insecurity of Lancastrian dynastic claims.

[79] 'For he was afraid to seem not only proud but also ungrateful.'

rhetorical flourish, for it strongly resembles other addresses in the poem, not to characters in the exempla, but to Prince Henry himself: 'O worthy Prince, this, lo, meeveth me' (2451); 'Prince excellent, have your lawes cheer' (2773); 'Excellent Prince, have in hem good savour' (3310, referring to pity and mercy).[80] These parallels blur the distinction between the historical/fictional kings in the exempla, and the future king, the primary reader of the poem. By addressing Marcus Marcellus directly, Hoccleve draws him into the arena of current affairs, especially with the pointed question 'who shal thy steppes sue?'. The final connection between historical exemplum and modern figurehead is made fifty lines later, when Hoccleve addresses Prince Henry at the end of a story about Alexander: 'Yit hope y seen his heir in this province; / And that shal yee be, my good lord the Prince' (3268–9).

In these brief snatches of speech and forms of address Hoccleve keeps up the pressure on Henry as an interlocutor in the poem, using overlapping patterns of direct speech. Henry is addressed directly by Hoccleve, Hoccleve addresses Henry's historical models, and those model kings are in turn addressed by their subjects.[81] Henry's involvement in the poem means that he, too, is the subject of the exempla, tested by each dilemma that presents itself in the poem's narratives. The movement of address from Classical exempla to Henry himself is illustrated in an earlier passage of the *Regiment*, lines 2857–84. It starts with the story of the tomb-makers, who consulted each new Roman emperor about the design of his tomb as a *memento mori*. This exchange is followed by a moralization on the transitory nature of man. Hoccleve then talks about an unspecified king 'That kyng that kyngly is of governance' (2873) and imagines how the people would speak of him once dead: 'In hevene moot this kynges soule reste' (2878). Finally, Prince Henry is addressed directly: 'O gracious Prince, swich be your wirkynge!' (2884). Henry is here the final link in a chain of exemplification, moving through a Roman narrative, moral *sententia*, imagined speech and finally to an apostrophe to the Prince.

These networks of exhortation and example constitute what one might call a strategy of redirection on Hoccleve's part. His adaptation of narratives from *De ludo scaccorum* introduces far more direct, advisory speech into the poem, but it is voiced by the wise or foolhardy

---

[80] Hoccleve frequently uses apostrophe when addressing Prince Henry. In addition to the examples quoted in the text, see 2017–18, 2055–6, 2157, 2185, 2390, 2884, 3268–9, 3344–5, 3347, 3407–8, 3963, 4387, 4740, 4747, 4866–7, 4891, 4964–5, 5321, 5332, 5363 and 5412. Each time, Hoccleve addresses Henry by the title 'Prince'.

[81] Stevens suggests that rhyme royal was associated with ceremonial addresses to real and imagined kings (Stevens 1979, 63–6). This connotation would make Hoccleve's use of the form particularly appropriate here, though he also uses rhyme royal in other situations and moods.

counsellors of an authoritative literary tradition. Likewise, themes of public dialogue and public responsibility are explored, but their destabilizing potential is initially effaced by their status as reported fictions. Their applicability to current English concerns is re-established by Hoccleve's technique of matching classical legend to recent example, and of mimicking in his own address to Prince Henry the dialogues contained in his exempla.

At the heart of Hoccleve's interventions and alterations to *De ludo scaccorum*'s narratives is the story of John of Canace, the longest exemplum in the *Regiment* (4180–354; Aster 52). Here, both Hoccleve and Prince Henry are involved in the exemplum's meaning and application. As in the other stories examined above, Hoccleve adds dialogue to the narrative and includes some extra details. For example, in the Latin text John's daughters are reported to ask him how much gold he really has in his chest: 'Die vero altera generi et filiae a patre interrogant, quanta esset pecunia in scrinio obstructo deposita.'[82] Hoccleve emphasizes the daughters' deviousness by having them ask about the money as if in jest:

His doghtres bothe with lawhynge cheere
Unto hir fadir spak and thus they seide [...]
'Now, goode fadir, how mochil moneye
In your strong bownden chiste is, we yow preye?'   (4301–2, 4304–5)

John of Canace is equally characterized in his reply, and matches their sly intent:

'Ten thousand pounde,' he seide, and lyed lowde,
'I tolde hem,' quod he, 'nat ful longe ago,
And that as redily as that I cowde.'   (4306–8)

Hoccleve adds the ironic detail of John mentioning that he counted the money, an event which, of course, he staged for their edification (as 'redily' neatly implies), with borrowed gold. There is more than a hint of mischief, too, in John's assurance that

          alle tho
I in my testament dispose shal
For your profyt.   (4310–12)

In this case the empty chest and grim warning that John of Canace's heirs do receive serve as a 'profitable' lesson in morality, if not financial management. Equally disconcerting, however, is the message that John

---

[82] 'Then on another day, the sons-in-law and daughters asked their father how much money was kept in the locked chest.'

leaves his family. In *De ludo scaccorum*, John's avaricious heirs find a club in his chest:

> Scrinium aperientes solemniter, nihil invenerunt in ipso, nisi clavam enormiter grossam et magnam, in cuius manubrio scriptum erat [...] Johannes ego Cavaza tale condo testamentum, ut quilibet hac clava mactetur qui se ipso neglecto alterius gerit curam. Stolidissimum opus est propria prodige expendere et aliena postmodum appetendo sperare sive filii sive filiae. (Aster 52)

> [Opening the chest solemnly, they found nothing in it, except a club of huge weight and size, on the handle of which was written [...] 'I John of Canace make this will, that whosoever has care of others while neglecting themselves should be killed with this club. It is a most thankless task to spend your own money recklessly and afterwards to hope for others' [money] from the greed of either sons or daughters'.]

The lesson to be learned here concerns John's own profligacy. In Hoccleve's version, the moral is rather different:

> They opneden the chiste and fond right noght
> But a passyngly greet sergeantes mace
> In which ther gayly maad was and ywroght
> This same scripture: 'I, John of Canace,
> Make swich testament heere in this place:
> Who berith charge of othir men and is
> Of hem despysid, slayn be he with this.' (4348–54)

The lesson here is hardly applicable to spending money foolishly (though 'berith charge' implies a financial as well as political duty); it is, however, directly relevant to the rule of kings. For Scanlon, the lines teach that the king must 'acknowledge the ideological contingency of his own position'.[83] Hoccleve's reference to a 'sergeantes mace', Scanlon suggests, may refer to the Sergeant of the House of Commons. This potential connection with the authority of civil and parliamentary institutions is intriguing, but Scanlon goes on to claim that the motto also reasserts royal power: 'the point of the inscription is to reaffirm the material power of such authority [...] Those who bear charge of others can always draw on that power despite the contempt of those to whom they are superior.'[84] I believe that the inscription has the opposite effect

---

[83] Scanlon 1994, 321.
[84] Ibid., 320. Strohm (1998, 196–214) finds a potential threat to the Lancastrian regime in the story, but, for him, Hoccleve's intention is to veil by silence the troublesome implications of John of Canace's deception. Strohm goes too far here in privileging 'our' reading of Lancastrian texts (unstable, ridden with ideological aporia) against the apparent complicity of Hoccleve and his contemporaries.

to this. Far from reinforcing royal power, Hoccleve manipulates the exemplum to produce a moral tied to his own agenda, in this case a warning that rulers cannot afford to ignore the welfare of their people. He repeats the point later:

> Ther may no prince in his estat endure,
> Ne therin any whyle stande sad,
> But he be loved. (4783–5)

These passages limit the absolute authority of the king rather than affirming it. They develop a monitory thread in the advisory tradition (including warnings in Aegidius's *De regimine principum*), which has an all-too-apparent relevance to recent English history. But if John of Canace's altered motto is to apply to Henry, as one who 'berith charge of othir men', then the next stanza also links the exemplum to Hoccleve:

> Amonges folies alle is noon, I leeve,
> More than man his good ful largely
> Despende in hope men wole him releeve
> Whan his good is despendid uttirly;
> The indigent men setten nothyng by.
> I, Hoccleve, in swich cas am gilty; this me touchith.
> So seith povert, which on fool large him vouchith. (4355–61)

The first four lines of the stanza are a fairly close rendering of the second part of the Latin motto. Hoccleve, then, returns to the lesson about profligacy that Jacobus's exemplum appears to require, but in this case it is Hoccleve himself who has to learn the lesson. One exemplum is made to articulate two morals, the first concerning governance (applicable to the Prince), the second concerning money (applicable to the poet). Hoccleve steps out of his role as advisor and turns his own prodigality into a moral story, placing himself in the text as an example. Anthony Hasler points out that Hoccleve 'is here a foreign body in the figuring of the body politic; even his name (4360) can only be read as metrically excessive to the line'.[85] Hoccleve is literally drawn into the text from outside, physically affected by the exemplum: 'this me touchith'. In the following passage, the central one of the poem for Hoccleve's stance as suppliant, Henry is also inscribed into the text as an exemplum of liberality: 'O, liberal Prince, ensample of honour' (4387). These stanzas contain the full range of Hoccleve's approaches to the Prince: self-deprecation, underlying threat, direct appeal, assurances of good faith and duty: 'In al my book yee shul nat see ne fynde / That I youre deedes lakke or hem dispreise' (4397–8). This protestation betrays Hoccleve's anxiety about his dangerously

[85] Hasler 1990, 178.

unwelcome reminders, and of course its embedding in a passage on the dangers of 'fool largesse' deepens the implications of Hoccleve's own indigence for the nation as a whole. These modes of address – encompassing threat and flattery – shade into one another, just as the rhetorical space between public and private realms is breached in Hoccleve's doubled conclusion to the John of Canace story.

This carefully staged appeal is the climax of the many appeals, supplications and debates that the *Regiment* contains. Through Hoccleve's changes to *De ludo scaccorum*, public dialogue becomes a feature of the *Regiment*'s narratives. Subjects are seen to address their kings, giving them counsel, reproving their vices, voicing uncomfortable opinions, asking for help. Meanwhile Hoccleve directs their historical voices and actions to issues of current concern and to the matter of Henry's personal *regiment*. This directive mode of writing consistently encourages the inclusion of Henry as a participant in constructing and ultimately exemplifying the *Regiment*'s teaching. Henry must not only listen, but also act, in order to live up to his title of 'liberal Prince'.

VI. THE IMAGERY OF COUNSEL

Finally in this chapter, I consider two points of the *Regiment* at which an image of Hoccleve's relationship with advisory authority is placed before the reader. In the earliest extant manuscripts of the *Regiment*, two pictures survive. These are the presentation miniature in BL MS Arundel 38, folio 37r, and the marginal picture of Chaucer in BL MS Harley 4866, folio 88r.[86] Both manuscripts once contained two pictures; Arundel 38 lacks one leaf after folio 90, where the image of Chaucer would have appeared, and Harley 4866 lacks one after folio 36, where a presentation scene would have been placed.[87] Five stanzas are missing from the text at this point, which indicates that the picture would have taken up three-quarters of a page, as it does in the Arundel manuscript. Both manuscripts were presentation copies made in Hoccleve's lifetime, probably under his supervision. Given these circumstances, and the fact that Hoccleve draws attention to the Chaucer portrait in the poem itself, it is legitimate to ask what role the pictures play in the advisory scheme of the *Regiment*.

---

[86] See plates 1 and 2, between pp. 116 and 117. I discuss the pictures' artistic affiliations and place in the *Regiment*'s manuscript tradition below, in Chapter 5, section II (pp. 155–9).

[87] Not after fol. 37, as Seymour states (Seymour 1974, 269). He also says that lines 2003–51 are missing at this point; in fact, lines 2017–51 are missing.

Voices of Translation

The placement and function of the presentation scene in Arundel 38 are intriguing. It does not appear at the beginning of the poem, as is normally the case with such scenes, but after the Dialogue with the Old Man. The picture thus forms an important division between the apparently spoken Dialogue and the formal written treatise addressed to the Prince, a division that in other manuscripts of the poem is often marked by a large initial or new page. This interplay between oral and textual is a characteristic part of Hoccleve's poetic, and in the *Regiment* he self-consciously signals the move from remembered speech to written text:

Recordyng in my mynde the lessoun
That he me yaf, I hoom to mete wente.
And on the morwe sette I me adoun,
And penne and ynke and parchemeyn I hente,
And [...]
Unto my lord the Prince thus I wroot.   (2010–14, 2016)

Then follows the presentation picture in the Arundel manuscript, as if it were the first folio of a self-contained volume – the very volume, indeed, that is handed to the Prince in the picture. It is only at this point that Hoccleve begins to address Prince Henry directly; lines 2017–23 (the only text written on folio 37r of Arundel 38) can stand on their own as an epigraph of dedication to the Prince: 'Hy noble and mighty Prince excellent' (2017).[88]

If the Arundel picture is unusual in appearing so far into the poem, it also stands in a complex relationship to fictional and historical contexts. Here we could place the picture beside comparable images in works by Gower and Lydgate.[89] Two pictures are most commonly found in *Confessio* manuscripts: Nebuchadnezzar's dream, and the confession scene itself, in which Gower's alter ego Amans usually kneels before the priest of Venus, Genius. The confession scene is thus played out by two 'invented' figures. It is inside the fictional conceit of the poem, as well as physically placed within the text, though some *Confessio* manuscripts do complicate this fictionality by depicting Amans as the elderly Gower.[90] Lydgate presentation pictures generally record a genuine, or hoped-for, event: the delivery of the finished work to a patron. For example, Bodleian MS Rawlinson C. 446, fol. 1r has Lydgate presenting *The Siege of Thebes* to Henry V; Bodleian MS Digby 232, fol. 1r includes another presentation scene with Henry V, also of *The Siege of Thebes*; Bodleian MS Ashmole 46, fol. 1r, shows Henry VI

---

[88] See plate 1; and on the picture's placement, Simpson 1995a, 172, note 29. Salter and Pearsall (1980) survey the tradition of frontispiece illustrations from which, due to its position, the Arundel picture deviates.

[89] See Griffiths 1983.

[90] See below, p. 121, note 109.

receiving *The Life of St Edmund* from the kneeling poet. These scenes are not uncomplicatedly 'real', but they appear outside the fiction of the work, and also outside its textual space. Gower similarly describes his meeting with Richard II within fifty lines of the *Confessio*'s opening, in the poetic equivalent of a commissioning portrait; subsequently, the implied parallels between Richard and the fictive action of the *Confessio* mostly remain below the surface. The *Regiment*'s scene is more involved. Prince Henry is both patron and subject of a 'text' already well under way; his continuing presence is integral to the construction of the *Regiment* proper. The Arundel picture thus either 'historicizes' the poetic moment of address to Prince Henry, or 'fictionalizes' the real Henry, in the sense that it draws him, both metaphorically and literally, into the already-invented scenario of Hoccleve's poem.

Hoccleve's transformation from despair and isolation at the start of the poem to the presentation scene's physical proximity with his future sovereign is another striking feature of the picture; it is almost too much of a change to be credible. The habitual identification of the kneeling figure in the Arundel scene as Thomas Hoccleve has, indeed, been questioned. In her catalogue of illuminated manuscripts, Kathleen Scott describes the picture as showing a 'finely dressed young man, kneeling and presenting (or possibly receiving) book from young male figure in royal dress and crown, almost certainly Prince Henry of Lancaster'.[91] She suggests that the kneeling man may be John Mowbray, Lord Mowbray and Segrave, later the second Duke of Norfolk (1392–1432). The initial just below the picture includes the Mowbray arms; the Segrave arms are depicted on folio 71r. The manuscript would then be a gift copy, paid for by the young nobleman.[92] Scott's theory has its attractions but is also problematic. In 1411–12, when the manuscript was almost certainly produced, Mowbray was nineteen years old, and

---

[91] Scott 1996, II, 158.

[92] In 1423 Mowbray paid Hoccleve for writing a petition to the Council for him, along with the subsequent Privy Seal warrant; see Burrow 1994, 17. Mowbray also had close links to other of Hoccleve's patrons. In 1411 Henry IV placed Mowbray in the care of Ralph Nevill. Nevill's brother Thomas was the Lord Fourneval to whom Hoccleve addressed the *Male Regle*. Mowbray subsequently married the daughter of Ralph Nevill and Joan Beaufort, Countess of Westmorland, to whom Hoccleve later dedicated the Durham manuscript of the *Series*. The circumstances of Mowbray's possible sponsorship of the Arundel manuscript merit closer attention. He was the son of Thomas Mowbray I (1366?–99), who may have been responsible for the death of Thomas, Duke of Gloucester in 1397, and whose dispute with Henry of Derby (Henry Bolingbroke, later King Henry IV) in 1398 had precipitated the exile of them both. John Mowbray's elder brother Thomas II had been executed as one of the Scrope conspirators in 1405, and Mowbray himself was given livery of his arms only two weeks before Henry IV's death. He was then summoned to Henry V's first Parliament as Earl Marshall; see entries in *DNB*, Pryor 1968, 58 and Allmand 1992, 11–15.

Plate 1. London, BL MS Arundel 38, fol. 37r
Reproduced by permission of the British Library.

Howe she þt bar ihu was mayden marie
And law his loue floure and fructifie

Al þogh his lyfe be queynt þe resemblaunce
Of him haþ in me so fressh lyflynesse
Þat to putte othir men in remembraunce
Of his persone I haue heere his lyknesse
Do make to þis ende in soothfastnesse
Þat þei þat haue of him lest þought & mynde
By þis peynture may ageyn him fynde

The ymages þt in þe chirche been
Maken folk þenke on god & on his seyntes
Whan þe ymages þei be holden & seen
Were oft vnsyte of hem causith restreyntes
Of þoughtes gode Whan a þing depeynt is
Or entailed if men take of it heede
Thoght of þe lyknesse it wil in hym brede

Yit somme holden oppynyoun and sey
Þat none ymages schuld I maked be
Þei erren foule & goon out of þe wey
Of trouthe haue þei skant sensibilitee
Passe ovir þt now blessid trinitee
Vppon my maistres soule mercy haue
ffor him lady eke þi mercy I craue

More othir þing wolde I fayne speke & touche
Heere in þis booke but sochuch is my dulnesse
ffor þt al voyde and empty is my pouche
Þat al my lust is queynt wt heuynesse
And heuy spirit comaundeth stilnesse

Plate 2. London, BL MS Harley 4866, fol. 88r
Reproduced by permission of the British Library.

Prince Henry (b. 1387) about five years his senior. The man kneeling in the picture, however, looks older than the Prince: his rather straggly dark hair seems to cover an area of greyness and his complexion is more worn. In addition, his gown, while generously cut, is not fur-lined or decorated in any way; Sylvia Wright describes it as a courtier's 'houpelleande', effectively Hoccleve's working clothes.[93] Another presentation scene survives in BL MS Royal 17 D. vi, a manuscript of the *Regiment* dating from the second quarter of the fifteenth century. Here the figures are quite clearly a prince and poet, the latter looking distinctly nervous and with a prominent (presumably empty) purse hanging from his waist. This scene seems more likely to have been copied from a picture that was believed to show prince and poet rather than prince and patron, though of course those two models are very similar, and an adaptation would be possible. Even if one should be cautious about Scott's identification, however, her description should encourage a closer consideration of the portrait, not simply as a textbook image of authorial deference, but as part of Hoccleve's poetic transformation from melancholy outsider to royal counsellor. The Mowbray arms that accompany the picture in Arundel 38 suggest that Hoccleve's approach to Prince Henry is not achieved alone; he has not yet gained the confidence of an English Aristotle, but instead relies on the support of others in order to make his counsel heard. In the portrait itself, Hoccleve's gown trails out of the frame, and his slightly awkward position – half-kneeling – gives the impression that he has just arrived on the scene; Prince Henry dominates the centre of the frame, and the book is offered, it seems, as advice from the edge of his world.

Like the Arundel presentation scene, the Chaucer portrait in Harley 4866 stands in close relationship to the text. Hoccleve clearly intended it to be integral to his project, and he shows a keen awareness of the boundaries between written text and marginal space in the manuscript. Rather than simply quote Chaucer's works, Hoccleve lays claim to a para-textual authority (that of the portrait) in order to reinforce his personal and literary connections with the great poet:

Althogh his lyf be qweynt, the resemblance
Of him hath in me so fressh lyflynesse
That to putte othir men in remembrance
Of his persone, I have heere his liknesse
Do make, to this ende, in soothfastnesse,
That they that han of him lost thoght and mynde
By this peynture may ageyn him fynde. (4992–8)

---

[93] Wright 1992, 199–200. The matching of ages and features is in no way definitive, of course, but may give an idea of what the picture is intended to portray, or what model it follows.

Hoccleve here implies his own proximity to the memory, and thus the literary inheritance, of Chaucer by claiming that 'the resemblance / Of him hath in me so fressh lyflynesse' whereas other men have 'lost thoght and mynde' of Chaucer. In particular, Hoccleve emphasizes the fact that the picture is true. It is a 'liknesse' made 'in soothfastnesse' – implying both that the portrait is true to life, and that it is made with a true intention.[94] Hoccleve seeks to combine the symbolic power of the picture with the empirical authority of a genuine portrait.

The Harley portrait is much discussed. David Carlson argues that it serves Hoccleve's need for patronage by presenting Chaucer as a successful forerunner.[95] James McGregor suggests that it canonizes Chaucer, who himself becomes one of the icons, the 'ymages' (4999), whose value in worship Hoccleve defends.[96] Building on this, Derek Pearsall links Chaucer's appearance with Hoccleve's anti-Lollard rhetoric in this section of the poem, particularly since Chaucer holds a rosary in his left hand.[97] I shall explore a different layer of resonances in the picture. Chaucer undoubtedly provides a powerful figure of vernacular written authority in the *Regiment*. It is significant, then, that Hoccleve places the Chaucer portrait in his section on taking counsel (lines 4859–5019). Indeed, Hoccleve's introduction of Chaucer appropriates Chaucer's own works as advisory ones; discussing the reception and interpretation of advice, Hoccleve says:

> The firste fyndere of our fair langage
> Hath seid, in cas semblable, and othir mo,
> So hyly wel that it is my dotage
> For to expresse or touche any of tho. (4978–81)

McGregor interprets Chaucer as an advisor-philosopher figure here, a surrogate Aristotle to Prince Henry's Alexander.[98] Though McGregor's claims for a close relationship between this part of the *Regiment* and Chaucer's *Melibee* are questionable,[99] the view that Chaucer is an exemplary advisory figure is attractive. The role of respected advisor is one that Hoccleve cannot claim unequivocally because of his own ad-

---

[94] Pearsall claims much for the accuracy and originality of the portrait, calling it 'marvellously expressive' (Pearsall 1992a, 287–9, at 288); see also Krochalis 1986–7. The picture may be lifelike, but the value of Chaucer's appearance lies as much in his symbolic potential as in his features. I have profited from conversations about the Chaucer portrait with Jessica Brantley and Martin Kaufmann.
[95] Carlson 1991.
[96] McGregor 1977. The portrait certainly plays a significant role in Hoccleve's discussion of icons in church.
[97] Pearsall 1994, 402–3.
[98] McGregor 1977, 342–3.
[99] He proposes that this section of the *Regiment* 'is a more or less abbreviated version of Chaucer's own *Melibee*'; ibid., 342.

missions of failure and misrule. Another source of authority is therefore needed, and Chaucer (whose texts such as *Lak of Stedfastnesse*, *Boece* and *Melibee* are highly relevant to royal governance) is the ideal candidate, since he has the status of a vernacular *auctor* (England's first) and he has already been claimed as Hoccleve's 'fadir' (1961).[100] In addition, his writing bridges the political rupture between Richard II and Henry IV. Chaucer survived to address the *Complaint to his Purse* to Henry IV, supporting the King's legitimacy by referring to him as 'conquerour of Brutes Albyon'; he could thus be reclaimed as a 'Lancastrian' poet. These factors make him an accessible figure of authority who reinforces Hoccleve's own advice. The picture functions as a *translatio auctoritatis* – boldly carrying Chaucer's textual and conciliar authority into Hoccleve's poem by visual means, in parallel to the textual *translatio* with which Hoccleve moulds and appropriates his written sources. Hoccleve is then able to adopt the mantle of advisor left by his dead poet-father.[101]

There are, in addition, aspects of the portrait's iconography that deepen the authoritative, advisory role played by Chaucer. In Harley 4866, Chaucer points at the text to indicate the passage describing the portrait. The gesture is reminiscent of the pointing hands that act as *nota bene* marks in many medieval manuscripts, but it also reproduces a common gesture in manuscript illustrations to denote teaching and instruction. For example, a fifteenth-century manuscript of an English *Secretum secretorum* shows Aristotle teaching Alexander, his pointing

---

[100] See Scanlon 1994, 240–1 and Pearsall 1994, 402. Bragg (1996, 129) suggests that the inclusion of a rosary in the portrait is a visual pun on Paternoster Row, the street at the centre of the London book trade (rosaries were commonly known as 'paternosters'). The reference is more likely to be religious, but another possibility – that the beads refer instead to Chaucer as Hoccleve's 'pater noster' – is not out of the question. Black beads also appear in Gower's *Confessio amantis*; see below, p. 121, note 109. The main claim of Bragg's article (that Chaucer's gesture represents his initials in a 'finger alphabet') rests on the flimsiest of evidence. The reference to Chaucer as a vernacular *auctor* is apposite, as Chaucer's garb bears a close resemblance to manuscript portraits of Italian *auctores* such as Petrarch; see Trapp 1992–3. This association would only have strengthened Chaucer's authoritative presence in the portrait.

[101] For Hoccleve's implied challenge to Chaucer in these passages, see Knapp 1999b. About five years before Hoccleve's *Regiment*, Henry Scogan (?1361–1407) had written his *Moral Balade*, a monitory poem addressed to Henry IV's four sons, to whom he was a tutor. Scogan uses a similar technique of praising and lamenting his friend Chaucer in order to bolster his own authority; in his case he incorporates Chaucer's balade *Gentilesse* into his poem (Scogan, *Moral Balade*, lines 105–25). Hoccleve may well have known Scogan's poem, and perhaps here is attempting to supersede its merely textual appropriation of Chaucer with a new, pictorial *translatio*. Stanzas from Hoccleve's own *Male Regle* were later adapted to form a moral balade in a Canterbury Cathedral manuscript; see Trudgill and Burrow 1998.

finger appearing to tick off a series of instructions to the seated king.[102] A manuscript of Henri de Gauchi's translation of Aegidius contains a similar standing figure (this time Aegidius) talking to a king, book in hand.[103] The only extant copy of Trevisa's English version of *De regimine principum* includes an image of Aegidius kneeling before his prince and pointing to the royal household, which forms the subject of that section of the work.[104] These parallels place the Chaucer picture in Harley 4866 in a tradition not only of author portraiture, but also of advisory iconography, an iconography that manuscripts of Hoccleve's sources employ. A picture of an academic or religious figure has been placed just before the *Regiment* in Coventry City Record Office MS Acc. 325/1, perhaps taking this type of illustration as a model.[105]

One further reference suggests itself, this time to manuscripts of the other poet whom Hoccleve eulogizes in the *Regiment*: John Gower. Numerous *Confessio amantis* manuscripts are illustrated with a picture of Amans, kneeling in confession before Genius. In Cambridge, Pembroke College MS 307, folio 9r, the dark-robed Genius stretches out a hand, with two fingers extended in blessing or instruction, while his other hand is held in a position analogous to that of Chaucer in the Harley portrait.[106] A similar scene occurs in Bodleian MS Bodley 294, folio 9r.[107] These manuscripts were illustrated by artists working in the same milieu – possibly the same workshops – as those who illustrated

---

[102] Oxford, University College MS 85, p. 70; reproduced as the frontispiece to *Secretum Secretorum*, ed. Manzalaoui. There is a substantial tradition of pictures showing Aristotle teaching Alexander. BL MS Add. 47680 (a version of the *Secretum* presented by Walter of Milemete to Edward III) contains several such illustrations; see *The Treatise of Walter of Milemete* and Sandler 1986, I, plates 219–21; II, 93–4. Sherman 1995 discusses a series of elaborately illustrated manuscripts containing Nicole Oresme's translations of Aristotle, made for King Charles V of France in the late fourteenth century.

[103] Reproduced in Henri de Gauchi, *Livres du gouvernement*, frontispiece, from a manuscript belonging (in 1899) to Mr J.E. Kerr Jnr of New York (now New York, Pierpont Morgan Library, MS M. 122). On illustrative programmes in Aegidius manuscripts, see further Briggs 1999, 30–42.

[104] Bodleian MS Digby 233, fol. 62r; reproduced in Pächt and Alexander 1966–73, III, plate LXXX; see also Scott 1996, II, 123–5.

[105] The three-quarter page picture (which is badly rubbed) shows a pensive figure in an open landscape with green hills behind him. Doyle suggests that the figure may represent Aristotle or Aegidius (Doyle and Pace 1968, 24). His downcast eyes and troubled expression nevertheless match the mood of the *Regiment*'s opening (the first stanza of the *Regiment* is the only text on fol. 1r). It is possible to discern some words in the upper right margin of fol. 1r, but they are not distinct enough to judge whether they refer to the picture.

[106] Reproduced in Wright 1992, 193.

[107] Other *Confessio* manuscripts show the same scene, for example BL MS Egerton 1991, Oxford, Corpus Christi College MS 67 and Bodleian MS Bodley 693.

the Harley and Arundel manuscripts of the *Regiment*.[108] In Harley 4866, Chaucer's sober academic dress, rosary and demonstrative gesture carry the same quasi-religious advisory authority that the pictures of Genius and Amans possess.[109]

The parallels that I have drawn here with advisory illustrations suggest a wider frame of reference for the Chaucer picture. If Chaucer is depicted in Harley 4866 to uphold the value of icons, then his iconography may point towards royal governance as much as religious sensibility. Chaucer's role as the authoritative genius behind Hoccleve's advice helps to legitimize both Hoccleve's claim of friendship with Chaucer and his claim to inherit from his 'fadir' the status of royal counsellor. Further, not only does Chaucer here exemplify the royal advisor in the mould of Aristotle or Aegidius, but his picture may also provide a link with Hoccleve's other 'maister' – Gower. The Chaucer portrait provides an image of a vernacular author as authoritative advisor that Hoccleve cannot hope to achieve by himself. Instead, and in keeping with the *Regiment* as a whole, Hoccleve plays both cards, mingling the image of deferential servant (the presentation scene) with that of serious counsellor (the Chaucer portrait).

Hoccleve's translations in the *Regiment*, both textual and pictorial, promote his strategy of advisory redirection. To make himself heard, Hoccleve enlists the voices of others. In an act of ventriloquism he directs his own political and advisory agenda through the exemplary figures who debate with and criticize their rulers, and through the marginal voices of the opening Dialogue. Meanwhile, an image of true advice is channelled back into the text through the pointing finger of the ample Chaucer, a finger that redirects our attention towards the claim to 'sothfastnesse' that Hoccleve mounts throughout the *Regiment*.

---

[108] For the close community of London scribes and artists in this period, see Christianson 1989. The text hand of Pembroke MS 307 has been identified in three other manuscripts of English poetry with Bury St Edmunds connections; see Hanna and Edwards 1996, 17–18, and below, p. 174, note 90.

[109] The black rosary is also reminiscent of the 'Peire of Bedes blak as Sable' that Venus gives Gower at the moment of his absolution in *Confessio* VIII. 2904. Some *Confessio* manuscripts show Amans as an elderly Gower, and Gaylord has drawn a parallel between the aged poet in these illustrations and Chaucer in Harley 4866 (Gaylord 1997, 133–8). Curiously, however, he does not address parallels between Genius in the Gower pictures and Chaucer in Harley 4866.

Table of Borrowings for Lines 2017–5463 of the *Regiment*

Notes

1. Numbers in square brackets refer to the numbers given to borrowings in Aster 1888 and Marzec 1982 (A and M), but to the page number in Gilbert 1928 (G). A star shows either where Aster is unsure about the correspondence, or where the *Regiment* acknowledges a source, but Aster has not identified the Latin passage.
2. The line numbers given are those lines cited from the *Regiment* by Aster, Marzec and Gilbert as being parallel to the sources.

Opening line number and section heading	Jacobus	Aegidius	*Secretum*
2017 Prologus			
2157 De fide observanda	2171–84 [A33] 2248–86 [A22] 2300–31 [A7] 2360–6 [A8]		2199–212 [A8] 2227–37 [A9] 2423–8 [A5]
2465 De justicia	 2528–41 [A21] 2570–83 [A1] 2584–642 [A23] 2654–74 [A24] 2675–88 [A16] 2731–68 [A17] 2815–35 [A18] 2950–89 [A20]	2500–6 [A9] 2724–30 [A10] 2836–51 [A4]	2507–9 [A*; G94–5] 2523–7 [A10]

Opening line number and section heading	Jacobus	Aegidius	Secretum
2997 De pietate	2997–3000 [A25] 3004–38 [A9] 3062–6 [A42] 3200–13 [A27] 3235–45 [A29] 3246–8 [A28] 3249–67 [A30] 3270–304 [A41]		3102–8 [G94] 3109–15 [A7]
3312 De misericordia	3361–7 [A10] 3375–85 [A26] 3389–406 [A6] 3417–20 [A3] 3426–44 [A4]		
3459 De paciencia	3496–512 [A34] 3513–28 [A35] 3529–35 [A36] 3536–42 [A37] 3543–70 [A5] 3590–1 [A31]		
3627 De castitate	3676–710 [A11] 3711–17 [A46] 3718–31 [A43] 3732–55 [A12] 3760–6 [A44] 3767–73 [A45] 3774–87 [A13] 3802–5 [A49] 3844–50 [A51] 3854–7 [A50]	3645–7 [A1] 3830–6 [A21]	3655–61 [A6]

Hoccleve's Regiment of Princes: *Counsel and Constraint*

Opening line number and section heading	Jacobus	Aegidius	*Secretum*
3900 De magnanimitate	3949–59 [A19]	3928–34 [A5] 3942–4 [A20]	
4005 Quod rex non debet felicitatem suam ponere in diuiciis	4033–46 [A15] 4047–74 [A2] 4075–9 [A14]		
4124 De virtute largitatis et de vicio prodigalitatis	4180–359 [A52]	4145–7 [A11]	4124–30 [A1] 4131–43 [A2] 4404–10 [A3] 4413–17 [A4]
4474 De vicio avaricie	4491 [A47] 4495–501 [A48] 4744–6 [M18]	4504–5 [M12] 4512–13 [M12] 4549–50 [M13] 4576–7 [M14] 4579–606 [A*] 4607–13 [A12] 4614–20 [A13] 4621–7 [A14] 4628–34 [A15] 4635–41 [A16] 4645–8 [A17] 4649–55 [A18] 4656–9 [A19] 4659–62 [M15] 4665–8 [M16] 4677–8 [M17]	4722–853 [parallels with English texts of the *Secretum*, M25–30]

Opening line number and section heading	Jacobus	Aegidius	*Secretum*
4747 De regis prudencia		4747–53 [A6] 4754–5 [M19] 4761–2 [M20] 4766–7 [M21] 4775 [M22] 4782 [M23] 4838–9 [A7] 4840–4 [A8] 4845–9 [A2] 4850–1 [M24]	
4859 De consilio habendo in omnibus factis			4859–900 [G95–7] 4915–21 [G97–8] 4922–8 [G98] 4901–14 [A11]
5020 De pace			
5440 Verba compilatoris ad librum			

Chapter 4

Regiment and the Governing Body

I. THEORIES AND DEFINITIONS

George Lakoff and Mark Johnson's influential book *Metaphors We Live By* describes the ways in which large metaphorical structures – such as ARGUMENT IS WAR or TIME IS MONEY – shape our language and assumptions.[1] THE STATE IS A BODY was a metaphor the Middle Ages lived by, and whose implications form a recurring imaginative field in medieval political and literary texts. If the state is a body, then it has limbs and a brain; it can be injured and healed. Its corporeality is available for comparison with individual human bodies, which themselves bear the stamp of the divine image, but also of earthly corruption. This chapter asks how Hoccleve's *Regiment* takes its place in the ongoing body-political constructions of medieval theory, practice and poetry, and how it imagines the relationship between the bodies of poet, prince and state to operate.[2]

The theory that the human body is a template for the organization of society was current in the Classical period,[3] and gains its most influential medieval expression in John of Salisbury's *Policraticus*. John makes a detailed comparison between the limbs and organs of the body and the groups of people who form the state: the king is the head; the senate the heart; judges and governors the eyes, ears and tongue; king's attendants the sides; financial officers the stomach; labourers the feet.[4] In this formulation, priests are the soul of the body politic.[5] An important feature of John of Salisbury's analogy is the interdependence of

---

[1] Lakoff and Johnson 1980.
[2] Bodies and the body politic in the *Regiment* have already received some perceptive commentary with which I engage in this chapter, for example in Medcalf 1981, Hasler 1990, Scanlon 1990 and 1994.
[3] The *locus classicus* is Livy's story of how Menenius Agrippa prevented a riot by recounting a dispute between a body's belly and its limbs; see Struve 1984, 303–4.
[4] *Policraticus*, V. 2. On various aspects of John of Salisbury's formulation, see Struve 1978, 123–48, Struve 1979–80 and Struve 1984. For his continued importance in the later medieval period, see Ullmann 1978.
[5] See Le Goff 1989 for the Church's place in the imagined body politic.

the organs.⁶ He emphasizes that the prince himself is vulnerable if damage occurs elsewhere:

> Dum autem singulorum officia in integritate uirtutis et suauitate opinionis conseruat, quandam quasi membris sanitatem procurat et decorum. Cum uero ex negligentia aut dissimulatione potestatis circa officia sit uirtutis aut famae dispendium, quasi in membra eius morbi et maculae incurrunt. Nec diu subsistit incolumitas capitis, ubi languor membrorum inualescit.⁷

> [And so, while he preserves each individual office in integrity of virtue and purity of reputation, he procures as it were a certain health and fitness in his own members. When, however, through the negligence or dissimulation of the prince there is a loss of virtue or good reputation from these offices, it is as if diseases and blemishes infect his own members. Nor does the well-being of the head last for long when sickness weakens the members.]

This analogy was a commonplace of political writing throughout the medieval period. *Mum and the Soothsegger*, for example, uses the image of the body to complain of poor government: 'For there the heede aketh alle the lymes after / Pynen' (763–4), with the marginal note 'Dum caput infirmum cetera membra dolent.' Christine de Pizan's *Livre du Corps de Policie* is structured around the metaphor of the body. She identifies parts of the body with different classes (the prince, the knights and the commoners) and prescribes how each is to behave. The aim is that the people of France may have a 'regimine de preservation de santé', just as a doctor advises a patient.⁸ In *The Descryvyng of Mannes Membres*, an English poem of the early fifteenth century,⁹ the writer initially reverses this analogy, explaining the functions of the head, limbs and so on by relating them to the state:

> The shuldres and the bakebon,
> I likne to lordis of the lond;
> The armes, to knyghtes, to fende fro fon. (33–5)

---

⁶ Struve 1984, 309, Nederman 1987 and Quillet 1988 all stress the importance of this physiological rather than strictly hierarchical conception of the state in John of Salisbury. See also Chroust 1947, 438, on the development of the corporate idea in Aegidius's *De regimine principum*.
⁷ *Policraticus* IV. 12 (ed. Webb, I, 279). I have drawn on the translations by Dickinson and Nederman.
⁸ Christine de Pizan, *Corps de policie*, III. 3. On Christine's conception of the body politic, see Forhan 1992.
⁹ *Twenty-Six Political Poems*, ed. Kail, 64–9.

Soon, however, he inverts the image once again to uncover his political message (a marginal 'Nota bene' in the manuscript draws attention to this stanza):

> I likne a kyngdom in good astate,
> To stalworthe man, myghty in hele.
> While non of his lymes other hate,
> He is myghty, with another to dele.
> Yif eche of his lymes with other debate,
> He waxeth syk, for flesch is frele. (121-6)

The political impulse behind the analogy is never far from the surface – here especially in the vocabulary of 'astate' and 'debate' – while a central feature of these texts is the interdependence of the limbs in the body-state. This discursive field is integral to Hoccleve's own political imagination, as for example in the *Regiment*, where, attacking the lawless actions of the powerful ('cobbes grete' (2806)), he complains that 'swich unbuxumnesse / Suffred us make wole of seurtee lame' (2796-7), while 'He that our heed is, sore it shal repente' (2809).

One branch of political thought in which the body played a vital role was that of monarchic theory. The idea that the king represents part of the body politic – usually the head, as in the *Policraticus, The Descryvyng of Mannes Membres* and the last quotation from the *Regiment* – has close links to the concept of the 'king's two bodies', investigated in Ernst Kantorowicz's influential study.[10] In the terminology of the political theorists and jurists whom Kantorowicz discusses, the king's endowment of grace and authority enabled him to have both a body physical (subject to weakness and death) and body political (imbued with grace, infallible, and able to be passed on to his successor):

> The value of immortality or continuity [...] was vested in the *universitas* 'which never dies', in the perpetuity of an immortal people, polity, or *patria*, from which the individual king might easily be separated, but not the Dynasty, the crown, and the Royal Dignity.[11]

Kantorowicz traces the origins of the theory to Antiquity, but its main impetus, he argues, came from the analogous concept of Christ as both man and God.[12] This pseudo-theological formulation worked to counter the potential difficulty of having so much divinely bestowed

---

[10] Kantorowicz 1957. See 207-32 for the image of the state as *corpus republicae mysticum*.
[11] Ibid., 272.
[12] Ibid., esp. 194, 270-2; on theocratic kingship and its limits, see also Ullmann 1966, 117-49.

authority residing in a human frame. As a consequence, the distancing of the king's body political from the instability of the body natural became a prominent feature of monarchic rhetoric.

The texts discussed by Kantorowicz needed to maintain a careful distinction, on the one hand identifying the office of king with the head of the body politic, and on the other separating the physical body of the king from the ongoing exercise of royal power. This separation was not easy to uphold, especially when a disruption of legitimate authority occured; the idea of an undying political body runs into difficulty if there is a violent transfer of power such as happened in England when Richard II was deposed. By this time, however, Richard's own attempts to generate an image of strongly personal kingship had already been threatening the theoretical distinction posited by Kantorowicz between the office of the king as part of a consensual body politic, and the actions of the current incumbent.[13]

The potential connections between the condition of the king's physical body and the management of the realm were made more apparent by the dubious legitimacy of the Lancastrian kings. Without the stability of a continuous political inheritance, Lancastrian claims to rule were vested all the more in the personal qualities of its individual representatives; physical weakness became all the more significant in the sphere of political debate. Henry IV's increasing incapacity during the last five years of his reign created an atmosphere of uncertainty around the throne, and allowed speculation to develop that the King's malady was a divine punishment for his past crimes, including the usurpation in 1399 and the execution of Archbishop Scrope in 1405.[14] The fact that Hoccleve passes over Henry IV with barely a mention in the *Regiment* suggests how difficult the subject of Henry's kingship had become. Hoccleve's allusions to the health of royal bodies have an urgent contemporary charge, and the physically frail, paternal Old Man of the *Regiment*'s Dialogue can in some respects be read as a textual shadow of the ailing King. The reign of Henry VI was to see an even closer link between the health of the state and the physical body of its head, first as an infant, and then as an enfeebled and childless monarch.[15] Such breaches of the imaginative space between the body politic and the royal natural body undermine theories that attempt to

---

[13] See Walker 1995 and Saul 1997. The latter, for example, argues that by the late fourteenth century in England, a brand of personal kingship had replaced Kantorowicz's model: 'king and man became virtually one' (446).

[14] Several chronicles refer to Henry IV's illness as leprosy, but the evidence is conflicting. McNiven argues that Henry's chronic and ultimately fatal attacks of illness were probably due to a circulatory or heart problem (McNiven 1985).

[15] For the urgent search in the late 1450s for an elixir to heal Henry VI's mental illness and solve the realm's financial problems, see Gross 1995, 64–5, and Rawcliffe 1996, 11–12.

separate physical decay from political immortality. In Lancastrian England, the currency of monarchic representation was not nearly as stable as Kantorowicz's work encourages us to think; instead, competing traditions of the body are at work in political rhetoric. These plural interpretations of the king's relationship to the body politic give a particular point to Hoccleve's portrayal of the king's body in all its forms, and especially to the separation or interdependence of the mortal natural body and the mystical political body. Which model of the state does Hoccleve use, and how does he resolve the potential conflict between the king's two bodies and the integral body of the state?

Before turning to the *Regiment* to ask these questions, I should like to consider the implications of the Middle English word *regiment* itself. The Latin word *regimen* was, of course, common in descriptions of ruling and in the titles of mirrors for princes, such as *De regimine principum* by Aegidius Romanus; in the heading to one of the *Regiment*'s envoys in San Marino, Huntington Library MS HM 111, Hoccleve himself refers to his poem as the 'livre del Regiment de Princes'. In the *MED*, the noun *regiment* has three principal meanings: 'government, sovereignty, rule', 'a rule or set of rules for good conduct or healthful living' and finally 'planetary influence; a region governed by certain astronomical signs'.[16] The last meaning is rare and is not found in Hoccleve's poem.

Though familiar in Latin texts, *regiment* was relatively new in English when Hoccleve used it. Its first cited uses in the *MED* are by John Gower. The word appears eight times in Gower's *Confessio amantis*, twice with the meaning of planetary influence (*Confessio* VII. 915 and 1245). In Book VII, for example, it is used to describe the effect that planets have on human characteristics:

> And whom this planete [Jupiter] underfongeth
> To stonde upon his regiment,
> He schal be meke and pacient. (914–16)

These lines articulate the relationship that Gower develops in the *Confessio* between the macrocosm of the universe and the microcosm of the individual – 'The man [...] is as a world in his partie' (*Confessio*, Prologue, 955–6).[17] Of the other six times that *regiment* appears in *Confessio amantis*, four are cited by the *MED* to illustrate the meaning 'government, sovereignty, rule'. For example, talking of the young Alexander, Genius comments:

---

[16] *MED*, s.v. 'regiment'.
[17] On medieval theories of microcosm and macrocosm, see Saxl 1957, D'Alverny 1976, and on the *Confessio* itself, Porter 1983.

> Lo, thus this worthi yonge king
> Was fulli tauht of every thing,
> Which mihte yive entendement
> Of good reule and good regiment
> To such a worthi prince as he. (VII. 1699–703)

Here, however, *regiment* applies not only to the government of the kingdom, but also to the self-regulation of the prince. Genius's remark is made in the context of the three parts of 'policie': 'etique', 'iconomique' and 'mechanique' (*Confessio* VII. 1641–710). 'Etique' is designed to teach the king about ruling the state, but in addition 'It makth a king also to lerne / Hou he his bodi schal governe' (VII. 1659–60). The word 'regiment' in line 1702 is, then, not merely a synonym for 'reule', but extends and deepens 'reule' to include the control of the prince's own conduct and body. It implies another relationship between the macrocosm (this time of the kingdom) and the microcosm of the body. Gower's usage of *regiment* in the *Confessio* gathers physical, moral and political meanings within its scope. Of the eight times that *regiment* is used by Gower, seven are in *Confessio* Book VII, Gower's own mirror for princes.[18] His usage establishes *regiment* in English as a word relating to physical and moral self-control as well as the exercise of political authority.

Hoccleve is the next author cited by the *MED* as using *regiment*, and he no doubt assimilated Gower's deployment of the word along with its Latin traditions.[19] Hoccleve translates the title of Aegidius's treatise as 'Gyles of Regiment / Of Princes' (2052–3). He calls the *Secretum secretorum* Aristotle's 'book of governance' (2051), written in order that Alexander can sustain his honour 'In reule' (2044); these descriptions retain the crucial ambiguity between governing the realm and controlling oneself that are found in Latin usage and in the *Confessio*. Hoccleve employs the word once more in the *Regiment* when Alexander the Great is reproved by a knight:

> O Alisaundre, it is uncovenable
> Thee for to have of peple regiment
> Syn thy lust bestial and miserable
> Hath qweynt thy reson and entendement. (3501–4)

Once again, the reader's attention is directed to the discrepancy between Alexander's political rule and personal misrule. Examples

---

[18] See Manzalaoui 1981.
[19] John Trevisa's version of Aegidius (Trevisa, *The Governance of Kings and Princes*) might be expected to use *regiment*, but instead Trevisa opts for *gouernans* as his regular equivalent to the Latin *regimen*.

such as this draw on the Latin satirical tradition, which frequently links kingship to self-governance by etymological punning. In a passage of *Piers Plowman* closely concerned with the power and limitations of kings, a 'goliardeis' quotes the lines 'Dum "rex" a "regere" dicatur nomen habere, / Nomen habet sine re, nisi studet iura tenere' (B-text Prologue, 141–2: 'Since "a king" is said to have his name from "to rule", he has the name without the actuality, unless he takes care to maintain the laws'). Jill Mann comments on the type of goliardic wordplay evident here that 'language is not just the means of expressing moral standards, it also embodies them'.[20] Etymology and political practice are here mutually reinforcing and generating, and the metaphorical field in which *regiment* operates insistently returns the discussion of politics to physical concepts and vocabulary. The metaphor THE STATE IS A BODY fundamentally shapes political argument even when the analogy is not directly invoked. While the passages quoted above are the only two occasions where Hoccleve uses the word *regiment*, he explores the relationship between the rule of the state and that of the body in striking ways throughout the poem.

II. THE SPECIAL BODY OF THE KING

The theory of the king's two bodies sets the king apart from his subjects in its analogy between the king and God.[21] The king's political body is put at a distance from any infections of public scrutiny or debate; this is done by separating the king from his subjects, and the king's office from his own natural body. At the start of the *Regiment* proper, Hoccleve uses elaborate, impersonal forms of address that seem to reinforce this separation. Prince Henry is described by the abstract qualities of his superior position: 'the altitude / Of your estat' (2059–60); 'so hy presence' (2072); 'your excellence' (2074, 2133); 'your noblesse' (2126); 'your innat sapience' (2130); 'your hynesse' (2143). A passage on making oaths quotes the view that different standards should apply to kings: 'Quintilian seith [...] A kyng or princes word oghte souffyse / Wel more than oghte a marchantes ooth' (2360, 2364–5). These formulae stress the ruler's difference from his subjects (and in this case also refer pointedly to current royal financial dealings). In lines 2409–50 of the *Regiment*, Hoccleve appears to reinforce such monarchic apotheosis when he warns Prince Henry against speaking too much:

---

[20] Mann 1980, 67–8.
[21] Kantorowicz 1957, 62–5.

> And syn a kyng by way of his office
> To God yliknèd is, as in maneere,
> And God is trouthe itself, than may the vice
> Of unthrouthe nat in a kyng appeere,
> If his office shal to God refeere.
> A bisy tonge bryngith in swich wyt,
> He that by word nat giltith is parfyt. (2409–15)

If the king is to emulate God, Hoccleve continues, he must restrain his natural body, and guard it against over-exposure: 'Bet is the peples eres thriste and yerne / Hir kyng or princes wordes for to heere' (2423–4). This advice seems to establish a distance between the common people and the special body of the king, though it also draws on a wider proverbial tradition of guarding one's tongue. The tongue's activities, however, threaten to introduce a dangerous physicality to the realm of royal speech:

> Silence of tonge is wardeyn of good fame,
> And aftir repreef, fissheth clap and foulith.
> The tonge of man al the body deffoulith. (2441–3)

The mouth and tongue, at the frontier of the body, are the most susceptible to damaging the king's honour; he must guard his special nature, his distance, by constraining a potentially destructive part of his physical body.[22] This passage has been taken by Larry Scanlon to indicate Hoccleve's ideological conservatism.[23] In his analysis, Scanlon acknowledges both the performative aspect of the king's oath (he has to keep his 'trouthe' (2411) in order to emulate God) and the danger to the king of too much speech: 'a king who speaks too much is likely to expose himself as no more in control of language than its other users'. However, he also argues that these factors reinforce the authority of the king precisely by being revealed in the poem: 'This view of political authority is both profoundly conservative and yet self-consciously constructive at the same time.'[24] I would prefer to see the performative aspect of the king's oath as important in itself. Lines 2409–15 (quoted above) carefully state that the 'office' (2409, 2413) of the king may be likened to God only if the king is in no way untruthful. There is a clear contingency about the clause: the king's office loses its likeness to God

---

[22] In Isidore of Seville's hugely influential *Etymologiae*, XI. 49 (col. 403), 'os', a mouth, is connected to 'ostium', a door, since the mouth takes in food and gives out speech. For the portrayal of the mouth as a dangerous area of exchange in medieval medical texts, see Pouchelle 1990, 147 and Camille 1994, 70–4.
[23] Scanlon 1990, 238–9.
[24] Ibid., both quotations from 239.

if it falls into 'untrouthe' (2412). Elsewhere in the *Regiment*, Hoccleve makes it plain that a king is not like God:

> For a kyng is but a man soul, par fay,
> And be his wit nevere so good, he may
> Erre and mistake him othirwhyle among. (4862–4)

Hoccleve, then, makes use of the comparison between king and God in the *Regiment*, but the analogy is contingent on the king's standards of 'trouthe', not only on the fact of his being a king. That the king is in danger of compromising his status by unguarded speech shows how fragile such 'trouthe' can be.

While warning of the dangers of royal speech, this section of the *Regiment* does demonstrate the important role that the king's voice plays in his relationship with the people. The royal voice projects the presence of the king beyond his body, influencing others through speech: 'that out of the tonge of kyng procedith, / The peple specially beren away' (2444–5). What the people 'beren away' is, in a sense, part of the king's wider body, since the laws voiced by the king represent his authority in the realm.[25] This aspect of the king's voice is portrayed in the exemplum of Lycurgus (called simply 'a knyght' by Hoccleve (2950–89)), who leaves his country, promising the 'froward peple' (2953) that he will ask permission of Apollo to mitigate the current unpopular, strict laws. Instead of looking for Apollo, however, he goes into exile, thus ensuring that the laws will continue to be obeyed. In this exemplum, the ruler's physical body becomes absent from the site of his power, but Lycurgus controls his subjects even from the grave by the word of his laws and his promise to return. Lycurgus's political body may be said to be present in his realm through the enactment of his voice, the continuing influence of his corpus of laws.

Scanlon draws attention to the fictive element of Lycurgus's ploy: 'he replaces his person with his story, and controls the state [...] by having constructed a story that will always maintain the distance between the story and the reality it claims to represent – a story, that is, that will always maintain its fiction'.[26] Such distance may correspond to Hoccleve's advice to control the king's tongue – another way of separating the king's natural body from the exercise of his power – but the advice also has disturbing implications. Both passages that I have discussed indicate how precarious is the separation between the authority of the imagined political body and the vulnerability of the

---

[25] Ibid., 222–3. For the relationship between the law and the king's own body in early modern constructions, see Foucault 1979, 47–54.

[26] Scanlon 1990, 245, and see also 225, where he posits a more general parallel between the ideology of kingship and the narrative form.

real, physical body. The exemplum of Lycurgus shows the fiction of royal authority to be more powerful than the fact of the royal body. The more the royal body is familiar to the people (the more 'factual' it is), the more negotiable the king's power becomes. Lycurgus has to absent himself, because he cannot in person persuade his people to obey the 'sharp lawes' (2953) that he has established. His own natural body is the victim of his desire for continued control of the state, as he spends the rest of his life in exile and his body is eventually thrown into the sea, to prevent news of his death releasing the people from their oath to keep the laws. In a bleak vision of absent kingship, Lycurgus must relinquish his country in order to rule it.

The authority of Lycurgus relies on his promise to return with an answer from the god, which he hopes will be repaid by the faith of his people. In the *Regiment*'s Dialogue, an unsettling shadow of this story is encountered in the debate over the 'real presence' of Christ in the Eucharist. The bitter disputes that developed surrounding the doctrine of transubstantiation were fought over the borders between physical and metaphorical or spiritual bodies. In the Dialogue, the Old Man describes how the heretic John Badby denied the real presence of Christ in the host:

The precious body of oure Lorde Jhesu
In forme of brede he leeved nat at al;
He was in nothyng abassht ne eschu
To seye it was but brede material. (288–91)

By denying the real presence, Badby also questions the system of analogy and metamorphosis on which it relies. In addition, he undermines the delicate balance between 'forme' and 'material' on which much monarchic theory rests. Appropriately, it is Prince Henry himself who tries to convince Badby of the dual nature of Christ's body, physical and spiritual, for it is the two equivalent aspects of the king's body – natural and political – that are at the heart of the Prince's own claim to authority. In this context it is easy to see why the views of Badby and others on the Eucharist were portrayed by the orthodox establishment as politically seditious.[27] The reflex of Christ's physical presence in the Eucharist is the ability of the king's physical body to signify for the wider spiritual or political body of the state. Hoccleve

---

[27] See Aston 1960. Lollard denial of the real presence was seen as the beginning of the end for all ecclesiastical and, eventually, temporal authority; the question of transubstantiation thus became intertwined with that of political power. For a reading of this passage in the context of unease over Lancastrian legitimacy, see Strohm 1997b, and on the power of Christ's body as a symbol of political and religious community, see James 1983 and Beckwith 1993, 33–6.

himself never questions the doctrine of transubstantiation, but this passage does not resolve the debate, rather it forms an uncomfortable reminder of the potential instability of royal and religious authority: Badby has to be burnt to silence his dissenting voice.[28]

The execution of Badby averts a crisis of authority in the Dialogue, but the image of a king's extended physicality, his continued 'real presence' is explored and questioned later in the *Regiment*. For example, Alexander the Great is taken to task by one of his own knights over his plans for world domination:

> He seide, 'If oure goddes thy body smal
> To thy greedy desir had maad egal,
> Al the world hadde nat be souffissant
> To han receyved so large a geant.' (4050–3)

The knight brings to the fore the disjunction that exists between the ruler's imagined giant political body and his actual physical frame: 'syn that thy body answerith nat / Unto thy wil, what may I seye, what?' (4057–8).[29] A similar image of the ruler swollen to giant size is given by John of Salisbury in his *Policraticus*:

> Plato: Perinde est cum subditos opprimit magistratus, ac si caput corporis intumescat, ut a membris aut omnino aut sine molestia ferri non possit.[30]
>
> [Plato says, 'When the magistrate oppresses his subjects, it is as though the head of the body were to swell up, so that the members cannot sustain it, either at all, or not without trouble.']

In John's conception of political organization, each member must keep in proportion to the others. Hoccleve's exemplum applies this theory to the bodies of the ruler. Far from supporting the proposition that Alexander has a transferable authoritative presence, the exemplum directs attention back to his physical body, showing that Alexander is mortal and that his power will come to nothing. The knight refers specifically to the fate of the ruler's body after death: 'By deeth a leon maad is briddes mete, / And beestes also his flessh gnawe and frete' (4071–2). This restores the balance between the forces of nature and the

---

[28] See Hasler 1990, 172. Hasler says that it is Badby's 'silence' that makes him 'out of order', but the passage makes clear that it is Badby's continued willingness to speak out that sets him at odds with the authorities.

[29] Alexander's overbearing will is also commented on in Gower's *Confessio amantis* III. 1278–92 and 2363–417; see Simpson 1995b, 297–8.

[30] *Policraticus* V. 7 (ed. Webb, I, 308).

royal body, a balance threatened by Alexander's bid to take over the world.[31] Hoccleve's final reference to Alexander again explores his physical presence, extended during his rule, shrunken in death. Several philosophers gather around the ruler's tomb, and one comments:

> Al this world yistirday was nat ynow
> To stoppen Alisaundres covetyse;
> And now three elnes of clooth him souffyse.   (5360–2)[32]

The fate of Alexander is a pointed reminder to the Princes of France and England whom Hoccleve addresses in this part of the poem: 'O worthy Princes two, now takith heede' (5363). These Alexander exempla put pressure on the theory of the king's political, immortal body by drawing attention to the physical contingency of political power. It is once again the philosophers who have the last word. Hoccleve does indeed use ideas associated with the king's two bodies and the separation of the royal body from the people, but their appearance also raises serious questions about the theory itself. The narrative of Lycurgus does show a ruler replacing his physical body with a judicial corpus, but other potential discrepancies between the king's natural body and his political jurisdiction (as with Alexander) come under critical scrutiny. When discussing the operation of political authority in the *Regiment*, the physical (and thus fallible and mortal) body of the king cannot be left out of consideration.

III. THE KING AND THE BODY POLITIC

While the theory of the king's two bodies separates the powerful political body of the king both from his own physical body and the bodies of his subjects, the analogy of the corporate body politic draws sovereign and subjects together as part of a single system, an organic whole, albeit with a hierarchy of members.[33] This conception of social organization draws on the Aristotelian view that social groups are a natural feature of human interaction, making externally imposed

---

[31] Such dangerous expansion was a common theme of the Alexander legend. In Walter of Châtillon's twelfth-century epic the *Alexandreis*, Nature recalls that Alexander 'nimis angustum terrarum dixerat orbem' [had said that the sphere of the earth was too narrow [for him]] (*Alexandreis*, X. 8).

[32] This description of death narrowing the boundaries of the body echoes the 'constantly diminishing world ground' that Elaine Scarry explores in literary depictions of old age and its consequent loss of power; see Scarry 1985, 33.

[33] See Strohm 1989, 3–5 for the influence of such theories of 'functional interdependence' (ibid., 4).

hierarchies unnecessary.³⁴ Aristotle was, of course, the presumed author of the *Secretum secretorum*, whose mixture of advice on health, household management and politics brought the body of the king into the field of political discussion, and which is one of Hoccleve's major sources. The previous section of this chapter suggests that Hoccleve's attitude to the separation of the king's body from the people is equivocal. Does the *Regiment* instead draw the physical body of the ruler into the workings of the state?

In the *Regiment* proper, the physical body is used to signify moral positions to a striking degree. The bodies of rulers and subjects are made the field of action for Hoccleve's exempla. This is found most clearly in the *Regiment*'s section on chastity ('De castitate', 3627–899), since the principles of constraint taught there must be practised on the king's own body. In this section of the *Regiment*, Hoccleve begins with the Christian and moral arguments for chastity, illustrates them with positive examples taken from his sources, and goes on to discuss overindulgence in food and drink.³⁵

Far from distancing the body of the ruler from the discussion of chastity and lust, Hoccleve heightens the physical immediacy of this section by alluding to the bodily senses. Thus in the section's first stanza (3627–33), chastity is paradoxically described as something 'covenable [...] Unto a kyng for to savoure and taaste' (3628–9). In the exempla themselves, different senses are brought to bear on the problem of lust. The 'seemly, fressh yong man' (3718) of lines 3718–31 has 'favour [...] of shap and beautee' (3719–20); every woman that 'had a look on him despent' (3721) gives 'flesshly consent' (3722) to him in her heart. He, however, 'eschued [...] the taast / Of unclennesse' (3723–4). In order to keep the women off, he mutilates himself: 'with his nayles cracchid he his face, / And scocchid it with knyves and torente' (3726–7). Touch, sight and taste are integral to these narratives, and in the next exemplum (3732–59) smell is the important component. The loyal Roman wife Ulie does not tell her husband that he has bad breath.

---

³⁴ The influence of Aristotle's *Politics* was enormous, both directly and through figures such as Aquinas and Aegidius Romanus; see Wilks 1963, 200–27, and Dunbabin 1982, and for a discussion of natural political organization and the restriction of royal power, Luscombe 1982. Strohm (1989, 3–5, 145–51) relates these ideas to currents of thought in fourteenth-century England: 'The Aristotelian/Thomist view of the natural state, in which the ruler enjoyed a consensual or contractual relation with his subjects, was to dominate fourteenth-century English thought' (147).

³⁵ The physical connection between eating and sex is explained by Hoccleve in terms familiar from medieval medical and moral works: 'Excesse of mete and drynke is wombes freend, / And wombe is next to our membres pryvee' (3802–3). For the connection between the belly and sexual organs in medical and religious texts, see respectively Pouchelle 1990, 181–5 and Le Goff 1989, 14–17.

When he discovers his embarrassing condition from an enemy and asks his wife why she never mentioned it, Ulie replies that she did not realize it was a problem, as she has never kissed another man. In the next exempla, Plato's followers blind themselves to avoid temptations of the flesh (3760–6), Demosthenes shows his contempt for a prostitute by placing his hands on her breasts (3767–73) and two women put rotting chicken meat under their breasts so that the putrid smell will ward off invading soldiers (3774–87).

These stories – some playful, some disturbing in their use of mutilation and decay – powerfully combine sight, touch, smell, taste and their potential influence on the body. They recall Hoccleve's earlier warning about the uncontrollable tongue that 'deffoulith' (2443) the whole body. The senses were traditionally thought of as points of entry for temptations, and their physical role of interacting with the outside world could easily allow them to become breaches in the body's defences against evil. Medieval penitential and devotional texts frequently organized discussion of sin around the senses.[36] Gower draws on such traditions in Book I of the *Confessio amantis*, using the analogy of a military assault:

> Visus et auditus fragilis sunt ostia mentis,
> Que viciosa manus claudere nulla potest.
> Est ibi larga via, graditur qua cordis ad antrum
> Hostis, et ingrediens fossa talenta rapit.   (*Confessio* I. before 289)

> [Sight and hearing are doors of the fragile mind, which no sinful hand is able to shut. A broad path is there, by which the enemy advances to the recesses of the heart and, entering, snatches the buried treasure.][37]

The senses are, then, a powerful way to connect physical experience with moral danger and corruption; they also invite analogy with military and political action. The use of the senses in the 'De castitate' section of the *Regiment* highlights this dangerous area of exchange between the outside world and the inner feelings, between physical and moral environments. The violent physicality of many of the exempla about chastity illustrates Hoccleve's comment that 'whoso chaast lyve schal / Moot scourge his flesshly lust with abstinence' (3796–7). As Anthony Hasler comments: 'Many of the *exempla* [...] foreground the degree to which regulation of the body can only be upheld through its

---

[36] As, for example, the thirteenth-century treatise *Ancrene Wisse*, which was copied and adapted into the fifteenth century.
[37] For discussion and translations of Gower's Latin, see Gower, *Latin Verses*, trans. Echard and Fanger (I have adapted their translation here).

mutilation.'[38] Such solutions to problems of the body, both physical and political, are not an innovation in Hoccleve, but correspond to medical theory and the Christian penitential tradition.[39] Nevertheless, the scarred bodies of Hoccleve's exemplary characters hardly contribute to a sense of the royal body as inviolate or somehow set apart from physical conflict. The 'De castitate' section's insistent return to the physical body and its desires instead poses the body of the ruler as a site of moral conflict.

In 'De castitate', mutilation or constraint serve to inhibit vices of the body, but equally drastic measures are also found outside the section, in stories where the problem has implications for the body politic as much as the body natural. In one exemplum, a Persian judge is found to be corrupt (2675–88). As a punishment, he is flayed, and his skin used to cover the chair on which his son is to sit in judgement. Later in the same section, a Roman senator's son commits adultery (2731–72). Rather than disrupt the course of justice and pardon his son (as he is begged to do by the people), the senator has one of his own eyes put out so that his son can also save one eye. The exemplary figure here accepts physical injury in order to uphold the integrity of the *polis*. In these cases, ruptures in the political body find solutions, albeit drastic ones, in the physical bodies of its members, while the roles of father and son in each narrative reinforce the connection between physical sacrifice and political integrity.

The interrelation of physical and political can work in the other direction, too; in some exempla, physical and moral dilemmas lead to 'political' solutions. The 'De castitate' section itself establishes a clear link between virtues of the physical body and the conduct of political affairs. The exemplum of Scipio Africanus (3676–710), for example, tells how the Roman commander returns a beautiful hostage when he discovers that she is engaged to be married:

> And in him multiplied thoghtes breeme.
> But nathelees, for al his bysy thoght,
> Enquere he gan if shee wyf were or noght. (3687–9)

Scipio's action wins him the town he is besieging when the girl's betrothed describes Scipio's actions to the town's leaders:

> And they this lord gaf laude and hy renoun
> For that; and alle with oon herte and wil
> Submittid hem to this prince gentil. (3706–8)

---

[38] Hasler 1990, 176.
[39] See Rawcliffe 1995, 64–71 on the importance of bleeding in medieval medicine. In *Policraticus* IV. 8, John of Salisbury compares a rebellious section of the body politic to an ailing member that might eventually need amputation.

The submission of the town is suggestive of a sexual submission, the lesson being that 'tendre gentillesse / Conquereth hertes' (3709–10). The implication is that Scipio has won a prize as satisfying to the needs of the body politic as the girl would perhaps have been to Scipio's physical desires. This Ovidian parallel between war and sex is equally at work in the *Regiment*'s next exemplum, where the Roman general Marcus Marcellus besieges Syracuse:

> Or Marcus Marcellus had the citee
> Of Ciracuse taken or ynome,
> He leet do crye amonges his meynee
> That, whan the citee he had overcome
> And his folk therin entred were and come,
> Noon be so hardy the wommen oppresse,
> Ne touche hem by no way of unclennesse. (3711–17)

The fates of the city and of the women are held in balance. Just as the words for the capture of the city – 'taken', 'ynome', 'entred' – indicate a sexual encounter, so 'oppresse', and the phrase 'Noon be so hardy', carry political overtones.[40] In these two exempla, restraint of the physical body is directly linked to achieving the desires of the political body.[41] The two spheres are not separated by the exercise of power, but joined, these stories suggest, both morally and practically. The lesson of power restrained, of the potentially overwhelming and destructive body of the king held in check, is delineated earlier in the *Regiment*:

> Whoso that in hy dignitee is set
> And may do grevous wrong and crueltee,
> If he forbere hem, to commende is bet,
> And gretter shal his meede and meryt be,
> Than they that nat may kythe iniquitee. (2843–7)

The ultimate example of such restraint would be the death of the ruler for the good of the realm. Just as mutilation of the body is paradoxically presented as a way of preserving it intact, such an action by the ruler could benefit the whole body. In the section of the *Regiment* called 'De regis magnanimitate', the Athenian leader Codrus makes just such a sacrifice, going to his death so that his army can win a battle:

> Him lever was himselven for to dye
> And his men lyve, than see hem bystad
> So streite. (3956–8)

---

[40] Hoccleve uses 'oppresse' elsewhere in a political sense: 'ministres to seelde hem wel governe; / Oppressioun regneth in every herne' (2540–1). 'Noon be so hardy' anglicizes a phrase common in prohibitory statutes; see above, p. 33 note 83.

[41] See Sigal 1984.

If Codrus has 'another' body, it is not a distant political one, but the body of his army and its men. His action is introduced by a direct invocation of the body politic:

> Right as we seen by reson and nature
> Part of mannes body deffendith al,
> As an arm puttith him in aventure
> For the body that nat perisshe it shal,
> Right so a kynges cheertee special,
> If he God love and his peple and his land,
> Whan neede is, moot deffende hem with his hand. (3928–34)

Here, the 'special' nature of the king resides in his duty to protect the body of the community of which he is an integral part, to put himself 'in aventure' for his people. A few lines earlier Hoccleve introduces the idea of *magnanimitas* with a direct reference to Prince Henry. The physical connection between the king and the concept of *magnanimitas* is not lost on Hoccleve, who explains the etymology of the word: 'Of magnanimitee now wole I trete, / That is to seyn, strong herte or greet corage' (3900–1). He completes the connection between *magna-anima* and Henry's own body by a reference to the Prince's noble blood: 'Yee, gracious Prince, of blood and of lynage / Descendid been to have it in usage' (3903–4). Here Henry's physical make-up, his own blood, is directly responsible for his ability to aspire to the virtue of *magnanimitas*. Hoccleve certainly draws on the theory that aristocratic blood was physically more suited to ruling than that of commoners. In the context of the passages on the body politic and on Codrus, however, to acknowledge Henry's special body is not to remove the Prince from the concerns of the body politic. Rather, the royal blood flowing in Henry's veins is to make a vital contribution to his role as protector of the physical, moral and political body of England.

These fictions in the *Regiment* powerfully associate the bodies of rulers and subjects with the health of the body politic, and Prince Henry's future role is intimately connected to the community of his subjects. The *Regiment*'s exempla consistently address issues of the social body through the medium of the physical bodies of subjects and rulers. Political problems are shown to impinge upon the well-being of the physical body, while the voluntary physical restraint of the ruler is not merely symbolically apt, but directly related to the regulation of the state. These lessons are applied to the current condition of England later in the *Regiment*, where Hoccleve warns against internal division:

The riot that hath been withyn this land
Among ourself many a wyntres space
Hath to the swerd put many a thousand. (5216–18)

In this part of the poem, Hoccleve draws together images of divided countries and wounded bodies in an appeal against civil war and conflict with France, matching for the last time in the poem the value of personal, political and spiritual *regiment*.[42]

IV. HOCCLEVE'S BODY IN THE DIALOGUE

'*What* do you call him? Nemo?' says Mr Tulkinghorn.
'Nemo, sir. Here it is. Forty-two folio. Given out on the Wednesday night, at eight o'clock; brought in on the Thursday morning, at half after nine.'
'Nemo!' repeats Mr Tulkinghorn. 'Nemo is Latin for no one.'
'It must be English for some one, sir, I think,' Mr Snagsby submits, with his deferential cough. 'It is a person's name. Here it is, you see, sir! Given out, Wednesday night, eight o'clock; brought in, Thursday morning, half after nine.'[43]

In contrast to the exemplary landscape of the *Regiment* proper, the Dialogue depicts the physical circumstances of Hoccleve and the Old Man in some detail. The opening of the *Regiment*, for example, immediately establishes the physical environment of the poem's action: Hoccleve is lying in bed 'At Chestres In, right faste by the Stronde' (5). Numerous critics have remarked on the 'realism' of the *Regiment*'s Dialogue, a quality that scholars used to regard as one of Hoccleve's few redeeming features.[44]

Hoccleve's concern with his own physicality is not, however, only a function of the Dialogue's realism, and is as much a response to absence as presence. Anthony Hasler, for example, has explored the relationship between the decrepit bodies of Hoccleve and the Old Man in the Dialogue, and the ideal body of the king imagined in the *Regiment*

---

[42] The section on Peace also proceeds partly by excluding or refiguring possible threats to that peace – and even, it is implied, to Hoccleve himself – from Lollards and women. See Nissé 1999 for a reading that aligns Hoccleve's gender and religious politics.

[43] Dickens, *Bleak House*, 161. Although separated by several hundred years from Hoccleve's *Regiment*, this exchange about a powerfully absent copyist takes place just a few hundred yards from the site of Hoccleve's lodgings.

[44] For example, Bennett 1947, 146–50 and Baugh 1950, 298–9.

proper: 'Those aspects of the body rejected in the construction of the ideal prince are thus projected off onto the body of the subject.'[45] Hasler here cites Louise Fradenburg's discussion of *The Thrissill and the Rose* by Dunbar, in which, she claims, 'the poetics of sovereignty purchases glory through dis-embodiment', leading to 'the projection of somatic unpleasure onto the poem's beginning and end'.[46]

Fradenburg's reading of Dunbar, and by analogy other court literature, sees the poet's energies overwhelmed by royal power. Hoccleve's 'poetics of sovereignty' is, however, more equivocal than this, juxtaposing competing impulses in the projection of royal bodies and royal power: accommodation and threat; regulation and excess. By bringing the body of the ruler to bear on questions of physical and political restraint, Hoccleve challenges any separation between the natural and political body, and between the sovereign's body and the realm as a whole. The *Regiment*'s Dialogue depicts the constraints under which Hoccleve operates before he has the chance to construct his version of the integrated royal body. In this part of the *Regiment*, the fact that Hoccleve's own body is the focus of our attention disturbs the boundaries between the rejected features of royal representation and the construction of poetic self-representation.

The *Regiment*'s Dialogue certainly provides examples of 'textual dehiscence', in Fradenburg's Lacanian terminology. Hoccleve's own body has been pushed to the margins of the poem. It is only at the edges of the text that his own life can be depicted.[47] In addition, the integrity and boundaries of Hoccleve's body are themselves in doubt at the beginning of the *Regiment*. This focus on the body, its margins and confines, helps to define the textual space in which the Dialogue proceeds. The first passages of the poem see Hoccleve troubled by anxieties such as 'thoght' and 'wach': 'Thoght me byrefte of sleep' (7); 'Ageyn my lust wach proferred his servyse, / And I admittid him in hevy wyse' (76–7). Stephen Medcalf has drawn attention to the 'substantial quality' of these abstract nouns.[48] In these passages, Hoccleve's body, rather than being actively engaged, becomes a field of action for other personified qualities. In Hasler's formulation, Hoccleve is 'defined by a reversible allegorical space';[49] the reader is left unsure where the abstractions stop and the physical body begins:

---

[45] Hasler 1990, 167.
[46] Fradenburg 1984, 514.
[47] Simpson 1995a, 173, note 29, remarks on 'the marginal quality of the Prologue's dialogue'.
[48] Medcalf 1981, 134.
[49] Hasler 1990, 168–9.

> The smert of thoght I by experience
> Knowe as wel as any man dooth lyvynge.
> His frosty swoot and fyry hoot fervence,
> And troubly dremes drempt al in wakynge,
> My mazid heed sleeplees han of konnynge
> And wit despoillid. (106–11)

At this stage of the poem, Hoccleve seems no more real than 'thoght' itself, becoming the object or vessel of external anxieties; he himself admits that 'The thoghtful wight is vessel of torment' (81). Hoccleve's dislocation from his own body is reflected in his neglect of the physical environment: 'My seekly distresse / Forbad myn eres usen hir office' (124–5). The Old Man eventually recognizes that Hoccleve is ill from his 'deedly colour pale and wan' (128), and other passages reinforce the impression that Hoccleve is hovering at the margins of life and death, being and nothingness:

> My tremblynge herte so greet gastnesse hadde
> That my spirites were of my lyf sadde. (20–1)

Thought is seen as an enemy attacking the defenceless writer, an idea most strikingly conveyed in this passage:

> [Thoght] that fretynge adversarie
> Myn herte made to him tributarie
> In sowkynge of the fressheste of my blood. (88–90)

Hoccleve here subtly combines an imagined symptom of thought – sucking his very blood – with its root cause, lack of money.[50] Later in the *Regiment* he returns to the figurative connection between money and blood:

> Evene as a mannes blood is norisshynge
> To his body if it corrupt nat be,
> So been richesses to soules feedynge
> Holsum. (4159–62)

Just as royal economics can be imagined as an issue of healthy circulation, so Hoccleve's haemorrhaging expenditure is figured in the Dialogue as a payment of blood-money to Thought. It is significant that Hoccleve uses a political analogy to describe his condition. Thought is an 'adversarie' demanding tribute in the currency of Hoccleve's own body, an analogy that foreshadows the use of the physical body to describe political actions later in the poem.

[50] I take 'sowkynge' here as a form of 'souken'; see *MED*, s.v. 'souken', meaning 4a: 'to suck on; feed on; torture by sucking'.

This network of images highlights the insubstantiality of Hoccleve's body, just as the imagery of the empty purse or pouch marked his financial and literary need. But as with the movement from constraining silence to public advice examined above in Chapter 1, so Hoccleve's physical absence – even symbolic death – at the start of the poem is countered by an embodied, medical tradition that identifies his ailment and seeks to cure it. Medical imagery permeates Hoccleve's discussion with the Old Man – described sarcastically as a 'fair leeche' (162). The Old Man identifies 'thoght' as a poison; the act of speaking thus parallels the bleeding or vomiting traditionally recommended for ridding the body of such a toxin:

> In whom that he his mortel venym shedith,
> But if a vomyt aftir folwe blyve,
> At the port of despeir he may arryve. (271–3)

The Old Man tells Hoccleve to reveal the cause of his problems, literally by speaking about his depression, metaphorically by uncovering a wound: 'The verray cause of thyn hid maladie / Thow moot deskevere and telle out al thyn herte' (262–3).[51] Numerous manuscripts of the *Regiment* note the source of this advice as the *De consolatione Philosophiae*, where Philosophia tells Boethius: 'Quid fles, quid lacrimis manas? [...] Si operam medicantis expectas, oportet vulnus detegas.'[52] This telling out is, for the Old Man, the key to re-establishing Hoccleve's senses. By literalizing Hoccleve's sickness, and then applying a medical treatment, the Old Man engages a powerfully embodied tradition to overcome the absence and silence characteristic of Hoccleve's melancholic state.[53] The subsequent flow of fevered speech returns the Dialogue to the concrete world of London and the state of Hoccleve's finances,[54] participating in the poem's movement

---

[51] Wounds and the mouth were closely linked in the language of medieval medical texts; see Pouchelle 1990, 182–4. 'Searching' or 'discovering' a wound was also a common medical procedure, but one rich in symbolic potential. See also Scarry 1985, 28, for continuing figurative connections between confession and wounds.

[52] Boethius, *De consolatione Philosophiae*, I. pr. 4; in Chaucer's *Boece*: 'Why wepistow, why spillestow teeris? Yif thou abidest after helpe of thi leche, the byhoveth discovre thy wownde.' The ellipsis covers a Greek quotation in Boethius's text, 'Speak out and hide not thy thoughts', from Homer's *Iliad*, I. 363. For Boethian glosses in the *Regiment*, see below, p. 181.

[53] Compare the powerful medical imagery in *Mum and the Soothsegger*, 1121–4.

[54] Hasler calls these parts of the Dialogue 'magnificently unmotivated', displaying 'neurotic loquacity' (Hasler 1990, 172 and 173). Claridge et al. 1990 assesses Hoccleve's fevered speech as a symptom of his mental instability. Hoccleve's tumbling words do, however, underline his release from the constraints of his position, and allow for pointed discussion of political and personal issues.

from internal anxiety to dialogue, and then towards public speech in the *Regiment* proper.[55]

Another embodied tradition challenges the constrictions under which the Privy Seal clerks must work. They are depicted without supporters or voices; when the Old Man asks whether anyone looks after the clerks' interests, Hoccleve sarcastically replies:

> Yis, fadir, yis. Ther is oon clept Nemo:
> He helpith hem, by him been they chericed;
> Nere he, they weren poorely chevyced. (1487–9)[56]

This powerful absence acts as the ironic standard by which to judge the corrupt servants and indifferent lords who leave the clerks friendless. The vocabulary of patronage here – 'helpith', 'chericed', 'chevyced' – is comically overloaded to suggest just how much support the clerks lack.

While its rewards might be intangible, however, Hoccleve describes the act of writing itself as intensely physical, a matter of the body. Writing is not merely compared to agricultural labour; instead, Hoccleve claims that the strain of writing has damaged his back so that he cannot work in the fields:

> My bak unbuxum hath swich thyng forsworn,
> At instaunce of wrytynge, his werreyour,
> That stowpynge hath him spilt with his labour. (985–7)

The connection here with farming ironically echoes the familiar metaphor of a writer gathering blooms from the fields of literature.[57] Here, by contrast, the harsh world of the 'plow' and 'harwe', the effort required to 'lade a cart or fille a barwe' (983), is brought to the work of the scribe. Hoccleve also refers to the bodily constraint that such a labour imposes on the clerks:

> Thise artificers see I day be day,
> In the hootteste of al hir bysynesse,
> Talken and synge and make game and play,

---

[55] See Knapp 1994, 70 and Simpson 1995a, 167.

[56] Hoccleve's use of 'nemo' is rooted in the Latin satirical tradition (see Bayless 1996, 57–86), though its use here specifically points to a subculture of bureaucratic irony and subversion.

[57] The tradition, of course, stretches back to the Greek bucolic poets and the *Eclogues* of Virgil. In the C-text of *Piers Plowman*, Will excuses himself from working in the fields in terms similar to Hoccleve's: 'Y am to wayke to worche with sykel or with sythe' (V. 23). His labour is to pray and say psalms (42–7). Hoccleve may well have known this passage, but he goes further than Langland in claiming that the physical effects of writing itself have crippled him. On Langland's portrayal of the labour of writing, see Kerby-Fulton and Justice 1997 and Kerby-Fulton 1997.

> And foorth hir labour passith with gladnesse;
> But we laboure in travaillous stilnesse;
> We stowpe and stare upon the sheepes skyn,
> And keepe moote our song and wordes yn. (1009–15)

The scribe acts here as a frustrated labourer or herdsman, restricted to staring 'upon the sheepes skyn'. His inability to speak is figured as a physical harm or lack, while his scribal work afflicts him 'In every veyne and place of his body' (1026). In the process of describing constraints on the clerks, then, Hoccleve also literalizes, and thus makes present, an occupation that otherwise is marked by insubstantiality and absence. In effect, he turns a Latinate 'no one' into an English, embodied 'some one'. A later passage resonates with these depictions of the physical labour of writing. Hoccleve describes the Incarnation, and at the same time introduces the image of a written text:

> Him lothid nat His precious body sprede
> Upon the Crois, this lord benigne and good;
> He wroot our chartre of mercy with His blood. (3337–9)

This passage refers to the popular Middle English tradition of the 'Charter of Christ'.[58] Sometimes written in the form of a land charter, with diplomatic vocabulary and layout, sometimes presented as if spoken by Christ, these texts elaborate the idea of Christ as feudal lord, granting the estate of Heaven to mankind in return for the due service of devotion and repentance. Some versions develop the idea of Christ's body itself as the text, His skin as parchment, His blood as ink:

> Herknyth and ye schall wete
> How this chartour was y-wrete
> Of my face fill downe the ynke
> Whan thornys on my hed gan synke
> the pennys that the lettris were with wrytene
> were skorges that y was with betyne.[59]

The *Regiment*'s image of Christ's blood as ink takes to a logical conclusion the concept of writing as physical labour, again calling to mind Hoccleve's work as a scribe, which 'smertith [...] ful sore / In every veyne' (1025–6). It also constructs the body as a field of meaning. Christ's body here becomes a signifying text: flesh made word. Whereas in Hoccleve's earlier exemplum the ruler Lycurgus leaves disembodied

---

[58] See *Middle English Charters of Christ*, ed. Spalding, Hughes 1992 and Rubin 1991, 306–8.
[59] *Middle English Charters of Christ*, ed. Spalding, 58–60, from CUL MS Ii. iii. 26. A version of the *Charter of Christ* immediately follows the *Regiment* in BL MS Harley 116.

laws to his people, here the law is inscribed on the body of the lawmaker; Christ the King is intimately physically involved with the process of justice and the social body of His people.

Shortly before this passage, Hoccleve tells the story of a Roman veteran who, on trial for his life, calls on Caesar for help (3270–311). Caesar acknowledges a debt to his former soldier, and sends him an advocate. This indirect verbal assistance is not good enough for the veteran, who reminds Caesar of his service in battle:

And advocat ne sente I noon to yow,
But myself putte in prees and for yow faght;
My wowndes beren good witnesse ynow
That I sooth seye. (3284–7)

He then bares his wounded body as if a text on which the history of his loyalty is written, and a chastened Caesar intercedes for the veteran himself. While the Dialogue figures words as bleeding wounds, this Roman exemplum imagines a scarred body more eloquent than any verbal petition. In the same way, perhaps, Hoccleve can deploy his physical condition, his sacrifice in writing, in support of his petitionary claims. With the idea of the text as a made object, something sweated and suffered over, comes also the idea that such concrete labour is worth a concrete reward. Hoccleve's description of his work and its effect on his body comes immediately after a complaint about his small annuity: 'Six marc yeerly and no more than that, / Fadir, to me me thynkith is ful lyte' (974–5). He goes on to describe how his fellow clerks are cheated of the money 'that is us due / For our labour' (1501–2). Further, the whole venture of writing a book of advice for Prince Henry is described by the Old Man as a practical service: 'To thee good lord, good servant thow thee qwyte / To him, and treewe' (1945–6). This phrase is powerfully echoed in a later passage, which also recalls Hoccleve's description of writing as a physically debilitating labour:

He that his flessh despendith and his blood,
My Lord, in your service, him giftes beede;
There is largesse mesurable good.
A kyng so bownde is, he moot do so neede.
Service unqwit and murdre, it is no dreede,
As clerkes writen, and desheritance,
Byfore almighty God axen vengeance. (4173–9)

Hoccleve's claim for recognition from Henry is thus inscribed on his body by his labour in writing, while his 'service' in writing a book of advice is placed in the same category as manual work.[60] But the other side of the coin is the threat of vengeance: unrewarded service, murder, disinheritance, all of them charges that were laid at the door of Prince Henry's father, here are assimilated to the flesh-and-blood struggle of the court writer. The phrase 'as clerkes writen' is here a reminder of the rules of engagement discussed above in Chapter 2; by writing, clerks control the imagined moral arena in which kings must ultimately be judged. Clerks are here allied to a divine authority that trumps that of the king on earth.[61] Unlike 'thoght' and 'wach' at the start of the poem, the animated nouns in this stanza are directly marshalled against the criminal King.

As this passage shows, Hoccleve is also highly conscious of the *Regiment*'s value as a physical text, despite the strongly imagined dialogic setting of much of the poem. Hoccleve's description of the physical labour of a scribe is one of several ways in which his anxieties and constraints are projected on to his own body. The imagery deployed in the Dialogue establishes a physiological discourse that will be echoed and extended in the rest of the *Regiment*, where the mirror for princes tradition is directed towards the integration of the natural body of the prince with the social body of the state. Despite using some of the vocabulary of disembodied royal power, it is to an organic model of the polity that the *Regiment* owes most, however much this model is compromised by the fear that inheritance, law, reward and belief will disintegrate in the post-Ricardian polity. Since political actions have physical consequences, and vice versa, the *regiment* of princes must apply closely both to the control of the king's own body and that of the state in Hoccleve's poem, with the failing, absent or scarred body of the subject as a potent site of alternative signification.

---

[60] An analogue of Hoccleve's strategy is that of the *Richard the Redeless* poet: 'And as my body and my beste oute to be my liegis, / So rithffully be reson my rede shuld also' (I. 47–8). This strategy is also employed in *The Prince*, which begins by comparing Machiavelli's 'knowledge of the conduct of great men' to the tangible gifts of horses, jewels and other objects conventionally offered by those approaching a ruler (Machiavelli, *The Prince*, 3).

[61] 'As clerkes writen' also alerts the reader to a possible biblical allusion here, in this case perhaps to Genesis 4: 10, where God tells Cain that the blood of Abel 'crieth out to me from the ground'. The significance of the Cain and Abel story for Henry IV's deposition and murder of his cousin Richard II would not have been lost on contemporary observers.

Chapter 5

The Afterlife of the Poem:
Hoccleve Manuscripts, Readers and Critics

The previous chapters have examined how the pressures imposed by historical environment, intellectual and political traditions and literary genres are represented and refigured in Hoccleve's poem. This final chapter is concerned with the responses that the *Regiment* itself generated in its early scribes and readers, examining the traditions in which it was read and the audiences for whom it was rewritten. I briefly characterize the manuscripts as a whole, and then discuss aspects of their artistic affinities, manuscript partners, milieux of production and their ownership. Finally, I consider the ways in which readers tried to interpret the genre and meaning of the first part of the *Regiment* by means of glossing, annotation and headings. These multiple acts of writing and reading help not only to evaluate the poem(s) that the *Regiment* became during its manuscript dissemination, but also to re-focus the reader's attention on features of the text that have provoked more recent debate.[1]

I. THE CORPUS OF *REGIMENT* MANUSCRIPTS

The great popularity of the *Regiment* may in part be gauged by the number of manuscripts in which it survives: forty-three complete or substantial copies, and two fragments of another copy.[2] These provide a significant corpus of information about the poem's production,

---

[1] There is no 'authorial' text of the *Regiment*, though Hoccleve may have supervised the production of the two earliest surviving copies of the poem, BL MSS Arundel 38 and Harley 4866. Furnivall's edition of 1897 uses the latter as his base text; Charles Blyth's recent edition employs the former, but emends its spellings using evidence from Hoccleve's own scribal practice.

[2] The *Regiment* may be compared with *The Canterbury Tales* (fifty-seven complete manuscripts), *Piers Plowman* (fifty-one), the *Confessio amantis* (forty, not including excerpts) and Lydgate's *The Fall of Princes* (thirty-four, as well as extracts in numerous other manuscripts); see Edwards and Pearsall 1989, 270, and for Lydgate manuscripts, Edwards 1983.

readership and early interpretation which has yet to be fully investigated.³ The surviving manuscripts range from some magnificent early volumes such as BL MSS Arundel 38 and Harley 4866 to small, unadorned paper books such as BL MSS Sloane 1212 and Royal 17 C. xiv.⁴ Differences in value and circumstances of production are also betrayed, of course, by the handwriting, layout and (where the original survives) binding. The manuscripts range in date from the second decade of the fifteenth century to the turn of the sixteenth century. Despite its wide circulation, however, the *Regiment* did not receive an early printing; its *editio princeps*, by Thomas Wright, did not appear until 1860.⁵ Marcia Smith Marzec argues that the poem's popularity was short-lived partly because of its language, which was already becoming dated by the third quarter of the fifteenth century,⁶ though this would not wholly account for the lack of an early edition. Hoccleve's overt Catholic piety would certainly have told against the *Regiment* after the Reformation.⁷ In addition, the *Regiment*'s personal and topical references, while they received attention from some readers, would have made the poem seem dated for others, especially amongst a new wave of Tudor political texts in the early sixteenth century. However, the manuscripts do contain

---

3   For descriptions of *Regiment* manuscripts, see Seymour 1974, to be treated with caution and supplemented by Edwards 1978, Green 1978 and Marzec 1980, lii–xciii. Seymour lists two manuscripts that were sold in the nineteenth century and have since been lost (his numbers 38a and 38b). Marzec (1987b, 269–70) estimates that at least as many *Regiment* manuscripts have been lost as survive, perhaps twice as many. Burrow (1994, 50–5) provides a useful list of extant Hoccleve manuscripts and editions (though he mistakenly identifies Philadelphia, Rosenbach Foundation MS 1083/30 as 'MS 1983/10').

4   Thirty-two of the manuscripts are wholly or mainly of membrane.

5   The first 'modern' edition of any poems by Hoccleve was that of Mason in 1796. He printed six poems, including the *Male Regle*, from the manuscript that is now San Marino, Huntington Library MS HM 111.

6   See Marzec 1987a, who discusses scribal emendation in *Regiment* manuscripts as a consequence of language change. There is similar evidence from later additions and glosses in the manuscripts. For example, in the late-fifteenth century CUL Gg. vi. 17, a late-fifteenth/early-sixteenth-century hand adds occasional glosses in Latin. These include 'effugias' (line 264, 'astert') and 'statim' (line 272, 'blive'), both on fol. 5v. See Harris 1983 for comparable scribal emendation in *Confessio* manuscripts. Cannon 1998, 179–89, elegantly traces the ways in which Chaucer's cultural authority overcame the feeling that his language had become outdated.

7   Due to a misinterpretation of Walsingham's *Chronicle*, some sixteenth-century commentators spoke of Hoccleve as a Wycliffite (for example, Bale, *Catalogus*, 537) but the *Regiment* itself clearly demonstrates Hoccleve's orthodox Catholic beliefs. Later readers of some *Regiment* manuscripts display their disapproval of Catholic references. For example, in BL MS Harley 4866, fols 6r–v, stanzas 42 and 45–7 of the *Regiment* (which support transubstantiation and the authority of the Church) have been crossed out in pen. In Bodleian MS Laud Misc. 735, fol. 53r, during Lydgate's *Danse Macabre*, the word 'pope' has been scored out each time it occurs.

numerous sixteenth-century names, and Hoccleve was still known in antiquarian circles, albeit mainly through his connection with Chaucer.[8]

The *Regiment* proper is only rarely separated from the Dialogue with the Old Man. For example, only lines 1–2016 appear in BL MS Harley 7333, but a catchword on folio 211v shows that the *Regiment* proper was originally meant to continue on the next quire. In BL MS Harley 372 a paper strip once covered the top few lines of folio 71r, in order to hide the fact that the copy was at one time more complete.[9] The fact that so few manuscripts divide the *Regiment* argues for an early awareness of the poem's integrity, something that is also suggested by the number of manuscripts – at least eighteen – in which the poem appears alone.[10]

A.S.G. Edwards and Derek Pearsall note that eighteen of the manuscripts have a similar layout, that is, in a quarto volume with four spaced stanzas to the page. This occurs not only in the early presentation manuscripts BL MSS Arundel 38 and Harley 4866, but also in late copies such as BL MS Royal 17 D. xix and CUL MS Hh. iv. 11. The arrangement was probably for practical reasons as much as anything: the long lines of the rhyme royal stanza militate against the double-column format in which so many copies of, for example, the *Confessio amantis* are written. Only two *Regiment* manuscripts are written in double columns: BL MS Harley 7333 and Coventry City Record Office MS Acc. 325/1. Both of these are large collections that include works by Chaucer, Lydgate and, in the case of Harley 7333, extracts from the *Confessio*; the miscellaneous character of the manuscripts and the inclusion of texts with other traditions of layout have in these cases influenced the way in which the *Regiment* is presented. The single-

---

[8] For example, Bale, *Catalogus*, 537: 'Thomas Occleue, vel Ocklefe, uir tam bonis disciplinis quam generis prosapia clarus, exquisita quadam Anglici sermonis eloquentia, post Chaucerum, cuius fuerat discipulus, patriam ornavit linguam. Praeter alia literatorum hominum studia, poesim ipse amore summo coluit, in quo exercitii genere lepidus ac facundus & ille tandem euasit.' [Thomas Occleve, or Ocklefe, a man as outstanding in good learning as in the nobility of his family, ornamented our mother tongue with a certain exquisite eloquence of English speech after Chaucer, whose disciple he had been. Besides other studies of men of letters, he himself practised poetry with the utmost love, in which manner of skill he too at length turned out to be charming and fluent.] Bale's description is repeated in Thomas Speght's Chaucer edition. A.S.G. Edwards (1997a) discusses the poet William Browne, a Hoccleve enthusiast from the early seventeenth century, and another serious reader of Hoccleve from this period deserves mention: Richard James (1592–1638), scholar, poet and librarian to Sir Robert Cotton. James copied Hoccleve's *Remonstrance to Oldcastle* in Bodleian MS James 34, along with copious notes defending Oldcastle as a proto-protestant martyr.

[9] See Green 1978, 41.

[10] This is a conservative figure, not including copies that have subsequently been bound with other material, such as Harley 372, or, conversely, divided from texts with which they were previously bound, as in Bodleian MS Rawlinson poet. 168.

column, spaced-stanza format of most *Regiment* manuscripts is shared by many copies of Chaucer's *Troilus and Criseyde* and Lydgate's *Life of Our Lady*.[11] Edwards and Pearsall suggest that this layout was partly for reasons of economy: a regular number of stanzas to a page meant that it was simpler to estimate how much parchment would be needed to copy the text. In the case of the *Regiment*, other considerations could also come into play. Spaced stanzas allow enough room for the Latin apparatus to be written in the margins. They also make the text easier to read and to copy. In addition, a four-stanza arrangement means that the first few sections of the *Regiment* proper would start at the top of a leaf. While highly unlikely that this arrangement was intended by Hoccleve, it too makes the text easier to follow.[12]

The hands that copied the *Regiment* generally wrote in some form of cursive script, based on an Anglicana or Secretary model. The scribes of the English text were usually also responsible for the marginal glosses, in Latin of varying proficiency and abbreviation. The standard set of Latin glosses is usually written by the scribe of the main text, though frequently in a more formal script, and with paraphs or underlining that establish a textual hierarchy. The most expensive manuscripts have elaborate border decoration at the divisions of the text, prominent *litterae notabiliores* and coloured and flourished initials to mark the beginning of stanzas. Nearly all the manuscripts have some form of decoration, if only a simple mark in red crayon through some initial letters. The *Regiment* manuscripts are more variable in quality than, for example, those of Gower's *Confessio amantis*, whose sheer size meant that producing a new copy was a substantial undertaking. Neither do they match the decorative profusion of some Lydgate manuscripts, which became such fashionable accoutrements for royal and noble libraries in the fifteenth century. Nevertheless, their very variety – from exceptional presentation copies to privately written paper books – prompts questions about the nature of early responses to the poem.

---

[11] See respectively Chaucer, *Troilus and Criseyde*, ed. Windeatt, 68–75 and Edwards and Pearsall 1989, 264 and note 64. See also their table of information about material, size, scribes and decoration in manuscripts of nine major Middle English poems, including the *Regiment*, ibid., 270. On the layout of Lydgate's *Life of Our Lady*, see Keiser 1991 and 1995.

[12] The Dialogue, with 288 stanzas, should take up exactly 36 folios, as it does in, for example, Bodleian MS Ashmole 40. After this there are 20 stanzas in Hoccleve's prologue to Prince Henry, 44 in the section on keeping oaths and the law, and 76 in the section on justice. The pattern breaks down in the next section, 'De pietate', which has 45 stanzas. However, in Arundel 38 (perhaps the earliest extant manuscript) a three-quarter-page dedication picture means that the *Regiment* proper starts at the bottom of fol. 37r, and so subsequent sections begin in the middle of pages.

The Afterlife of the Poem

II. THE PICTURE TRADITION

Two pictures in early manuscripts of the *Regiment* have attracted much art-historical and critical attention. These are the presentation miniature in BL MS Arundel 38, folio 37r, and the marginal picture of Chaucer in BL MS Harley 4866, folio 88r.[13] Both manuscripts are presentation copies made shortly after the *Regiment* was written. Arundel 38 includes the arms of the Mowbray family,[14] and in Harley 4866, leaves that may have contained coats of arms associated with a patron or dedicatee have been excised.

The Arundel presentation miniature has been linked on stylistic grounds to the workshop of Herman Scheere, one of the best-known contemporary illuminators working in England.[15] Scheere was probably from Flanders, and brought with him a distinctive and influential style of portraiture. Features of this style include solid, compact figures, a three-dimensional frame, and decoration more restrained than the sometimes overpowering exuberance of the English fourteenth-century school. In addition, the Scheere school employs a characteristic gold scrollwork pattern in the background to pictures, while figures frequently break out of the frames in which they are depicted. Manuscripts with miniatures by Scheere include Bodleian MS lat. liturg. f. 2 (for example, the execution of Archbishop Scrope, folio 146v) and BL MS Royal 2 A. xviii (the Beaufort Hours; Scheere's painting of the Annunciation is on folio 23v). With his collaboration on BL MS Add. 42131 (the Bedford Psalter-Hours), Scheere was working for the same patron – John, Duke of Bedford – that Hoccleve addresses in an envoy to the *Regiment*. Scheere's influence has been found in numerous manuscripts of this period, including Bodleian MSS Bodley 294, 693 and 902, BL MS Egerton 1991, and Cambridge, Pembroke College MS 307 (all copies of Gower's *Confessio*),[16] while Bodleian MS Selden supra 53, which contains Hoccleve's *Regiment* and *Series*, includes a miniature on folio 118r illustrating *Lerne to Die*, perhaps painted by an artist of the same atelier.[17]

---

[13] See above, plates 1 and 2 and pp. 114–21.

[14] See Harris 1984.

[15] For the work of Scheere and his followers in numerous manuscripts of the early fifteenth century, see Kuhn 1940, Rickert 1954, 185–9, Turner 1962, Spriggs 1962–7 and Wright 1995.

[16] See Kuhn 1940, Spriggs 1962–7, 193–8 and, for the Pembroke manuscript, Wright 1992, 193.

[17] Reproduced in Pächt and Alexander 1966–73, III, plate 84. See Spriggs 1962–7 and Seymour 1974, 278. In the picture, a fearful, dying man in a bed is threatened by Death, while a robed figure stands beside the bed, hands crossed across his breast. This bedridden vision in the Selden manuscript may be compared to the dream of Nebuchadnezzar depicted in numerous *Confessio amantis* manuscripts, based on

Hoccleve's Regiment of Princes: Counsel and Constraint

The Arundel presentation picture displays several features of the Scheere style. The grassy platform on which the figures are placed protrudes from the simple frame, while the robes of the kneeling figure flow over the frame's edge on the right-hand side. The figures are gracefully proportioned and solidly three-dimensional. The picture's background is decorated with gold scrollwork. The pose of the kneeling figure in the Arundel picture can be compared with that of John Beaufort, Earl of Somerset (d. 1410), who is probably depicted in Scheere's Annunciation scene in the Beaufort Hours.[18] Beaufort and his wife kneel on either side of the architectural frame in which the Virgin and the Angel Gabriel are shown. Beaufort's facial type, his high-necked courtier's robe and the way that he breaks out of the picture's frame are all reminiscent of the Arundel picture.[19]

There is no doubt that the Arundel manuscript contained a picture of Chaucer, and, indeed, J.J.G. Alexander and C.M. Kaufmann note that the portrait leaves an 'offprint' on folio 90v.[20] Fortunately, it is the Chaucer picture that survives in Harley 4866. Here, too, the figure breaks out of its frame: Chaucer points at the text (lines 4995–6) with his right hand, while a rosary dangles below the frame from his left hand. This picture has also been associated with the workshop of Herman Scheere, and certainly shows the influence of his style.[21] The Harley portrait is closely related to the famous image of Chaucer on horseback in the Ellesmere copy of *The Canterbury Tales*.[22] The Harley and Ellesmere pictures were probably copied from the same model. The relationships between Arundel 38, Harley 4866 and Ellesmere are further strengthened when one considers that the layout of Arundel 38

---

the same model of a man lying in a bed on the left of the picture. The robed figure in the Selden manuscript has been compared by Seymour (1974, 278) to the pose of Genius in the confession scenes commonly found in manuscripts of the *Confessio amantis*.

[18] Reproduced in Gordon 1993, 43.

[19] Seymour (1982, 622) notes the similarity, but mistakenly refers to the manuscript as Royal 2 A. xvii. There is not general agreement in identifying other pictures painted by the Arundel miniaturist. Seymour (1982, 622) says that the artist also worked on Cambridge, Gonville and Caius MS 433, BL MSS Egerton 1991 and Royal 8 G. iii. Turner (1962, 269) links him to some portrait miniatures in BL MS Add. 42131 (the Bedford Psalter-Hours). Alexander (1983, 149) identifies him with the 'Master of the Pentecost', and says that the same workshop produced the initials (including one showing Henry IV) in the first volume of the Great Cowcher books of the Duchy of Lancaster (now in the Public Record Office, London).

[20] Alexander and Kaufmann 1973, 109.

[21] Carlson (1991, 287) even suggests that the Harley and Arundel pictures may be by the same artist.

[22] San Marino, Huntington Library MS EL 26 C. 9, fol. 153v. See Brusendorff 1925, 14–21, Margaret Rickert's essay in Manly and Rickert 1940, I, 588–615, Seymour 1982, Carlson 1991 and Pearsall 1992a, 285–9.

– in particular its illuminated initials and presentation of marginal glosses – corresponds very closely to the Ellesmere manuscript.[23] Such affiliations between Arundel, Harley and Ellesmere suggest that Hoccleve probably knew the Ellesmere manuscript.[24] He had, of course, collaborated with its scribe on the *Confessio amantis* in Cambridge, Trinity College MS R. 3. 2.[25] Another scribe of the Trinity Gower (scribe 'D') wrote some of the Bodleian manuscripts (including MS Bodley 294) whose illustrations show close affinities with Arundel 38 and Harley 4866.[26] These networks of scribal collaboration and influence reinforce Hoccleve's connections with the production and dissemination of the poetry of Gower and Chaucer, just as his eulogies to them in the *Regiment* claim a personal association with his illustrious predecessors.

There is no substantial corpus of presentation and Chaucer pictures in the later *Regiment* manuscripts, since the Chaucer picture, due no doubt to its very value, was excised from manuscripts such as Arundel 38 at an early stage in transmission. BL MS Royal 17 D. vi includes lively though crude presentation and Chaucer pictures, clearly copied from an early model similar to Arundel or Harley,[27] while Philadelphia, Rosenbach MS 1083/30 has an eighteenth-century copy of the Harley picture.[28] Some manuscripts note the absence of the picture with a marginal comment,[29] and in BL MS Harley 4826 only the margin of the

[23] See Doyle and Parkes 1978, 203, note 106. Another 'homage' to the Ellesmere manuscript appears later in the fifteenth century. This is BL MS Arundel 119, a copy of Lydgate's *Siege of Thebes* written for William de la Pole, Duke of Suffolk; its imitation of Ellesmere's *ordinatio* is a particularly appropriate design for Lydgate's own Canterbury tale. See Edwards and Pearsall 1989, 264, and Hanna and Edwards 1996, 16–19.

[24] Arguing that the Chaucer pictures share a common exemplar, Pearsall comments: 'The best supposition would be that Hoccleve had such an exemplar in his possession before or soon after Chaucer's death [...] and made it available to the editor of Ellesmere (if indeed he was not himself the editor)' (Pearsall 1992a, 289). That Hoccleve had access to such an exemplar is quite possible; the idea that he was the 'editor' of the Ellesmere manuscript is, of course, extremely speculative.

[25] See Doyle and Parkes 1978. The Ellesmere copyist is their scribe 'B', Hoccleve scribe 'E'.

[26] Ibid., 203, note 106.

[27] BL MS Royal 17 D. vi is placed in the 'alpha' section of Marzec's stemma of *Regiment* manuscripts (reproduced in Greetham 1987, 66–7). Its exemplar is her putative '4', from which she supposes BL MS Harley 7333 and the Coventry manuscript also to have been copied. Bodleian MS Digby 185 was, according to the stemma, copied in turn from Royal 17 D. vi, but it does not contain the presentation or Chaucer pictures. The scribe of the Digby manuscript notes 'Chaucers ymage' on fol. 139r, where the portrait would have appeared.

[28] See Edwards 1993.

[29] For example, Bodleian MSS Laud Misc. 735, fol. 128r, 'The figure of Chaucer'; Digby 185, fol. 139r, 'Chaucers ymage'; Ashmole 40, fol. 90r, 'The figure of Chaucer', and Cambridge, Fitzwilliam MS McClean 185, fol. 76r, 'The Figure of

'Chaucer page' has been removed, leaving the edge of the figure visible. At the bottom of the page (folio 139r) a brief poem laments its loss:

> Off worthy Chaucer
> here the pickture stood
> That much did wryght
> and all to doo us good.
>
> Summe ffuryous ffoole
> have Cutt the Same in twayne
> His deed doo shewe
> He bare a barren Brayne.[30]

In other manuscripts, different evidence of the loss of the picture tradition can be found. Cambridge, Queens' College MS 12 is missing a whole quire, which may have contained a Chaucer picture.[31] M.C. Seymour suggests that in the cases both of Bodleian MS Dugdale 45 and CUL MS Gg. vi. 17, a page containing the picture was missing in the manuscripts' exemplars.[32] If this is the case, however, the loss of just five stanzas in these manuscripts (stanzas 712–16, lines 4978–5012) is curious. It suggests either that only a portion of the exemplar's page was cut out (still unlikely to remove an odd number of stanzas), or that a portrait of Chaucer in the exemplar took up three-quarters of a page, leaving five stanzas of text on the folio. Marzec's stemma of *Regiment* manuscripts suggests that Gg. vi. 17 was in any case copied from another extant manuscript, Edinburgh, NLS MS Adv. 19. I. II, part 3, which has no text loss at this point.[33] In the case of Gg. vi. 17, at least, it seems that we should look for other explanations for the loss, such as careless copying or an effort to edit the text.[34] Another case for caution is that of San Marino, Huntington Library MS HM 135, where the *Regiment* is incomplete, breaking off after line 4928. The text loss includes the portion of the poem where a Chaucer picture may have

---

Chaucer'. In the margin of BL MS Harley 372, fol. 103r, the Tudor antiquary John Stow has written 'Chaucer' and further down 'his picture shuld be here'.

[30] See Pearsall 1992a, 289.

[31] The quire was probably missing before the manuscript was rebound in the sixteenth century, because the wooden sewing supports seem too narrow to have accommodated another quire. I am very grateful to Elizabeth Bradshaw for showing me this manuscript in its disbound state during conservation.

[32] Seymour 1974, 258.

[33] In Greetham 1987, 66–7.

[34] Apart from those five stanzas, Seymour does not notice any text loss in Gg. vi. 17. In fact, the manuscript is missing a substantial amount of text at numerous points, amounting to 651 lines in all, which suggests a conscious editorial process either on the part of the manuscript's compiler or in its exemplar. Marginal marks and notes have been added to indicate where text is missing.

The Afterlife of the Poem

appeared, but the manuscript is lacking pages elsewhere, and its late date and plain quality make it unlikely to have included a portrait.[35]

The tradition of one other early Chaucer picture survives in an engraving made by the artist George Vertue in 1717, which appeared in Urry's edition of Chaucer, posthumously published in 1721.[36] George Lam and Warren Smith suggest that Vertue had access to a picture of Chaucer inserted into BL MS Cotton Otho A. xviii, one of the manuscripts destroyed in the Cotton fire of 1731; a description of Chaucer, most probably from the same picture, occurs in the notes on *Troilus and Criseyde* made by the scholar and antiquary Sir Francis Kinaston (1587–?1642).[37] The Vertue engraving, in which Chaucer's right hand fingers a penknife around his neck, is similar to that made by John Speed for the frontispiece of Speght's Chaucer edition of 1598. Speght's claim to have seen an original of this Chaucer picture may be (as Pearsall suggests) merely a marketing ploy.[38] It is quite possible, however, that he had seen such a portrait, whether the one described by Kinaston, or in a manuscript now lost, or in Arundel 38 or Harley 4826 before they were excised.

Regiment manuscripts, then, soon lost their pictorial tradition, unlike the marginal dream and confession scenes that are commonly found in manuscripts of Gower's *Confessio*, or the ambitious illustrative programmes in some copies of Lydgate's *Troy Book* and *The Lives of St Edmund and St Fremund*. The *Regiment* did not have the canonical status of Gower's work or the picturesque narrative of Lydgate's poems with which to sustain a pictorial tradition.[39] However, the early pictures play an important part in the strategy of the *Regiment* (as shown above in Chapter 3) and in the development of Chaucer portraiture. They situate the production of the poem not only in a context of London patrons, scribes and artistic ateliers, but also in a revealing rhetorical, literary and iconographic environment.

---

[35] These features militate against Seymour's speculation that Huntington MS HM 135 is the manuscript described in a nineteenth-century sale catalogue as being 'cruelly mutilated [...] for the sake of the illumination' (Seymour 1974, 291). See Dutschke 1989, I, 181.

[36] See Lam and Smith 1944 and Pearsall 1992a, 302–3, and plate 21.

[37] See Beadle 1990, 227–8.

[38] Pearsall 1992a, 301–3. This image may also have been the one depicted on Chaucer's tomb in Westminster Abbey; see ibid., 295–6.

[39] For the *Confessio*, see Griffiths 1983; and for Lydgate, Lawton 1983 and Scott 1989a. Unfortunately, I do not have space here to discuss the other images that appear in copies of the *Regiment*, such as the monks in the large initials of BL MS Harley 4826, fols 52r and 84r and the men, birds and fanciful creatures in the borders of CUL MS Hh. iv. 11.

III. THE REGIMENT AND ITS MANUSCRIPT PARTNERS

The range of style and quality in the surviving manuscripts of the *Regiment* provides initial evidence of the variety of readers that the poem had during the fifteenth century. This information can be supplemented by studying the texts that accompany Hoccleve's poem in manuscripts, and by identifying individual readers and owners. As mentioned above, nearly half the extant copies of the *Regiment* are alone in a manuscript. The poem's length made it suitable for an average-sized copy that was easily portable and not too expensive. It was also, however, grouped with various combinations of texts, usually poetic, and usually in English. Seymour characterizes the *Regiment* as 'always making a serious contribution to a serious volume'.[40] In the next two sections I briefly consider three aspects of this compilation: collections of regiminal texts, copies of the *Regiment* alongside Hoccleve's *Series*, and evidence for the *Regiment* as a distinct booklet in some manuscripts.

The *Regiment* was frequently copied alongside other regiminal texts. Numerous Latin and French versions of such texts were circulating in the later fourteenth century, but by the beginning of the fifteenth century an English readership was developing whose members were interested not only in romance and devotional literature, but in philosophical and political writing, too. This readership included the small but educated group, based around Westminster and London, that formed much of Gower's and Chaucer's early-fifteenth-century audience.[41] It was a group of which Hoccleve and his associates were themselves members. Indeed, the administrative offices around Westminster were fertile ground for the production and, no doubt, discussion of vernacular literature in the late-medieval period, generating a reading community with a professional and personal interest in the intersections of writing, morality and governance. One of Hoccleve's colleagues as a Privy Seal clerk, William Donne, has, for example, been identified with the William 'Denne' who was an executor of Gower's will.[42] Hoccleve was bequeathed five marks by a senior clerk at the Privy Seal, Guy de Rouclif, along with 'uno libro vocato Bello Troie'.[43] Another government official, Thomas Kent, who subsequently became Secondary in the Privy Seal, owned a copy of *The Canterbury Tales*, now

---

[40] Seymour 1974, 255. Varieties of vernacular compilation are analysed in Boffey and Thompson 1989, Boffey and Meale 1991, Edwards 1996 and Hanna 1996b.

[41] See Middleton 1978, Scattergood 1983, Strohm 1982b, 1988 and 1989, and Kerby-Fulton and Justice 1997. Two early owners of a *Canterbury Tales* manuscript, both Chancery clerks, are discussed in Richardson 1990. See also Briggs 1999, esp. 53–73, for English owners of Aegidius manuscripts.

[42] Parkes 1995, 97.

[43] Burrow 1994, 9 and 33, and Ingram 1973.

Cambridge, Fitzwilliam Museum MS McClean 181.[44] George Ashby had been in the bureaucratic service since the early 1420s, though it was not until the early 1460s that he wrote his *A Prisoner's Reflections* and *Active Policy of a Prince*.[45] It is possible that Ashby had met Hoccleve; his own advisory texts are certainly indebted to Hoccleve's works, and his poetic persona of Boethian complainant and servant-advisor has close affinities with Hoccleve's self-projection.

The *Regiment* takes a prominent place amongst the vernacular works written in this environment, and is coupled in manuscripts with other regiminal texts, including Lydgate and Burgh's *Secrees of Old Philisoffres*, Lydgate's *Danse Macabre*, and Gower's *Confessio amantis*.[46] In addition, Walton's translation of *De consolatione Philosophiae* is associated with Hoccleve's poem in three manuscripts.[47] Many of these texts are translations of well-known Latin treatises. One reason for the *Regiment*'s popularity, indeed, could be its service of 'translating' parts of three Latin works for an audience that preferred to read English rather than Latin.[48] *Regiment* manuscripts frequently note the passage in which Hoccleve introduces his three major sources, and the *Regiment* is also sometimes described in the manuscripts as being a translation of Aegidius's work.[49] Hoccleve could be thought to be bringing important texts to the attention of those who could not read Latin, or would not read it habitually. This strengthens the *Regiment*'s links with Lydgate and Burgh's *Secrees*, Walton's Boethius translation, and Burgh's version of one of the most popular teaching texts of the Middle Ages, the

---

[44] See Manly and Rickert 1940, I, 166–9. Although Kent was not promoted to this post until 1444, he had been in the King's service since at least 1409, and probably knew Hoccleve. Manly and Rickert suggest (I, 169) that the manuscript was written by a Privy Seal clerk.

[45] For the dating of Ashby's works, see Scattergood 1990.

[46] The *Secrees* appears in BL MS Arundel 59, MS Harley 4826 and Fitzwilliam Museum MS McClean 182; the *Danse Macabre* in BL MS Harley 116, Bodleian MSS Laud Misc. 735, Selden supra 53 and Bodley 221, and in Coventry Record Office MS Acc. 325/1, San Marino, Huntington MS EL 26 A. 13 and New Haven, Yale MS Beinecke 493. Extracts from the *Confessio* are found in BL MS Harley 7333, Bodleian MS Rawlinson poet. 168 and Society of Antiquaries MS 134.

[47] Fitzwilliam MS McClean 185 (Walton's *Boethius* is now McClean 184), Society of Antiquaries MS 134 and Rosenbach MS 1083/30.

[48] For the burgeoning use of English for official business in the early fifteenth century, see Richardson 1980 and Fisher 1992. For the debate over John Trevisa's translation of Aegidius and its lack of circulation, see above, pp. 89–90.

[49] For example, Bodleian MS Rawlinson poet. 10, fol. 25v notes 'Gayles' and 'egidius' beside stanza 296. Manuscripts that call the *Regiment* a translation of Aegidius include Bodleian MSS Ashmole 40 ('Explicit Egidius de regimine principum' on fol. 98v) and Laud Misc. 735 ('Explicit Egidius de regimine principum' on fol. 134r).

Disticha Catonis.⁵⁰ Hoccleve's version of his sources is much freer and more politically pointed than these texts, but the impression that the *Regiment* is a translation is also, of course, a valuable protective feature of his poetic strategy.

Such compilations of regiminal material allow multiple readings of Hoccleve's poem to emerge. To take one example: in Cambridge, St John's College MS I. 22, a hybrid regiminal text has been created by pairing an incomplete copy of the *Regiment* with extracts from Lydgate's *The Fall of Princes*. The *Regiment* stops at the bottom of folio 93v, after line 5369: 'Deth threwe him doun to grounde, and lete him lye.'⁵¹ This passage refers to the devastation caused by war and the illusory value of worldly riches. Specifically, it describes the death of Alexander the Great, and warns the Princes of England and France to beware his example. At this point in the *Regiment*, the addition of passages from *The Fall of Princes* (folios 94r–99v, including a missing leaf) is extremely apt. The passages are all from the first book of Lydgate's poem, lines 4551–844 (with some out of order and 4712–67 excised) and 6350–77. Extracts from *The Fall of Princes* are usually taken from Lydgate's moralizing envoys.⁵² Such is the case in Fitzwilliam MS McClean 182, for example, where the *Regiment* is preceded by seven balades chosen from various books of *The Fall of Princes*. In the St John's College manuscript, however, two sections are used that contain some narrative. The first warns princes not to be hasty in judgement or believe all they are told, and to beware slanderers and flatterers:

> But off alle chaungis, that chaung is most to dreede,
> And most feerful is that variaunce,
> Whan that pryncis, which may the peeple leede,
> Be founde vnstable in ther gouernaunce. (*Fall of Princes*, I. 4565–8)

> There is no damage that men can purpose,
> Mor to be drad nor more lamentable,
> Than a prynce his eris to onclose
> To eueri tale and to eueri fable;

---

⁵⁰ Burgh's *Cato* appears in BL MSS Harley 116 and Harley 7333. It is also found in Bodleian MS Rawlinson poet. 35, once joined to the copy of the *Regiment* in MS Rawlinson poet. 168.

⁵¹ Lines 4259–354 are also missing. After 4257–8, written at the top of fol. 75v, the rest of the page is blank. Fol. 76r then begins with line 4355. This lacuna is not noticed by Seymour (1974, 284) or James (1913, 256–7).

⁵² See Edwards 1971 and Mortimer 1995b. Another Hoccleve manuscript with *Fall of Princes* extracts is BL MS Harley 172, which contains *Lerne to Die*. The Lydgate passages there are I. 4558–662 and 4817–44, lines that also occur in the St John's College manuscript.

> It is a tokne ther hertis be nat stable,
> Whan thei to flatereris ther eris do applie,
> Namli to such that can weel forge and lie. (I. 4593–9)

The passage includes the exemplum of the clean-living Hippolytus, who despised the company of flattering women. After more warnings about false speech and hasty judgement, the final excerpt tells another antifeminist story (6350–77), this time of how Delilah betrayed the secret of a riddle that Samson had made. The compiler of this manuscript (or its exemplar) has clearly recognized a major theme of the *Regiment* – the ambiguous status of royal counsel and advisory speech – and has concluded the book with narratives that reinforce their own reading. The excerpts from Lydgate match the form of the *Regiment* (rhyme royal stanzas) and its rhetorical framework (direct advice to princes), and they promote the warnings that underlie Hoccleve's advice. It is significant, too, that the compiler should include Lydgate's antifeminist attacks, for shortly before the *Regiment* ends in this manuscript, Hoccleve has been ostentatiously (though rather disingenuously) praising women and asserting their superiority (*Regiment*, 5097–194). The Lydgate passages close off the dangerous potential contained in Hoccleve's image of a powerful female audience, instead reinscribing women as flatterers and deceivers. The textual intervention here should remind us of the many other appropriations and rewritings that the *Regiment*'s varied manuscript dissemination allowed for, and that we can no longer recover because the manuscripts have been lost.

The juxtaposition of the *Regiment* with these passages from *The Fall of Princes* in St John's MS I. 22 appears to have been prompted by the incomplete state of the *Regiment* there. I now consider two other works that appear alongside the complete *Regiment* in several manuscripts. These are Hoccleve's *Series* and Lydgate's *Danse Macabre*. They are both, like the *Regiment*, translations in some sense: the *Danse Macabre* is said by Lydgate to be translated 'Owte of the frensshe' (lines 24 and 665) and the *Series* includes two stories from the *Gesta Romanorum*, as well as a version of Heinrich Suso's *De arte moriendi*. Five *Regiment* manuscripts contain complete copies both of the *Series* and the *Danse Macabre*.[53] Four of the five belong to the so-called 'Bodley Group' of *Regiment* copies,

---

[53] These are Bodleian MSS Bodley 221, Laud Misc. 735 and Selden supra 53, New Haven, Yale Beinecke MS 493 and Coventry City Record Office MS Acc. 325/1. Parts of the *Series* are also found in BL MS Royal 17 D. vi (*Jereslaus, Lerne to Die, Jonathas*) and Bodleian MS Digby 185 (*Jereslaus, Jonathas*). The *Danse Macabre* is also found in BL MS Harley 116 and Huntington MS EL 26 A. 13. Edwards 1978 notes the connection between the contents of Beinecke 493 and the Bodleian manuscripts, but states that the Coventry manuscript does not contain *Jonathas*. This tale is in fact part of the Coventry manuscript, fols 64v–69v.

which also share some distinctive textual features.[54] (Indeed, the only manuscript of the complete *Series* that does not also contain the *Regiment* is Durham, University Library MS Cosin V. iii. 9, most of which is in Hoccleve's own hand.) The collocation in these manuscripts of Hoccleve's two longest poems is at first sight reminiscent of his holograph books of 'collected' shorter poems,[55] and also raises the question of why Lydgate's poem is included so regularly in *Series* manuscripts.

There is no evidence that Hoccleve himself included the *Regiment* and *Series* in a single manuscript; nevertheless, the combination of the *Regiment* and *Series* would have been attractive for any reader interested in Hoccleve's life as depicted in his poems.[56] Both works have extended 'autobiographical' sections that frame the texts to follow; both see the poet move from solitary despair to a more confident, socialized status as an author.[57] The idea that a major subject of Hoccleve's poems is the process of composition itself, the moments before and after the

---

[54] The group was named by Green (1978, 37–9), who included the Bodley, Laud and Selden manuscripts, along with Ashmole 40 (the only manuscript of the group not to contain the *Series* and Lydgate's *Danse Macabre*). Green did not know about Beinecke 493, whose layout is similar to Bodley and Laud, and which can also be placed in the same textual grouping. Indeed, Linne Mooney has identified Beinecke 493 and Laud 735 as being written by the same scribe (my thanks to her for this information).

[55] These are San Marino, Huntington MSS HM 111 and HM 744; see Bowers 1989. Seymour says of the *Series* that it 'survives in whole or in part in eight manuscripts, though Hoccleve himself probably "published" some, if not most, of these' (Seymour 1974, 255). There are in fact eleven complete or fragmentary manuscripts of the *Series* (listed in Burrow 1994, 51–2). Two of these are holographs. Of the other nine, seven are dated c. 1450 or later, and two are dated to the second quarter of the fifteenth century. (Two of these manuscripts are not given dates in Burrow 1994: Bodleian MS Eng. poet. d. 4 and BL MS Harley 172. The Bodleian catalogue dates the former to the second half of the fifteenth century, and the latter, since it contains extracts from Lydgate's *Fall of Princes*, is unlikely to have been written before about 1440.) Since Hoccleve died in 1426, it is highly unlikely that he had direct involvement in the production of any extant *Series* manuscripts apart from the two holograph copies, Durham University Library MS Cosin V. iii. 9, and San Marino, Huntington Library MS HM 744 (which contains, of the *Series*, only part of *Lerne to Die*, fols 53r–68v).

[56] This is not to suggest that a 'biographical' reading in a modern sense would have been a normal part of fifteenth-century reading practice, but that Hoccleve's persona is thematically important to both works and may have encouraged a parallel reading. On the scarcity of single-author compilations in Middle English, see Edwards 2000.

[57] The self-referential characteristics of the *Regiment* and *Series* have been analysed by Burrow 1982a and 1984, and Greetham 1989. Greetham suggests that these manuscripts (he includes BL MS Royal 17 D. vi, but does not mention Yale Beinecke MS 493) are 'attempts at "collected works" ', which may reflect a 'perceived unity to the Hoccleve corpus' (246, note 15). He does not, however, discuss the appearance of Lydgate's *Danse Macabre* in the manuscripts.

'text', has only recently been advanced by modern critics of Hoccleve.[58] However, by placing the *Regiment* and the *Series* together – two major poems where Hoccleve dramatizes his own life, his illness, the motives for and means of writing – the fifteenth-century compilers of these manuscripts have already highlighted Hoccleve's autobiographical and intertextual progress in a striking way.[59]

The *Danse Macabre* is not attributed to Hoccleve in these manuscripts (indeed Lydgate names himself as its author (line 670)), but neither is attention drawn to the change of authorship.[60] In all five manuscripts the Lydgate poem follows the *Tale of Jonathas*, the last major section of the *Series*. This does not disrupt the sense of an ending in the *Series*, however, for the work itself invites readers to participate in shaping its progress. We are given a model for this (re)shaping both in Hoccleve's *Dialogue with a Friend*, and in the dialogues that surround the tales, where Hoccleve and his friend discuss the texts and their interpretation, and where decisions about compilation are made. For a later compiler to add the *Danse Macabre* to the *Series* merely takes this participation one step further. Like most of the *Series* and the *Regiment*, Lydgate's poem is written in decasyllabic lines (he uses eight-line stanzas, the same form as Hoccleve's envoy to the *Regiment*). The *Danse Macabre* is roughly the same length as the individual sections of the *Series*. In addition, its subject matter neatly complements the theme of *Lerne to Die*. The texts approach the same problems of death and salvation, but from different perspectives. *Lerne to Die* focuses on the private struggle by which a human soul must face up to the 'last things' through individual contrition and repentance. Lydgate's *Danse Macabre* imagines a public arena, in which Death challenges representatives of society with their sinful conduct. *Lerne to Die* is placed after the first *Gesta Romanorum* tale, *Jereslaus' Wife*, while in these manuscripts, the *Danse Macabre* follows *Jonathas*. This brings a balance to the structure of the *Series*: each fictional narrative is mirrored by a didactic moral text.

---

[58] For example, Burrow 1984, Greetham 1989, Simpson 1991.

[59] The *Regiment* and *Series* are intertextual in ways apart from the shared backdrop of Hoccleve's career. For example, the *Series* contains references to Hoccleve's *Letter of Cupid*, as well as discussing its own progress towards completion, while the *Regiment*, as well as adapting its Latin authorities, signals Hoccleve's relationship to Chaucer and Gower through its eulogy of their influence and writings.

[60] So, for example, in the Coventry manuscript, Hoccleve's *Series* ends on fol. 70r. Below it, the start of Lydgate's *Danse Macabre* has its usual rubric 'Verba translatoris', but there is no note of the change of authorship. After the *Danse Macabre* finishes (towards the end of fol. 74v), some short poems by Chaucer are introduced by a note (fol. 75r) identifying his authorship.

Indeed, Lydgate's monitory poem could be said to provide an ending for the *Series* more in accordance with Hoccleve's stated wishes. After the sombre *Lerne to Die*, Hoccleve's alter ego Thomas wants to stop; it is his friend that persuades him to add another tale:

> This booke thus to han endid had y thoght,
> But my freend made me change my cast;
> Cleene out of that purpos hath he me broght. (*Minor Poems*, XXIV, 1–3)

The concerns of human frailty and the mutability of fortune that the *Series* and the *Danse Macabre* raise in these manuscripts are mirrored in the *Regiment*, too.[61] Lydgate warns of the power of death to disrupt human society:

> Dethe spareth not low ne hye degre,
> Popes, kynges ne worthi Emperowrs;
> When thei schyne moste in felicite
> He can abate the fresshness of her flowres. (*Danse Macabre*, 9–12)

Hoccleve, meanwhile, describes his own anxious thoughts:

> Bysily in my minde I gan revolve
> The welthe unseur of every creature [...]
> My tremlyng herte so greet gastnesse hadde
> That my spirites were of my lyf sadde. (*Regiment*, 15–16, 20–1)

Hoccleve's alter ego might almost be reacting to Lydgate's poem in his personal despair about the instability of worldly fortune. But he too reflects on figures of 'hye degre' who have suffered misfortune:

> Me fil to mynde how that nat longe agoo
> Fortunes strook doun thrast estat rial
> Into mescheef; and I took heede also
> Of many anothir lord that hadde a fal. (*Regiment*, 22–5)

It is not simply fortuitous that political and moral lessons can be carried across from one text to another: these poems invite intertextual responses because of the way they are framed by their authors. Lydgate's

---

[61] Boyd 1990, 77–122 and 1993 proposes that the idea of 'governance' links the poems found in Yale Beinecke MS 493, but his arguments stem mainly from assumptions about Hoccleve's and Lydgate's ideologies, rather than the style and content of the poems themselves.

Danse Macabre is, he says, inspired by a famous mural that he had seen in Paris:[62]

> Considereth this, ye folkes that ben wyse,
> And hit enprenteth in yowre memorialle,
> Like the exawmple whiche that at Parise
> I fownde depicte ones on a walle. (*Danse Macabre*, 17–20)

Lydgate also specifies that his poem is translated from French. While he claims a painted and written inspiration for the text, however, the body of the poem is presented as a spoken event. The poem is laid out in the manuscripts like speeches in a play, with the characters' names in the margin beside their words. Similar interplay between textual and spoken forms occurs in Hoccleve's *Series*. In the *Complaint*, for example, Thomas recalls reading about the consolation of a man by Reason 'in a boke' (310), while in *Lerne to Die*, a book containing a didactic dialogue provides the basis for fuller self-knowledge and spiritual preparation.[63] These imagined bookish conversations are paralleled and contrasted with Thomas's 'real' dialogue with his friend, while in the *Regiment*, the textual, translated, authoritative *Regiment* proper is also juxtaposed with the apparently spontaneous conversation that Hoccleve has with the Old Man. Placed together in this way, the *Regiment*, *Series* and *Danse Macabre* strengthen one another's engagement with monitory and religious themes, textual and verbal boundaries, and the experience of the poet.[64]

---

[62] The painting of the Dance of Death was at Holy Innocents in Paris. There was also a well-known version painted on a cloister wall at St Paul's Cathedral in London, with which Lydgate's verses were associated. In his *Survey of London*, John Stow says that 'the metres or poesie of this daunce, were translated out of French into English, by John Lidgate, the Monke of Bery [...] at the speciall request and dispence of Jankin Carpenter' (quoted in *Danse Macabre*, ed. Warren, xxii–xxiii). John Carpenter, Town Clerk of London 1417–38, was the recipient of one of Hoccleve's begging poems (*Minor Poems*, XVI). For Carpenter's activities, especially his literary interests and ownership of books, see Brewer 1856, MacCracken 1911 and Scase 1992.

[63] The book of consolation in the *Complaint* has been identified as a short version of Isidore's *Synonyma*; see Rigg 1970 and, further, Burrow 1998.

[64] I am grateful to Lee Patterson for allowing me to read an essay on Yale Beinecke MS 493 and the Bodley Group in advance of publication. Patterson speculates that John Carpenter himself promoted the copying of this group of manuscripts, and that the Lydgate poem is a protective decoy, allowing the poetry of the now-disregarded Hoccleve to be disseminated under the guise of the massively authoritative Lydgate. His article raises some fascinating questions over Hoccleve's reputation, audience and relationship to Carpenter, though I read these manuscripts rather differently.

IV. PRODUCTION AND OWNERSHIP

The *Regiment*'s manuscripts can suggest much about the circumstances of production and audience of the poem in the century or so after it was written, and often a book that has undergone alteration reveals more than a pristine volume does. Of the five *Regiment–Series–Danse Macabre* manuscripts discussed above, four appear to have been produced as complete entities. The exception is Coventry City Record Office MS Acc. 325/1, which shows signs of having been altered and rearranged. A.I. Doyle notes that there has been some disturbance at the beginning of the book, with folios 1–4 being substituted (but still written by the same scribe); he calls the picture of a robed figure on folio 1r 'another device of adaptation'.[65] After the metrical version of *Mandeville's Travels*, folios 77v–95v, there are two blank leaves before a different scribe starts *The Siege of Jerusalem* on a new quire with different signatures (folios 98r–129v). The third section (folio 137r onwards) contains Lydgate's *Siege of Thebes*. The Coventry manuscript is laid out in double columns, and its textual exemplars are of high quality, especially in the short poems by Chaucer that follow Lydgate's *Danse Macabre*.[66] It may have been put together on order for a wealthy patron, using booklets that had already been produced, or was perhaps rearranged after being acquired. The fact that the first pages of the *Regiment* are rewritten by the same hand as the rest of the poem suggests either that the owner could call on the scribe to rearrange the beginning of the manuscript, or that the initial adaptation took place before the manuscript was sold or passed on by its compilers.

Coventry MS Acc. 325/1 is one of several *Regiment* manuscripts displaying signs of compilation using booklets.[67] The production of separately written groups of quires was common in the fifteenth century; some circulated as unbound texts, others were used as units in compiling larger manuscripts, either as a convenient way of copying lengthy works, or as a form of anthologizing.[68] Indeed, compilation from different sources using separate booklets as exemplars is described in (and also exemplified by) Hoccleve's *Series*. Hoccleve goes to fetch his newly written tale of *Jereslaus' Wife* for his friend: 'my tale anoon y fette and he it nam / In-to his hand' (*Minor Poems*, XXII; Prologue to the Moralization of *Jereslaus' Wife*, 5–6). Later, the friend

---

[65] Doyle and Pace 1968, 24. The manuscript's quire signatures suggest that at some time there were a substantial number of leaves before the *Regiment*.

[66] Ibid., 25–6 and 33–4.

[67] For the definition and limits of the term, see Robinson 1980 and Hanna 1986.

[68] See Boffey and Thompson 1989, especially 290. Though not strictly speaking in booklets, Gower's *Confessio amantis* in Cambridge, Trinity College MS R. 3. 2 was copied in separate locations by several London scribes including Hoccleve; see above, p. 157, and Doyle and Parkes 1978.

The Afterlife of the Poem

tells Hoccleve that he has missed out the story's moralization; he goes home and collects his own copy so that Hoccleve can add it to the tale. The friend subsequently fetches a copy of *Jonathas* in the same way.

Scribes and compilers of several *Regiment* manuscripts shared Hoccleve's willingness to construct or add to their books in this fashion. For example, BL MS Arundel 59 begins with the *Regiment* on folios 1r–89v. Folios 90–1 are blank. The same scribe starts Lydgate and Burgh's *Secrees* on a new quire, with different preparation of the written space, different marks at stanza beginnings, and more elaborate initials. This could be explained by using another rubricator, or different parchment stock, but could also suggest that the two parts were written independently and later joined together for a buyer. This hand (the 'Hammond scribe') has been identified in fifteen manuscripts dating from around the reign of Edward IV, including the *Regiment* in BL MS Harley 372.[69] There, only lines 3309 onwards of the *Regiment* survive, but it is clear that the copy was at one time more complete. The *Regiment* has been joined to an independent section containing works by Chaucer, Lydgate and Roos, and Richard Firth Green suggests that 'some time in their history the two sections must have circulated as independent booklets'.[70] As Green notes, the fact that a large number of this scribe's manuscripts survive, many of them passing through the hands of John Stow, argues strongly for a London provenance and some form of commercial production. The probable commercial background of the Hammond scribe strengthens the chance that the two texts of Arundel 59 were written separately, and bound together at the behest of the manuscript's buyer.

The Hammond scribe is one of several whose activities are now coming to light, and who produced copies of the *Regiment* along with other vernacular texts. For example, the scribe of Bodleian MS Selden supra 53 was identified by Doyle as the hand of MS Digby 230 (also in the Bodleian), a manuscript containing Lydgate's *Siege of Thebes* and *Troy Book*, along with the anonymous *Siege of Jerusalem*.[71] This hand, the 'Selden scribe', was also at work in at least four other manuscripts identified by Linne Mooney, including another copy of the *Regiment*, Cambridge, Queens' College MS 12, and a further copy of Lydgate's *Troy Book*. The work of this scribe points to a professional, London-based workshop, though he was active well before the Hammond scribe.[72] Another *Regiment* manuscript whose scribe has been identified

---

[69] See Hammond 1929–30, Doyle 1959, Green 1978, 39–41, Mooney 1995–6 and Mooney 2000.
[70] Green 1978, 41.
[71] Doyle and Pace 1968, 25.
[72] I am grateful to Professor Mooney for sharing her expert knowledge of this and other fifteenth-century scribes. The additional manuscripts in which the Selden scribe has been found are: Bristol, Public Library MS 8 (Lydgate, *Troy Book*);

at work elsewhere is Bodleian MS Dugdale 45. The hand that wrote this copy was also responsible for a *Canterbury Tales* manuscript in Oxford: New College MS 314.[73]

In the Hammond scribe's manuscript BL MS Arundel 59, the use of booklets can suggest something about the circumstances of production. Many other manuscripts show some differences between texts, but the evidence is often too slight to form any conclusions about separate or speculative copying. For example, in BL MS Harley 4826 the *Regiment* begins on a new quire with its own set of quire signatures, but the layout of the manuscript remains the same, and the two scribes who work in the rest of the manuscript are used in the *Regiment*, too. Scribe A appears to have had two copying stints (folios 4–81 and 100–4), while Scribe B wrote a short section in the middle (folios 84–100 – the start of the *Regiment*). In Cambridge, Trinity College MS R. 3. 22, the *Regiment* starts on a new quire (quire 15). Quire 14 contains six leaves, rather than the eight used for quires 1–13, and its last leaf (folio 110) is blank, after the end of Lydgate's *Life of Our Lady*.[74] At the bottom of folio 110v is a scribbled note apparently about the illumination of the manuscript. The *Regiment* has different sets of quire signatures from those in the first part of the manuscript, though due to cropping they are only partially visible. These features suggest that some distinction between the texts was intended, but since the scribe and basic layout of the texts is the same, it is difficult to make a substantial case for the production of the manuscript as two completely separate booklets. Another manuscript with different sets of signatures is Bodleian MS Digby 185. Here there is one set for the prose *Brut* at the beginning, another for the Hoccleve poems (parts of the *Series*, and the *Regiment*), and a third for the romance *King Ponthus*, which concludes the manuscript. Blank pages are left on folios 79v and 165v at the end of sections. A leaf has also been excised after folio 79, and two leaves after folio 165, probably to keep the individual parts within separate blocks of quires. However, the text hand and style of illustration (including family coats of arms) is the same throughout; Digby 185 was probably conceived as a collection rather than pieced together from previously copied booklets.

In the case of Bodleian MS Rawlinson poet. 168, a diaspora has taken place. This copy of the *Regiment* was once connected to at least six other sections (of which it was the fourth) that now form separate books.[75] The others contained Burgh's *Cato* and Lydgate's *Dietary*, prose

---

Manchester, John Rylands Library MS Eng. 98 (Nicholas Love, *Mirror*); and Bodleian MS Rawlinson C. 446 (Lydgate, *Troy Book*). My own examination of the Queens' and Selden manuscripts would support Mooney's identification.

[73] See Partridge 1997.
[74] R. 3. 22 is described by Seymour (1974, 284–5), but he fails to mention quire 14 at all in his collation.
[75] See Smith 1966.

versions of the *Siege of Thebes* and *Siege of Troy*, along with extracts from the *Confessio*, the romance *Gawain and Galeron*, Mandeville's *Travels*, Dame Juliana Berners's *Book of Hunting* and, finally, a treatise for the instruction of parishioners.[76] The complete book would have formed a weighty source of stories, classical and moral teaching, and practical advice, amongst which the *Regiment* could fulfil both narrative and didactic functions.

Evidence about milieux of production and scribal practice can extend our knowledge of the different types of readers who owned *The Regiment of Princes* in the fifteenth century. The two earliest extant copies – BL MSS Arundel 38 and Harley 4866 – were undoubtedly made for presentation to Hoccleve's patrons. The arms in Arundel 38 are those of John Mowbray, Duke of Norfolk, and a later name written on folio 99r suggests that the manuscript was again in the Mowbray family during the fifteenth century.[77] Seymour speculates that Harley 4866 was presented to John, Duke of Bedford, or Edward, Duke of York, but the first and last folios of the manuscript, which might have given clues as to its initial ownership, are missing.[78] Hoccleve's dedicatory verses to Bedford accompany the *Regiment* in BL MS Royal 17 D. xviii and Bodleian MS Dugdale 45.

A further connection with John, Duke of Bedford, may perhaps be found in the miniatures that decorate in such profusion the Bedford Psalter-Hours (BL MS Add. 42131), a manuscript written for the Duke in the 1410s. The miniatures in this book are closely related to pictures in the Gower, Chaucer and Hoccleve manuscripts whose artistic affiliations have been described above; in addition, Sylvia Wright has recently identified representations of the three poets in the Bedford manuscript. She discusses ten miniatures of Gower, three of Chaucer (two, she argues, by the artist of the Harley 4866 portrait) and three which, she claims, show Hoccleve.[79] If Wright is correct, these pictures provide an illuminating insight into the associations that the three poets' works generated. For example, she argues persuasively that the Gower pictures reflect political currents in his poetry and his status as a prophetic, admonitory voice. The texts that the Chaucer miniatures accompany are less clearly related to his poetry, but the pictures

---

[76] Now respectively Bodleian MSS Rawlinson poet. 35; Rawlinson D. 82; Douce 324; Rawlinson D. 99; Rawlinson poet. 143; Rawlinson D. 913, fols 10–21. (A fragment of another *Regiment* manuscript is bound in this last volume, fol. 63; it comes from the same copy as fragment 90 in BL MS Harley 5977; see Green 1978, 37–8.)

[77] See Harris 1984.

[78] An envoy to Edward of York is included by Hoccleve in San Marino, Huntington MS HM 111, but probably does not refer to the *Regiment*; see Burrow 1994, 23.

[79] Wright 1992. She reproduces the Gower and Chaucer portraits, 198, 200; one of the portraits that she identifies as Hoccleve (fol. 118r) is reproduced in Wright 1997, 269. On Bedford's collection of manuscripts, see Stratford 1987.

nevertheless correspond to the Ellesmere–Harley image of the poet. The identification of Hoccleve is less certain, since Wright bases her claim on his appearance in the Arundel presentation scene, something which has itself been questioned by Kathleen Scott's description.[80] The pictures do show a writer in a gown and tonsure close to psalm texts that suggest the operation of royal counsel; if accepted as representations of Hoccleve, they may (as Wright suggests) indicate his status as a commentator on royal governance soon after the *Regiment* was written.

The dedicatees of the *Regiment*'s envoys, Prince Henry and John, Duke of Bedford, may be added to those noble patrons mentioned elsewhere in Hoccleve's poetry whom he attempted to cultivate throughout his career, such as Joan FitzAlan, Countess of Hereford, Edward, Duke of York, Humphrey, Duke of Gloucester, and Joan Beaufort, Countess of Westmorland. Patrons such as these were undoubtedly recipients of some early copies of the *Regiment*.[81] Hoccleve's audience, however, was not confined to these powerful court circles; while books such as BL MSS Arundel 38 and Harley 4866 are unusually well made and beautifully decorated, other manuscripts of the *Regiment* have been adapted no less appropriately to the requirements of religious, gentry or professional owners. Bodleian MS Digby 185, for example, was written for the family of Sir William Hopton of Swillington in Yorkshire (d. 1484). As mentioned above, the manuscript contains the prose *Brut*, Hoccleve's *Regiment*, *Tale of Jereslaus' Wife* and *Jonathas*, and the anonymous romance *King Ponthus*, while family arms adorn five *litterae notabiliores*.[82] This judicious mixture of historical, regiminal and narrative matter is enlivened by the elaborate armorial

---

[80] Scott 1996, II, 158. The 'Hoccleve' picture on fol. 118r is the most like the Arundel portrait, though the figure in the Bedford Psalter-Hours has a tonsure. In the picture on fol. 199r, the figure looks older; his face is slightly upturned and he too wears a high-necked robe. On fol. 206r the figure is bald except for a ring of hair round the side of his head, with a slightly longer face.

[81] For Henry V's books, see Krochalis 1988–9, and for Hoccleve's patrons, Pryor 1968, 55–70. More general comments on patronage can be found in Green 1980 and Lucas 1997, 249–80. Hoccleve also addressed poems to influential but non-aristocratic figures such as John Carpenter (*Minor Poems*, XVI; see above, p. 167, note 62) and the prominent London stationer Thomas Marleburgh (*Minor Poems*, part 2, VI; for Marleburgh's activities see Christianson 1989).

[82] Fols 1r, 80r, 104r, 157v, 166r. Of these, two are part of the *Regiment* section of the manuscript: fol. 80r is the start of the *Regiment*, and fol. 104r is above line 2017. Pächt and Alexander (1966–73, III, plate 194) reproduce part of fol. 80r. Friedman has assessed northern English books, showing that there is more evidence for book use and ownership than has previously been thought (Friedman 1989, 1995). However, he does not discuss MS Digby 185 or the Hoptons. Sir William Hopton himself was a substantial figure, treasurer of the household to Richard III in 1483; see Pächt and Alexander 1966–73, III, 86, and Sutton and Visser-Fuchs 1997, 129–30. *King Ponthus* is edited from MS Digby 185 in Mather 1897.

decorations and numerous small pictures that are designed to illustrate the manuscript's catchwords.[83] Both Seymour and Marzec suggest that the *Regiment* in Digby 185 was copied from BL MS Royal 17 D. vi.[84] If the tales from the *Series* were also copied from the Royal manuscript, the compiler made a conscious decision to omit from this family anthology the edifying but dark *Lerne to Die*, extracting the translated narratives from the *Series* without their extratextual commentary, and giving a rather different colour to the stories when compared to the Bodley Group manuscripts that I discussed earlier.

Another compilation owned and perhaps written outside London is BL MS Harley 7333 (c. 1450–60), which Manly and Rickert identify with St Mary de Pré, a house of Augustinian canons in Leicester.[85] The manuscript is a large, double-column collection, mainly of poetry, including *The Canterbury Tales*, extracts from the *Confessio amantis*, some religious and political works by Lydgate, and the *Gesta Romanorum* in prose. It appears to have been produced in seven separable units. The manuscript partly derives from a collection made by John Shirley (d. 1456), and the text of the *Regiment* ends at line 2016, thus excluding the *Regiment* proper (and suggesting that the *Regiment* was read at least in some quarters primarily for its autobiographical or Boethian content). The collection in Harley 7333 suggests a developed taste in secular literature amongst at least some of the Leicester canons, though they baulked at the 'naked text' of *The Canterbury Tales*, editing it to remove objectionable material.[86]

These compilations and their initial owners can be localized with some certainty; many other *Regiment* manuscripts contain the names of early readers about whom less is known, but they included priests such as the Henry Beighton 'capellan[us]' in BL MS Royal 17 D. xix and, in one case, a surgeon.[87] A note records that BL MS Royal 17 C. xiv was the property of 'Nicholai Saunder et amicorum' in the early sixteenth

---

[83] The punning catchword illustrations include fol. 87v ('Gold Sylver' enclosed in gold and silver coins), fol. 119v ('it is to leve' inside a leaf) and fol. 135v ('Senec sayth' in a scroll issuing from the mouth of a bearded philosopher).

[84] Seymour 1974, 277 and Marzec's stemma in Greetham 1987, 66–7. Seymour suggests (1974, 273) that the Royal manuscript itself may have been taken to the north of England in the fifteenth century.

[85] Manly and Rickert 1940, I, 207–18; for the library at Leicester, see Webber 1997 and *Libraries of the Augustinian Canons*, ed. Webber and Watson, 104–400.

[86] For the link with Shirley, whose notes and explicits are reproduced at various points in the manuscript, and for alterations to *The Canterbury Tales*, see Manly and Rickert 1940, I, 212–13 and Lerer 1993, 123–6. The changes include ending *The Pardoner's Tale* after VI. 918 (cutting out the Pardoner's offer to sell relics to the pilgrims and the Host's testy reply) and the complete omission of *The Shipman's Tale*.

[87] 'surgon correll' (or 'torrell' ?) in BL MS Harley 116; see Seymour 1974, 294–5.

century,[88] and it is certain that other manuscripts were passed between friends or jointly owned in this way: already mentioned above is Bodleian MS Digby 185, written for the Hopton family, and BL MS Royal 17 D. xviii contains the (fifteenth-century) names of various members of the Wikes family. Likewise, Doyle characterizes BL MS Royal 17 D. vi as 'a sort of *album amicorum* for members of a number of noble and gentle families in the later fifteenth century'.[89]

One gentry family with literary interests who probably owned a copy of Hoccleve's poem were the Drurys of Suffolk. BL MS Harley 4826 contains an epitaph on Sir William Drury (d. 1579). A note in the Ellesmere manuscript of *The Canterbury Tales* associates that manuscript with Sir Robert Drury (1455–1536), while in 1493 Robert's brother William was left 'ii. Inglyshe bocks called Bochas of Lydgats makyng' (i.e. *The Fall of Princes*) in the will of their father, Roger. The inclusion in Harley 4826 of Lydgate's *Lives of St Edmund and St Fremund* and Lydgate and Burgh's *Secrees* points to a Bury St Edmunds provenance, and the manuscript has been linked to several other literary books read or owned by the Drurys and their associates, including Lydgate's *Siege of Thebes* in BL MS Arundel 119.[90]

I have already remarked on the literary interests of Hoccleve's associates and colleagues in Westminster. A significant number of *Regiment* manuscripts are themselves connected with career administrators and writers.[91] BL MS Sloane 1212 includes the name 'Lucas', probably Sir Thomas Lucas, who was secretary to Jasper Tudor, Duke of Bedford (d. 1495).[92] Huntington MS EL 26. A. 13 belonged to John Shirley (1366–1456), whose literary activities were combined with service in the retinue of Richard Beauchamp, Earl of Warwick (1382–1439).[93] It is also

---

[88] Seymour (1974, 272) suggests that this Saunder was father of Sir Nicholas Saunder, MP for Penryn in 1588.

[89] Doyle 1983, 176. The manuscript includes the arms (after 1438) of Joan Nevill, Countess of Salisbury (d. 1462) and her husband, William FitzAlan, Earl of Arundel (d. 1487). Other family names include Courtenay, Berkeley, Duddeley and Roos; see Seymour 1974, 272–3.

[90] For the Drurys and their connections with De Vere and Bury manuscripts, see Hanna and Edwards 1996. Roger Drury's will is quoted in Seymour 1974, 268. As noted above (p. 157, note 23), BL MS Arundel 119 imitates the *ordinatio* of the Ellesmere manuscript. Arundel 119's scribe also wrote Cambridge, Pembroke College MS 307 (*Confessio amantis*; its *ordinatio* is also reminiscent of Ellesmere's), Tokyo, Takamiya MS 54 (*South English Legendary*) and Oslo and London, Schøyen Collection MS 615 (Walton, *Boethius*); see Hanna and Edwards 1996, 17–18.

[91] This mirrors the readership of the Latin *De regimine principum*. See Briggs 1999, 66–70 for ways in which that text came into the hands of non-noble readers in the fifteenth and sixteenth centuries.

[92] Seymour 1974, 274.

[93] On Shirley's career and literary interests as scribe, compiler and translator of regiminal texts, see Doyle 1961, Edwards 1997b and Connolly 1998.

signed by Avery Corneburgh, a Yeoman of the Chamber to Edward IV; Corneburgh married Shirley's sister-in-law, Beatrice. Another name in the manuscript, 'necolas gaynsford' probably refers to an Usher to the Chamber of Edward IV.[94] The name of Sir John Allyn appears in BL MS Royal 17 D. xix, probably the Allyn who was Lord Mayor of London in 1525 and 1535. This was the period when Nicholas Brigham (d. 1558) was building his career in London. A lawyer and energetic writer and antiquary, he became a Teller of the Exchequer in 1545, advancing to be First Teller in 1555. He must also have owned Hoccleve manuscripts, since John Bale cites him as a source for his knowledge of Hoccleve's life and works.[95]

As a further example of the milieux in which the *Regiment* circulated, we could take BL MS Arundel 59, a copy of the *Regiment* written by the Hammond scribe, which was bought in 1525 by Thomas Wall, who held the post of Windsor Herald, and was also a Garter King of Arms, 1534–6.[96] The other manuscripts written by this scribe include vernacular literature, law and science; their ownership points to a network of readers and interests in the professional and knightly classes of the late fifteenth and early sixteenth centuries.[97] Indeed, one recent addition to the Hammond scribe canon is BL MS Add. 29901, a collection of documents on state ceremonial and heraldry which, Linne Mooney suggests, may have been produced for a Garter King of Arms, Earl Marshall or Constable in the late fifteenth century.[98] The scribe's involvement in such texts, and Thomas Wall's later ownership of Arundel 59, underlines how the *Regiment* could have been of special interest to those with a professional or personal concern in heraldry, the duties of a king, political theory, administration, the workings of royal bureaucracy and public spectacle.

A few other sources, such as references to the *Regiment* in booklists and wills, provide evidence of Hoccleve's readership in the fifteenth century. In the will of Robert Norwich, in 1443, 'one book called Hocclef' is mentioned. It was bequeathed to Nicholas Frenge, a priest.

---

[94] Dutscke 1989, I, 38–9.

[95] Bale, *Index*, 447–8. Brigham was a crucial source for Bale about many authors. He clearly had a large manuscript collection, but only a few of these can now be identified; see Bale, *Index*, xx, and for Brigham's career, Alsop 1981. Apart from his antiquarian interests, Brigham's position in the Exchequer and possible Catholic allegiances (Alsop 1981, 63) would have added to the attraction of Hoccleve's poetry for him. Bale names two other sources of information on Hoccleve in the *Index*: 'domin[us] de Russell' (Francis Russell, Second Earl of Bedford, d. 1585) and 'Iohann[es] bibliopol[a]', who remains unidentified.

[96] Wall also owned a copy of the *Libelle of English Policy*; see Seymour 1974, 265, and for the *Libelle*'s background in mercantile London, Meale 1995.

[97] See Mooney 1995–6 and 2000.

[98] Mooney 2000, 116–19.

Seymour notes references to 'de regimine principum' in an inventory of goods confiscated from Sir Thomas Charlton in 1461, and in another made by John Goodyere of Monken Hadley in 1504.[99] These references, however, like the 'liber de regimine dominorum' left in John Carpenter's will, may be to other works in the genre.[100] A more secure reference to the *Regiment* is found in Bodleian MS Fairfax 10, whose front flyleaf contains a booklist from the late fifteenth century. The list includes 'Legenda sanctorum', 'Vita Christi', 'Boicius de consolacione philosophie', 'The boke of good maners', 'Egidius de regimine principis et al', 'Medecinus', 'The talys of Caunterbury', 'The Chesse', 'De regimine sanitatis diuersi tractatus' and 'De multis diuersis liber rubeus'. Bracketed together are 'Speculum vite Christi; Incendium amoris; Hocklyf de regimine; Vita sancti Jeronimi episcopi; Expositio propheciarum Merlini'.[101] In Cambridge, Pembroke College MS 227 (an astrological compilation) a parchment wrapper survives that lists three of the works in the same order: 'Speculum vite Christi', 'Incendium amoris' and 'Hoccleve de regimine principum'.[102] Pembroke 227 was probably given to the college by a cleric called Woodcock, whose name appears on the recto of the wrapper. On his death in 1488 he left to Pembroke College several books resembling those on the list in Fairfax 10, including 'a boke called *de vita Christi* and my rede boke of astronomy' and also a 'bok of physyk'.[103]

Pembroke 227 belonged previously to Roger Marchall, Fellow of Peterhouse from 1437/8 and physician to Edward IV. The manuscript contains a contents list in Marchall's hand.[104] Does the list in Bodleian MS Fairfax 10 also relate to books owned by Marchall? Fairfax 10 contains Latin notes on the endleaves relating to the Broughton family of Toddington, Bedfordshire, the town where Roger Marchall was born

---

[99] Seymour 1974, 257. Seymour quotes the Norwich bequest as 'a book called Hocclef'; I have followed the wording in Cavanaugh 1980, 625. Other books left by Norwich include a versified work on the kings of England, statutes, meditations of St Bernard and St Anselm and a book of the Duke of York's household.

[100] For Carpenter's bequest see Brewer 1856, 123 and Seymour 1974, 256.

[101] The list is edited in Dean 1939, 84–5; see also Doyle and Pace 1968, 25 and note 26. Doyle (24–5) suggests that the text called 'Incendium amoris' may be Hoccleve's *Complaint*, since this work is introduced by the words 'incipit prologus de Incendio Amoris' in Coventry MS Acc. 325/1, fol. 40r.

[102] See Doyle and Pace 1968, 25, note 26 and James 1905, 206.

[103] See Emden 1963, 644. Compare with this bequest the 'Vita Christi', 'De multis diuersis liber rubeus' and 'De regimine sanitatis diuersi tractatus' in the Fairfax list.

[104] Doyle mistakenly calls Marchall a Fellow of Pembroke (Doyle and Pace 1968, 25, note 26). See Voigts 1995, who identifies over forty manuscripts that show signs of Marchall's ownership, and reveals much about his activities in medicine, astrology and money-lending.

and where one of his brothers was living at the time of Marchall's death in 1477.[105] However, Linda Ehrsam Voigts has shown that Marchall displays little interest in works other than medical or astrological treatises, and owned virtually no texts in the vernacular.[106] Thus while the Fairfax booklist has a tantalizing connection with Roger Marchall, it is more likely that William Woodcock owned the books listed on the Pembroke wrapper (including the *Regiment*), and that he acquired them from the Broughtons.[107] We know that John Broughton of Toddington owned a Latin copy of Aegidius's *De regimine principum*, now BL MS Royal 6 B. v, and so it would not be surprising if some of the other books mentioned on the list also came from his family.[108]

Whoever owned the books listed in Fairfax 10, their collection provides a valuable context for Hoccleve's *Regiment* in the reading public of the fifteenth century. Here are two of his major sources (Aegidius and *De ludo scaccorum*), the manuals of deportment and health so vital in maintaining the physical bodies of the social and political elite, religious and legal tracts and two of Hoccleve's most important authorities – Boethius and Chaucer. This collection projects onto a larger scale the collections of regiminal texts that are found in manuscript compilations of the fifteenth century. Its probable owner, William Woodcock, was a member of the clerical and professional classes, while his associate Roger Marchall was charged with caring for the physical body of King Edward IV.

The evidence of manuscript ownership confirms that the *Regiment* enjoyed a wide range of readers, not only amongst the nobility, but also amongst the class of clerics and bureaucrats to which Hoccleve himself belonged. These politically aware and highly literate readers, many of whom held positions in and around the royal household, represent a major audience for vernacular regiminal texts in the late medieval and early Tudor period. Just as Chaucer and Langland were keenly read by an identifiable group of administrators in Westminster and London, so too Hoccleve's work was disseminated along similar channels in the fifteenth and early sixteenth centuries. The existence of this wider readership shifts the focus of the poem in a significant way, towards individual self-fashioning and moral education, rather than towards the exercise of royal authority or image-making.

---

[105] See Doyle and Pace 1968, 25, note 26 and Voigts 1995, 253–8.
[106] Voigts 1995, 261 and 263–4.
[107] Doyle notes that 'John Broughton, who founded the Toddington hospital in 1433, lived long enough to have owned all the listed books' (Doyle and Pace 1968, 25, note 26).
[108] Briggs 1999, 67. Doyle (Doyle and Pace 1968, 25, note 26) notes references to John Broughton's activities in 1433, 1451 and 1462. The last of these, his returning to Bury St Edmunds Abbey a register (now CUL MS Ff. ii. 29) that he bought from a London stationer, gives further evidence of his interest in books.

V. THE PROBLEM OF GENRE IN THE *REGIMENT*'S 'PROLOGUE'

So far, I have discussed the production, illustration, compilation and ownership of *Regiment* manuscripts. In this section I consider the ways in which early editors and readers glossed and interpreted the first part of the *Regiment*, and ask what other evidence about the interpretative priorities and interests of readers may be found in the extant manuscripts. In this case, valuable information about genre and early reactions to the poem can be gained from close attention to the manuscripts – information that may reorientate our own response to the poem.

The *Regiment* proper has a consistent and clearly recognizable set of section divisions which are reproduced in most of the manuscripts and signposted within the text. So, for example, the section marked 'De pietate' in many manuscripts also begins 'Pitee nat elles is to undirstonde' (2997). In contrast, the first part of the poem (called the 'Prologue' by most critics) has no such straightforward divisions, even though it takes up over a third of the work. This part of the poem is also stylistically distinct from the *Regiment* proper, although the two are transmitted together in most manuscripts. These differences raise the question of how the first 2016 lines of the *Regiment* were approached by their early audience, and what generic or stylistic expectations fifteenth-century readers brought to Hoccleve's poem.

First, is the opening of the poem a 'prologue'? A running header in BL MS Add. 18632 does call it 'Prologus', but no other manuscripts use that word to refer to the first 2016 lines of the poem. However, 'prologus' or 'prohemium' is used in numerous copies to describe the next 140 lines (2017–156). For example, Bodleian MS Dugdale 45, folio 37r has a scribal heading above line 2017 'Sequitur prologus de Regimine Principum', and on folio 39r after line 2156 notes 'Explicit prologus'. BL MS Arundel 59, folio 36r, has 'Explicit Prohemium' after line 2156.[109] It makes good sense to call this passage a prologue; as I have already discussed, this is the formal beginning of 'the regiment of princes', signalled by Hoccleve's textual cues and the presentation picture. The passage certainly contains elements of the academic prologue as adapted by vernacular writers.[110] The marking out of this passage as a prologue divides the *Regiment* proper into thirteen roughly equal sections, not including the envoy. Doing this also, however, deprives

---

[109] Similar headings and explicits appear in, for example, BL MSS Arundel 38, fol. 39v; Harley 116, fol. 36r; Royal 17 D. xviii, fol. 40r; Sloane 1212, fol. 38r, Oxford, Bodleian MS Douce 158, fol. 37r ('hic incipit prologus de principum regimine': the foliation in Douce is wrong here; this folio is marked 36) and Chicago, Newberry Library MS f 33.7, fol. 30r.

[110] For the use made of these conventions by Chaucer, Gower and others, see Minnis 1981 and Minnis 1984, 160–210.

the opening of the poem of its commonly used title.[111] Frederick J. Furnivall called this part of the *Regiment* Hoccleve's 'preliminary talk with his beggar',[112] which itself raises another question of naming and interpretation: who is the old man who engages an unwilling Hoccleve in conversation? This problem was also faced by editors and scribes of *Regiment* manuscripts.

If the 'Prologue' to the *Regiment of Princes* is lines 2017–156, how should lines 1–2016 be thought of? Do they belong to any identifiable genre? Hoccleve seems to present various generic possibilities that are questioned or negotiated in the rest of the poem. The opening of the *Regiment* sees the narrator lying in bed, unable to sleep for anxiety. He goes out to some fields and encounters a 'poore old hoor man' (122) who gives him advice. These features of the *Regiment*'s opening, in particular the time of the encounter (morning), its place, and Hoccleve's solitude and troubled psychological state all suggest the topoi of a dream-vision, a genre that could be used to frame narratives about love, religion and politics.[113] In Hoccleve's poem, the conventional spring- or summertime opening is disturbed in the very first stanza. Hoccleve's despair is brought on by

> Musynge upon the restlees bysynesse
> Which that this troubly world hath ay on honde,
> That othir thyng than fruyt of bittirnesse
> Ne yildith naght, as I can undirstonde. (1–4)

An expected reference to nature's fruitful abundance is undermined, preparing the reader for Hoccleve's own 'angwissh and pyne' (10).[114] The intemperate feeling here is strengthened by references to 'this stormy nyght' (113) and 'this worldes stormy wawes' (51). The *Regiment*'s beginning can be contrasted with a famous springtime opening that Hoccleve certainly knew, that of *The Canterbury Tales*. There Chaucer describes 'shoures soote' (I. 1) and 'tendre croppes' (I. 7); here Hoccleve has 'fruyt of bittirnesse'. The *Regiment*'s opening, then, initiates a troubling vision; as Hoccleve later admits to the Old Man: 'Thogh I nat slepte, yit my spirit mette / Ful angry dremes' (759–60).

---

[111] Disappointingly, Blyth's recent edition persists in calling the first part the 'prologue' despite the lack of manuscript support, on the grounds that it is 'traditional' (his note to line 2017).
[112] *Regiment*, ed. Furnivall, xi.
[113] See Spearing 1976, 1–6, and Davidoff 1983, 103–19.
[114] Larry Scanlon compares the 'moment of psychic disturbance' with which the *Regiment* begins, with the troubled opening of Chaucer's *The Book of the Duchess* (Scanlon 1990, 234).

Another expected feature of the dream-vision is an encounter with a guide or authority figure.[115] In the *Regiment*, Hoccleve again overturns the reader's expectations of the scene. Instead of falling asleep and meeting a guide, Hoccleve is woken from his daze by the insistent 'poore olde hoor man' (122): 'He stirte unto me and seide, "Sleepstow, man? / Awake!" and gan me shake wondir faste' (131–2). The poem itself is shaken out of sleep by the Old Man, whose rough clothes and colloquial manner mark him as a 'real' Londoner rather than a supernatural messenger. This shift away from the visionary authenticates the autobiography of Hoccleve's encounter with the Old Man, and focuses the reader's attention more securely on the pressing nature of Hoccleve's melancholia and financial problems, not circumscribing them by a generic, literary pattern.

While Hoccleve modifies the conventional dream-vision opening, his description of meeting the Old Man does have something in common with 'waking' visions such as those that initiate Boethius's *De consolatione Philosophiae* and Alan of Lille's *De planctu Naturae*.[116] In Boethius's work, the author's dramatic, even self-indulgent lament is interrupted by the straight-talking (if hardly down-to-earth) figure of Philosophia. Boethius's speechless astonishment at Philosophia's arrival is reminiscent of Hoccleve's mute reaction to the Old Man, but whereas Boethius is in awe of Philosophia, Hoccleve regards the Old Man as a nuisance: 'go thy way, talke to me no more' (139). The first marginal gloss that regularly occurs in *Regiment* manuscripts is written beside lines 54–6:

And how in bookes thus writen I fynde,
'The werste kynde of wrecchidnesse is
A man to han be weleful or this.'

Lines 55–6 are quoted from *De consolatione Philosophiae* II. pr. 4. Numerous manuscripts note the Latin *sententia* in the margin, as for example in BL MS Harley 4866, folio 1v: 'Boecius de consolatione philosophiae; maximum genus infortunii est, fuisse felicem etc.' This is by no means the only reference to Boethius in the first part of the *Regiment*: the discussion of the fickleness of fortune and the Old Man's advice to disregard worldly riches also echo positions articulated by Philosophia. In Cambridge, Queens' College MS 12, folio 1r, an eighteenth-century note adopts a Boethian model for its description of

---

[115] See, for example, *Mum and the Soothsegger* and, more problematically, *Piers Plowman*. Chaucer plays with the convention by having a scientifically minded eagle as his guide in *The House of Fame*.

[116] Compare, too, the opening of *Confessio amantis*, Book I, in which the melancholy Amans goes 'Unto the wode' (110).

Hoccleve's poem, 'This Poem is usually call'd "Consolatio sibi a sene oblata" ' [Consolation offered to him by an old man].

Some support for this note is given by Thomas Tanner's apparent use of the same words in referring to the *Regiment*.[117] These descriptions place the *Regiment* in a Boethian milieu, but they are too late in date to be relied upon as evidence for early interpretation of Hoccleve's poem. The *Regiment* is, though, copied alongside Walton's near-contemporary translation of *De consolatione Philosophiae* in Society of Antiquaries MS 134 and Rosenbach MS 1083/30, while Fitzwilliam MS McClean 185 was previously bound with the Walton (now kept separately as MS McClean 184). Additions to another *Regiment* manuscript, CUL MS Gg. vi. 17, highlight Hoccleve's debt to Boethius. Here, a fifteenth-century hand slightly later than that of the main scribe has added some marginal glosses, including a quotation from Boethius not usually found in the manuscripts. Next to line 246, which initiates the exemplum of a beggar who gains relief by speaking out, the hand writes 'si medicum expectas oportet vt vulnus detegas' (from *Consolatio* I. pr. 4), advice paraphrased by the Old Man two stanzas later. The same glossing hand marks some of the changes of speaker in Hoccleve's conversation with the Old Man. Hoccleve's speeches are marked 'Egenus', and the Old Man's are marked 'Sapiens'.[118] This reader, at any rate, was in no doubt about the authority of Hoccleve's interlocutor; rather than seeing the Old Man as a beggar (as the glosses in Furnivall's editon encourage readers to do), in Gg. vi. 17 it is Hoccleve who is indigent.

As well as philosophical – and specifically Boethian – elements, more general moral and religious questions are highlighted by annotators of the *Regiment*, such as the post-medieval hand who wrote the heading 'The vertuouse doctrine of Hoccleue vpon the Rewle of Princes' in CUL MS Gg. vi. 17 (folio 1r). The Old Man tells Hoccleve 'I every day heere at the Carmes messe' (2007; that is, at Whitefriars); in addition, his comments on the heretic John Badby, his frequent allusions to the Bible and moral works and his role as Hoccleve's advisor have suggested to some that he is a religious.[119] In BL MS Harley 4826, Hoccleve's conversation with the Old Man has the running header 'dialogus inter Occlyff et mendicum'. The word 'mendicus' originally simply meant 'poor', 'beggar', but by the fifteenth century was also the usual word for 'friar',[120] and included a 'regular' beggar or almsman.

---

[117] Tanner 1748, 557.

[118] The *DML* defines 'egenus' as needy, pauper, poor in spirit, deficient, lacking in substance, jejune. These definitions certainly chime with Hoccleve's imagined lack of substance in the *Regiment*; see above, pp. 143–6.

[119] See Hoccleve, *De Regimine Principum*, ed. Wright, xi, and Pearsall 1994, 407.

[120] For instance, in Chaucer's *The Summoner's Tale*, 'we mendynantz, we sely freres' (III. 1906).

The mention of the Carmelites in line 2007 might encourage a reader to identify the Old Man as a friar, but we cannot be certain which meaning of 'mendicus' the header in Harley 4826 intends. It does, however, point to the ambiguity of the Old Man's position – financially needy, but nevertheless in a position to help and encourage Hoccleve.[121]

Further affinities with moral and didactic dialogues are suggested in Bodleian MS Douce 158, which has a scribal explicit after line 2016, folio 36v: 'Explicit diologus inter patrem et filium.' Hoccleve calls the Old Man 'fader' on numerous occasions, and he in turn calls Hoccleve 'sone', so this designation is readily understandable. Another manuscript, CUL MS Hh. iv. 11, occasionally marks the speakers 'senex' and 'Iuuenis'.[122] These additions suggest links with the parent–child didactic texts that were popular throughout the fifteenth century, such as Peter Idley's *Instructions to his Son*,[123] and, indeed, several *Regiment* manuscripts situate the conversation within such didactic and textual boundaries by drawing attention to biblical allusions and moral commonplaces in the text.

One other manuscript note suggests links with a particular type of moral dialogue, perhaps even a particular poem. This is Cambridge, Corpus Christi College MS 496, copied probably in the 1440s by William Wilflete (d. 1470), a Fellow of Clare Hall (later Clare College), Cambridge. Wilflete writes occasional extra notes in the margins; on folio 12r beside lines 995–1001 he writes in a more formal hand 'Labores Scribentium' (a subject undoubtedly close to his heart, as he still had nearly fifty pages to go!). More significantly, where the Old Man begins to talk about his reckless youth (line 610), Wilflete has written 'Confessio'. Wilflete had quite probably read manuscripts of Gower's *Confessio amantis*, many of which have just such marginal 'confessio' or 'confessio amantis' glosses at appropriate moments in the text.[124] There is only one 'confessio' mark in the Corpus Christi manuscript of the *Regiment*, but it is nevertheless suggestive of the thematic and generic links between Gower's and Hoccleve's poems. *Confessio amantis* manuscripts regularly label the speeches of Genius ('Confessor') and Amans as part of the complex *ordinatio* that governs the production of

---

[121] Pearsall (1994, 407) raises the possibility that the picture at the start of the Coventry manuscript of the *Regiment* may represent a Carmelite friar.

[122] For example, fol. 7v, line 374, 'nunc Iuuenis loquitur'; fol. 8r, line 396, 'juuenis'; fol. 31v, lines 1772, 1773, 1775, 'Senex', 'juuenis', 'senex'.

[123] Idley's poem survives in seven manuscripts; see Idley, *Instructions*, 60–75.

[124] Some are printed in Gower, *English Works*, from Bodleian MS Fairfax 3 (for example at *Confessio* IV. 24 and IV. 270). They also appear in two first recension manuscripts in Cambridge, CUL MSS Dd. viii. 19 (for example, fols 82r and 84r) and Mm. ii. 21 (for example, fol. 48v).

Gower's poem.[125] Readers and 'editors' of the *Regiment* would have been thoroughly acquainted with the layout of *Confessio* manuscripts; as noted above, the two poems were frequently copied and read in the same milieux. Hoccleve himself wrote part of the text of Gower's poem in Cambridge, Trinity College MS R. 3. 2, and extracts from the *Confessio* appear in three *Regiment* manuscripts: BL MS Harley 7333, Society of Antiquaries MS 134 and (after reconstruction) Bodleian MS Rawlinson poet. 168. The 'Confessio' gloss in the Corpus Christi manuscript thus draws attention to the literary and bibliographical connections between Hoccleve and 'my maistir Gower' (*Regiment*, 1975). Wilflete's gloss, and the other annotations that I have considered, situate the *Regiment* in parallel traditions of religious, moral and philosophical texts, giving advice, preaching the virtues of fortitude and patience, contrasting the fortunes of youth and old age.

Underlying these traditions is the dialogue, a flexible form that can encompass political, satirical and religious debate (for example, *Winner and Waster*), technical and moral instruction (Idley's *Instructions*) and philosophical teaching (Boethius; Usk's *Testament of Love*). It is to this genre, if any, that the opening of the *Regiment* belongs. Hoccleve, of course, later wrote an extended dialogue that frames and comments on other texts in his *Series*, and as we have seen, the *Series* appears in five manuscripts with the *Regiment*. Three manuscripts in particular are of interest here – Bodleian MSS Laud Misc. 735 and Bodley 221, and New Haven, Yale Beinecke MS 493 – because in them the layout and headings of Hoccleve's *Dialogue with a Friend* seem to have influenced the layout of the *Regiment*. All three are part of the Bodley Group of *Regiment* manuscripts; they are textually close, and very similar in layout and decoration.[126]

The Bodley, Laud and Beinecke manuscripts set out their texts in a distinctive way, separating the stanzas by horizontal red lines, and indicating the rhyme royal stanza scheme with interlocking red lines in the margin. They have similar frames and *litterae notabiliores*, though the text of Bodley 221 stops at line 5270 due to an incomplete final quire. In the *Dialogue with a Friend*, they indicate the speakers with marginal cues, for example Laud Misc. 735, folio 10r, 'Amicus'; folio 10v, 'Thomas'; folio 11r, 'Amicus'. Similar glosses occur in Lydgate's *Danse*

---

[125] For the relationship between languages and between text and gloss in the *Confessio*, see Wetherbee 1991 and Yeager 1987b.

[126] See Marzec's stemma of *Regiment* manuscripts in Greetham 1987, 66–7. Marzec's work is based on a full collation of two sections of the *Regiment* (Marzec 1980). With such a large number of extant manuscripts, the relationships are inevitably complex, and complicated still further by conflation and contamination. Marzec also considers (1987b) the manuscripts' affiliations in the light of the marginal glosses, which, she says, generally support the textual evidence.

Macabre.¹²⁷ The idea is then transferred to the *Regiment*. Hoccleve's speeches are labelled 'Occleve' (for example, Laud Misc. 735, folios 87r, 87v, 88v) and the Old Man's 'Amicus' (folios 81v, 83r, 86r). In Bodley 221, there are four marks beside the passage where Hoccleve reveals his name, showing each change of speaker (folio 86v; lines 1863–9).¹²⁸ While the label 'pater', which some *Regiment* manuscripts use, could easily be supported by the many times Hoccleve calls the Old Man 'fadir', there is no similar use of 'frend' in the *Regiment*: the 'Amicus' labels were undoubtedly borrowed from the *Series* and applied to the *Regiment*. This continuity of speaker-labels emphasizes the thematic and autobiographical continuities between the poems that I have already noted; they give the impression that Hoccleve simply resumes a conversation interrupted by the end of the *Series*.

The first part of the *Regiment* employs a restless, colloquial style, the discussion moving from one topic to another without formal divisions. Whether seen as a deliberate stylistic decision or a result of Hoccleve's weak-mindedness,¹²⁹ the Dialogue closely mimics patterns of speech rather than writing. The speeches of Hoccleve and the Old Man usually follow one another without a break (I count ten speech-markers ('quod he', 'thus I seide') in the first 2016 lines of the *Regiment*). There are also far fewer marginal glosses in the Dialogue than in the *Regiment* proper. This is, of course, a consequence of the *Regiment* proper being based on identified Latin sources, but that fact in itself tells us much about the contrasting discourses of the two parts. In Charles Blyth's edition, based on BL MS Arundel 38, there are thirty-four early glosses giving citations or summaries in lines 1–2016, leaving much of the text free from any apparatus. By contrast, in the *Regiment* proper's section on justice (2465–996; just over a quarter of the Dialogue's length at 531 lines) there are twenty-five.

Hoccleve's decision to free the Dialogue from literary apparatus may be contrasted with Gower's *Confessio amantis*.¹³⁰ There, Gower himself establishes the firm 'textual' basis of his poem by describing his own persona in traditional literary terms; in a note beside *Confessio* I. 61, Gower describes himself as an 'auctor' pretending to be a lover ('fingens se [...] esse Amantem'). Many *Confessio* manuscripts reflect the 'textual' nature of the poem in their organization, indeed Gower is

---

¹²⁷ 'Deth to the [Pope]'; 'The [Pope] answeres', and so on with an emperor, constable and others.

¹²⁸ Complications arise when Hoccleve addresses the Old Man as 'ffadir' (e.g. 1891); at this point the manuscripts label his words 'ffilius'.

¹²⁹ Many critics opt for the latter. Furnivall calls this part 'chat' (*Regiment*, ed. Furnivall, xi), Claridge (1990, 239) talks of 'uncontrolled and obsessive digressions', Hasler (1990, 172) of 'manic excess'.

¹³⁰ The early appearance and stable textual tradition of the glosses supports the view that Hoccleve was responsible for the standard set of Latin apparatus.

known to have exercised control over the production of some copies, carefully establishing the hierarchy of the *Confessio*'s layout, with English text, Latin headnotes and summaries, and glosses denoting the speakers.[131] The *Regiment*'s speaker-labels in MSS Bodley 221, Laud Misc. 735 and Beinecke 493 (like those in CUL Gg. vi. 17) have two contradictory effects on Hoccleve's Dialogue with the Old Man. By marking the speeches they acknowledge and even draw attention to the dramatic, dialogic quality of the writing, and bring to the fore parallels between Hoccleve's framing of the *Series* and the *Regiment*. Hoccleve himself, in his holograph copy of the *Dialogue with a Friend*, marks the start of some speeches with paraphs.[132] On the other hand, by labelling the speakers, defining the limits of the speeches and hemming in the text on the page, the marginal apparatus 'retextualizes' the Dialogue. It places the speeches back within the boundaries of conventional, literary form, and so deprives the Dialogue of its feeling of spontaneity.[133] The glosses are designed for a reader who can silently absorb the extra information, rather than for a listener eavesdropping on the conversation. Paradoxically, by recognizing and defining Hoccleve and the Old Man as speakers, the extra apparatus loses the immediacy of spoken dialogue which Hoccleve's writing does so much to foster; it could be said to impose a 'Gowerian' sense of literary form and textual layout on the *Series* and the *Regiment*.

The first 2016 lines of the *Regiment* can, then, aptly be called Hoccleve's Dialogue with the Old Man, while the next section is more accurately described as the Prologue to the *Regiment* proper. This renaming helps to reveal the various generic affinities to which the Dialogue points, including the dream-vision, Boethian dialogue and moral or instructional dialogue, as well as Hoccleve's own *Dialogue with a Friend*. The annotators of *Regiment* manuscripts highlight different aspects of these affiliations in their own attempts to elucidate the identity of the protagonists and the meaning of the Dialogue, and their interventions in turn refocus the reader's field of vision.

---

[131] See Gower, *English Works*, I, cxxx–cxxxviii; Yeager 1987b; Doyle and Parkes 1978; Parkes 1995.

[132] These are printed in the editions of the *Dialogue* from the Durham manuscript by Furnivall (*Minor Poems*, 95–242) and Burrow. No paraphs appear in the first 252 lines of the *Dialogue*, which were copied by the Tudor antiquary John Stow in the Durham manuscript, after the loss of the first two quires, but they are in any case nearly all taken up with a long speech by Hoccleve.

[133] The speaker-labels do perform a practical function. Since the Dialogue with the Old Man lacks the regular section divisions of the *Regiment* proper, the marginal marks help to find one's place in a manuscript, as I can testify from experience.

VI. SCHEMES OF READING

The previous section identified attempts to categorize or frame the opening sections of the *Regiment*, but the poem's manuscripts include many types of intervention and annotation throughout the text that affect the experience of reading. A few contain no, or only a few, marginal glosses, such as Bodleian MSS Rawlinson poet. 10 and Rawlinson poet. 168, both dating from the second half of the fifteenth century; in another late manuscript, BL MS Royal 17 C. xiv, notes have been added by a sixteenth-century reader. The absence of glosses and relatively simple appearance of these books suggest that they were cheap copies intended for non-Latinate readers. While Rawlinson poet. 10 and Royal 17 C. xiv contain the *Regiment* alone, Rawlinson poet. 168, noted above, had at one time been compiled with a variety of didactic and poetic works that would give an introduction to moral, exemplary and educational themes. Other copies incorporate the Latin glosses into the main body of the text, saving the problem of crowded margins, and implying a firmer connection between the Latin text and Hoccleve's 'translation'.[134] In some passages, the effect is reminiscent of Ashby's later *Dicta philosophorum*, which is laid out in just this way, with Latin *sententiae* followed by their English translation.

CUL MS Hh. iv. 11 (late fifteenth century) contains only a few (heavily abbreviated) Latin notes, but has its own distinctive apparatus in the form of the vine-leaf decoration, heraldic signs and vigorous illustrations of men, birds and animals that crowd sixteen of its pages. Written in scrolls are mottoes containing proverbial advice such as: 'Say trouthe be not fals: Telle no talis', 'Whanne thou begynnyst a thyng, thynk on the endynge' and 'Say the best and bere the softe; ontaught tunge greuith ofte.'[135] Surrounding a text so keenly aware of the complications of advisory speech, these scrolls issue double-edged warnings from the margins. Their provocative wisdom applies equally to advisor and to prince. On folio 1r appears the message 'Be war; stodi not to sore', just as Hoccleve's capitulation to anxious 'thoght' is being described. On folio 44r a prince is shown in an initial, reading a book; the mottoes include 'Wan in thy most thynke on thyn ende / Deth sparith no creature.' On folio 21r appears 'In wele be wyis and war or thu be wo / Though thou mow sle yit do nothyng so', accompanying the Old Man's exempla of the restraint shown by the King of Sicily and Scipio Africanus. These proverbial verses are deployed separately, and significantly, later in the manuscript. On folio 60v appears 'yff thou may sle yit do not so' beside the opening of the section on Patience,

---

[134] For example, CUL MS Gg. vi. 17 (notes in a more formal hand); CUL MS Kk. i. 3 (notes in red); BL MS Sloane 1825 (notes in red).

[135] Fols 36r (first two) and 44r.

while 'In wele be war or thow be woo' is written on folio 78v, at the start of the section on Avarice and how it can ruin a king. On folio 88v, at the start of the section on Peace, is written 'Mekenes passeth alle maner thynges.' These gnomic additions place the *Regiment*'s dilemmas of speech and silence into sharp focus, and reorientate the authority of the text towards the marginal and vernacular. Their querulous voices would no doubt have appealed to the later owner of the manuscript, the recusant Nicholas Roscarrock (?1549–?1634), who wrote a collection of lives of the saints while companion to another Catholic and bibliophile, Lord William Howard (1563–1640) in Naworth Castle, near Carlisle, at England's geographical and religious margin.[136]

The Latin apparatus in the *Regiment* proper mainly cites, apart from Hoccleve's proximate sources, biblical and patristic works. Several manuscripts include additional marginalia from such texts in the Dialogue with the Old Man, establishing a didactic framework within which the discussion takes place. In Bodleian MS Laud Misc. 735 the text hand makes more general notes drawing attention to moral issues raised by the text, for example:

fol. 67r,	line 400:	'Of pridd and of waste clothyng of lordis mene which is a yens her astate'
fol. 69v,	line 561:	'How vertuous age moaneth for the wastfull expenses of youth'
fol. 72r,	line 743:	'How a man may be sufferance of vertu [...] be brought to a good mene'
fol. 121r,	line 4439:	'contra adulatores'
fol. 127r,	line 4915:	'consilium ab adulatore', and under this 'nota de avaro'.

In another copy, BL MS Arundel 59, additional notes by the text hand in the Dialogue reflect the established set of headings and glosses in the *Regiment* proper, for example 'de fide', 'De paupertate', 'De fragilitate iuuenali'.[137] These glosses, more descriptive than the occasional Latin references normally found in this part of the poem, provide easier access to specific points of interest in the discussion. They also bring the layout and meaning of the Dialogue closer to that of the *Regiment* proper, whose divisions are often accompanied by similar explanatory glosses or headings ('De regis magnanimitate', 'De vicio avaricie'). Like

---

[136] Roscarrock's name appears on fol. 1r, and his family arms have been drawn in ink on fol. 68v. For his career, see Roscarrock, *Lives of the Saints*, 1–14. Two other *Regiment* manuscripts (BL MSS Arundel 38 and Arundel 59) belonged to Lord William's nephew, Thomas Howard, Earl of Arundel (d. 1646; Seymour (1974, 264) mistakenly calls him Thomas FitzAlan). Arundel 59 had previously belonged to Sir Robert Cotton, a friend of both the Howards; for the antiquarian and political circles in which they moved, see Sharpe 1979, esp. 205–15.

[137] Fol. 5v, stanza 40 (line 274); fol. 10v, stanza 81 (561); fol. 18v, stanza 150 (1044).

the speaker cues that I discussed in the previous section, these glosses impose a new *ordinatio* – this time that of the *Regiment* proper – on Hoccleve's discussion with the Old Man, bringing to the fore issues of morality and governance, and subtly directing the experience of reading the poem.

Only a minority of manuscripts display this kind of consistent annotation or alteration, but almost all of them include notes of some sort marking passages of interest, such as references to Henry IV and Henry V,[138] Hoccleve's attack on unsuitable clothing, his name and other information about his life.[139] These annotations, though informal, build a picture of the reading habits and interests of the *Regiment*'s early audience. Many manuscripts, for example, demonstrate an interest in the stories and exempla of the poem by marking these passages. They suggest a perception of the *Regiment* as a story collection in the tradition of *Confessio amantis* and *The Canterbury Tales*, a connection that modern scholarship has not adequately explored. Hoccleve himself draws attention to this aspect of the poem by recommending it to Prince Henry as a text to read 'if yow list of stories taken heede' (2138). To give some examples: BL MS Harley 4866 includes numerous glosses that summarize or mark off exempla.[140] In Bodleian MSS Laud Misc. 735 and Bodley 221 *litterae notabiliores* mark the beginnings of exempla, including lines 3529, 3851 and 3858. In Cambridge, Magdalene College Pepys MS 2101, the beginning of the John of Canace exemplum is

---

[138] For example, Bodleian MSS Laud Misc. 735, fol. 65v (beside stanzas 42 and 43, one stanza too early), and Bodley 221, fol. 66r.

[139] For example, BL MS Arundel 38 has pointing hands on fol. 21r (line 1128, on the King of Sicily), fol. 25r (line 1345, on Hoccleve's wife) and on fol. 34r, line 1864, 'Nota nominis auctoris huius libri.' Many manuscripts draw attention to the moment when Hoccleve connects his own poverty to the moral of the John of Canace exemplum; one example is Edinburgh University MS 202, fol. 78v, 'nota de prodigalitate Thome hoccleve'. By contrast, a marginal gloss in Cambridge, Corpus Christi MS 496 notes the absence of this passage. Stanzas 598 to 627 (lines 4180–389) are missing, cutting the whole of the exemplum and Hoccleve's subsequent act of self-revelation. Blyth (1996, 15) assumes that the manuscript's scribe, William Wilflete, omitted the passage deliberately because he thought it was of 'no value'. But if so, why should he draw attention to the omission with a note? Wilflete's note is more likely to be a genuine query about the lacuna (which may have derived from a deficiency in his exemplar); it reads 'Nota saltum et quaere / quia non valet' (fol. 48v), which could perhaps be translated as 'Note the jump and inquire, because it does not work.' Blyth also does Wilflete a disservice by calling him simply a 'Clare College student' (1996, 15). In a colophon on fol. 60v Wilflete describes himself as 'magist[er]' and a Fellow of the college. He was indeed Master of Clare from 1448 to 1455 and Chancellor of Cambridge University in 1458, 1464 and 1466; see James 1909–13, II, 447, Venn and Venn 1922–7, I, 408 and Leader 1988, 164.

[140] Thus lines 3676, 'De castitate Scipionis Africani'; 3718, 'De castitate cuiusdam iuuenis'; 3732, 'De castitate cuiusdam femine Vlie nuncupate'.

marked by a three-line flourished initial on folio 65v. Bodleian MS Selden supra 53 contains a large number of two-line initials to show where stories appear, and 'Exemplum' is written in red above the stanzas where exempla begin, for example on folio 45r, lines 3711, 3718 and 3732. Similar interest in the narratives of the *Regiment* is shown in Bodleian MS Rawlinson poet. 168 (which, as mentioned above, lacks the standard Latin apparatus). Passages on folios 12v (line 2731 – the consul and his adulterous son) and 19r (line 3123 – a murderer pardoned by a king) are marked 'ffabula' in the margin. In this case, Hoccleve himself provides a precedent for such an annotation. He gives the label 'ffabula' to *Jereslaus' Wife* and *Jonathas* in Durham MS Cosin V. iii. 9.[141]

I noted earlier that BL MS Arundel 59 adds glosses in Hoccleve's Dialogue with the Old Man that echo those in the *Regiment* proper. The pattern of notes in Arundel 59 suggests a scheme of reading the *Regiment* as a collection of stories and as a store of wisdom on subjects of moral or political value. Two glosses in particular provide a brief literary (or moral) judgement of the stories: 'Nota bona narracio de quodam rege cecilie' (folio 20r, line 1135) and 'hic incipit [?]locutio bona' (folio 15v, line 862). Their taste and critical vocabulary match the comments of an early reader of Chaucer – Jean d'Angoulême, a hostage in England from 1412 to 1445.[142] Of *The Knight's Tale*, for example, Jean notes 'Explicit fabula militis valde bona.'

Another attempt at generic naming in Arundel 59 occurs at the point where Hoccleve apologizes to the Old Man for his distracted state and rudeness; here the scribe marks 'contemplacio dolentis' (folio 13v, line 750). In his *Complaint*, Hoccleve uses similar language to refer to a book that he has been reading: 'This othar day, a lamentacion / Of a wofull man in a boke I sye' (*Minor Poems*, XX, 309–10). Here Hoccleve's description corresponds to the subtitle of Isidore's *Synonyma*, 'De lamentacione animae dolentis', the book on which Hoccleve draws in the *Complaint*.[143] These terms – 'fabula', 'narracio', 'contemplacio', 'lamentacion' – waver between the status of casual descriptive tags, and formal or generic titles. Julia Boffey has analysed numerous such glosses and headings that occur in manuscripts of Chaucer's *Troilus and Criseyde*.[144] Criseyde's speech at IV. 742–98 is marked 'lamentacio' in three manuscripts. Parts of *Troilus* are, of course, marked 'litera' and 'cantus' in some copies, and in others, speech cues like those in copies of the *Regiment* are found. Boffey argues that these labels, primarily

---

[141] Fols 26v and 77v respectively.
[142] Paris, BN fonds anglais MS 39; see Strohm 1971.
[143] See Rigg 1970 and Burrow 1998. In Princeton MS Garrett 137, fol. 28v, a hand larger than the text hand has written after the Dialogue 'Fynitur lamentacio compilatoris T. hokcleffe, et incipit prologus, ut sequitur.'
[144] Boffey 1995; the glosses are recorded in Benson and Windeatt 1990. See also Butterfield 1996 and Hardman 1995.

devices to aid understanding, were probably the result of additions by scribes, editors or readers rather than being original to Chaucer. However, she suggests that some of the self-contained lyric sections of the poem may have been added by Chaucer to his working copy from separate manuscript sheets bearing a heading.[145] Chaucer himself provides an impetus for defining Criseyde's lament in literary terms by the way he introduces it: 'And she spak, sobbyng in hire compleynte' (IV. 741). Here, 'compleynte' could simply be taken descriptively, but also suggests a literary form and frame of reference. Hoccleve seems more conscious of the word as a literary category than is Chaucer at this point in *Troilus and Criseyde*. After the opening five stanzas of Hoccleve's *Series* comes the explicit/incipit: 'here endythe my prologe and folowythe my complaynt'. (This part of the Durham manuscript is John Stow's hand, but the line is probably authorial.) Hoccleve again refers to 'my complaynt' in the *Dialogue with a Friend* (*Minor Poems*, XXI, 1 and 17), references that could either be descriptive or titular. The *Complaint* has now become the standard title for this part of the *Series*.[146] In these cases, both Chaucer and Hoccleve draw attention to the literary form of a passage by calling it a complaint. Later readers and editors follow this precedent in their own attempts to define and explain other parts of their poems. While the *Regiment*'s glosses such as 'exemplum', 'fabula', 'narracio' and 'contemplacio' do not redefine the genre of the poem as a whole, they nevertheless show an interest in the genre and hence interpretation of its component parts, defining the small-scale narratives from which the poem is constructed.

These observations on the *Regiment*'s manuscripts will, I hope, encourage more questions about the readings and rewritings that Hoccleve's poem received in the century or so after its composition. Its audience was by no means restricted to the circle of Prince Henry's intimates who would have received presentation copies, but included the poet's successors as royal servants, administrators or clerics. The *Regiment*'s scribes, compilers and readers provide the first available evidence of people's reactions to and engagement with Hoccleve's text, whether by placing it alongside other works, adopting a distinctive layout or apparatus, or by exploring the identity of the speakers and genres that Hoccleve draws together. At the level of textual intervention, of compilation and production, and of ownership and subsequent annotation, these manuscripts are valuable testimony to the poem(s) that the *Regiment* became. They help to answer the question of how such a widely copied poem did not make it into print early. The great interest that readers showed in the *Regiment*'s narratives, in its moral concerns,

---

[145] Boffey 1995, 12; see also *Troilus and Criseyde*, ed. Windeatt, 38–9.
[146] Bale's *Catalogus* latinizes the name as 'planctum proprium' (I, 537).

and in its historical and political information did not overcome its apparent historical specificity and mixture of authorized advice and private despair. By the 1470s–80s, when Caxton was printing *The Game of Chess* as well as Chaucer and Gower, a book of advice written for Henry V, father of the failing Henry VI, was not a likely success. A translation of Jacobus de Cessolis's *De ludo scaccorum* was a safer bet for a suggestive tale collection, laundered as it was through the impeccable channels of French literary fashion. Despite this, Hoccleve's readers were numerous, and the variety of manuscript responses generated by *The Regiment of Princes* suggests that it resisted a monolithic reading. Instead, the *Regiment*'s dissemination opens the poem to many readerly approaches: exemplary, philosophical, narrative, historical, biographical and educational.

Conclusion

On a flyleaf of one manuscript of *The Regiment of Princes*, an anonymous poem of dedication appears, perhaps addressed to William FitzAlan, Earl of Arundel (d. 1487).[1] The poem's subject and style draw together many strands from Hoccleve's own writing:

> My lord, whan ye thys boke wolle ovyr redde,
> hast nowte to blyne – yt wolle yow more avayll.
> god of hys merssy do hys sowlle mede
> that up-on hyme take the labbur and travayll   4
> on-to hys prynce to geve suche counssell,
> wyche ys to yow a very memery,
> and un-to al othyr lorddys how they schale hem gy.
>
> Enprente hys worddys and al heye entent,   8
> to boddy and sowll he schall fynd yt veyllabyl;
> Follow yt for he hathe trewlly mente;
> to god and to the world yt ys commendabbyll.
> A counsseller to hys prynce ys wys and proffytabbyll   12
> to say the trowthe and no thyng to hyde;
> ye so to do, I pray god be your only gyde.[2]

Like the *Regiment*, these verses are addressed by a servant to his reader, patron and lord. The writer adopts the rhyme royal form of the *Regiment* and the imprecatory tone of its second-person address. The emphasis on authorial 'entent' (line 8) and the true, or loyal, meaning of the verse (line 10) echoes a major concern of Hoccleve's. The poem includes both an acknowledgement of the patron's ability to discard the advice (lines 1–2), and a bolder statement of its value: 'A counsseller to hys prynce ys wys and proffytabbyll / to say the trowthe and no thyng to hyde'. There is also a nice ambiguity about the direction of the *Regiment*'s – and the verses' – advice. Is it given in order to govern the life of the lord being addressed (line 10)? Or does it provide a template for the lord's own advice to his king (lines 12–14)? In this way, the verses in the Royal manuscript deflect and refocus the significance of Hoccleve's work.

---

[1] BL Royal 17 D. vi, recto of second front flyleaf. FitzAlan's arms appear on fol. 40r; see above, p. 174, note 89.

[2] *Secular Lyrics*, ed. Robbins, 93 (some forms regularized).

Conclusion

The Regiment of Princes has the same quality of redirection. It moves between the official rhetoric of royal counsel and the vernacular mode in which Hoccleve's fictional and autobiographical creations debate, advise and criticize. These plural voices both dramatize and overcome the constraints imposed by law, tradition and self-preservation. They create the space for an advisory discourse to emerge based on public dialogue, in which the meaning of political language and power is subject to interpretation and realignment.[3] Hoccleve's approach is that of the long-serving veteran in the *Regiment*, who displays his wounds to Caesar in order to get him to listen and act for him by speaking 'On heighte wel that al the peple it herde' (3278). This thread of verbal – and hence political – engagement runs through Hoccleve's treatment of the specular tradition, the major sources of the poem and the governance of England's ruling bodies.

Hoccleve's model of dialogic engagement is always subject to fracture from the pressure that constraining ideologies bring to bear, but the very fissures in his text are also creative; they energize Hoccleve's urgent need to speak, and power his brilliant and dangerous metaphorical excess. Hoccleve's poetic instinct is for the personal above the institutional, for diverse and often competing voices above a calm and empty absolutism. For these reasons, I depart from those who view the *Regiment* as a more or less convincing exercise in Lancastrian hero-making. While much was hoped of Prince Henry (especially after the taint of the Lancastrian usurpation and the disappointments of Henry IV's reign), the *Regiment* does not give merely a burnished image of the ideal future monarch. Along with the offer to the Prince to become an exemplum of royal virtue comes a threat of discovery if the reality of Henry's rule did not match the projected image; the model for such a failed contract between vernacular poet and young ruler was close at hand in Gower's *Confessio amantis*.[4] Hoccleve's relationship to the Lancastrian regime is, then, not simply one of anxious complicity, but of mutual negotiation and pressure.[5]

It is not possible to make wide claims about the *Regiment*'s impact on Prince Henry. Part of Hoccleve's overdue annuity was paid on 8 July

---

[3] See the influential work of J.G.A. Pocock, who describes language as 'an effective medium for political communication [...] because it is relatively uncontrollable and so hard to monopolize' (1973, 35).

[4] For a complementary assessment of Gower's own rhetorical and political position, see Dimmick 1998, 194–5: '[B]y making the rhetoric of praise dependent on, and inseparable from, the rhetoric of counsel, Gower also speaks to the king on behalf of his subjects' (194).

[5] An analogous view of royal representations in the Tudor period is offered by Greg Walker, who describes the production of art and literature for Henry VIII's court as 'more a matter of contest, of political negotiation and persuasion, than [...] an arena for royal ego-massage' (Walker 1996, 74).

1411, and brought up to date in February 1412.⁶ At the start of Henry V's reign, Hoccleve wrote some public poems that were probably commissioned by the King,⁷ though his spell as an official poet was shortlived. Henry's reign was marked by spectacular political and military triumphs, but his achievements were in the end unsustainable. The *Regiment*, however, is not contained by its relationship to Prince Henry, its primary imagined reader, or by the operations of Lancastrian power. Just as vital is the way in which the *Regiment* inscribes the Prince in an ethical and monitory tradition, and presents him to a wider audience, which will overhear the voice of the counsellor, or veteran, or poet, and judge royal actions accordingly. The *Regiment* was no doubt keenly read by Hoccleve's associates in London and Westminster (just as Hoccleve knew or read Chaucer, Gower, Langland and perhaps the poet of *Mum and the Soothsegger*) and it continued to be widely disseminated throughout the fifteenth century. The plural voices of the poem thus also have plural destinations, modulating themes of counsel, constraint and governance for other reading communities, members of a literate political society beyond the royal *familia*.

This broadening network of participation suggests a further line of inquiry. The *Regiment* helped to establish a tradition of vernacular writing on issues of governance which gave an English vocabulary to the process of political engagement. As legal structures came under increasing pressure during the fifteenth century, the discourse of governance, of the mirrors for princes, paradoxically became more widely disseminated and deployed.⁸ The involvement of regiminal texts in the development of political language and organization in late-medieval England is a subject that deserves more attention. In any such investigation, *The Regiment of Princes* should play a major part.

---

⁶ Burrow 1994, 41, appendix nos 33–4.
⁷ *Minor Poems*, II, IV and VIII, on Oldcastle, Henry V's accession and the reburial of Richard II.
⁸ See McIntosh 1996, who describes how concepts and vocabulary from regiminal texts became part of the language of local courts during the fifteenth century. Other writers whose work is relevant to a study of the late-medieval language of governance include Lydgate, Shirley, Ashby, Fortescue and Malory.

Bibliography

I. MANUSCRIPTS

An asterisk indicates manuscripts consulted on microfilm only.

Copies of *The Regiment of Princes*

Cambridge
CUL MS Gg. vi. 17
—— MS Hh. iv. 11
—— MS Kk. i. 3, part 11
Corpus Christi College MS 496
Magdalene College MS Pepys 2101
Queens' College MS 12 (Horne 24)
St John's College MS I. 22
Trinity College MS R. 3. 22
Fitzwilliam Museum MS McClean 182
—— MS McClean 185

Chicago, IL
*Newberry Library MS f 33. 7

Coventry
Coventry City Record Office MS Acc. 325/1

Edinburgh
NLS MS Adv. 19. 1. 11, part 3
Edinburgh University Library MS 202

London
BL MS Additional 18632
—— MS Arundel 38
—— MS Arundel 59
—— MS Harley 116
—— MS Harley 372
—— MS Harley 4826
—— MS Harley 4866
—— MS Harley 5977, fragment 90 (same copy as Bodleian MS Rawl. D. 913)
—— MS Harley 7333
—— MS Royal 17 C. xiv

—— MS Royal 17 D. vi
—— MS Royal 17 D. xviii
—— MS Royal 17 D. xix
—— MS Sloane 1212
—— MS Sloane 1825
Society of Antiquaries MS 134

New Haven, CT
*Yale University Beinecke Library MS 493

Oxford
Bodleian Library MS Ashmole 40
—— MS Bodley 221
—— MS Digby 185
—— MS Douce 158
—— MS Dugdale 45
—— MS Laud Misc. 735
—— MS Rawlinson D. 913, fol. 63 (same copy as BL MS Harley 5977)
—— MS Rawlinson poet. 10
—— MS Rawlinson poet. 168
—— MS Selden supra 53

Philadelphia, PA
*Rosenbach Foundation MS 1083/30

Princeton, NJ
*Princeton University MS Garrett 137

San Marino, CA
Huntington Library MS EL 26 A. 13
—— MS HM 135

Other Manuscripts

Cambridge

CUL MS Dd. viii. 19	*Confessio amantis*
—— MS Ff. i. 6	Chaucer, Gower, Hoccleve
—— MS Mm. ii. 21	*Confessio amantis*
Corpus Christi College MS 177	Jacobus de Cessolis, *De ludo scaccorum*
Pembroke College MS 227	Astronomy, etc.
—— MS 307	*Confessio amantis*
Fitzwilliam Museum MS McClean 181	*The Canterbury Tales*
—— MS McClean 184	Walton, *Consolation of Philosophy*

Bibliography

London
BL MS Arundel 119 — Lydgate, *Siege of Thebes*
—— MS Harley 172 — Religious/proverbial texts, incl. *Lerne to Die*
—— MS Royal 8 A. xxi — Theology (2 *Regiment* stanzas, fol. 1v)
—— MS Add. 24062 — Hoccleve's Formulary
—— MS Add. 41666 — *Mum and the Soothsegger*
*—— MS Add. 42131 — Bedford Psalter-Hours
—— MS Add. 47680 — *Secretum secretorum*

Oxford
Bodleian Library MS Bodley 638 — Chaucer, Lydgate, Hoccleve
—— MS Digby 233 — Trevisa, *Governance*; Vegetius
—— MS James 34 — Hoccleve, *Remonstrance to Oldcastle*

San Marino, CA
Huntington Library MS HM 111 — Hoccleve, shorter poems
—— MS HM 744 — Hoccleve, shorter poems
—— MS HM 1037 — Jacobus de Cessolis, *De ludo scaccorum*

II. PRINTED PRIMARY SOURCES

Accessus ad Auctores, ed. R.B.C. Huygens (Leiden: Brill, 1970)

Aegidius Romanus, *De regimine principum* (Venice: Bernardinus Vercelensis, 1502)

Alan of Lille, *The Plaint of Nature*, ed./trans. James J. Sheridan, Medieval Sources in Translation, 26 (Toronto: Pontifical Institute of Medieval Studies, 1980)

Albertanus of Brescia, *Ars loquendi et tacendi*, in *Brunetto Latinos Levnet og Skrifter*, ed. Thor Sundby (Copenhagen: Lunds, 1869), XCIII–CXIX

Annales Ricardi Secundi et Henrici Quinti, Regum Angliae, in *Johannis de Trokelowe et Henrici de Blaneford [...] Chronica et Annales*, ed. Henry Thomas Riley, Chronica Monasterii S. Albani 3, RS 28 (London: HMSO, 1866), 155–420

The Anonimalle Chronicle, ed. V.H. Galbraith (Manchester: Manchester UP, 1970)

Ashby, George, *George Ashby's Poems*, ed. Mary Bateson, EETS e.s. 76 (London: Kegan Paul, Trench, Trübner, 1899)

Bale, John, *Index Britanniae scriptorum*, ed. Reginald Lane Poole and Mary Bateson, repr. with introduction by Caroline Brett and James P. Carley (Cambridge: Brewer, 1990; orig. publ. Oxford: Clarendon Press, 1902)

——, *Scriptorum illustrium maioris Brytannie, quam nunc Angliam & Scotiam uocant: Catalogus*, 2 vols, facsimile edn (Basle, 1557; repr. Westmead: Gregg International, 1971)

Boethius, *De consolatione Philosophiae*, trans. S.J. Tester, 2nd edn, Loeb 74 (London: Heinemann; Cambridge, MA: Harvard UP, 1973)

The Boke of Noblesse: Addressed to King Edward the Fourth on his Invasion of France, ed. John Gough Nichols, Roxburghe Club (London: Nichols, 1860)

The Book of Curtesye, ed. Frederick J. Furnivall, EETS e.s. 3 (London: Trübner, 1868)

Bracton, Henry, *The Laws and Customs of England*, ed. G.E. Woodbine, trans. S.E. Thorne, 4 vols (Cambridge, MA: Harvard UP, 1968–77)

The Buke of the Chess, ed. Catherine van Buuren (Edinburgh: Scottish Text Society, 1997)

Caxton, William, *Caxton's 'Game and Playe of the Chesse', 1474*, ed. E.A. Axon (London, 1883; repr. St Leonard's on Sea: British Chess Magazine, 1960)

——, *Jacobus de Cessolis: 'The Game of Chess'; Translated and Printed by William Caxton c. 1483*, intr. N.F. Blake, facsimile edn (London: Scolar Press, 1976)

Chartier, Alain, *Curial*, ed. Paul Meyer and Frederick J. Furnivall, EETS e.s. 54 (London: Trübner, 1888)

Chaucer, Geoffrey, *The Riverside Chaucer*, gen. ed. Larry C. Benson (Oxford: OUP, 1988)

——, *The Workes of our Antient and Learned English Poet, Geffrey Chavcer, Newly Printed*, ed. Thomas Speght (London: Islip, 1598)

——, *Troilus and Criseyde*, ed. B.A. Windeatt (London: Longman, 1984)

——, *The Poetical Works of Geoffrey Chaucer: a Facsimile of Cambridge University Library MS Gg.4.27*, ed. M.B. Parkes and Richard Beadle, 3 vols (Cambridge: Brewer, 1979–80)

——, *'Troilus and Criseyde' – Geoffrey Chaucer: a Facsimile of CCCC MS 61*, ed. M.B. Parkes and Elizabeth Salter (Cambridge: Brewer, 1978)

Christine de Pizan, *Le Livre du Corps de Policie*, ed. Robert H. Lucas, Textes Littéraires Français (Geneva: Droz, 1967)

——, *The Book of the Body Politic*, ed./trans. Kate Langdon Forhan (Cambridge: CUP, 1994)

Chronicles of the Revolution, 1397–1400, ed. Chris Given-Wilson (Manchester: Manchester UP, 1993)

Concilia Magnae Britanniae et Hiberniae, a Synodo Verolamiensi A.D. CCCCXLVI ad Londiniensem A.D. MDCCXVII, ed. David Wilkins, 4 vols (London: Gosling et al., 1737)

Constitutional History of England in the Fifteenth Century, ed. B. Wilkinson (London: Longman, 1964)

The Crowned King, in *The Piers Plowman Tradition*, ed. Helen Barr (London: Dent, 1993), 205–10

Dickens, Charles, *Bleak House*, ed. Nicola Bradbury (Harmondsworth: Penguin, 1996)

Disticha Catonis, in *Minor Latin Poets*, trans. J. Wight Duff and Arnold M. Duff, rev. edn, Loeb 284 (London: Heinemann; Cambridge, MA: Harvard UP, 1968), 592–639

Bibliography

English Gilds, ed. Toulmin Smith and Lucy Toulmin Smith, EETS o.s. 40 (London: Trübner, 1870)
English Historical Literature in the Fifteenth Century, ed. Charles Lethbridge Kingsford (Oxford: Clarendon Press, 1913)
Four English Political Tracts of the Later Middle Ages, ed. Jean-Philippe Genet, Camden 4th series (London: Royal Historical Society, 1977)
Fifteenth-Century Verse and Prose, ed. Alfred W. Pollard (Westminster: Constable, 1903)
Fortescue, John, *On the Laws and Governance of England*, ed./trans. Shelley Lockwood (Cambridge: CUP, 1997)
Gesta Henrici Quinti, ed./trans. Frank Taylor and John S. Roskell (Oxford: Clarendon Press, 1975)
The Good Wife Taught her Daughter; The Good Wyfe Wold a Pylgremage; The Thewis of Gud Women, ed. Tauno F. Mustanoja, Annales Academiae Scientarum Fennicae, series B, 61(2) (Helsinki: Suomalaisen Kirjallisuuden Seuran, 1948)
Gower, John, *English Works*, ed. G.C. Macaulay, 2 vols, EETS e.s. 81–2 (London: OUP, 1900–1)
——, *Latin Works*, volume 4 of *The Complete Works of John Gower*, ed. G.C. Macaulay, 4 vols (Oxford: Clarendon Press, 1899–1902)
——, *The Major Latin Works of John Gower: the Voice of One Crying and the Tripartite Chronicle*, trans. Eric W. Stockton (Seattle: University of Washington Press, 1962)
——, *The Latin Verses in the Confessio Amantis: an Annotated Translation*, trans. Sian Echard and Claire Fanger, Medieval Texts and Studies, 7 (East Lancing, MI: Colleagues Press, 1991)
Henri de Gauchi, *Li Livres du gouvernement des rois*, ed. Samuel Paul Molenaer (New York: Columbia UP, 1899)
Historical Poems of the XIVth and XVth Centuries, ed. Rossell Hope Robbins (New York: Columbia UP, 1959)
Hoccleve, Thomas, *The Regiment of Princes*, ed. Charles R. Blyth, TEAMS Series (Kalamazoo, MI: Medieval Institute Publications, 1999)
——, *Poems by Thomas Hoccleve, Never before Printed*, ed. George Mason (London: Roworth, for Leigh and Sotheby, 1796)
——, *De Regimine Principum*, ed. Thomas Wright, Roxburghe Club, 79 (London: Nichols, 1860)
——, *Works, vol. III: 'The Regement of Princes'*, ed. Frederick J. Furnivall, EETS e.s. 72 (London: Kegan Paul, Trench, Trübner, 1897)
——, *Hoccleve's Works: The Minor Poems*, ed. Frederick J. Furnivall and I. Gollancz; rev. Jerome Mitchell and A.I. Doyle, EETS e.s. 61 and 73 (printed as one volume, London: OUP, 1970)
——, *Series*, in Pryor 1968 (see secondary bibliography)
——, *Selections from Hoccleve*, ed. M.C. Seymour (Oxford: Clarendon Press, 1981)
——, *Selected Poems*, ed. Bernard O'Donoghue (Manchester: Fyfield Books/Carcanet, 1982)
——, *Letter of Cupid*, in *Poems of Cupid, God of Love: Christine de Pizan's 'Epistre au dieu d'Amours' and 'Dit de la rose', Thomas Hoccleve's 'The Letter of Cupid':*

editions and translations, with George Sewell's *'The Proclamation of Cupid'*, ed. Thelma S. Fenster and Mary Carpenter Erler (Leiden: Brill, 1990), 176–203
——, *Thomas Hoccleve's Complaint and Dialogue*, ed. J.A. Burrow, EETS o.s. 313 (Oxford: OUP, 1999)
Household Books of John Duke of Norfolk and Thomas Earl of Surrey, ed. J. Payne Collier (London: Nicol, 1844)
The Household of Edward IV: The Black Book and the Ordinance of 1478, ed. A.R. Myers (Manchester: Manchester UP, 1959)
Idley, Peter, *Peter Idley's 'Instructions to his Son'*, ed. C. D'Evelyn (Boston, MA: Modern Language Association, 1935)
Isidore of Seville, *Etymologiae*, ed. J.-P. Migne, Patrologia Latina 82 (Paris: Migne, 1850), cols 9–728
Jacobus de Cessolis, *De ludo scaccorum*, in Burt 1957 (see secondary bibliography)
——, *De ludo scaccorum*, in *Das Schachzabelbuch Kunrats von Ammenhausen*, ed. Ferdinand Vetter, Bibliothek Älterer Schriftwerke der Deutschen Schweiz, supplementary volume (Frauenfeld: Huber, 1892), cols 25–504
John of Salisbury, *Policraticus*, ed. Clement C.I. Webb, 2 vols (Oxford: Clarendon Press, 1909)
——, *The Statesman's Book of John of Salisbury*, ed./trans. John Dickinson (New York: Knopf, 1927)
——, *Policraticus*, ed./trans. Cary J. Nederman (Cambridge: CUP, 1990)
Langland, William, *'The Vision of Piers Plowman': a Critical Edition of the B-text*, ed. A.V.C. Schmidt, rev. edn, Everyman (London: Dent, 1991)
——, *'Piers Plowman': an Edition of the C-text*, ed. Derek Pearsall (London: Arnold, 1978)
The Libraries of the Augustinian Canons, ed. T. Webber and A.G. Watson, Corpus of British Medieval Library Catalogues, 6 (London: BL, 1998)
Lydgate, John, *Danse Macabre*, ed. Florence Warren, EETS o.s. 181 (London: OUP, 1931)
——, *The Fall of Princes*, ed. Henry Bergen, 4 vols, EETS e.s. 121–4 (London: OUP, 1924–7)
——, *The Life of Our Lady*, ed. Joseph A. Lauritis, Ralph A. Klinefelter and Vernon F. Gallagher (Pittsburgh, PA: Duquesne University, 1961)
——, *Minor Poems, vol. II*, ed. Henry Noble McCracken, EETS o.s. 192 (London: Humphrey Milford for OUP, 1934)
——, *Troy Book*, ed. Henry Bergen, 3 vols, EETS e.s. 97, 103, 106 (London: Kegan Paul, Trench, Trübner, and Frowde for OUP, 1906–10)
——, and Benedict Burgh, *Secrees of Old Philisoffres*, ed. Robert Steele, EETS e.s. 66 (London: Kegan Paul, Trench, Trübner, 1894)
Machiavelli, Niccolò, *The Prince*, ed./trans. Quentin Skinner and Russell Price (Cambridge: CUP, 1988)
Manners and Meals in Olden Time, ed. Frederick J. Furnivall, EETS o.s. 32 (London: Trübner, 1868)
The Middle English Charters of Christ, ed. Mary Caroline Spalding (Bryn Mawr, PA: Bryn Mawr College, 1914)
Mum and the Soothsegger, in *The Piers Plowman Tradition*, ed. Helen Barr (London: Dent, 1993), 137–202

Bibliography

Ovid, *Ars amatoria*, trans. J.H. Mozely, 2nd edn, Loeb 232 (London: Heinemann; Cambridge, MA: Harvard UP, 1979)
——, *Metamorphoses*, trans. Frank Justus Miller, 2 vols, rev. edns, Loeb 42–3 (London: Heinemann; Cambridge, MA: Harvard UP, 1984)
——, *Tristia*, trans. Arthur Leslie Wheeler, 2nd edn, rev. G.P. Gould, Loeb 151 (London: Heinemann; Cambridge, MA: Harvard UP, 1988)
The Peasants' Revolt of 1381, ed. R.B. Dobson, 2nd edn (London: Macmillan, 1983)
The Piers Plowman Tradition, ed. Helen Barr (London: Dent, 1993)
Political Poems and Songs relating to English History, composed during the period from the Accession of Edw. III to that of Ric. III, ed. Thomas Wright, 2 vols, RS 14 (London: HMSO, 1859–61)
The Political Songs of England, ed. Thomas Wright (London: Camden Society, 1839)
Religious Lyrics of the XIVth Century, ed. Carleton Brown, 2nd edn, rev. G.V. Smithers (Oxford: Clarendon Press, 1952)
Repingdon, Philip, *Letter to Henry IV*, in *Official Correspondence of Thomas Bekynton*, ed. George Williams, 2 vols, RS 56 (London: Longman; Trübner, 1872), I, 151–4
Richard the Redeless, in *The Piers Plowman Tradition*, ed. Helen Barr (London: Dent, 1993), 101–33
Roscarrock, Nicholas, *Nicholas Roscarrock's Lives of the Saints: Devon and Cornwall*, ed. Nicholas Orme, Devon and Cornwall Record Society, n.s. 35 (Exeter: Devon and Cornwall Record Society, 1992)
Rymer, Thomas, *Foedera, Conventiones, Literae, et cujuscunque generis Acta Publica [...]*, 10 vols (1745; repr. Farnborough: Gregg, 1967)
Scogan, Henry, *Moral Balade*, in *The Complete Works of Geoffrey Chaucer*, ed. Walter W. Skeat, 7 vols (Oxford: Clarendon Press, 1894), VII, 237–44
Secretum Secretorum, in *Opera hactenus inediti Rogeri Baconi, Fasc. V*, ed. Robert Steele (Oxford: Clarendon Press, 1920), 25–175
Three Prose Versions of the Secreta Secretorum, ed. Robert Steele, EETS e.s. 74 (London: Kegan Paul, Trench, Trübner, 1898)
Secretum Secretorum: Nine English Versions, ed. M.A. Manzalaoui, EETS o.s. 276 (Oxford: OUP, 1977)
Secular Lyrics of the XIVth and XVth Centuries, ed. Rossell Hope Robbins, 2nd edn (Oxford: Clarendon Press, 1955)
Skelton, John, *The Complete English Poems*, ed. John Scattergood (Harmondsworth: Penguin, 1983)
The Statutes of the Realm, 12 vols (London, 1810–28; repr. Dawsons, 1963)
Trevisa, John, *The Governance of Kings and Princes*, ed. David C. Fowler, Charles F. Briggs and Paul G. Remley (New York and London: Garland, 1997)
Twenty-Six Political and other Poems, ed. J. Kail, EETS o.s. 124 (London: Kegan Paul, Trench, Trübner, 1904)
Usk, Adam, *The Chronicle of Adam Usk, 1377–1421*, ed./trans. C. Given-Wilson (Oxford: Clarendon Press, 1997)
Usk, Thomas, *The Testament of Love*, in *The Complete Works of Geoffrey Chaucer*, ed. Walter W. Skeat, 7 vols (Oxford: Clarendon Press, 1894), VII, 1–145

Vegetius, *The Earliest English Translation of Vegetius' 'De Re Militari'*, ed. Geoffrey Lester, Middle English Texts, 21 (Heidelberg: Winter, 1988)

Walsingham, Thomas, *Historia Anglicana*, ed. H.T. Riley, 2 vols, Chronica Monasterii S. Albani 1, RS 28 (London: HMSO, 1863–4)

Walter of Châtillon, *Alexandreis*, ed. Marvin L. Colker, Thesaurus mundi, 17 (Padua: Antenor, 1978)

Walter of Milemete, *The Treatise of Walter de Milemete, De Nobilitatibus, Sapientiis, et Prudentiis Regum*, facsimile edn, intro. by Montague Rhodes James (Oxford: Roxburghe Club, 1913)

Walton, John, *The Consolation of Philosophy*, ed. Mark Science, EETS o.s. 170 (London: Milford for OUP, 1927)

The Welles Anthology, MS. Rawlinson C. 813: a Critical Edition, ed. Sharon L. Jansen and Kathleen H. Jordan, Medieval and Renaissance Texts and Studies, 75 (Binghampton, NY: Center for Medieval and Early Renaissance Studies, 1991)

III. SECONDARY SOURCES

Manuscript catalogues are included only if cited in the text, or if published since M.C. Seymour's description of *Regiment* manuscripts (Seymour 1974).

Ainsworth 1990. Peter F. Ainsworth, *Jean Froissart and the Fabric of History: Truth, Myth, and Fiction in the 'Chroniques'* (Oxford: Clarendon Press)

Alexander 1983. J.J.G. Alexander, 'Painting and Manuscript Illumination for Royal Patrons in the Later Middle Ages', in *English Court Culture in the Later Middle Ages*, ed. V.J. Scattergood and J.W. Sherborne (London: Duckworth), 141–62

Alexander and Kaufmann 1973. J.J.G. Alexander and C.M. Kaufmann, *English Illuminated Manuscripts, 700–1500* (Brussels: Bibliothèque Royale Albert 1er)

Allen 1995. Rosamund S. Allen, 'John Gower and Southwark: the Paradox of the Social Self', in *London and Europe in the Later Middle Ages*, ed. Julia Boffey and Pamela King (London: Centre for Medieval and Renaissance Studies, Queen Mary and Westfield College), 111–47

Allmand 1992. Christopher Allmand, *Henry V* (London: Methuen)

Alsop 1981. James Alsop, 'Nicholas Brigham (d. 1558), Scholar, Antiquary, and Crown Servant', *The Sixteenth Century Journal*, 12, no. 2, 49–67

Ambrisco and Strohm 1995. Alan S. Ambrisco and Paul Strohm, 'Succession and Sovereignty in Lydgate's Prologue to *The Troy Book*', *ChR*, 30, 40–57

Anderson 1986. David Anderson, ed., *Catalogue of the Exhibition Sixty Bokes Olde and New* (Knoxville, TN: New Chaucer Society)

Bibliography

Antin 1968. David Antin, 'Caxton's *The Game and Playe of Chesse*', *Journal of the History of Ideas*, 29, 269–78

Armstrong 1932. Edward Armstrong, 'Italy in the Time of Dante', in *The Decline of the Empire and Papacy*, vol. VII of *The Cambridge Medieval History*, gen. ed. J.R. Tanner, C.W. Previté-Orton and Z.N. Brooke (Cambridge: CUP), 1–48

Aster 1888. Friedrich Aster, *Das Verhältniss des Altenglischen Gedichtes 'De Regimine Principum' von Thomas Hoccleve zu Seinen Quellen nebst einer Einleitung über Leben und Werke des Dichters* (Leipzig: Peters)

Aston 1960. Margaret Aston, 'Lollardy and Sedition, 1381–1431', *Past & Present*, 17, 1–44

—— **1984.** *Lollards and Reformers: Images and Literacy in Late Medieval Religion* (London: Hambledon Press)

Baldwin 1981. Anna P. Baldwin, *The Theme of Government in 'Piers Plowman'* (Cambridge: Brewer)

Barney 1973. Stephen A. Barney, 'The Plowshare of the Tongue: the Progress of a Symbol from the Bible to *Piers Plowman*', *Mediaeval Studies*, 35, 261–93

Barnie 1974. John Barnie, *War in Medieval Society: Social Values and the Hundred Years War, 1337–99* (London: Weidenfeld and Nicolson)

Barr 1989. Helen Barr, 'A Study of *Mum and the Soothsegger* in its Political and Literary Contexts' (unpublished doctoral thesis, University of Oxford)

—— **1994.** *Signes and Sothe: Language in the 'Piers Plowman' Tradition* (Cambridge: Brewer)

—— **1995.** 'Poetic Tradition', *Yearbook of Langland Studies*, 9, 39–64

Barr and Ward-Perkins 1997. Helen Barr and Kate Ward-Perkins, ' "Spekyng for one's sustenance": the Rhetoric of Counsel in *Mum and the Soothsegger*, Skelton's *Bowge of Court*, and Eliot's *Pasquil the Playne*', in *The Long Fifteenth Century: Essays for Douglas Gray*, ed. Helen Cooper and Sally Mapstone (Oxford: Clarendon Press), 249–72

Barron 1968. Caroline M. Barron, 'The Tyranny of Richard II', *Bulletin of the Institute of Historical Research*, 41, 1–18

—— **1990.** 'The Deposition of Richard II', in *Politics and Crisis in Fourteenth-Century England*, ed. John Taylor and Wendy Childs (Gloucester: Sutton), 132–49

Batt 1996. Catherine Batt, 'Hoccleve and ... Feminism? Negotiating Meaning in *The Regiment of Princes*', in *Essays on Thomas Hoccleve*, ed. Catherine Batt (London: Centre for Medieval and Renaissance Studies, Queen Mary and Westfield College; Turnhout: Brepols), 55–84

Baugh 1950. Albert C. Baugh, ed., *A Literary History of England* (London: Routledge & Kegan Paul)

Bayless 1996. Martha Bayless, *Parody in the Middle Ages: the Latin Tradition* (Ann Arbor: University of Michigan Press)

Beadle 1990. Richard Beadle, 'The Virtuoso's *Troilus*', in *Chaucer Traditions: Studies in Honour of Derek Brewer*, ed. Ruth Morse and Barry Windeatt (Cambridge: CUP), 213–33

Beckwith 1993. Sarah Beckwith, *Christ's Body: Identity, Culture and Society in Late Medieval Writings* (London: Routledge)

Bennett 1947. H.S. Bennett, *Chaucer and the Fifteenth Century* (Oxford: OUP)

—— 1955. *Six Medieval Men and Women* (Cambridge: CUP)
M. Bennett 1992. Michael J. Bennett, 'The Court of Richard II and the Promotion of Literature', in *Chaucer's England: Literature in Historical Context*, ed. Barbara A. Hanawalt (Minneapolis: University of Minnesota Press), 3–20
W. Bennett 1992. William Fremont Bennett, 'Interrupting the Word: "Mankind" and the Politics of the Vernacular' (unpublished doctoral dissertation, University of Harvard)
Benson and Blanchfield 1997. C. David Benson and Lynne S. Blanchfield, *The Manuscripts of Piers Plowman: the B-Version* (Cambridge: Brewer)
Benson and Windeatt 1990. C. David Benson and Barry A. Windeatt, 'The Manuscript Glosses to Chaucer's *Troilus and Criseyde*', *ChR*, 25, 33–53
Bentley 1965. Elna-Jean Young Bentley, 'The Formulary of Thomas Hoccleve' (unpublished doctoral dissertation, Emory University)
Berges 1938. Wilhelm Berges, *Die Fürstenspiegel des hohen und späten Mittelalters*, Schriften des Reichsinstituts für ältere deutsche Geschichtskunde, 2 (Leipzig: Hiersemann)
Black 1984. Antony Black, *Guilds and Civil Society in European Political Thought from the Twelfth Century to the Present* (London: Methuen)
Blyth 1993. Charles R. Blyth, 'Thomas Hoccleve's Other Master', *Mediaevalia*, 16, 349–59
—— 1996. 'Editing *The Regiment of Princes*', in *Essays on Thomas Hoccleve*, ed. Catherine Batt (London: Centre for Medieval and Renaissance Studies, Queen Mary and Westfield College; Turnhout: Brepols), 11–28
Boffey 1995. Julia Boffey, 'Annotation in Some Manuscripts of *Troilus and Criseyde*', *EMS*, 5, 1–17
Boffey and Meale 1991. Julia Boffey and Carol M. Meale, 'Selecting the Text: Rawlinson C. 86 and some Other Books for London Readers', in *Regionalism in Late Medieval Manuscripts and Texts*, ed. Felicity Riddy (Cambridge: Brewer), 143–69
Boffey and Thompson 1989. Julia Boffey and John J. Thompson, 'Anthologies and Miscellanies: Production and Choice of Texts', in *Book Production and Publishing in Britain, 1375–1475*, ed. Jeremy Griffiths and Derek Pearsall (Cambridge: CUP), 279–315
Borges 1970. Jorge Luis Borges, 'Partial Magic in the *Quixote*', in his *Labyrinths: Selected Stories and Other Writings*, ed./trans. Donald A. Yates and James E. Irby (Harmondsworth: Penguin), 228–31
Born 1928. Lester K. Born, 'The Perfect Prince: a Study in Thirteenth- and Fourteenth-Century Ideals', *Speculum*, 3, 470–504
Bornstein 1975. Diane Bornstein, *Mirrors of Courtesy* (Hamden, CT: Archon Books)
—— 1976. 'Reflections of Political Theory and Political Fact in Fifteenth-Century Mirrors for the Prince', in *Medieval Studies in Honor of Lillian Herlands Hornstein*, ed. Jess B. Bessinger and Robert R. Raymo (New York: New York UP), 77–85
Boswell and Holton 1996–7. Jackson Campbell Boswell and Sylvia Wallace Holton, 'References to Chaucer's Literary Reputation', *ChR*, 31, 291–316

Bibliography

Bourdieu 1991. Pierre Bourdieu, *Language and Symbolic Power*, ed. John B. Thompson, trans. Gino Raymond and Matthew Adamson (Cambridge: Polity Press)

Bowers 1989. John M. Bowers, 'Hoccleve's Huntingdon Holographs: the First "Collected Poems" in English', *FCS*, 15, 27–51

Boyd 1990. David Lorenzo Boyd, 'Recapturing Readings: Middle English Literature in its Manuscript Contexts' (unpublished doctoral dissertation, Yale University)

—— 1993. 'Reading Through the *Regiment of Princes*: Hoccleve's *Series* and Lydgate's *Dance of Death* in Yale Beinecke MS 493', *FCS*, 20, 15–34

Bragg 1996. Lois Bragg, 'Chaucer's Monogram and the "Hoccleve Portrait" Tradition', *Word & Image*, 12, 127–42

Brewer 1856. Thomas Brewer, *Memoir of the Life and Times of John Carpenter* (London: Taylor)

Briggs 1993. Charles F. Briggs, 'Manuscripts of Giles of Rome's *De regimine principum* in England, 1300–1500: a Handlist', *Scriptorium*, 47, 60–73

—— 1998. 'MS Digby 233 and the Patronage of John Trevisa's *De regimine principum*', *EMS*, 7, 249-63

—— 1999. *Giles of Rome's 'De Regimine Principum': Reading and Writing Politics at Court and University, c. 1275 – c. 1525* (Cambridge: CUP)

Brown 1964. A.L. Brown, 'The Commons and the Council in the Reign of Henry IV', *EHR*, 79, 1–30

—— 1971. 'The Privy Seal Clerks in the Early Fifteenth Century', in *The Study of Medieval Records: Essays in Honour of Kathleen Major* ed. D.A. Bullough and R.L. Storey (Oxford: Clarendon Press), 260–81

—— 1981. 'Parliament, c. 1377–1422', in *The English Parliament in the Middle Ages*, ed. R.G. Davies and J.H. Denton (Manchester: Manchester UP), 109–40

—— 1989. *The Governance of Late Medieval England, 1272–1461* (London: Arnold)

Bruni 1932. Gerardo Bruni, 'Il "De Regimine Principum" Di Egidio Romano: Studio Bibliografico', *Aevum*, 6, 339–72

Brusendorff 1925. Aage Brusendorff, *The Chaucer Tradition* (London: Milford for OUP)

Burrow 1971. J.A. [John] Burrow, *Ricardian Poetry: Chaucer, Gower, Langland and the 'Gawain' Poet* (London: Routledge & Kegan Paul)

—— 1981. 'The Poet as Petitioner', *SAC*, 3, 61–75

—— 1982a. *Medieval Writers and their Work: Middle English Literature and its Background, 1100–1500* (Oxford: OUP)

—— 1982b. 'Autobiographical Poetry in the Middle Ages: the Case of Thomas Hoccleve', *PBA*, 68, 389–412

—— 1984. 'Hoccleve's *Series*: Experience and Books', in *Fifteenth-Century Studies: Recent Essays*, ed. Robert F. Yeager (Hamden, CT: Archon Books), 259–73

—— 1988. 'The Poet and the Book', in *Genres, Themes, and Images in English Literature*, ed. Piero Boitani and Anna Torti (Tübingen: Narr; Cambridge: Brewer), 230–45

—— 1990. 'Hoccleve and Chaucer', in *Chaucer Traditions: Studies in Honour of Derek Brewer*, ed. Ruth Morse and Barry Windeatt (Cambridge: CUP), 54–61
—— 1993. *Thinking in Poetry: Three Medieval Examples*, The William Matthews Lectures 1993 (London: Birkbeck College)
—— 1994. *Thomas Hoccleve* (Aldershot: Variorum)
—— 1995. 'Thomas Hoccleve: Some Redatings', *RES*, 46, 366–72
—— 1997. 'Hoccleve and the Middle French Poets', in *The Long Fifteenth Century: Essays for Douglas Gray*, ed. Helen Cooper and Sally Mapstone (Oxford: Clarendon Press), 35–49
—— 1998. 'Hoccleve's *Complaint* and Isidore of Seville Again', *Speculum*, 73, 424–8
Burt 1957. Marie Anita Burt, 'Jacobus de Cessolis: Libellus de Moribus Hominum et Officiis Nobilium ac Popularium super Ludo Scachorum' (unpublished doctoral dissertation, University of Texas)
Butterfield 1996. Ardis Butterfield, '*Mise-en-page* in the *Troilus* Manuscripts: Chaucer and French Manuscript Culture', in *Reading from the Margins: Textual Studies, Chaucer, and Medieval Literature*, ed. Seth Lerer (San Marino, CA: Huntington Library), 49–80 (volume also publ. as *Huntington Library Quarterly*, 58, no. 1)
—— 1997. 'French Culture and the Ricardian Court', in *Essays on Ricardian Literature in Honour of John Burrow*, ed. Alastair Minnis, Charlotte C. Morse and Thorlac Turville-Petre (Oxford: Clarendon Press), 82–120
Cam 1970. H.M. Cam, 'The Theory and Practice of Representation in Medieval England', in *Historical Studies of the English Parliament, I: Origins to 1399*, ed. E.B. Fryde and Edward Miller (Cambridge: CUP), 262–78
Camille 1994. Michael Camille, 'The Image and the Self: Unwriting Medieval Bodies', in *Framing Medieval Bodies*, ed. Sarah Kay and Miri Rubin (Manchester: Manchester UP), 62–99
Cannon 1998. Christopher Cannon, *The Making of Chaucer's English: a Study of Words* (Cambridge: CUP)
Carey 1992. Hilary M. Carey, *Courting Disaster: Astrology at the English Court and University in the Later Middle Ages* (Basingstoke: Macmillan)
Carley 1985. James P. Carley, 'The Manuscript Remains of John Leland, "The King's Antiquary" ', *Text*, 2, 111–20
Carlson 1991. David R. Carlson, 'Thomas Hoccleve and the Chaucer Portrait', *Huntington Library Quarterly*, 54, 283–300
—— 1993. *English Humanist Books: Writers and Patrons, Manuscript and Print, 1475–1525* (Toronto: University of Toronto Press)
Carpenter 1995. Christine Carpenter, 'Political and Constitutional History: Before and After McFarlane', in *The McFarlane Legacy: Studies in Late Medieval Politics and Society*, ed. R.H. Britnell and A.J. Pollard (Stroud: Sutton), 175–206
Carruthers 1990. Mary Carruthers, *The Book of Memory: a Study of Memory in Medieval Culture* (Cambridge: CUP)
Catto 1985. Jeremy Catto, 'The King's Servants', in *Henry V: the Practice of Kingship*, ed. G.L. Harriss (Oxford: OUP), 75–95

Bibliography

Cavanaugh 1980. Susan H. Cavanaugh, 'A Study of Books Privately Owned in England, 1300–1450' (doctoral dissertation, University of Pennsylvania; facsimile produced by University Microfilms International, 1983)

Childs 1932. Herbert Ellsworth Childs, 'A Study of the Unique Middle English Translation of the *De Regimine Principum* of Aegidius Romanus (MS Digby 233)' (unpublished doctoral dissertation, University of Washington)

Christianson 1989. C. Paul Christianson, 'A Community of Book Artisans in Chaucer's London', *Viator*, 20, 207–18

Chroust 1947. Anton-Herman Chroust, 'The Corporate Idea and the Body Politic in the Middle Ages', *Review of Politics*, 9, 423–52

Claridge et al. 1990. Gordon Claridge, Ruth Pryor and Gwen Watkins, *Sounds from the Belljar: Ten Psychotic Authors* (Basingstoke: Macmillan)

Classen 1990. Albrecht Classen, 'Hoccleve's Independence from Chaucer: a Study of Poetic Emancipation', *FCS*, 16, 59–81

Coleman 1981. Janet Coleman, *English Literature in History 1350–1400: Medieval Readers and Writers* (London: Hutchinson)

Connolly 1998. Margaret Connolly, *John Shirley: Book Production and the Noble Household in Fifteenth-Century England* (Aldershot: Ashgate)

Copeland 1987. Rita Copeland, 'Rhetoric and Vernacular Translation in the Middle Ages', *SAC*, 9, 41–75

—— **1991.** *Rhetoric, Hermeneutics, and Translation in the Middle Ages: Academic Traditions and Vernacular Texts* (Cambridge: CUP)

Courthope 1895–7. W.J. Courthope, *A History of English Poetry*, 2 vols (London: Macmillan)

Crane 1992. Susan Crane, 'The Writing Lesson of 1381', in *Chaucer's England: Literature in Historical Context*, ed. Barbara A. Hanawalt (Minneapolis: University of Minnesota Press), 201–21

Craun 1997. Edwin D. Craun, *Lies, Slander, and Obscenity in Medieval English Literature: Pastoral Rhetoric and the Deviant Speaker* (Cambridge: CUP)

D'Alverny 1976. Marie-Thérèse D'Alverny, 'L'Homme comme symbole. Le microcosme', *Settimane di Studio del Centro Italiano di Studi sull'Alto Medioevo*, 23, 123–83

Dällenbach 1989. Lucien Dällenbach, *The Mirror in the Text*, trans. Jeremy Whitely with Emma Hughes (Cambridge: Polity Press)

Davidoff 1983. Judith M. Davidoff, 'The Audience Illuminated, or New Light Shed on the Dream Frame of Lydgate's *Temple of Glas*', *SAC*, 5, 103–25

Dean 1939. Ruth J. Dean, 'An Essay in Anglo-Norman Palaeography', in *Studies in French Language and Literature Presented to Professor Mildred K. Pope*, n. ed. (Manchester: Manchester UP), 79–87

Deansley 1920. M. Deansley, 'Vernacular Books in England in the Fourteenth and Fifteenth Centuries', *Modern Language Review*, 15, 349–58

de la Mare 1988–91. A.C. de la Mare, 'Manuscripts Given to the University of Oxford by Humphrey, Duke of Gloucester', *BLR*, 13, 30–51; 112–21

del Punta and Luna 1993. Francesco del Punta and Concetta Luna, *Catalogo dei Manuscritti: De regimine Principum (Italian MSS)*, Aegidii Romani: Opera Omnia, I. 1/11 (Florence: Olschki)

Dimmick 1998. Jeremy Dimmick, 'Patterns of Ethics and Politics in John Gower's *Confessio Amantis*' (unpublished doctoral thesis, University of Cambridge)

Douglas 1973. Mary Douglas, *Natural Symbols: Explorations in Cosmology*, 2nd edn (London: Barrie & Jenkins)

Doyle 1959. A.I. Doyle, 'An Unrecognised Piece of *Piers the Ploughman's Creed* and Other Work by its Scribe', *Speculum*, 34, 428–36

—— 1961. 'More Light on John Shirley', *MÆ*, 30, 93–101

—— 1983. 'English Books in and out of Court from Edward III to Henry VII', in *English Court Culture in the Later Middle Ages*, ed. V.J. Scattergood and J.W. Sherborne (London: Duckworth), 163–81

Doyle and Pace 1968. A.I. Doyle and George B. Pace, 'A New Chaucer Manuscript', *PMLA*, 83, 22–34

Doyle and Parkes 1978. A.I. Doyle and M.B. Parkes, 'The Production of Copies of the *Canterbury Tales* and *Confessio Amantis* in the Early Fifteenth Century', in *Medieval Scribes, Manuscripts and Libraries: Essays Presented to N.R. Ker*, ed. M.B. Parkes and Andrew G. Watson (London: Scolar Press), 163–210

Dunbabin 1982. Jean Dunbabin, 'The Reception and Interpretation of Aristotle's *Politics*', in *The Cambridge History of Later Medieval Philosophy*, ed. Norman Kretzmann, Anthony Kenny and Jan Pinborg (Cambridge: CUP), 723–37

—— 1988. 'Government', in *The Cambridge History of Medieval Political Thought*, ed. J.H. Burns (Cambridge: CUP), 477–519

Dunham and Wood 1976. William Huse Dunham Jnr and Charles T. Wood, 'The Right to Rule in England: Depositions and the Kingdom's Authority, 1327–1485', *American Historical Review*, 81, 738–61

Dunlop 1998. Lynn M. Dunlop, 'Cities without Walls: the Politics of Melancholy from Machaut to Lydgate' (unpublished doctoral thesis, University of Cambridge)

Dutschke 1989. C.W. Dutschke et al., *Guide to Medieval and Renaissance Manuscripts in the Huntington Library*, 2 vols (San Marino, CA: Huntington Library)

Eales 1986. Richard Eales, 'The Game of Chess: an Aspect of Knightly Culture', in *The Ideals and Practice of Medieval Knighthood: Papers from the First and Second Strawberry Hill Conferences*, ed. Christopher Harper-Bill and Ruth Harvey (Woodbridge: Boydell Press), 12–34

Eberle 1985. Patricia J. Eberle, 'The Politics of Courtly Style at the Court of Richard II', in *The Spirit of the Court: Selected Proceedings of the Fourth Congress of the International Courtly Literature Society*, ed. Glyn S. Burgess and Robert A. Taylor (Cambridge: Brewer), 168–78

Edwards 1971. A.S.G. Edwards, 'Selections from Lydgate's *Fall of Princes*: a Checklist', *The Library*, 5th series, 26, 337–42

—— 1978. 'Hoccleve's *Regiment of Princes*: a Further Manuscript', *Edinburgh Bibliographical Society Transactions*, 5, part 1, 32

—— 1983. 'Lydgate Manuscripts: Some Directions for Future Research', in *Manuscripts and Readers in Fifteenth-Century England: the Literary*

Implications of Manuscript Study, ed. Derek Pearsall (Cambridge: Brewer), 15–26

—— 1993. 'The Chaucer Portraits in the Harley and Rosenbach Manuscripts', *EMS*, 4, 268–71

—— 1996. 'Bodleian Library MS Arch. Selden B.24: A "Transitional" Collection', in *The Whole Book: Cultural Perspectives on the Medieval Miscellany*, ed. Stephen G. Nichols and Siegfried Wenzel (Ann Arbor: University of Michigan Press), 53–67

—— 1997a. 'Medieval Manuscripts Owned by William Browne of Tavistock (1590/1? – 1643/5?)', in *Books and Collectors, 1200–1700: Essays Presented to Andrew Watson*, ed. James P. Carley and Colin G.C. Tite (London: BL), 441–9

—— 1997b. 'John Shirley and the Emulation of Courtly Culture', in *The Court and Cultural Diversity: Selected Papers from the Eighth Triennial Congress of the International Courtly Literature Society*, ed. Evelyn Mullally and John Thompson (Cambridge: Brewer), 309–17

—— 2000. 'Fifteenth-Century Middle English Verse Author Collections', in *The English Medieval Book: Studies in Memory of Jeremy Griffiths*, ed. A.S.G. Edwards, Vincent Gillespie and Ralph Hanna (London: BL), 101–12

Edwards and Pearsall 1989. A.S.G. Edwards and Derek Pearsall, 'The Manuscripts of the Major English Poetic Texts', in *Book Production and Publishing in Britain, 1375–1475*, ed. Jeremy Griffiths and Derek Pearsall (Cambridge: CUP), 257–78

J. Edwards 1970. J.G. Edwards, 'The Parliamentary Committee of 1398', in *Historical Studies of the English Parliament I: Origins to 1399*, ed. E.B. Fryde and Edward Miller (Cambridge: CUP), 316–28

Elliot 1973. Thomas J. Elliot, 'Middle English Complaints against the Times: To Contemn the World or to Reform it?', *Annuale Medievale*, 14, 22–34

Embree 1975. Dan Embree, '*Richard the Redeless* and *Mum and the Soothsegger*: a Case of Mistaken Identity', *Notes & Queries*, 220, 4–12

—— 1985. ' "The King's Ignorance": a Topos for Evil Times', *MÆ*, 54, 121–6

Emden 1963. A.B. Emden, *A Biographical Register of the University of Cambridge to 1500* (Cambridge: CUP)

Emmerson 1997. Richard K. Emmerson, 'Text and Image in the Ellesmere Portraits of the Tale-Tellers', in *The Ellesmere Chaucer: Essays in Interpretation*, ed. Martin Stevens and Daniel Woodard (San Marino, CA: Huntington Library), 143–70

Epstein 1996. Steven A. Epstein, *Genoa & the Genoese, 958–1528* (Chapel Hill and London: University of North Carolina Press)

Ferguson 1955. Arthur B. Ferguson, 'The Problem of Counsel in *Mum and the Soothsegger*', *Studies in the Renaissance*, 2, 67–83

—— 1965. *The Articulate Citizen and the English Renaissance* (Durham, NC: Duke UP)

Ferster 1996. Judith Ferster, *Fictions of Advice: the Literature and Politics of Counsel in Late Medieval England* (Philadelphia: University of Pennsylvania Press)

Fisher 1992. John H. Fisher, 'A Language Policy for Lancastrian England', *PMLA*, 107, 1168–80

Forhan 1992. Kate Langdon Forhan, 'Polycracy, Obligation, and Revolt: the Body Politic in John of Salisbury and Christine de Pizan', in *Politics, Gender, and Genre: the Political Thought of Christine de Pizan*, ed. Margaret Brabant (Boulder, CO: Westview Press), 33–52

Foucault 1979. Michel Foucault, *Discipline and Punish: the Birth of the Prison*, trans. Alan Sheridan (Harmondsworth: Penguin)

Fowler 1995. David C. Fowler, *The Life and Times of John Trevisa, Medieval Scholar* (Seattle: University of Washington Press)

Fradenburg 1984. Louise O. Fradenburg, 'Spectacular Fictions: the Body Politic in Chaucer and Dunbar', *Poetics Today*, 5, 493–517

—— **1985.** 'The Manciple's Servant Tongue: Politics and Poetry in *The Canterbury Tales*', *ELH*, 52, 85–118

Friedman 1989. John B. Friedman, 'Books, Owners and Makers in Fifteenth-Century Yorkshire: the Evidence from some Wills and Extant Manuscripts', in *Latin and Vernacular: Studies in Late-Medieval Texts and Manuscripts*, ed. A.J. Minnis (Cambridge: Brewer), 111–27

—— **1995.** *Northern English Books, Owners, and Makers in the Late Middle Ages* (Syracuse, NY: Syracuse UP)

Gaylord 1997. Alan T. Gaylord, 'Portrait of a Poet', in *The Ellesmere Chaucer: Essays in Interpretation*, ed. Martin Stevens and Daniel Woodard (San Marino, CA: Huntington Library), 121–42

Gilbert 1928. Allan H. Gilbert, 'Notes on the Influence of the *Secretum Secretorum*', *Speculum*, 3, 84–98

Gillingham 1987. John B. Gillingham, 'Crisis or Continuity? The Structure of Royal Authority in England, 1369–1422', in *Das Spätmittelalterliche Königtum im Europäischen Vergleich*, ed. Reinhard Schneider (Sigmaringen: Thorbecke), 59–80

Given-Wilson 1986. Chris Given-Wilson, *The Royal Household and the King's Affinity: Service, Politics and Finance in England 1360–1413* (New Haven, CT: Yale UP)

—— **1987.** *The English Nobility in the Late Middle Ages: the Fourteenth-Century Political Community* (London: Routledge & Kegan Paul)

—— **1994.** 'Richard II, Edward II, and the Lancastrian Inheritance', *EHR*, 109, 553–71

Gordon 1993. Dillian Gordon, *Making and Meaning: the Wilton Diptych* (London: National Gallery Publications)

Grabes 1982. Herbert Grabes, *The Mutable Glass: Mirror-Imagery in Titles and Texts of the Middle Ages and Renaissance*, trans. Gordon Collier (Cambridge: CUP)

Gradon 1980. Pamela Gradon, 'Langland and the Ideology of Dissent', *PBA*, 66, 179–205

Grady 1995. Frank Grady, 'The Lancastrian Gower and the Limits of Exemplarity', *Speculum*, 70, 552–75

Gransden 1982. Antonia Gransden, *Historical Writing in England II: c. 1307 to the Early Sixteenth Century* (London: Routledge & Kegan Paul)

Green 1976–7. Richard Firth Green, 'Three Fifteenth-Century Notes', *English Language Notes*, 14, 14–17

Bibliography

—— 1978. 'Notes on Some Manuscripts of Hoccleve's *Regiment of Princes*', *British Library Journal*, 4, 37–41

—— 1980. *Poets and Princepleasers: Literature and the English Court in the Late Middle Ages* (Toronto: University of Toronto Press)

—— 1983. 'The *Familia Regis* and the *Familia Cupidinis*', in *English Court Culture in the Later Middle Ages*, ed. V.J. Scattergood and J.W. Sherborne (London: Duckworth), 87–108

—— 1999. *A Crisis of Truth: Literature and Law in Ricardian England* (Philadelphia: University of Pennsylvania Press)

Greetham 1985. D.C. [David] Greetham, 'Normalisation of Accidentals in Middle English Texts: the Paradox of Thomas Hoccleve', *Studies in Bibliography*, 38, 121–50

—— 1987. 'Challenges of Theory and Practice in the Editing of Hoccleve's *Regement of Princes*', in *Manuscripts and Texts: Editorial Problems in Later Middle English Literature*, ed. Derek Pearsall (Cambridge: Brewer), 60–86

—— 1989. 'Self-Referential Artifacts: Hoccleve's Persona as a Literary Device', *Modern Philology*, 86, 242–51

Griffiths 1983. Jeremy Griffiths, '*Confessio Amantis*: the Poem and its Pictures', in *Gower's Confessio Amantis: Responses and Reassessments*, ed. A.J. Minnis (Cambridge: Brewer), 163–78

Griffiths 1980. R.A. Griffiths, 'Public and Private Bureaucracies in England and Wales in the Fifteenth Century', *Transactions of the Royal Historical Society*, 5th series, 30, 109–30

Gross 1995. A.J. Gross, 'K.B. McFarlane and the Determinists: the Fallibilities of the English Kings, c.1399–c.1520', in *The McFarlane Legacy: Studies in Late Medieval Politics and Society*, ed. R.H. Britnell and A.J. Pollard (Stroud: Sutton; New York: St Martins), 49–75

Hammond 1914. Eleanor Prescott Hammond, 'Poet and Patron in the *Fall of Princes*: Lydgate and Humphrey of Gloucester', *Anglia*, 38, 121–36

—— 1929–30. 'A Scribe of Chaucer', *Modern Philology*, 27, 27–33

Hanna 1986. Ralph Hanna III, 'Booklets in Medieval Manuscripts: Further Considerations', *Studies in Bibliography*, 39, 100–11

—— 1989. 'Sir Thomas Berkeley and his Patronage', *Speculum*, 64, 878–916

—— 1992. 'Pilate's Voice/Shirley's Case', *South Atlantic Quarterly*, 91, 793–812

—— 1996a. *Pursuing History: Middle English Manuscripts and their Texts* (Stanford, CA: Stanford UP)

—— 1996b. 'Miscellaneity and Vernacularity: Conditions of Literary Production in Late Medieval England', in *The Whole Book: Cultural Perspectives on the Medieval Miscellany*, ed. Stephen G. Nichols and Siegfried Wenzel (Ann Arbor: University of Michigan Press), 37–51

Hanna and Edwards 1996. Ralph Hanna III and A.S.G. Edwards, 'Rotheley, the De Vere Circle, and the Ellesmere Chaucer', in *Reading from the Margins: Textual Studies, Chaucer, and Medieval Literature*, ed. Seth Lerer (San Marino, CA: Huntington Library), 11–35 (volume also publ. as *Huntington Library Quarterly*, 58, no. 1)

Hanning 1984. Robert W. Hanning, 'Chaucer and the Dangers of Poetry', *CEA Critic*, 46, 17–26

Hardman 1995. Phillipa Hardman, 'Chaucer's Articulation of the Narrative in *Troilus*: the Manuscript Evidence', *ChR*, 30, 111–33

Harris 1983. Kate Harris, 'John Gower's *Confessio Amantis*: the Virtues of Bad Texts', in *Manuscripts and Readers in Fifteenth-Century England: the Literary Implications of Manuscript Study*, ed. Derek Pearsall (Cambridge: Brewer), 27–40

—— **1984.** 'The Patron of BL MS Arundel 38', *Notes & Queries*, n.s. 31, 462–3

—— **1989.** 'Patrons, Buyers and Owners: the Evidence for Ownership and the Rôle of Book Owners in Book Production and the Book Trade', in *Book Production and Publishing in Britain, 1375–1475*, ed. Jeremy Griffiths and Derek Pearsall (Cambridge: CUP), 163–99

Harriss 1985a. G.L. [Gerald] Harriss, 'Introduction: the Exemplar of Kingship', in *Henry V: the Practice of Kingship*, ed. G.L. Harriss (Oxford: OUP), 1–29

—— **1985b.** 'Financial Policy', in *Henry V: the Practice of Kingship*, ed. G.L. Harriss (Oxford: OUP), 159–79

—— **1993.** 'Political Society and the Growth of Government in Late Medieval England', *Past & Present*, 138, 28–57

—— **1994–6.** 'Good Duke Humphrey', *BLR*, 15, 119–23

—— **1995.** 'The Dimensions of Politics', in *The McFarlane Legacy: Studies in Late Medieval Politics and Society*, ed. R.H. Britnell and A.J. Pollard (Stroud: Sutton), 1–20

Hasler 1990. Anthony J. Hasler, 'Hoccleve's Unregimented Body', *Paragraph*, 13, 164–83

Hazelton 1960. R. Hazelton, 'Chaucer and Cato', *Speculum*, 35, 357–80

Heal 1996. Felicity Heal, 'Reciprocity and Exchange in the Late Medieval Household', in *Bodies and Disciplines: Intersections of Literature and History in Fifteenth-Century England*, ed. Barbara A. Hanawalt and David Wallace (Minneapolis: University of Minnesota Press), 179–98

Horrox 1995. Rosemary Horrox, 'Caterpillars of the Commonwealth? Courtiers in Late Medieval England', in *Rulers and Ruled in Late Medieval England: Essays Presented to Gerald Harriss*, ed. Rowena E. Archer and Simon Walker (London: Hambledon Press), 1–15

Hudson 1988. Anne Hudson, *The Premature Reformation: Wycliffite Texts and Lollard History* (Oxford: Clarendon Press)

—— **1991.** 'The Mouse in the Pyx: Popular Heresy and the Eucharist', *Trivium*, 26, 40–53

—— **1994.** '*Piers Plowman* and the Peasants' Revolt: a Problem Revisited', *Yearbook of Langland Studies*, 8, 85–106

Hughes 1992. M.E.J. Hughes, ' "The Feffement that fals hath ymaked": a Study of the Image of the Document in *Piers Plowman* and some Literary Analogues', *NM*, 93, 125–33

Ingram 1973. Elizabeth Morley Ingram, 'Thomas Hoccleve and Guy de Rouclif', *Notes & Queries*, 218, 42–3

James 1983. Mervyn James, 'Ritual, Drama and Social Body in the Late Medieval English Town', *Past & Present*, 98, 3–29

James 1905. Montague Rhodes James, *A Descriptive Catalogue of the Manuscripts in the Library of Pembroke College* (Cambridge: CUP)

Bibliography

—— 1909–13. *A Descriptive Catalogue of the Manuscripts in the Library of Corpus Christi College Cambridge*, 2 vols (Cambridge: CUP)

—— 1913. *A Descriptive Catalogue of the Manuscripts in the Library of St John's College Cambridge* (Cambridge: CUP)

Jones 1968. Richard H. Jones, *The Royal Policy of Richard II: Absolutism in the Later Middle Ages* (Oxford: Blackwell)

Justice 1994. Steven Justice, *Writing and Rebellion: England in 1381* (Berkeley: University of California Press)

—— 1997. 'Introduction: Authorial Work and Literary Ideology', in *Written Work: Langland, Labor, and Authorship*, ed. Steven Justice and Kathryn Kerby-Fulton (Philadelphia: University of Pennsylvania Press), 1–12

Kaepelli 1960. Tommaso Kaepelli, 'Pour la biographie de Jacques de Cessole', *Archivum Fratrum Praedicatorum*, 30, 149–62

Kane 1986. George Kane, 'Some Fourteenth-Century "Political" Poems', in *Medieval English Religious and Ethical Literature: Essays in Honour of G.H. Russell*, ed. Gregory Kratzmann and James Simpson (Cambridge: Brewer), 82–91

Kantorowicz 1957. Ernst H. Kantorowicz, *The King's Two Bodies: a Study in Medieval Political Theology* (Princeton, NJ: Princeton UP)

Keiser 1991. George R. Keiser, 'Ordinatio in the Manuscripts of John Lydgate's *Lyf of Our Lady*: Its Value for the Reader, Its Challenge for the Modern Editor', in *Medieval Literature: Texts and Interpretation*, ed. Tim William Machan (Binghampton, NY: Center for Medieval and Early Renaissance Studies), 139–57

—— 1995. 'Serving the Needs of Readers: Textual Division in some Late-Medieval English Texts', in *New Science out of Old Books: Studies in Manuscripts and Early Printed Books in Honour of A.I. Doyle*, ed. Richard Beadle and A.J. Piper (Aldershot: Scolar Press), 207–26

Kelly 1987. Douglas Kelly, 'The Genius of the Patron: the Prince, the Poet, and Fourteenth Century Invention', *Studies in the Literary Imagination*, 20, no. 1, 77–97

Kerby-Fulton 1997. Kathryn Kerby-Fulton, 'Langland and the Bibliographic Ego', in *Written Work: Langland, Labor, and Authorship*, ed. Steven Justice and Kathryn Kerby-Fulton (Philadelphia: University of Pennsylvania Press), 67–143

Kerby-Fulton and Justice 1997. Kathryn Kerby-Fulton and Steven Justice, 'Langlandian Reading Circles and the Civil Service in London and Dublin, 1380–1427', *New Medieval Literatures*, 1, 59–83

Kindermann 1978. Udo Kindermann, *Satyra: Die Theorie der Satire im Mittellateinischen: Vorstudie zu einer Gattungsgeschichte*, Erlanger Beiträge zur Sprach- und Kunstwissenschaft, 58 (Nuremberg: Carl)

Kleinecke 1937. Wilhelm Kleinecke, *Englische Fürstenspiegel vom Policraticus Johanns von Salisbury bis zum Basilikon Doron König Jakobs I* (Halle: Niemeyer)

Knapp 1994. Ethan Knapp, 'Bureaucratic Identity and Literary Practice in Lancastrian England', *Medieval Perspectives*, 9, 63–72

—— 1999a. 'Bureaucratic Identity and the Construction of the Self in Hoccleve's *Formulary* and *La Male Regle*', *Speculum*, 74, 357–76

—— **1999b**. 'Eulogies and Usurpations: Hoccleve and Chaucer Revisited', *SAC*, 21, 247–73
Knowles 1954. C. Knowles, 'Caxton and his Two French Sources', *Modern Language Review*, 49, 417–23
Kohl 1988. Stephan Kohl, 'More than Virtues and Vices: Self-Analysis in Hoccleve's "Autobiographies" ', *FCS*, 14, 115–27
Kohler 1900–6. Charles Kohler, 'Traité du recouvrement de la Terre Sainte adressé vers l'an 1295 à Philippe le Bel, par Galvano de Levanto, médecin génois', in his *Mélanges pour servir à l'histoire de l'Orient latin et des Croisades*, 2 vols (Paris: Leroux), I, 213–40
Krochalis 1986–7. Jeanne E. Krochalis, 'Hoccleve's Chaucer Portrait', *ChR*, 21, 234–45
—— **1988–9.** 'The Books and Reading of Henry V and his Circle', *ChR*, 23, 50–77
Kuhn 1940. Charles L. Kuhn, 'Herman Scheere and English Illumination of the Early Fifteenth Century', *The Art Bulletin*, 22, 138–56
Kurdzialek 1971. Marian Kurdzialek, 'Der Mensch als Abild des Kosmos', in *Der Begriff der Repraesentatio im Mittelalter: Stellvertretung, Symbol, Zeichen, Bild*, ed. Albert Zimmerman (Berlin: de Gruyter), 35–75
Lakoff and Johnson 1980. George Lakoff and Mark Johnson, *Metaphors We Live By* (Chicago, IL: University of Chicago Press)
Lam and Smith 1944. George L. Lam and Warren A. Smith, 'George Vertue's Contributions to Chaucerian Iconography', *Modern Language Quarterly*, 5, 303–22
Lapsley 1934. Gaillard Lapsley, 'The Parliamentary Title of Henry IV', *EHR*, 49, 423–49; 577–606
Lawton 1981. David Lawton, 'Lollardy and the *Piers Plowman* Tradition', *Modern Language Review*, 76, 780–93
—— **1987.** 'Dullness and the Fifteenth Century', *ELH*, 54, 761–99
Lawton 1983. Lesley Lawton, 'The Illustration of Late Medieval Secular Texts, with Special Reference to Lydgate's *Troy Book*', in *Manuscripts and Readers in Fifteenth-Century England: the Literary Implications of Manuscript Study*, ed. Derek Pearsall (Cambridge: Brewer), 41–69
Leader 1988. Damien Riehl Leader, *A History of the University of Cambridge, I: The University to 1546*, gen. ed. Christopher Brooke (Cambridge: CUP)
Le Goff 1989. Jacques Le Goff, 'Head or Heart? The Political Use of Body Metaphors in the Middle Ages', in *Fragments for a History of the Human Body*, ed. Michel Feher, with Ramona Naddaff and Nadia Tazi, 3 vols (New York: Urzone), III, 13–26
Lerer 1993. Seth Lerer, *Chaucer and his Readers: Imagining the Author in Late-Medieval England* (Princeton, NJ: Princeton UP)
Linder 1977. Amnon Linder, 'The Knowledge of John of Salisbury in the Late Middle Ages', *Studi Medievali*, 3rd series, 18, 315–66
Lucas 1997. Peter J. Lucas, *From Author to Audience: John Capgrave and Medieval Publication* (Dublin: University College Dublin Press)
Luscombe 1982. D.E. Luscombe, 'The State of Nature and the Origin of the State', in *The Cambridge History of Later Medieval Philosophy*, ed. Norman Kretzmann, Anthony Kenny and Jan Pinborg (Cambridge: CUP), 757–70

Bibliography

MacCracken 1911. Henry Noble MacCracken, 'King Henry's Triumphal Entry into London, Lydgate's Poem, and Carpenter's Letter', *Archiv für das Studium der Neueren Sprachen und Literaturen*, 126, 75–102

MacDonald 1966. Donald MacDonald, 'Proverbs, *Sententiae*, and *Exempla* in Chaucer's Comic Tales: the Function of Comic Misapplication', *Speculum*, 41, 453–65

Machan 1992. Tim W. Machan, 'Textual Authority and the Works of Hoccleve, Lydgate, and Henryson', *Viator*, 23, 281–99

Manly and Rickert 1940. John M. Manly and Edith Rickert, *The Text of the 'Canterbury Tales'*, 8 vols (Chicago, IL: University of Chicago Press)

Mann 1980. Jill Mann, 'Satiric Subject and Satiric Object in Goliardic Literature', *Mittellateinisches Jahrbuch*, 15, 63–86

—— 1983. 'Satisfaction and Payment in Middle English Literature', *SAC*, 5, 17–48

Manzalaoui 1961. M.A. [Mahmoud] Manzalaoui, 'The *Secreta Secretorum*: the Mediaeval European Version of *Kitāb Sirr-al-asrār*', *Bulletin of the Faculty of Arts, Alexandria University*, 15, 83–107

—— 1981. ' "Noght in the Registre of Venus": Gower's English Mirror for Princes', in *Medieval Studies for J.A.W. Bennett aetatis suae LXX*, ed. P.L. Heyworth (Oxford: Clarendon Press), 159–83

Mapstone 1987. Sally Mapstone, 'The Advice to Princes Tradition in Scottish Literature, 1450–1500' (unpublished doctoral thesis, University of Oxford)

—— 1997. 'Kingship and the *Kingis Quair*', in *The Long Fifteenth Century: Essays for Douglas Gray*, ed. Helen Cooper and Sally Mapstone (Oxford: Clarendon Press), 51–69

Markus 1983. Manfred Markus, 'Truth, Fiction and Metafiction in Fifteenth-Century English Literature, Particularly in Lydgate and Hoccleve', *FCS*, 8, 117–39

Marzec 1980. Marcia Smith Marzec, 'Thomas Hoccleve's *De Regimine Principum*, Sections 12 and 13: a Critical Edition' (doctoral dissertation, University of Northern Illinois)

—— 1982. 'The Sources of Hoccleve's *Regiment* and the Use of Translations', *Équivalences*, 13, 9–21

—— 1987a. 'Scribal Emendation in Some Later Manuscripts of Hoccleve's *Regiment of Princes*', *Analytical and Enumerative Bibliography*, n.s. 1, 41–51

—— 1987b. 'The Latin Marginalia of the *Regiment of Princes* as an Aid to Stemmatic Analysis', *Text*, 3, 269–84

Mather 1897. F.J. Mather Jnr, 'King Ponthus and the Fair Sidone', *PMLA*, 12, 1–150

Mathew 1968. Gervase Mathew, *The Court of Richard II* (London: Murray)

Matthews 1972. William Matthews, 'Thomas Hoccleve', in *A Manual of the Writings of Middle English, 1050–1500*, new edn, gen. ed. J. Burke Severs and Albert E. Hartung (New Haven: Connecticut Academy of Arts and Sciences, 1967– (vol. III pub. 1972)), III, 746–56, 903–8

McFarlane 1973. K.B. McFarlane, *The Nobility of Later Medieval England: the Ford Lectures for 1953 and Related Studies* (Oxford: Clarendon Press)

—— 1981. *England in the Fifteenth Century: Collected Essays*, intro. by G.L. Harriss (London: Hambledon Press)

McGregor 1977. James H. McGregor, 'The Iconography of Chaucer in Hoccleve's *De Regimine Principum* and in the *Troilus* Frontispiece', *ChR*, 11, 338–50

McIntosh 1996. Marjorie K. McIntosh, 'Finding Language for Misconduct: Jurors in Fifteenth-Century Local Courts', in *Bodies and Disciplines: Intersections of Literature and History in Fifteenth-Century England*, ed. Barbara H. Hanawalt and David Wallace (Minneapolis: University of Minnesota Press), 87–122

McMillan 1988. Douglas J. McMillan, 'The Single Most Popular of Thomas Hoccleve's Poems: *The Regement of Princes'*, *NM*, 89, 63–71

McNiven 1980. Peter McNiven, 'Prince Henry and the English Political Crisis of 1412', *History*, 65, 1–16

—— 1985. 'The Problem of Henry IV's Health, 1405–1413', *EHR*, 100, 747–72

—— 1987. *Heresy and Politics in the Reign of Henry IV: the Burning of John Badby* (Woodbridge: Boydell Press)

—— 1994. 'Rebellion, Sedition, and the Legend of Richard II's Survival in the Reigns of Henry IV and Henry V', *Bulletin of the John Rylands Library*, 76, 93–117

McRee 1987. Ben R. McRee, 'Religious Gilds and Regulation of Behaviour in Late Medieval Towns', in *People, Politics and Community in the Later Middle Ages*, ed. Joel Rosenthal and Colin Richmond (Gloucester: Sutton), 108–22

Meale 1989. Carol M. Meale, 'Patrons, Buyers and Owners: Book Production and Social Status', in *Book Production and Publishing in Britain, 1375–1475*, ed. Jeremy Griffiths and Derek Pearsall (Cambridge: CUP), 201–38

—— 1995. '*The Libelle of Englyshe Polycye* and Mercantile Literary Culture in Late-Medieval London', in *London and Europe in the Later Middle Ages*, ed. Julia Boffey and Pamela King (London: Centre for Medieval and Renaissance Studies, Queen Mary and Westfield College), 181–227

Medcalf 1981. Stephen Medcalf, 'Inner and Outer', in *The Later Middle Ages*, ed. Stephen Medcalf (London: Methuen), 108–71

Mehl 1978. J.M. Mehl, 'L'exemplum chez Jacques de Cessoles', *Le Moyen Age*, 4th series, 33, 227–46

Mertes 1988. Kate Mertes, *The English Noble Household, 1250–1600: Good Governance and Politic Rule* (Oxford: Blackwell)

Middleton 1978. Anne Middleton, 'The Idea of Public Poetry in the Reign of Richard II', *Speculum*, 53, 94–114

Mills 1996. David Mills, 'The Voices of Thomas Hoccleve', in *Essays on Thomas Hoccleve*, ed. Catherine Batt (London: Centre for Medieval and Renaissance Studies, Queen Mary and Westfield College; Turnhout: Brepols), 85–107

Minnis 1979. Alastair J. Minnis, 'Late-Medieval Discussions of *Compilatio* and the Rôle of the *Compilator*', *Beiträge zur Geschichte der Deutschen Sprache und Literatur*, 101, 385–421

—— 1981. 'The Influence of Academic Prologues on the Prologues and Literary Attitudes of Late-Medieval English Writers', *Medieval Studies*, 43, 342–83

—— 1984. *Medieval Theory of Authorship: Scholastic Literary Attitudes in the Later Middle Ages* (Aldershot: Scolar Press)

Minnis and Scott 1988. A.J. Minnis and A.B. Scott, *Medieval Literary Theory and Criticism c.1100–c.1375: the Commentary Tradition* (Oxford: Clarendon Press)

Bibliography

Mitchell 1968. Jerome Mitchell, *Thomas Hoccleve: a Study in Early Fifteenth-Century Poetic* (Urbana: University of Illinois Press)
—— **1984.** 'Hoccleve Studies, 1965–1981', in *Fifteenth Century Studies: Recent Essays*, ed. Robert F. Yeager (Hamden, CT: Archon Books), 49–63
Mooney 1995–6. Linne R. Mooney, 'More Manuscripts Written by a Chaucer Scribe', *ChR*, 30, 401–7
—— **2000.** 'A New Manuscript by the Hammond Scribe Discovered by Jeremy Griffiths', in *The English Medieval Book: Studies in Memory of Jeremy Griffiths*, ed. A.S.G. Edwards, Vincent Gillespie and Ralph Hanna (London: BL), 113–23
Morgan 1987. D.A.L. Morgan, 'The House of Policy: the Political Role of the Late Plantagenet Household, 1422–1485', in *The English Court: From the Wars of the Roses to the Civil War*, ed. David Starkey et al. (London: Longman), 25–70
—— **1997.** 'The Political Afterlife of Edward III: the Apotheosis of a Warmonger', *EHR*, 112, 856–81
Morgan 1995. Philip Morgan, 'Henry IV and the Shadow of Richard II', in *Crown, Government and People in the Fifteenth Century*, ed. Rowena E. Archer (Stroud: Sutton), 1–31
Mortimer 1995a. Nigel Mortimer, 'A Study of John Lydgate's *Fall of Princes* in its Literary and Political Contexts' (unpublished doctoral thesis, University of Oxford)
—— **1995b.** 'Selections from Lydgate's *Fall of Princes*: a Corrected Checklist', *The Library*, 6th series, 17, 342–4
Murray 1913. H.J.R. Murray, *A History of Chess* (Oxford: Clarendon Press)
Nederman 1987. Cary J. Nederman, 'The Physiological Significance of the Organic Metaphor in John of Salisbury's *Policraticus*', *History of Political Thought*, 8, 211–23
Nicholls 1985. Jonathan Nicholls, *The Matter of Courtesy: Medieval Courtesy Books and the Gawain Poet* (Cambridge: Brewer)
Nissé 1999. Ruth Nissé, ' "Oure Fadres Olde and Modres": Gender, Heresy, and Hoccleve's Literary Politics', *SAC*, 21, 275–99
Nolan and Farley-Hills 1971. Barbara Nolan and David Farley-Hills, 'The Authorship of *Pearl*: Two Notes', *RES*, n.s. 22, 295–302
Orme 1984. Nicholas Orme, *From Childhood to Chivalry: the Education of the English Kings and Aristocracy, 1066–1530* (London: Methuen)
Owen 1987. Charles A. Owen, Jnr, '*Troilus and Criseyde*: the Question of Chaucer's Revisions', *SAC*, 9, 155–72
Pächt and Alexander 1966–73. Otto Pächt and J.J.G. Alexander, *Illuminated Manuscripts in the Bodleian Library, Oxford*, 3 vols (Oxford: Clarendon Press)
Parkes 1995. M.B. Parkes, 'Patterns of Scribal Activity and Revisions of the Text in Early Copies of Works by John Gower', in *New Science out of Old Books: Studies in Manuscripts and Early Printed Books in Honour of A.I. Doyle*, ed. Richard Beadle and A.J. Piper (Aldershot: Scolar Press), 81–121
Partridge 1997. Stephen Partridge, 'A Newly Identified Manuscript by the Scribe of the New College *Canterbury Tales*', *EMS*, 6, 229–36

Patterson 1984. Annabel Patterson, *Censorship and Interpretation: the Conditions of Writing and Reading in Early Modern England* (Madison: University of Wisconsin Press)

Patterson 1989. Lee Patterson, ' "What Man Artow?": Authorial Self-Definition in *The Tale of Sir Thopas* and *The Tale of Melibee*', *SAC*, 11, 117–75

—— **1991.** *Chaucer and the Subject of History* (London: Routledge)

—— **1992.** 'Court Politics and the Invention of Literature: the Case of Sir John Clanvowe', in *Culture and History, 1350–1600: Essays on English Communities, Identities and Writing*, ed. David Aers (New York: Harvester Wheatsheaf), 7–41

—— **1993a.** 'Making Identities in Fifteenth-Century England: Henry V and John Lydgate', in *New Historical Literary Study: Essays on Reproducing Texts, Representing History*, ed. Jeffrey N. Cox and Larry J. Reynolds (Princeton, NJ: Princeton UP), 69–107

—— **1993b.** 'Perpetual Motion: Alchemy and the Technology of the Self', *SAC*, 15, 25–57

Patton 1992. Celeste A. Patton, 'False "Rekenynges": Sharp Practice and the Politics of Language in Chaucer's *Manciple's Tale*', *Philological Quarterly*, 71, 399–417

Pearsall 1970. Derek Pearsall, *John Lydgate* (London: Routledge & Kegan Paul)

—— **1989.** 'Gower's Latin in the *Confessio Amantis*', in *Latin and Vernacular: Studies in Late-Medieval Texts and Manuscripts*, ed. A.J. Minnis (Cambridge: Brewer), 13–25

—— **1992a.** *The Life of Chaucer: a Critical Biography* (Oxford: Blackwell)

—— **1992b.** 'Lydgate as Innovator', *Modern Language Quarterly*, 53, 5–22

—— **1994.** 'Thomas Hoccleve's *Regement of Princes*: the Poetics of Royal Self-Representation', *Speculum*, 69, 386–410

—— **1997.** 'The Ellesmere Chaucer and Contemporary English Literary Manuscripts', in *The Ellesmere Chaucer: Essays in Interpretation*, ed. Martin Stevens and Daniel Woodard (San Marino, CA: Huntington Library), 263–80

Peck 1978. Russell A. Peck, *Kingship and Common Profit in Gower's 'Confessio Amantis'* (Carbondale: Southern Illinois UP)

—— **1986.** 'Social Conscience and the Poets', in *Social Unrest in the Late Middle Ages*, ed. Francis X. Newman (Binghampton, NY: Center for Medieval and Early Renaissance Studies), 113–48

Perkins 1999a. Nicholas Perkins, 'Counsel and Constraint in Thomas Hoccleve's *The Regement of Princes*' (unpublished doctoral dissertation, University of Cambridge)

—— **1999b.** 'Musing on Mutability: a Poem in the Welles Anthology and Hoccleve's *The Regement of Princes*', *RES*, n.s. 50, 493–8

Peterson 1977. Clifford Peterson, 'Hoccleve, the Old Hall Manuscript, Cotton Nero A. x, and the *Pearl*-Poet', *RES*, n.s. 28, 49–55 (reply by Edward Wilson, 55–6)

Pocock 1973. J.G.A. Pocock, 'Verbalizing a Political Act: Toward a Politics of Speech', *Political Theory*, 1, 27–45

Bibliography

Pollard 1995. A.J. Pollard, 'The Lancastrian Constitutional Experiment Revisited: Henry IV, Sir John Tiptoft and the Parliament of 1406', *Parliamentary History*, 14, 103–19

Porter 1983. Elizabeth Porter, 'Gower's Ethical Microcosm and Political Macrocosm', in *Gower's 'Confessio Amantis': Responses and Reassessments*, ed. A.J. Minnis (Cambridge: Brewer), 135–62

Pouchelle 1990. Marie-Christine Pouchelle, *The Body and Surgery in the Middle Ages*, trans. Rosemary Morris (Cambridge: Polity Press)

Powell 1989. Edward Powell, *Kingship, Law, and Society: Criminal Justice in the Reign of Henry V* (Oxford: Clarendon Press)

—— **1994.** 'After "After McFarlane": The Poverty of Patronage and the Case for Constitutional History', in *Trade, Devotion, and Governance: Papers in Later Medieval History*, ed. Dorothy J. Clayton, Richard G. Davies and Peter McNiven (Gloucester: Sutton), 1–16

Powell 1992. James M. Powell, *Albertanus of Brescia: The Pursuit of Happiness in the Early Thirteenth Century* (Philadelphia: University of Pennsylvania Press)

Pryor 1968. Mary Ruth Pryor, 'Thomas Hoccleve's Series: an Edition of MS Durham Cosin V. iii. 9' (unpublished doctoral dissertation, University of California, Los Angeles)

Quillet 1988. Jeannine Quillet, 'Community, Counsel and Representation', in *The Cambridge History of Medieval Political Thought, c. 350–1450*, ed. J.H. Burns (Cambridge: CUP), 520–72

Rawcliffe 1995. Carole Rawcliffe, *Medicine and Society in Later Medieval England* (Stroud: Sutton)

—— **1996.** 'The Insanity of Henry VI', *The Historian*, 50, 8–12

Reeves 1974. A. Compton Reeves, 'Thomas Hoccleve, Bureaucrat', *Medievalia et Humanistica*, n.s. 5, 201–14

—— **1979.** 'The World of Thomas Hoccleve', *FCS*, 2, 187–201

Rezneck 1927–8. Samuel Rezneck, 'Constructive Treason by Words in the Fifteenth Century', *American Historical Review*, 33, 544–52

Richardson 1936. H.G. Richardson, 'Heresy and the Lay Power under Richard II', *EHR*, 51, 1–28

Richardson 1980. Malcolm Richardson, 'Henry V, the English Chancery, and Chancery English', *Speculum*, 55, 726–50

—— **1986.** 'Hoccleve in his Social Context', *ChR*, 20, 313–22

—— **1990.** 'The Earliest Known Owners of *Canterbury Tales* Manuscripts and Chaucer's Secondary Audience', *ChR*, 25, 17–32

Richmond 1983. Colin Richmond, 'After McFarlane', *History*, 68, 46–60

—— **1988.** 'Hand and Mouth: Information Gathering and Use in England in the Later Middle Ages', *Journal of Historical Sociology*, 1, 233–52

Rickert 1954. Margaret Rickert, *Painting in Britain: the Middle Ages* (Harmondsworth: Penguin)

Rigg 1970. A.G. Rigg, 'Hoccleve's *Complaint* and Isidore of Seville', *Speculum*, 45, 564–74

—— **1992.** *A History of Anglo-Latin Literature, 1066–1422* (Cambridge: CUP)

Robbins 1955. Rossell Hope Robbins, 'An Epitaph for Duke Humphrey', *NM*, 56, 241–9

Robinson 1980. P.R. Robinson, 'The "Booklet": a Self-Contained Unit in Composite Manuscripts', in *Codicologica 3: Essais typologiques,* ed. A. Gruys and J.P. Gumbert (Leiden: Brill), 46–69

Roskell 1981–3. J.S. Roskell, *Parliament and Politics in Late Medieval England,* 3 vols (London: Hambledon Press)

Rosser 1988. Gervase Rosser, 'Communities of Parish and Guild in the Late Middle Ages', in *Parish, Church and People: Local Studies in Lay Religion 1350–1750,* ed. S.J. Wright (London: Hutchinson), 29–55

—— **1989.** *Medieval Westminster, 1200–1540* (Oxford: Clarendon Press)

Rubin 1991. Miri Rubin, *Corpus Christi: the Eucharist in Late Medieval Culture* (Cambridge: CUP)

—— **1994.** 'The Person in the Form: Medieval Challenges to Bodily Order', in *Framing Medieval Bodies,* ed. Sarah Kay and Miri Rubin (Manchester: Manchester UP), 100–22

Rychner 1955. J. Rychner, 'Les traductions françaises de la *Morilisatio super ludum scaccorum* de Jacques de Cessoles', in *Recueil de travaux offert à M. Clovis Brunel,* no ed., 2 vols (Paris: École des chartes), II, 480–93

Saenger 1989. Paul Saenger, *A Catalogue of the Pre-1500 Western Manuscript Books at the Newberry Library* (Chicago, IL: University of Chicago Press)

Salter and Pearsall 1980. Elizabeth Salter and Derek Pearsall, 'Pictorial Illustration of Late Medieval Poetic Texts: the Role of the Frontispiece or Prefatory Picture', in *Medieval Iconography and Narrative,* ed. Fleming G. Andersen et al. (Odense: Odense UP), 100–23

Sandler 1986. Lucy Freeman Sandler, *Gothic Manuscripts, 1285–1385,* 2 vols; part 5 of *A Survey of Manuscripts Illuminated in the British Isles,* gen. ed. J.J.G. Alexander (London: Miller)

Saul 1997. Nigel Saul, *Richard II* (New Haven, CT: Yale UP)

Saxl 1957. F. Saxl, 'Macrocosm and Microcosm in Medieval Pictures', in his *Lectures,* 2 vols (London: Warburg Institute), I, 58–72 (plates in volume II)

Scanlon 1990. Larry Scanlon, 'The King's Two Voices: Narrative and Power in Hoccleve's *Regement of Princes',* in *Literary Practice and Social Change in Britain, 1380–1530,* ed. Lee Patterson (Berkeley: University of California Press), 216–47

—— **1994.** *Narrative, Authority, and Power: the Medieval Exemplum and the Chaucerian Tradition* (Cambridge: CUP)

Scarry 1985. Elaine Scarry, *The Body in Pain: the Making and Unmaking of the World* (New York: OUP)

Scase 1992. Wendy Scase, 'Reginald Peacock, John Carpenter and John Colop's "Common Profit" Books: Aspects of Book Ownership and Circulation in Fifteenth-Century London', *MÆ,* 61, 261–74

Scattergood 1969. V.J. [John] Scattergood, 'Two Medieval Booklists', *The Library,* 5th series, 23, 236–9

—— **1971.** *Politics and Poetry in the Fifteenth Century* (London: Blandford Press)

—— **1974.** 'The Manciple's Manner of Speaking', *Essays in Criticism,* 24, 124–46

—— **1983.** 'Literary Culture at the Court of Richard II', in *English Court Culture in the Later Middle Ages,* ed. V.J. Scattergood and J.W. Sherborne (London: Duckworth), 29–43

—— 1987. 'Social and Political Issues in Chaucer: an Approach to Lak of Stedfastnesse', *ChR*, 21, 469–75
—— 1990. 'The Date and Composition of George Ashby's Poems', *Leeds Studies in English*, 21, 167–76
—— 1996. 'George Ashby's *Prisoner's Reflections* and the Virtue of Patience', in his *Reading the Past: Essays on Medieval and Renaissance Literature* (Blackrock: Four Courts Press), 266–74
Schlauch 1945. Margaret Schlauch, 'Chaucer's Doctrine of Kings and Tyrants', *Speculum*, 20, 133–56
Schmitt and Knox 1985. Charles B. Schmitt and Dilwyn Knox, *Pseudo-Aristoteles Latinus: a Guide to Latin Works Falsely Attributed to Aristotle before 1500* (London: Warburg Institute)
Schulz 1937. H.C. Schulz, 'Thomas Hoccleve, Scribe', *Speculum*, 12, 71–81
Scott 1989a. Kathleen L. Scott, 'Design, Decoration and Illustration', in *Book Production and Publishing in Britain, 1375–1475*, ed. Jeremy Griffiths and Derek Pearsall (Cambridge: CUP), 31–64
—— 1989b. 'Caveat Lector: Ownership and Standardization in the Illustration of Fifteenth-Century English Manuscripts', *EMS*, 1, 19–63
—— 1996. *Later Gothic Manuscripts, 1390–1490*, 2 vols; part 6 of *A Survey of Manuscripts Illuminated in the British Isles*, gen. ed. J.J.G. Alexander (London: Miller)
Seymour 1974. M.C. [Michael] Seymour, 'The Manuscripts of Hoccleve's *Regiment of Princes*', *Edinburgh Bibliographical Society Transactions*, 4, part 7, 255–97
—— 1982. 'Manuscript Portraits of Chaucer and Hoccleve', *The Burlington Magazine*, 124, 618–23
Shailor 1984–92. Barbara A. Shailor, *Catalogue of Medieval and Renaissance Manuscripts in the Beinecke Rare Books and Manuscript Library, Yale University*, 3 vols (Binghampton, NY: Medieval and Renaissance Texts and Studies)
Sharpe 1979. Kevin Sharpe, *Sir Robert Cotton, 1586–1631: History and Politics in Early Modern England* (Oxford: OUP)
Sherman 1995. Claire Richter Sherman, *Imaging Aristotle: Verbal and Visual Representation in Fourteenth-Century France* (Berkeley: University of California Press)
Shoaf 1983. R.A. Shoaf, *Dante, Chaucer, and the Currency of the Word: Money, Images, and Reference in Late Medieval Poetry* (Norman, OK: Pilgrim Books)
Sigal 1984. Gale Sigal, 'The Rule of Pleasure: Chastity as Conquest in Hoccleve's *Regiment of Princes*', *Mid-Hudson Language Studies*, 7, 19–28
Silvia 1974. Daniel S. Silvia, 'Some Fifteenth-Century Manuscripts of the *Canterbury Tales*', in *Chaucer and Middle English Studies in Honour of Rossell Hope Robbins*, ed. Beryl Rowland (London: Allen & Unwin), 153–63
Simpson 1986a. James Simpson, 'Dante's "Astripetam Aquilam" and the Theme of Poetic Discretion in the *House of Fame*', *Essays and Studies*, 1–18
—— 1986b. 'From Reason to Affective Knowledge: Modes of Thought and Poetic Form in *Piers Plowman*', *MÆ*, 55, 1–23
—— 1990a. *'Piers Plowman': an Introduction to the B-text* (London: Longman)

—— 1990b. 'The Constraints of Satire in *Piers Plowman* and *Mum and the Soothsegger*', in *Langland, the Mystics, and the Medieval English Religious Tradition*, ed. Helen Phillips (Cambridge: Brewer), 11–30
—— 1991. 'Madness and Texts: Hoccleve's *Series*', in *Chaucer and Fifteenth-Century Poetry*, ed. Julia Boffey and Janet Cowan (London: King's College), 15–29
—— 1993. ' "After Craftes conseil clotheth yow and fede": Langland and London City Politics', in *England in the Fourteenth Century: Proceedings of the 1991 Harlaxton Symposium*, ed. Nicholas Rogers (Stamford: Paul Watkins), 109–27
—— 1995a. 'Nobody's Man: Thomas Hoccleve's *Regement of Princes*', in *London and Europe in the Later Middle Ages*, ed. Julia Boffey and Pamela King (London: Centre for Medieval and Renaissance Studies, Queen Mary and Westfield College), 149–80
—— 1995b. *Sciences and the Self in Medieval Poetry: Alan of Lille's 'Anticlaudianus' and John Gower's 'Confessio amantis'* (Cambridge: CUP)
—— 1996. 'Desire and the Scriptural Text: Will as Reader in *Piers Plowman*', in *Criticism and Dissent in the Middle Ages*, ed. Rita Copeland (Cambridge: CUP), 215–43
—— 1998a. 'The Other Book of Troy: Guido delle Colonne's *Historia destructionis Troiae* in Fourteenth- and Fifteenth-Century England', *Speculum*, 73, 397–423
—— 1998b. 'Ethics and Interpretation: Reading Wills in Chaucer's *Legend of Good Women*', *SAC*, 20, 73–100
Skinner 1978. Quentin Skinner, *The Foundations of Modern Political Thought*, 2 vols (Cambridge: CUP)
—— 1988. *Meaning and Context: Quentin Skinner and his Critics*, ed. and intr. by James Tully (Cambridge: Polity Press)
Smith 1966. Kathleen L. Smith, 'A Fifteenth-Century Vernacular Manuscript Reconstructed', *BLR*, 7, 234–41
Somerset 1998. Fiona Somerset, *Clerical Discourse and Lay Audience in Late Medieval England* (Cambridge: CUP)
Spearing 1976. A.C. Spearing, *Medieval Dream-Poetry* (Cambridge: CUP)
—— 1985. *Medieval to Renaissance in English Poetry* (Cambridge: CUP)
—— 1992. 'Prison, Writing, Absence: Representing the Subject in the English Poems of Charles D'Orleans', *Modern Language Quarterly*, 53, 83–99
Sponsler 1991–2. Claire Sponsler, 'Narrating the Social Order: Medieval Clothing Laws', *Clio*, 21, 265–83
Spriggs 1962–7. Gereth M. Spriggs, 'Unnoticed Bodleian Manuscripts, Illuminated by Herman Scheere and his School', *BLR*, 7, 193–203
Starkey 1981. David Starkey, 'The Age of the Household: Politics, Society and the Arts c. 1350–1550', in *The Later Middle Ages*, ed. Stephen Medcalf (London: Methuen), 225–90
—— 1987. 'Introduction: Court History in Perspective', in *The English Court: From the Wars of the Roses to the Civil War*, ed. David Starkey et al. (London: Longman), 1–24
Staley 2000. Lynn Staley, 'Gower, Richard II, Henry of Derby, and the Business of Making Culture', *Speculum*, 75, 68–96

Stevens 1979. Martin Stevens, 'The Royal Stanza in Early English Literature', *PMLA*, 94, 62–76

Straker 1998. Scott-Morgan Straker, 'Ethics, Militarism and Gender: John Lydgate's *Troy Book* as a Political Lesson for Henry V' (unpublished doctoral thesis, University of Cambridge)

Stratford 1987. Jenny Stratford, 'The Manuscripts of John, Duke of Bedford: Library and Chapel', in *England in the Fifteenth Century: Proceedings of the 1986 Harlaxton Symposium*, ed. Daniel Williams (Woodbridge: Boydell Press), 329–50

Strohm 1971. Paul Strohm, 'Jean of Angoulême: a Fifteenth-Century Reader of Chaucer', *NM*, 72, 69–76

—— 1979. 'Form and Social Statement in *Confessio Amantis* and *The Canterbury Tales*', *SAC*, 1, 17–40

—— 1982a. 'A Note on Gower's Persona', in *Acts of Interpretation: the Text in its Contexts, 700–1600: Essays on Medieval and Renaissance Literature in Honor of E. Talbot Donaldson*, ed. Mary J. Carruthers and Elizabeth D. Kirk (Norman, OK: Pilgrim Books), 293–8

—— 1982b. 'Chaucer's Fifteenth-Century Audience and the Narrowing of the "Chaucer Tradition" ', *SAC*, 4, 3–32

—— 1988. 'Fourteenth- and Fifteenth-Century Writers as Readers of Chaucer', in *Genres, Themes and Images in English Literature*, ed. Piero Boitani and Anna Torti (Tübingen: Narr; Cambridge: Brewer), 90–104

—— 1989. *Social Chaucer* (Cambridge, MA: Harvard UP)

—— 1990. 'Politics and Poetics: Usk and Chaucer in the 1380s ', in *Literary Practice and Social Change in Britain, 1380–1530*, ed. Lee Patterson (Berkeley: University of California Press), 83–112

—— 1992. *Hochon's Arrow: the Social Imagination of Fourteenth-Century Texts* (Princeton, NJ: Princeton UP)

—— 1996. 'The Trouble with Richard: the Reburial of Richard II and Lancastrian Symbolic Strategy', *Speculum*, 71, 87–111

—— 1997a. *Sir John Oldcastle: Another Ill-Framed Knight*, The William Matthews Lectures 1997 (London: Birkbeck College)

—— 1997b. 'Counterfeiters, Lollards, and Lancastrian Unease', *New Medieval Literatures*, 1, 31–58

—— 1998. *England's Empty Throne: Usurpation and the Language of Legitimation, 1399–1422* (New Haven, CT: Yale UP)

—— 1999. 'Hoccleve, Lydgate and the Lancastrian Court', in *The Cambridge History of Medieval English Literature*, ed. David Wallace (Cambridge: CUP), 640–61

—— 2000. *Theory and the Premodern Text* (Minneapolis and London: University of Minnesota Press)

Struve 1978. Tilman Struve, *Die Entwicklung der Organologischen Staatsauffasung im Mittelalter* (Stuttgart: Hiersemann)

—— 1979–80. 'Bedentung und Funktion des Organismusvergleichs in den Mittelalterlichen Theorien von Staat und Gesellschaft', in *Soziale Ordnungen im Selbstverständnis des Mittelalters*, ed. Albert Zimmermann, 2 vols (Berlin and New York: de Gruyter), I, 144–61

—— 1984. 'The Importance of the Organism in the Political Theory of John of Salisbury', in *The World of John of Salisbury*, ed. Michael Wilks (Oxford: Blackwell), 303–17

Stubbs 1874–8. William Stubbs, *Constitutional History of England in its Origin and Development*, 3 vols (Oxford: Clarendon Press)

Sutton 1994. Anne F. Sutton, 'Alice Claver, Silkwoman (d. 1489)', in *Medieval London Widows, 1300–1500*, ed. Caroline M. Barron and Anne F. Sutton (London: Hambledon Press), 129–42

Sutton and Visser-Fuchs 1997. Anne F. Sutton and Livia Visser-Fuchs, *Richard III's Books* (Stroud: Sutton)

Tanner 1748. Thomas Tanner, *Bibliotheca Britannia-Hibernica* (London: Bowyer)

Tolmie 2000. Sarah Tolmie, 'The *Prive Scilence* of Thomas Hoccleve', *SAC*, 22, 281–309

Torti 1986. Anna Torti, 'Mirroring in Hoccleve's *Regement of Princes*', *Poetica (Tokyo)*, 24, 39–57

—— 1991. *The Glass of Form: Mirroring Structures from Chaucer to Skelton* (Cambridge: Brewer)

—— 1992. 'Hoccleve's Attitude Towards Women: "I shoop me do my peyne and diligence / To wynne hir loue by obedience" ', in *A Wyf Ther Was: Essays in Honour of Paule Mertens-Fonck*, ed. Juliette Dor (Liège: University of Liège), 264–74

Tout 1920–37. T.F. [Thomas Frederick] Tout, *Chapters in the Administrative History of Medieval England*, 6 vols (Manchester: Manchester UP)

—— 1929. 'Literature and Learning in the English Civil Service in the Fourteenth Century', *Speculum*, 4, 365–89

Trapp 1992–3. J.B. Trapp, 'The Iconography of Petrarch in the Age of Humanism', *Quaderni Petrarcheschi*, 9–10, 11–73

Trigg 1986. Stephanie Trigg, 'Israel Gollancz's "Wynnere and Wastoure": Political Satire or Editorial Politics?', in *Medieval English Religious and Ethical Literature: Essays in Honour of G.H. Russell*, ed. Gregory Kratzmann and James Simpson (Cambridge: Brewer), 115–27

Trudgill and Burrow 1998. Marian Trudgill and J.A. Burrow, 'A Hocclevean Balade', *Notes & Queries*, 243 (1998), 178–80

Tuck 1971. J.A. Tuck, 'Richard II's System of Patronage', in *The Reign of Richard II: Essays in Honour of May McKisack*, ed. F.R.H. Du Boulay and Caroline M. Barron (London: Athlone Press), 1–20

Turner 1962. D.H. Turner, 'The Bedford Hours and Psalter', *Apollo*, 76, 265–70

Turville-Petre and Wilson 1975. Thorlac Turville-Petre and Edward Wilson, 'Hoccleve, "Maister Massy" and the *Pearl* Poet: Two Notes', *RES*, n.s. 26, 129–43

Ullmann 1966. Walter Ullmann, *Principles of Government and Politics in the Middle Ages*, 2nd edn (London: Methuen)

—— 1978. 'John of Salisbury's *Policraticus* in the Later Middle Ages', in *Geschichtsschreibung und Geistiges Leben im Mittelalter: Festschrift für Heinz Löwe zum 65. Geburtstag*, ed. Karl Hauck and Hubert Mordek (Cologne: Böhlau), 519–45

van der Linde 1874. Antonius van der Linde, *Geschichte und Litteratur des Schachspiels*, 2 vols (Berlin: Springer)

Bibliography

Venn and Venn 1922–7. John Venn and J.A. Venn, *Alumni Cantabrigiensis, Part I: From the Earliest Times to 1751*, 4 vols (Cambridge: CUP)

Vickers 1907. K.H. Vickers, *Humphrey, Duke of Gloucester: a Biography* (London: Constable)

Voigts 1995. Linda Ehrsam Voigts, 'A Doctor and his Books: the Manuscripts of Roger Marchall (d. 1477)', in *New Science out of Old Books: Studies in Manuscripts and Early Printed Books in Honour of A.I. Doyle*, ed. Richard Beadle and A.J. Piper (Aldershot: Scolar Press), 249–314

Waley 1988. Daniel Waley, *The Italian City-Republics*, 3rd edn (London: Longman)

Walker 1996. Greg Walker, *Persuasive Fictions: Faction, Faith and Political Culture in the Reign of Henry VIII* (Aldershot: Scolar Press)

Walker 1995. Simon Walker, 'Richard II's Views on Kingship', in *Rulers and Ruled in Late Medieval England: Essays Presented to Gerald Harriss*, ed. Rowena E. Archer and Simon Walker (London: Hambledon Press), 49–63

Wallace 1992. David Wallace, 'Chaucer and the Absent City', in *Chaucer's England: Literature in Historical Context*, ed. Barbara A. Hanawalt (Minneapolis: University of Minnesota Press), 59–90

—— 1997. *Chaucerian Polity: Absolutist Lineages and Associational Forms in England and Italy* (Stanford, CA: Stanford UP)

Watson 1995. Nicholas Watson, 'Censorship and Cultural Change in Late-Medieval England: Vernacular Theology, the Oxford Translation Debate, and Arundel's Constitutions of 1409', *Speculum*, 70, 822–64

Watts 1996. John Watts, *Henry VI and the Politics of Kingship* (Cambridge: CUP)

Wawn 1983. Andrew Wawn, 'Truthtelling and the Tradition of *Mum and the Soothsegger*', *Yearbook of English Studies*, 13, 270–87

Webber 1997. Teresa Webber, 'Latin Devotional Texts and the Books of the Augustinian Canons of Thurgarton Priory and Leicester Abbey in the Late Middle Ages', in *Books and Collectors, 1200–1700: Essays Presented to Andrew Watson*, ed. James P. Carley and Colin G.C. Tite (London: BL), 27–41

Weiss 1941. R. Weiss, *Humanism in England during the Fifteenth Century* (Oxford: Blackwell)

Wetherbee 1991. Winthrop Wetherbee, 'Latin Structure and Vernacular Space: Gower, Chaucer and the Boethian Tradition', in *Gower and Chaucer: Difference, Mutuality, Exchange*, ed. R.F. Yeager (Victoria, BC: University of Victoria), 7–35

Whiting 1968. B.J. Whiting, *Proverbs, Sentences and Proverbial Phrases from English Writings Mainly Before 1500* (Cambridge, MA: Harvard UP)

Wilks 1963. Michael Wilks, *The Problem of Sovereignty in the Later Middle Ages* (Cambridge: CUP)

Wilson 1975. Janet Wilson, 'Poet and Patron in Early Fifteenth-Century England: John Lydgate's *Temple of Glas*', *Parergon*, 11, 25–32

Winstead 1993. Karen A. Winstead, ' "I am al othir to yow than ye weene": Hoccleve, Women, and the *Series*', *Philological Quarterly*, 72, 143–55

Wright 1992. Sylvia Wright, 'The Author Portraits in the Bedford Psalter-Hours: Gower, Chaucer and Hoccleve', *British Library Journal*, 18, 190–201

—— 1995. 'Bruges Artists in London: the Patronage of the House of Lancaster', in *Flanders in a European Perspective: Manuscript Illumination around 1400 in*

Flanders and Abroad, ed. Maurits Smeyers and Bert Cardon (Leuven: Peeters), 93–109
—— **1997**. 'The *Gesta Henrici Quinti* and the Bedford Psalter-Hours', in *The Court and Cultural Diversity*, ed. Evelyn Mullally and John Thompson (Cambridge: Brewer), 267–85
Yeager 1987a. Robert F. Yeager, '*Pax Poetica*: On the Pacifism of Chaucer and Gower', *SAC*, 9, 97–121
—— **1987b**. 'English, Latin, and the Text as "Other": the Page as Sign in the Work of John Gower', *Text*, 3, 251–67
Zumkeller 1961. Adolar Zumkeller, 'Manuskripte von Werken der Autoren des Augustiner-Eremitenordens in mitteleuropäischen Bibliotheken', *Augustiniana*, 11, 27–86; 261–319

Index

I have attempted to index references to medieval texts and manuscripts comprehensively. References to modern critics are selectively indexed when described or discussed in the text or notes, not when simply cited. References to figures who appear in Hoccleve's *Regiment* are selectively included under their own names (for example, Alexander the Great, John of Canace). If relevant material appears in the text and footnotes of a page, there is no separate reference to the footnote.

accessus ad auctores, 81–2
advice: *see* counsel
Aegidius Romanus, 88–9, 120
   De ecclesiastica potestate, 88
   De regimine principum, 13, 85, 87, 88–90, 93–9, 102, 113, 174 n.91, 177
Alan of Lille: *De planctu Naturae*, 180
Albertanus of Brescia, 14, 16
   De arte dicendi et tacendi, 14–16, 22, 50 n.2
Alceste, 20–1
Alexander the Great, 47, 71–2, 75, 102 n.66, 105, 106–7, 118, 119–20, 131–2, 136–7, 162
Allyn, Sir John, 175
Anonimalle Chronicle, 30–4
Antin, David, 106 n.73
Aquinas, St Thomas, 88
Aristotle, 3 n.10, 21, 47, 47 n.115, 71, 85, 86, 88, 89, 95 n.47, 102 n.66, 118, 119–20, 137–8
Arundel, Thomas, Archbishop of Canterbury, 10–12, 66
Arundel Constitutions, 10–12
Ashby, George, 57, 161, 194 n.8
   Active Policy of a Prince, 161
   A Prinsoner's Reflections, 161
   Dicta philosophorum, 186
Asloan manuscript: *see* manuscripts, Edinburgh, NLS 16500
Aster, Friedrich, 94
Augustine of Hippo, St, 91

Bacon, Roger, 87
Badby, John, 10, 44, 135–6
Balbi, Giovanni: *Catholicon*, 90

Bale, John:
   Catalogus, 152 n.7, 153 n.8, 190 n.146
   Index, 175 n.95
Ball, John, 8
Bardolf, Lord Thomas, 66
Barr, Helen, 17 n.46, 65–6
Beauchamp, Richard, Earl of Warwick, 174
Beaufort, Henry, Chancellor and Cardinal, 54, 66 n.51
Beaufort Hours: *see* manuscripts, London, BL Royal 2 A. xviii
Beaufort, Joan, Countess of Westmorland, 116 n.92, 172
Beaufort, John, first Earl of Somerset, 156
Beaufort, John, first Duke of Somerset, 54
Bedford Psalter-Hours: *see* manuscripts, London, BL Additional 42131
Beighton, Henry, 173
Bennett, William Fremont, 11 n.29
Berges, Wilhelm, 55
Berkeley, Sir Thomas, 89
pseudo-Bernadus Silvestris: *Epistola de cura et modo rei familiaris gubernandi*, 91, 92
Berners, Dame Juliana: *Book of Hunting*, 171
Bennett, H.S., 93
Bible, 14 n.37, 23 n.63, 45 n.111, 80, 95, 150 n.61
Black Book of Edward IV, 18

227

Blyth, Charles R., 107–8, 179 n.111, 188 n.139
Boethius, 3 n.10, 47 n.115
  De consolatione Philosophiae, 146, 176–7, 180–1; *see also* Walton, John
body politic:
  and Christ's body, 128–9, 135–6, 148–9
  and Lancastrian kings, 129–30
  definitions of, 126–32
  in the *Regiment*, 132–50
Boffey, Julia, 189–90
Boniface VIII, Pope, 88–9
Book of Curtesye, 17–18
Borges, Jorge Luis, 83
Born, Lester K., 55
Bourdieu, Pierre, 5 n.3
Bragg, Lois, 119 n.100
Briggs, Charles F., 89–90
Brigham, Nicholas, 175
Broughton, John, and family, 176–7
Brown, A.L., 33
Browne, William, 153 n.8
Brunetto Latini: *Livres dou Tresor*, 86
Brut, 170, 172
Buke of the Chess, 91 n.28
bureaucratic/institutional language, 8, 20–1, 24–6
  in Hoccleve's work, 26, 35–7, 41–2
Burgh, Dominic:
  Cato, 161–2, 170
  Secrees: *see* Lydgate, John
Burrow, John, 3 n.8, 37
Burt, Marie Anita, 97 n.54

Carlson, David, 118
Carpenter, John, 38, 167 n.62, 172 n.81, 176
Cato: *see Disticha Catonis*, and Burgh, Dominic
Caxton, William: *Game of Chess*, 91, 106 n.73, 191
censorship: *see* constraint
Cervantes, Miguel de: *Don Quixote*, 83
'Charter of Christ', 148
Chastellain, Georges: *Temple de Boccace*, 54 n.15
Chaucer, Geoffrey, 2, 61, 152 n.6, 160, 165 n.60, 169, 178 n.110, 191, 194
  as advisor, 118–19, 121

  portraits of, 114, 117–21, 155–9, 171–2
  Book of the Duchess, 77, 179 n.114
  Canterbury Tales, 11, 12, 151 n.2, 160–1, 173, 174, 176, 178 n.110, 179, 188, 189
    Canon's Yeoman's Prologue and Tale, 27–9
    Clerk's Prologue and Tale, 12, 68
    Manciple's Tale, 21–4
    Melibee, 12, 14 n.40, 56, 119
    Monk's Tale, 12, 53
    Pardoner's Tale, 173 n.86
    Shipman's Tale, 173 n.86
    Summoner's Tale, 181 n.120
  Complaint to his Purse, 119
  Gentilesse, 119 n.101
  House of Fame, 51 n.5, 52, 180 n.115
  Legend of Good Women, 20–1, 50, 53, 54, 81
  Troilus and Criseyde, 51 n.5, 77 n.74, 78, 154, 159, 189–90
Chaucer, Thomas, 34 n.87
Charlton, Sir Thomas, 176
Christine de Pizan, 36, 127
Christ's body: *see* body politic
Church, 5, 24–6, 34 n.87; *see also* constraint; heresy and Lollardy
Cicero, 91
Clanvowe, John, 2
Cleanness, 10
Chartier, Alain: *Curial*, 19 n.55
clothing and language, 42–3, 46, 80–1
Cobham, Eleanor, 54
Commons, House of: *see* Parliament
Conrad von Ammenhausen: *Schachzabelbuch*, 91
constraint:
  concept of, 5–6
  and education, 12–17
  in households, 12–13, 17–29
  and the law, 6–9
  in Parliament, 29–38
  and rebellion, 8–9
  in the *Regiment*, 39–49, 106–8, 133–4, 138–43, 144–50, 192–4
  and religion, 9–12
  and royal power, 29–30, 50–1, 58–9, 64–5, 71–2, 83, 99–102, 111–14, 131–2, 133–7, 138–43, 193–4
Copeland, Rita, 81

228

Index

Copland, Robert: *Secrete of Secretes of Arystotle*, 82 n.82
Corneburgh, Avery, 175
Cotton, Sir Robert, 153 n.8, 187 n.136
counsel, 1–4, 5–6, 61–70
  historiography of, 57–61
  in the household, 18–23
  imagery of, 114–21
  'keeping counsel', 18, 27–9, 30–1
  King's Council: *see* King's Council
  parliamentary counsel, 29–35, 61–5
  'problem of counsel', 1, 5
  in the *Regiment*, 1–4, 45–7, 69–70, 75, 81, 82–3, 106–114, 116–17, 118–21, 192–4
  see also mirrors for princes
Cowcher Books: *see* manuscrips, London, Public Record Office D.L. 42
Cupid, 20–1, 35–6, 50 n.3

Dällenbach, Lucien, 83 n.85
de la Mare, Sir Peter, 33, 34 n.87
de la Pole, William, Duke of Suffolk, 157 n.23
De quatuor virtutibus cardinalibus, 91
de Rouclif, Guy, 160
Deschamps, Eustache, 37
Descryvyng of Mannes Membres, 127–8
Dickens, Charles: *Bleak House*, 143
Dimmick, Jeremy, 193 n.4
Disticha Catonis, 13–14, 16, 22–4, 28; *see also* Burgh, Dominic: *Cato*
Dives and Pauper, 11
Donne, William, 160
Drury, Sir William and family, 174
Dunbar, William: *The Thrissill and the Rose*, 144
Dunlop, Lynn, 77 n.73
Dymok, Roger: *Liber contra XII errores et hereses Lollardorum*, 9

Edward II, 53
Edward III, 30, 32, 34 n.87, 69 n.62, 75, 93, 120 n.102
Edward IV, 18, 176–7
Edward, Duke of York, 171, 172
Edwards, A.S.G., 153–4
Egidio Colonna: *see* Aegidius Romanus

Ellesmere manuscript: *see* manuscripts, San Marino, CA, Huntington Library EL 26 C. 9
Elmham, Thomas, 67–8
exchange:
  concept of, 5–6
  in households, 18
  in Parliament, 29–34
  in the *Regiment*, 39–48, 106, 145
Exchequer, 41, 175

Ferguson, Arthur B., 5 n.2, 55 n.20
Ferron, Jean, 91
Ferster, Judith, 6 n.4, 56
FitzAlan, Joan, Countess of Hereford, 172
FitzAlan, William, Earl of Arundel, 174 n.89, 192
Fortescue, Sir John, 59 n.36, 74 n.69, 194 n.8
Fourneval: *see* Nevill, Thomas
Fradenburg, Louise, 144,
fraternities: *see* guilds and fraternities
Frenge, Nicholas, 175
Froissart, Jean, 71 n.66
Frulovisi, Tito Livio, 69 n.62

Gawain and Galeron, 171
Gaynsford, Nicholas, 175
Genoa, 90, 99 n.59, 101
Geoffrey of Vinsauf: *Poetria nova*, 92
Gerald of Wales, 87
Gesta Romanorum, 92 n.31, 163, 173
Gide, André, 83 n.85
Gilbert, Allan, 94
Giles of Rome: *see* Aegidius Romanus
Goodyere, John, 176
Gower, John, 2, 53 n.9, 57, 61, 160, 171, 178 n.110, 191, 194
  Confessio amantis, 1, 5, 60–1, 66 n.50, 73–4, 86, 87, 102 n.66, 107–8, 130–1, 136 n.29, 139, 180 n.116, 184–5, 188, 193
  Aristotelian structure of, 13, 131
  illustrations, 115–16, 120–1, 155, 159
  manuscripts, 151 n.2, 152 n.6, 153, 154, 157, 161, 173, 174 n.90, 182–3, 184–5
  Chronica triperta, 66 n.50

'In Praise of Peace', 66 n.50, 96 n.51
'Rex celi deus', 66 n.50
Vox clamantis, 66 n.50
Grady, Frank, 67 n.53
Green, Richard Firth, 2, 22 n.61, 164 n.54, 169
Greetham, D.C., 164 n.57
guilds and fraternities, 26–7, 33–4

Hales, Robert, 8
Hammond scribe: *see* scribes
Hanna, Ralph, 8, 90
Harriss, Gerald, 6 n.5, 34–5
Hasler, Anthony, 93, 113, 136 n.28, 139–40, 143–4
Haxey, Thomas, 34 n.87
Heinrich von Berigen: *Schachgedichte*, 91
Henri de Gauchi: *Livres du gouvernement des rois*, 89, 120
Henry IV, 1, 6, 8, 9, 29, 31 n.80, 32, 34 n.87, 35 n.92, 58, 65–8, 116 n.92, 119, 129, 188
Henry V (Prince Henry), 1, 3, 37, 44, 47–8, 58, 66–70, 116 n.92, 135, 142, 149–50, 172, 188
  and English language, 10
  and Henry IV, 69 n.64
  portraits of, 114–17, 155–7
  as reader of the *Regiment*, 39, 46–8, 51, 72–3, 76–7, 82–4, 93, 102, 110–11, 113–14, 132–3, 193–4
Henry VI, 69 n.62, 129 n.15
Henry, Duke of Lancaster, 72
Hilton, Walter: *Scale of Perfection*, 10
heresy and Lollardy, 9–12, 24, 34 n.87, 68, 118, 135, 143 n.42, 152 n.7; *see also* Badby, John *and* Wyclif, John
Hoccleve, Thomas, 57, 61
  biography, 5, n.1, 6, 7, 18 n.50, 26, 160–1, 193–4
  and Chaucer, 2, 11 n.29, 117–21, 160
  as clerk, 16, 35–8, 41, 42, 85, 147–50
  and Gower, 120–1, 107–8, 131, 160
  as manuscript copyist, 36, 157, 164, 185
  balades, 26, 37, 38, 68,
  envoy to Duke of Bedford, 74 n.70, 78
  Letter of Cupid, 35–6, 165 n.59

Male Regle, 8, 19–20, 37–8, 43 n.108, 45, 116 n.92
Regiment of Princes, 32, 69
  and advice tradition, 1–4, 41–2, 45, 47–9, 50–7, 69–70, 70–6, 85–93, 99–102, 160–2, 177
  date, 1
  Dialogue with the Old Man, 39–40, 42–8, 79–82, 143–50, 178–85, 187–8
  direct speech, 103, 106–14
  and dream-visions, 179–80
  'dullness', 33, 40–2, 79, 85–6
  exempla, 70–8, 103–14
  flattery, 42–3, 75, 81, 104–5, 108
  intention, concept of, 71, 74, 76–8, 81–2, 192
  manuscripts, 151–91
    in general, 151–4
    compilation, 153, 160–7, 168–77, 183–5
    glossing and annotation, 152 n.6, 154, 156–7, 158 n.34, 178–85, 186–90
    illustrations, 114–21, 155–9, 172–3
    ownership, 155, 171–7, 182, 187, 192
  as petition, 38 n.98, 39, 44, 47–8
  and reading, 70–84
  and religion, 10–11, 135–6, 152
  sources, 85–114, 122–5
  and women, 3 n.9, 21, 143 n.42, 163
  see also body politic; constraint; counsel; exchange; Henry V; translation
Remonstrance to Oldcastle, 11, 153 n.8
Series, 77 n.73, 155, 162 n.52, 163–7, 168–9, 170, 172–3, 183–5, 189–90
Hopton, Sir William, 172
households, 13–15, 17–24
Howard, Thomas, Earl of Arundel, 187 n.136
Howard, Lord William, 187
Hudson, Anne, 10
Humphrey, Duke of Gloucester, 54, 172

Index

Idley, Peter: *Instructions to his Son*, 14, 182, 183
Isidore of Seville:
　Etymologiae, 133 n.22
　Synonyma, 167 n.63, 189

Jacobus de Cessolis, 90–1
　De ludo scaccorum, 41, 85, 86, 90–114, 176–7, 191
Jacobus de Voragine: *Legenda aurea*, 90
Jacqueline of Hainault, 54
James, Richard, 153 n.8
Jean d'Angoulême, 189
Jean de Vignay: *Livre de eschez*, 88 n.12, 91
Jerome, St, 91
Johannes Hispaniensis, 87
John II of France, 93
John, Duke of Bedford, 155, 171–2
John of Bridlington, 12 n.32
John, Duke of Burgundy, 53
John of Canace, 3 n.11, 46, 75–6, 98, 111–14, 188–9
John of Gaunt, 77
John of Salisbury, 19 n.55, 91, 126–7, 136, 140 n.39
Johnson, Mark, 126
Justinian, 91

Kaepelli, Tommaso, 90
Kantorowicz, Ernst, 128–9
Kent, Thomas, 160–1
Kerr manuscript: *see* manuscripts, New York, Pierpont Morgan Library M. 122
Kinaston, Sir Francis 159
King Ponthus, 170, 172
King's Council, 7 n.10, 9, 35, 58, 59
Kleinecke, Wilhelm, 55, 97 n.55
Knapp, Ethan, 36 n.94
Knighton, Henry: *Chronicle*, 8 n.12

Lakoff, George, 126
Lam, George, 159
Langland, William, 2, 8, 21, 53 n.9, 61, 194
　Piers Plowman, 10, 12 n.32, 24 n.68, 25 n.69, 105 n.70, 132, 147 n.57, 180 n.115
Lancastrian poetry, 2–3, 50–4, 119, 193

Lawton, David, 4 n.12, 40 n.104
Lerer, Seth, 40 n.104
Libelle of English Policy, 175 n.96
Love, Nicholas: *Mirror*, 169 n.72
Lucas, Sir Thomas, 174
Lydgate, John, 169, 194 n.8
　illustrations in works of, 115–16, 154, 159
　Danse Macabre, 152 n.7, 161, 163–7, 168, 183–4
　Dietary, 170
　Fall of Princes, 53–4, 151 n.2, 162–3, 174
　Life of Our Lady, 154, 170
　Lives of St Edmund and St Fremund, 159, 174
　Of the Sodein Fal of Princes in Oure Dayes, 53, 65
　(and Burgh) *Secrees of Old Philisoffres*, 161, 169, 174
　Siege of Thebes, 157 n.23, 168, 169, 174
　Troy Book, 51–4, 159, 169

McFarlane, K.B., 58
McGregor, James, 118
Machievelli, Niccolò: *The Prince*, 150 n.60
Machaut, Guillaume de, 37, 50 n.1
Malory, Sir Thomas, 194 n.8
Mandeville's Travels, 168, 171
Mann, Jill, 132
manuscripts:
　Berne, Bibliothèque de la Bourgeoisie 275: 91
　Bristol, Public Library 8: 169 n.72
　Cambridge:
　　CUL Dd. viii. 19: 182 n.124
　　CUL Ff. i. 33: 88 n.12
　　CUL Ff. ii. 29: 177 n.108
　　CUL Gg. vi. 17: 152 n.6, 158, 181, 186 n.134
　　CUL Hh. iv. 11: 153, 159 n.39, 182, 186–7
　　CUL Ii. iii. 26: 148 n.59
　　CUL Kk. i. 3, part 11: 186 n.134
　　CUL Mm. ii. 21: 182 n.124
　　Corpus Christi College 67: 120 n.107
　　Corpus Christi College 496: 182–3, 188 n.139

Gonville and Caius College 433: 156 n.19
Magdalene College Pepys 2101: 188–9
Pembroke College 227: 176
Pembroke College 307: 120, 121 n.108, 155, 174 n.90
Queens' College 12 (Horne 24): 158, 169, 180–1
St John's College I. 22: 162–3
Sidney Sussex College 56. 3. 11: 92
Trinity College R. 3. 2: 157, 168 n.68, 183
Trinity College R. 3. 22: 170
Trinity Hall 17: 9 n.22
Fitzwilliam Museum McClean 181: 160–1
Fitzwilliam Museum McClean 182: 161 n.46, 162
Fitzwilliam Museum McClean 184: 161 n.47, 181
Fitzwilliam Museum McClean 185: 157 n.29, 161 n.47, 181
Chicago, IL, Newberry Library f 33. 7: 178 n.109
Coventry, City Record Office Accession 325/1: 120, 153, 157 n.27, 161 n.46, 163 n.53, 165 n.60, 168, 176 n.101
Durham, University Library Cosin V. iii. 9: 164, 189–90
Edinburgh:
 NLS Adv. 19. 1. 11, part 3: 158
 NLS 16500 (Asloan manuscript): 91
 University Library 202: 188 n.139
London:
 BL Additional 18632: 178
 BL Additional 22283 (Vernon manuscript): 16
 BL Additional 24062 (Hoccleve's Formulary): 36
 BL Additional 29901: 175
 BL Additional 32097: 88 n.10
 BL Additional 41666: 23 n.65
 BL Additional 42131 (Bedford Psalter-Hours): 60 n.38, 155, 156 n.19, 171
 BL Additional 47680: 120 n.102
 BL Arundel 38: 83 n.87, 114–17, 151 n.1, 152, 153, 154 n.12, 155–7, 159, 171–2, 178 n.109, 184, 187 n.136, 188 n.139
 BL Arundel 59: 161 n.46, 169–70, 175, 178, 187, 189
 BL Arundel 119: 157 n.23, 174
 BL Cotton Otho A. xviii: 159
 BL Egerton 1991: 120 n.107, 155, 156 n.19
 BL Harley 116: 148 n.59, 161 n.46, 162 n.50, 163 n.53, 178 n.109
 BL Harley 172: 162 n.52, 164 n.55
 BL Harley 372: 153, 157 n.29, 169
 BL Harley 4826: 157–8, 159, 161 n.46, 170, 174, 181
 BL Harley 4866: 114, 117–21, 151 n.1, 152, 153, 155–7, 171–2, 180, 188
 BL Harley 5977: 171 n.76
 BL Harley 7333: 153, 157 n.27, 161 n.46, 162 n.50, 173, 183
 BL Royal 2 A. xviii (Beaufort Hours): 155, 156
 BL Royal 6 B. v: 177
 BL Royal 8 G. iii: 156 n.19
 BL Royal 12 D. iii: 88 n.10
 BL Royal 12 D. xv: 88 n.10
 BL Royal 12 E. xxi: 91 n.30, 92
 BL Royal 17 C. xiv: 152, 173–4, 186
 BL Royal 17 D. vi: 117, 157, 163 n.53, 164 n.57, 173, 174, 192
 BL Royal 17 D. xviii: 78 n.76, 171, 174, 178 n.109
 BL Royal 17 D. xix: 153, 173, 175
 BL Sloane 1212: 152, 174, 178 n.109
 BL Sloane 1825: 186 n.134
 Public Record Office D.L. 42 (includes Duchy of Lancaster Cowcher Books): 156 n.19
 Society of Antiquaries 134: 161 n.46, 161 n.47, 181, 183
Manchester, John Rylands Library Eng. 98: 169 n.72
New Haven, CT, Yale University Beinecke Library 493: 161 n.46, 163 n.53, 164 nn.54 and 57, 166 n.61, 167 n.64, 183–5
New York, Pierpont Morgan Library M. 122 (Kerr manuscript): 120 n. 103

Index

Oslo and London, Schøyen
  Collection 615: 174 n.90
Oxford:
  Bodleian Ashmole 40: 154 n.12,
    157 n.29, 161 n.49, 164 n.54
  Bodleian Ashmole 46: 115
  Bodleian Bodley 221: 161 n.46,
    163 n.53, 164 n.54, 183–5, 188
  Bodleian Bodley 294: 120, 155
  Bodleian Bodley 693: 120 n.107,
    155
  Bodleian Bodley 902: 155
  Bodleian Digby 185: 157 n.27,
    157 n.29, 163 n.53, 170, 172–3,
    174
  Bodleian Digby 230: 169
  Bodleian Digby 232: 115
  Bodleian Digby 233: 89, 120 n.104
  Bodleian Douce 95: 88 n.10
  Bodleian Douce 158: 178 n.109,
    182
  Bodleian Douce 324: 171 n.76
  Bodleian Dugdale 45: 78 n.76,
    158, 170, 171, 178
  Bodleian Eng. poet. d. 4: 164 n.55
  Bodleian Fairfax 3: 182 n.124
  Bodleian Fairfax 10: 176–7
  Bodleian Hatton 105: 91 n.30
  Bodleian James 34: 153 n.8
  Bodleian lat. liturg. f. 2: 155
  Bodleian Laud Misc. 735: 152 n.7,
    157 n.29, 161 n.46, 161 n.49,
    163 n.53, 164 n.54, 183–5, 187,
    188
  Bodleian Rawlinson C. 446: 115,
    169 n.72
  Bodleian Rawlinson D. 82:
    171 n.76
  Bodleian Rawlinson D. 99:
    171 n.76
  Bodleian Rawlinson D. 913:
    171 n.76
  Bodleian Rawlinson poet. 10:
    161 n.49, 186
  Bodleian Rawlinson poet. 35:
    162 n.50, 171 n.76
  Bodleian Rawlinson poet. 143:
    171 n.76
  Bodleian Rawlinson poet. 168:
    153 n.10, 161 n.46, 162 n.50,
    170, 183, 186, 189

  Bodleian Selden supra 53: 155,
    161 n.46, 163 n.53, 164 n.54,
    169, 189
  Corpus Christi College 67:
    120 n.107
  New College 314: 170
  University College 85: 88 n.12,
    120 n.102
Paris:
  BN fonds anglais 39: 189 n.142
  BN fonds français 5. 71: 88 n.11
  BN nouv. acquis. lat. 669:
    101 n.65
Philadelphia, PA, Rosenbach
  Foundation 1083/30: 152 n.3,
  157, 161 n.47, 181
Princeton, CT, Princeton
  University Garrett 137:
  189 n.143
San Marino, CA:
  Huntington Library EL 26 A. 13:
    161 n.46, 163 n.53, 174
  Huntington Library EL 26 C. 9
    (Ellesmere manuscript): 156–
    7, 172, 174
  Huntington Library HM 111:
    78 n.76, 130, 152 n.5, 164 n.55,
    171 n.78
  Huntington Library HM 135:
    158–9
  Huntington Library HM 744:
    164 n.55
Tokyo, Toshiyuki Takamiya 54:
  174 n.90
Manzalaoui, M.A., 55, 87, 93–4
Map, Walter, 19 n.55
Mapstone, Sally, 33 n.85
Marchall, Roger, 176–7
Marleburgh, Thomas, 172 n.81
Marzec, Marcia Smith, 86 n.2, 94,
  152, 158, 183 n.126
Medcalf, Stephen, 144
Minnis, Alastair, 60
Mirror for Magistrates, 54 n.15
mirrors for princes, 1, 12–13, 20–1,
  50–7, 57–61, 67–8, 76, 82–3, 85,
  87–93, 99–102, 131–2, 194; *see also*
  Hoccleve, Thomas, *Regiment of
  Princes*, and advice tradition
Mirror of Sinners, 11
mise en abyme, 82–3
Mitchell, Jerome, 3 n.9, 93

Molenaer, Samuel Paul, 89 n.15
Mooney, Linne R., 164 n.54, 169, 175
Mortimer, Sir Edmund (III), 66
Mowbray, John, second Duke of Norfolk, 116–17, 171
Mum and the Soothsegger, 12 n.32, 16–17, 23, 24–6, 30, 32–3, 35 n.91, 56 n.25, 59, 127, 146 n.53, 194
'Musyng uppon the mutabilitie', 54

Nevill, Joan, Countess of Salisbury, 174 n.89
Nevill, Thomas, Lord Fourneval, 20, 116 n.92
Norwich, Robert, 175
Nuttall, Jennifer, 39 n.101

Oldcastle, Sir John, 68 n.60; *see also* Hoccleve, Thomas, *Remonstrance to Oldcastle*
Oresme, Nicole, 120 n.102
Orosius, 91
Ovid, 92, 105–6, 141

Parliament, 5, 7, 8 n.13, 27, 29–34, 62–5, 66, 112
Patience, 10
Patterson, Annabel, 5 n.2, 12 n.32
Patterson, Lee, 52 n.7, 167 n.64
Paul the Deacon, 91
Pearl, 10, 78 n.77
Pearsall, Derek, 3, 11 n.29, 51, 118, 153–4, 157 n.24, 182 n.121
Peasants' Revolt, 7–9
Percy, Henry, first Earl of Northumberland, 66
Peter Alponsus, 91
petitions, 20 n.57, 34–8, 39, 44, 47–8, 149; *see also* Hoccleve, *Regiment of Princes*, as petition
Philip IV of France, 88
Philippus Tripolitanus, 87
Pickering, James, 61–2
Pocock, J.G.A., 193 n.3
Powell, Edward, 58 n.33
The Prick of Conscience, 11
Privy Seal, 6, 7, 35–6, 78 n.75, 160
prose *Brut*: see *Brut*
proverbs, 14, 15–17, 22–3

Repingdon, Philip, 67
Ricardian poetry, 2

Richard II, 6, 7 n.10, 18, 19 n.54, 19 n.55, 53, 56, 61–70, 90, 116, 119, 129
and heresy, 9, 10 n.23
Articles of Deposition, 63–5
Richard III, 172 n.82
Richard the Redeless, 18–19, 20, 26, 31 n.80, 59, 65, 150 n.60
Roos, Sir Richard, 169
Roscarrock, Nicholas, 187
Royce, Josiah, 83 n.85
Russell, Francis, Earl of Bedford, 175 n.95

St Mary de Pré, Leicester, 173
Saul, Nigel, 129 n.13
Saunder, Nicholas, 173–4
Savage, Sir Arnold, 34 n.87
Sawtre, William, 10 n.23
Scanlon, Larry, 3, 64–5, 89 n.15, 100–1, 112, 133–4
Scarry, Elaine, 137 n.32
Scattergood, John, 55 n.19
Scheere, Herman, 155–7
Scogan, Henry, 119 n.101
Scott, Kathleen, 116–17, 172
scribes, 154, 157, 164 n.54, 168–71, 189–90
  Hammond scribe, 169–70, 175
  Selden scribe, 169
  see also Hoccleve, Thomas, as manuscript copyist; Wilflete, William
Scrope, Richard, Archbishop of York, 129, 155
Secretum secretorum, 14 n.37, 21, 47, 85, 87–8, 93–8, 102
Seneca, 91, 100
Seymour, M.C., 93, 158, 164 n.55
Shakespeare, William: *Hamlet*, 83
Sherman, Claire Richter, 120 n.102
Shirley, John (labourer), 8
Shirley, John (writer), 173, 174–5, 194 n.8
  Governance of Kynges and of Pryncves, 71 n.67
Siege of Jerusalem, 168, 169
Siege of Thebes (prose), 171
Siege of Troy (prose), 171
Simpson, James, 6 n.4, 45, 47 n.115, 60, 109 n.78

Index

Sir Gawain and the Green Knight, 18 n.49
Skelton, John:
  Bowge of Courte, 19 n.55
  Collyn Clout, 46 n.113
Skinner, Quentin, 55 n.17, 58 n.33
Smith, Warren, 159
Sommer, Sir Henry, 26
South English Legendary, 174 n.90
Spearing, A.C., 40 n.104
Speght, Thomas, 153 n.8, 159
Steele, Robert, 55
Stevens, Martin, 110 n.81
Stow, John, 157 n.29, 169, 185 n.132, 190
  Survey of London, 167 n.62
Straker, Scott-Morgan, 69 n.64
Strohm, Paul, 3, 12, 26 n.70, 46 n.114, 67 n.53, 112 n.84
Stubbs, William, 58 n.30
Sudbury, Simon, Archbishop of Canterbury, 8
Suso, Heinrich: *De arte moriendi*, 163

Tanner, Thomas, 181
Thousand and One Nights, 83 n.85
Tiptoft, Sir John, 34 n.87
Tolmie, Sarah, 41 n.107
Tractatus consiliandi, 91
Tractatus de regimine sanitatis, 91
translation, 10–11, 86
  in the *Regiment*, 85–6, 93–9, 103–14, 119, 121, 161–2
  of Hoccleve's sources, 87, 89–90, 91, 92–3
Trevisa, John, 57, 61
  Governance of Kings and Princes, 89–90, 120, 131 n.19

Usk, Thomas: *Testament of Love*, 2, 21 n.59, 183

Valerius Maximus, 91
Vegetius: *De re militari*, 88 n.12, 89, 91, 92 n.31, 102 n. 67
Vernon manuscript: *see* manuscripts, London, BL Additional 22283
Vertue, George, 159
Vincent of Beauvais, 87, 91

Walker, Greg, 193 n.5
Wall, Thomas, 175

Wallace, David, 26 n.70, 53
Walsingham, Thomas, 62–3, 152 n.7
Walter of Châtillon: *Alexandreis*, 137 n.31
Walton, John: *Consolation of Philosophy*, 161, 174 n.90, 181
Ward, Thomas, 68
Watson, Nicholas, 10–12
Watts, John, 59–61
Wawn, Andrew, 16 n.45
Whate-ever thow sey, avyse thee Welle, 15–16
Wilflete, William, 182, 188 n.139
Winner and Waster, 19 n.55, 183
Woodcock, William, 176–7
Wright, Sylvia, 117, 171–2
Wright, Thomas, 152
Wyclif, John, 8, 9 n.19, 10

Yonge, James, 56 n.24

235

LIBRARY

s ou have